FUNDAMENTALS
OF PSYCHOLOGICAL
RESEARCH

FUNDAMENTALS OF PSYCHOLOGICAL RESEARCH

second edition

gordon wood
michigan state university

 little, brown and company   boston   toronto

TO THE MEMORY OF MY FATHER

Copyright © 1977, 1974 by
Little, Brown and Company (Inc.)

All rights reserved. No part of this book may be reproduced in any form or by any electronic or mechanical means including information storage and retrieval systems without permission in writing from the publisher, except by a reviewer who may quote brief passages in a review.

Library of Congress Catalog Card Number: 76-21560

THIRD PRINTING

Published simultaneously in Canada
by Little, Brown & Company (Canada) Limited

Printed in the United States of America

preface

Students taking their first course in methodology and statistics frequently have misconceptions about its usefulness. Many believe that methodology and statistics are important for some areas of psychology (for example, human memory, animal behavior, or perception) but not for others (such as personality, clinical, or social psychology). The fact is, however, that investigators in diverse areas of the social sciences use similar methods and statistical techniques to evaluate their ideas about behavior and mental activity. Thus this text should be as useful to the student interested in research in personality as it is to the student interested in research in perception. Many students believe that methodology and statistics are important for majors in psychology but not of particular use to students who will not pursue a major or minor in psychology. This is much too narrow a view. We are confronted daily with claims made by so-called experts and researchers in the social sciences that have important consequences for daily living. The citizen who can evaluate these claims is better able to separate good solutions from current fads. Finally, many students believe that one needs advanced mathematical skills to do research in the social sciences. This is clearly not the case. Statistics plays an important role in research, but it is not necessary to have a strong background in mathematics or statistics to evaluate or conduct psychological research. This text emphasizes the practical uses of statistics while keeping mathematical symbols to a minimum, in order to present statistical tests at a level that can be understood and used by students lacking a background in mathematics or statistics. In short, I believe most undergraduates can benefit from a course in methodology and statistics. I hope you have an enjoyable learning experience.

A number of people contributed to the two editions of this text. Joyce Pennington, James V. Hindrichs, Eugene A. Lovelace, Terrence M. Allen, two anonymous reviewers, and a number of my former students provided constructive criticism that helped shape the final version of the first edition. Christopher Hunter was instrumental in the development of the text, and Lynn Lloyd ably guided it through the various stages of production. A number of instructors who used the first edition provided suggestions for the second edition. I am particularly indebted to Harold O. Kiess and two anonymous reviewers for their extensive, constructive criticism. Marian R.

Ferguson and Jane E. Robbins, both of Little, Brown and Company, provided excellent editorial assistance for the second edition.

I am indebted to the Literary Executor of the late Sir Ronald A. Fisher, F.R.S., to Dr. Frank Yates, F.R.S., and to Oliver and Boyd, Edinburgh, for their permission to reprint material from Tables III and VI from their books *Statistical Methods for Research Workers* and *Statistical Tables for Biological, Agricultural and Medical Research*.

contents

SECTION I RESEARCH METHODOLOGY 1

CHAPTER 1 introduction 3

The Rationale for Studying
   Research Methodology 3
The Scientific Approach 6
Theories and Research 10
Criteria for Evaluating Ideas 13
Measurement 22
Summary 26
Questions 27

CHAPTER 2 methods of research 29

The Observational Approach 29
The Correlational Approach 34
The Experimental Method: Basic Properties 39
Subject Variables and the Experimental Method 41
The Quasi-experimental Approach 44
Classifying Research According to Method 45
The Experimental Method: Additional
   Properties 50
Summary 56
Questions 58

CHAPTER 3 estimation and hypothesis testing 60

Randomization 61
Probability 63
Estimation 70

Hypothesis Testing and the
    Experimental Method   70
The Logic Behind the Statistical Analysis
    of Experiments   73
Summary   81
Questions   81

CHAPTER 4   **between-subject designs**   83

The Logic of Analysis of Variance   83
The Random-groups Design   90
Matched-groups Designs   96
Summary   101
Questions   102

CHAPTER 5   **within-subject designs**   104

Properties of Within-subject Designs   104
Advantages of Within-subject Designs   106
Limitations of Within-subject Designs   108
Methodological and Interpretational
    Considerations   109
Selecting a Within-subject Design   115
Uses of Within-subject Designs   115
Summary   117
Questions   118

CHAPTER 6   **nonexperimental and quasi-experimental designs**   120

Nonexperimental Designs   120
Quasi-experimental Designs   129
Comparison of the Designs   136
Summary   139
Questions   140

CHAPTER 7   **performing the experiment**   141

Facilities, Special Skills, and Equipment   141
Subjects   145
Confounding   149
Testing the Subjects   154
Summary   155
Questions   156

SECTION II DESCRIBING, ANALYZING, AND REPORTING RESULTS   159

CHAPTER 8 methods and procedures for describing results   161

Level of Measurement and Performance Variables   161
Descriptive Measures   164
Standard Deviation as a Unit of Measurement   171
Describing the Results of Experiments   176
Evaluating Results   186
Summary   187
Questions   188

CHAPTER 9 correlation   190

Computing Correlation Coefficients   190
Scattergrams and Correlation   196
Understanding Correlation   202
Summary   209
Questions   210

CHAPTER 10 statistical analysis of between-subject designs: nominal and ordinal data   212

Selecting a Statistical Test   212
The Chi Square Test   213
Chi Square and Subject Variables   215
Chi Square and Nonsubject Variables   221
Restrictions on the Use of Chi Square   225
Wilcoxon-Mann-Whitney Test   226
Summary   229
Questions   229

CHAPTER 11 statistical analysis of between-subject designs: interval data   233

The t-Test   233
Logic of the Analysis of Variance   237
Analysis of Variance with One Independent Variable   238
Analysis of Variance with Two Independent Variables   247

Interactions   254
Assumptions of the Analysis of Variance   260
Summary   261
Questions   262

CHAPTER 12   **analysis of within-subject and matched-groups designs**   266

Nominal Data   266
Ordinal Data   269
Interval Data   271
Summary   277
Questions   278

CHAPTER 13   **evaluating and reporting results**   280

The Psychological Significance of Results   280
Reporting the Findings   282
Summary   290
Appendix   291

APPENDIX A   **proofs and examples**   305

1. Probability   305
2. Proof that Two Independent Estimates of Population Variance Can Be Obtained if the Null Hypothesis Is True   307
3. Proof that the $SS_{tot} = SS_{bg} + SS_{wg}$ 309
4. Computation of the Analysis of Variance with the Deviation Formulas   310
5. Proof that the Deviation and Computational Formulas for the Analysis of Variance Are Mathematically Equivalent   311

APPENDIX B   **research topics**   313

Topic 1. The Lost Letter Technique   313
Topic 2. Correlation of Abilities   314
Topic 3. Mnemonic Systems   316
Topic 4. Information Processing   317
Topic 5. Aggression   318
Topic 6. The Cocktail Party Phenomenon   320
Topic 7. Pupil Dilation   321

Topic 8. Reading 322
Topic 9. Machiavellianism 323
Topic 10. The Prisoner's Dilemma 324
Topic 11. Clothes and Behavior 325
Topic 12. The Eyewitness 326

APPENDIX C **tables** 328

1. Number Tables for Random Assignment 328
2. Table of Chi Squares 332
3. Critical Values of T in the Wilcoxon-Mann-Whitney Sum of Ranks Test 333
4. F Distribution 336
5. Values of t for Given Probability Levels 339
6. Critical Values of W for the Wilcoxon Test 340
7. Distribution of F_{max} Statistics 341
8. Critical Values of r_s (Rank-order Correlation Coefficient) 341
9. Critical Values of r (Pearson Product-moment Correlation) 342
10. Table of Squares and Square Roots 343
11. Random Numbers 352

APPENDIX D **answers for problems in chapters 8 through 12** 354

references 356

glossary 358

index 364

RESEARCH METHODOLOGY

introduction 1

THE RATIONALE FOR STUDYING RESEARCH METHODOLOGY

Research Methodology and the Citizen

Anyone who has completed a course in introductory psychology or who is reasonably well informed about current events knows that a vast amount of research is being conducted in the social sciences; she should also become aware of how such research is conducted. We are continually confronted with claims and findings that have important implications. An understanding of research methodology allows us to evaluate the claims, ideas, theories, and new research findings of investigators and "experts" in the social sciences.

One approach is to accept passively what the experts say without evaluating their statements critically. If you do not choose to believe what one investigator says, you may be able to find another who agrees with you. But a critical evaluation of the experts' statements is more satisfactory, because their conclusions are not always justified by the evidence. The person who wants to see evidence before deciding what to believe needs an understanding of research methodology. Let us look at some of the research behind findings that might be reported in newspapers.

We have all been confronted with the results of a poll at one time or another. For example, polls are used extensively during elections years to keep voters informed of the popularity of the candidates and, in some cases at least, to influence voter opinion. The results of political polls can be important to many citizens. People may be less willing to work for or send money to a candidate who has little chance of winning. If this is the case, then it is important to know whether the poll truly represents voter sentiment at the time the poll was taken. Does the poll accurately reflect the preferences of the voters who will actually vote on election day? How many people were polled? How were they selected? Was the poll conducted by telephone? By personal interview? What is the margin of error claimed for the prediction?

Since the election results provide a check on the accuracy of political polls, most independent pollsters (those not working for a political party) try to obtain representative samples. They lose credibility if they do not predict accurately. However, in most other surveys (for example, of sexual behaviors of high school students, views on busing to achieve racial balance in the public schools, views on foreign policy) there is no final check on accuracy, so the motivation to be accurate may not be as great. In the absence of a final check, the validity of the results can be evaluated only by examining the procedures used. The reader who has an understanding of what constitutes acceptable sampling techniques is equipped to evaluate the procedures. In some cases he may want to withhold judgment because insufficient information is presented. At the least, he should be able to decide whether the information presented is adequate; the uniformed reader will have no basis for an intelligent assessment of the facts.

There is usually a marked difference between the presentation of research in newspapers and that in journals. Although some newspaper reporters do an excellent job of presenting the evidence on which their conclusions are based, many do not, and most newspaper reports do not describe the methods used to obtain that evidence. Thus, newspaper articles are usually not the best source for information about recent scientific advances; a person who prefers to evaluate the evidence to determine whether the conclusions are justified requires more information than he can get from the newspaper. Fortunately, there are publications specifically intended for those who want to see detailed reports. Reports in journals typically include a detailed account of how the evidence was obtained, making it unnecessary for a reader to withhold judgment for lack of information. And, although many newspaper accounts of research may be incomplete, a knowledge of research methodology should still be useful for understanding and evaluating these accounts.

If you look for newspaper articles that raise questions about how knowledge is accumulated in the social sciences and medicine, you are likely to find articles discussing cures for cancer, the uses and abuses of sleeping pills, the effectiveness of psychotherapy, causes and treatments for alcoholism, coffee and heart disease, child rearing practices and anxiety in children, exercise and heart attacks, egg consumption and cholesterol level, the relative merits of breast versus bottle feeding, vitamins and schizophrenia, speed limits and traffic fatalities, handguns and homicides, violence on television and aggression, and so on. In short, it is unlikely that you will be able to find a metropolitan newspaper that does not contain articles making claims for particular products, techniques, or courses of action. In order to evaluate such claims, you will need to understand the methods used to test ideas.

Although to understand and to judge research in some areas of the social sciences requires specific technical knowledge, numerous research findings can be thoroughly understood, and in many cases critically evaluated, through a knowledge of general research methodology. Moreover, the methodology presented in this text is frequently applicable to the evaluation of research outside of the social sciences. For example, the evaluation of birth control pills, of gun control legislation and violence, and of monosodium glutamate in baby food are disparate problems which are nevertheless likely to involve the use of similar methodologies.

The primary reason for studying research methodology, then, is to develop critical judgment. But there are two additional reasons. One is that the student's view of the social sciences may change drastically as he absorbs the scientific approach to generating and testing ideas. Simply stated, there are two ways of evaluating ideas, people, and events: subjectively or on the basis of empirical evidence. Since it does not require any training to make subjective judgments, this method is readily available to everyone. But effort and training are necessary to understand the empirical method. Some students may opt to avoid it entirely; this is unfortunate because a knowledge of the empirical approach may have an influence on how ideas are evaluated, what is considered interesting and important, and what is learned from experience. Some students may be so impressed with the scientific approach that they will decide to pursue a career in the social sciences. It is extremely important that those who decide to major in psychology or the social sciences have a thorough understanding of methodology.

A second reason is that research can be fun. For most students, conducting research is a marked change from the typical educational experience. It allows them to test ideas rather than act primarily as sponges, soaking up others' thoughts. Of course, students can examine ideas without doing research. Yet, for many, conducting research will be a new and exciting way to evaluate ideas critically.

Research Methodology and Majors in Psychology

A casual reading of almost any introductory psychology text should convince most readers that our knowledge is limited. For example, we still do not have an adequate understanding of brain functioning, psychotherapy, the effects of viewing violence on television, drug and alcohol addiction, or human information processing. Yet, even though there are many unsolved problems, we know much more about behavior and mental activity than we did a decade ago. If we are to continue to extend our knowledge in psychology we have little choice but to encourage individuals to construct and test theories about behavior and mental activity. Research allows us to accumulate knowledge and make improvements without discarding old wisdom in favor of new fads (see Campbell & Stanley, 1963).

It is reasonable to expect psychology students to acquire the ability to understand and evaluate the research in their discipline. In less advanced areas of knowledge, such as the social sciences, it may be the most important ability the student can develop. The state of knowledge in any discipline changes with new research findings, but research methodology has remained fairly constant over the years. The student who is familiar with methodology should have a much easier time weighing new findings. The student who does not know methodology will be ill equipped to distinguish between inferior novelties and new wisdom.

Undergraduate psychology majors and minors who continue as graduate students in psychology are often surprised by the emphasis on statistics and methodology. As an undergraduate the student may have taken one or two methodology courses, but the scientific approach was probably not emphasized. Rather, it was probably viewed by the undergraduate as something to be tolerated only in order to achieve the bachelor's degree. Many undergraduates would prefer to learn about interesting psychological theories and findings without considering the steps by which knowledge is accumulated.

It *is* tempting, for the beginning student in particular, to take a dilettantish approach to psychology. Yet, advanced work in psychology requires a thorough understanding of the means by which psychologists accumulate knowledge. In addition, it is generally easier to understand the end results of an investigation if the intermediate steps are understood. A psychology major who masters the scientific approach can spend her graduate years doing research, not merely learning how.

Fortunately, the student who is considering becoming a researcher can receive research training and still have the option of pursuing other careers in psychology. The relatively incomplete state of knowledge in psychology can be an advantage in that the formal training necessary to become a researcher is very similar to that necessary to become a practitioner or teacher. That is, in psychology the "distance" between the acquisition and dissemination of knowledge is frequently so small that the effective teacher or practitioner should be able to evaluate research. In some areas of psychology it is, therefore, possible to prepare for an applied and research career at the same time; the decision to emphasize one or the other can be made later.

THE SCIENTIFIC APPROACH

Assumptions of the Scientific Approach

Order. The first assumption is that nature is ordered, not haphazard. Events follow each other in regular sequences; that is, an overall pattern or scheme of events, or *order,* is discernible. This assumption is usually easy to accept because there are so many instances of order: a child crawls before walking; eclipses of the moon can be accurately predicted; applying heat to ice causes it to melt.

Determinism. A second assumption is that events have causes, determinants, or antecedents that can be detected. The assumption that events are related and the relationships can be detected is known as *determinism*. Many investigators prefer terms like determinant and antecedent over cause because the former terms allow them to discuss the relationships among events without getting into the sticky problem of defining causality. Regardless of the preferred terminology, the critical aspect of determinism is the possibility of discovering the relationships among events.

Parsimony. The assumption of *parsimony* (simple over complex) is a general assumption about the organization of the universe. Scientists prefer simple explanations of natural phenomena over complex ones when both explanations account for the facts equally well. They also prefer general explanations over explanations that are appropriate for only a very limited range of phenomena. The assumption of parsimony is important because a science is not possible unless one can generalize the results of an experimental investigation.

Let us assume that an investigator studied the effect of alcohol consumption on motor performance by performing an experiment with twenty college sophomores. Let us also assume that the experiment was performed properly and that the results were clear. The students who consumed alcohol had poorer performance than the students who did not. The investigator now needs to ask whether this result can be generalized. Is it reasonable to conclude that the effect is general, or is this result limited to the conditions of his study? If the findings apply only to low anxiety, attractive, college females, from upper middle class backgrounds with IQs greater than 125, who drink 3 ounces of gin at 9 A.M., who vote republican, and so on, there is no way to arrive at general statements relating alcohol consumption and motor performance. In order to have a science we must be able to disregard most other variables (e.g., attractiveness, political party, IQ) when studying the effects of alcohol consumption on motor performance.

The extent to which generalization of research findings is possible depends, in part, on the research area considered. Investigators interested in physiological, perceptual, attention, and basic learning and memory phenomena usually do not have to be greatly concerned about the problem of generality. The phenomena that these investigators study are usually not affected by individual differences. For example, the visual system is pretty much the same for all people; differences in intelligence, beauty, socioeconomic status, personality, age, weight, and so on will not affect it. It is reasonable for these investigators to generalize their findings. Usually, they can embrace the parsimony assumption.

The situation appears to be considerably different for investigators interested in personality, social behavior, or instruction (see Cronbach, 1975). In these areas the effect of treatment manipulations frequently depends on the type of person participating in the experiment. For example, a new instructional technique may be effective for college students but not high school students. The same treatment manipulation frequently produces different effects for different people. And, it is usually difficult to predict an individual's behavior in a given situation unless a great deal is known about that individual. Thus, although simple theories are the goal of science, in general they do not account for personality, social behavior, or instructional effects very well. A simple theory that accounts for behavior studied under controlled conditions in the laboratory may fail to account for behavior observed in real life. Thus, investigators in these areas are usually much more cautious about generalizing their findings. They are more likely to view generalizations as assertions to be tested, not conclusions. Such investigators spend more of their experimental effort determining the generality of their findings. They are usually timid about embracing the parsimony assumption.

Empiricism. Empirical refers to a reliance on observation and experiment. Scientists insist their conclusions be based on observable, or *empirical,* experimental results. This assumption of *empiricism* implies more than just using observable events to test theories. The tests must be systematic and controlled as well as empirical. Most people use empirical data to support their views, but the data are often selectively obtained. We generally select evidence that is consistent with our position and ignore evidence that is not. The competent social scientist, however, avoids the tendency to select data; all the relevant data need to be considered. Much of this text is devoted to the methods and procedures used to obtain systematic, controlled, empirical tests.

The Goal of Science

The basic goal of science is to *understand* natural phenomena. Obviously, there are several levels of understanding; however, the social scientist who makes the more accurate predictions can be said to have a better understanding of the phenomenon. That is, we can compare the extent to which social scientists understand a phenomenon by requiring them to make predictions about future observable behaviors. There are usually three steps in understanding phenomena. The first step is accurate description. Basically, in describing a phenomenon the scientist determines whether that phenomenon exists and, if so, to what extent.

The second step in understanding phenomena is explanation. You have explained a phenomenon if you have specified conditions necessary to obtain it. If you can specify all the antecedent conditions for a phenomenon, you should have little difficulty in predicting the phenomenon. The extent to which a phenomenon is explained or understood is related to the number of different, plausible reasons for its existence. When there are many plausible reasons for a particular phenomenon, a state of ignorance exists. Initially, the number of theories or hypotheses for a phenomenon is far greater than the number that will be supported by empirical tests. That is, there are usually far more *plausible* solutions to a problem than there are solutions that actually work. The goal of experimentation is to reject the incorrect solutions (see Campbell & Stanley, 1963). If there is firm evidence to support only one explanation (that is, if all other explanations have been rejected), then the phenomenon can be considered explained or understood. Scientists regard all explanations as tentative, however, because additional evidence may reveal that a previously rejected or new explanation is better than the accepted one.

The third step in understanding is organization of the available evidence. This process is analogous to solving a jigsaw puzzle. At the early stages of investigation it is likely that scientists will primarily be trying to get a few pieces of the puzzle together. For example, scientists interested in how humans process information may study the mechanisms involved in the perception of printed material, the retention of information for short periods of time (e.g., remembering a telephone number long enough to dial it), the retention of information for long periods of time (e.g., material covered in methodology courses), and the subsequent use of stored information. As they gain more understanding of the components of human information processing, they should be able to determine how the components are related, that is, how the larger pieces of the jigsaw puzzle fit together.

Although the puzzle analogy is appropriate for emphasizing the point that scientists seek an overall picture of the relationships among their research findings, it is somewhat misleading to imagine that all the pieces of the puzzle are available. Additional phenomena may be discovered, and then new pieces can be added to the puzzle.

The Importance of Theory

Definition of Theory. A theory is a set of principles used to explain a particular phenomenon or set of phenomena. Although *theory* can be used as a synonym for *idea, view, notion,* or *hypothesis,* researchers tend to use these latter words — to extend the jigsaw analogy — as labels for tentative explanations of how two or more small pieces of the puzzle go together, whereas they frequently reserve *theory* for a tentative explanation of how larger pieces of the puzzle go together. *Theory* is also more likely to be used if there is considerable evidence to support the explanation. Yet, since all of these words can refer to tentative explanations, you can expect to find them used interchangeably by some investigators.

It is important to realize that theories are *tentative* explanations, and it is necessary to evaluate each theory by determining how well it accounts for the available research findings and how well it can predict new findings. A theory that cannot be used to make predictions about observable events is of no value to scientists. If the research findings do not support the theory, then it should be modified or discarded. Research findings should dominate the theory, not vice versa. The facts cannot be changed to accommodate the theory; the theory must be changed to accommodate the facts.

Functions of Theory. A theory has two important functions. One is to guide research. Because one of the important goals of science is to explain phenomena, it is reasonable to start with tentative explanations of phenomena, explanations typically derived from opposing theories, and then to test these explanations to eliminate those that are unsatisfactory. By gradually rejecting what is wrong, scientists can obtain a better estimate of the true state of affairs. Obviously, if numerous attempts to disprove a theory fail, then that theory is likely to be viewed as more plausible than one that has not been tested extensively. Theories are important to scientists because they stimulate inquiry by generating testable predictions.

A second function of theory is to organize facts — an important aid toward arriving at a systematic body of knowledge. Theories play a crucial role in clarifying knowledge by providing a basis for organization. If a theory has firm support, then research findings can be generated from it. The situation is analogous to remembering a rule instead of memorizing a vast number of specific instances. For example, it is much easier to remember the spelling rule "*i* before *e* except after *c*" than to memorize the ordering of *i* and *e* for all the words in which these letters appear consecutively.

THEORIES AND RESEARCH

The Purpose of Research

Why is scientific research needed to evaluate theories? If several approaches are available one might expect that, at least in the case of practical problems, each solution will be tried at one time or another. The process of "natural selection" should, in the long run, result in the retention of good solutions and the rejection of poor ones. Although such a process will undoubtedly yield some good solutions, it is crude, slow, and subject to considerable error, and chance is likely to play a large role. Research is preferred over natural selection because it minimizes the role of chance. Yet research should not be viewed as incompatible with a natural selection process, or a new source of ideas as necessarily incompatible with traditional wisdom. Research is simply a systematic procedure for testing plausible solutions (Campbell & Stanley, 1963).

Investigators

Most people believe that successful researchers are creative. Obviously, individuals differ in their problem-solving abilities, but does special ability account for these differences (see Campbell, 1960)? There is no question that some people are better equipped than others to store information. To use a computer analogy, some people have better hardware. It is also obvious that people differ in the kind and amount of information they process and store. Contrast the student who spends his leisure time in the library with the one who spends his watching television. People also differ in their desire to solve problems. A person who is highly motivated to solve a problem is likely to make more attempts to reach a solution and be more tolerant of failure; he or she is likely to continue generating ideas even if the first several attempts are not very fruitful.

You should not be too quick to conclude that you do not possess the characteristics of the active experimenter. If you are curious, reasonably intelligent, independent, and highly motivated you have the appropriate characteristics for research. For the most part, it is difficult to evaluate whether you have such characteristics until you have made a sincere effort to involve yourself in a research problem. Many apathetic, antiscientific individuals have developed a fondness for the scientific approach to problem solving. I expect that most researchers were apathetic toward research until they became involved in *their* research. The first task for the experimenter is to select a problem.

Selecting a Problem Area

Select a problem area that you find interesting and important. If you consider your problem to be dull or unimportant, you probably will not derive much satisfaction from your efforts. Moreover, if you cannot get excited about the research you are doing, it is improbable that you will continue doing research for any prolonged period. Choosing a research area is like selecting a mate. You should choose a problem that you can live with, one that you find exciting.

Resolving to select an important problem is decidedly easier than finding one. You may rule out entire areas of study because of ignorance; you may not understand an area well enough to evaluate it. The well-read investigator has an obvious advantage when it comes to finding an interesting problem. The basic task is to decide what you find appealing and valuable. Then you could examine an introductory psychology test or read Appendix B of this book, discuss your interests with your instructor, or read articles in the many psychology journals found in the library. By reading about the various areas and discussing them with others, you should be able to select one in which you would like to work. If no constraints are placed on your selection, you may prefer to choose an area in one of the other social sciences. Since the material presented in this text is applicable to many areas of social science, there is no compelling reason, from the author's point of view, why your selection has to be in the area of psychology.

Limiting the Scope of the Problem

You will probably be able to select a broad area of study fairly easily. You may decide that you are interested, say, in sociology, social psychology, clinical psychology, experimental psychology, or personality. However, deciding that you want to do research in one of these areas is analogous to deciding that you want to go to college; there are still many decisions to make. The task of narrowing your interests in order to isolate a researchable problem may prove to be difficult. It is a little like prospecting; the yield will depend on the area selected for investigation. Unfortunately, there are no road signs directing researchers to rich areas. It is quite understandable, therefore, that many students experience some anxiety while attempting to narrow their interests.

You should not be timid about isolating your research problem for fear of making a poor decision. At this point there is little reason to be overly concerned about how others view your selection. It is more important to find a problem that you consider worthwhile. It is particularly important to realize that a project does *not* have to be dull in order to have scientific respectability. If you continue to do research, you will probably experience a gradual shift in what you consider interesting and important. There will be ample time to worry about how others view your research if you continue with a research career.

Generating Ideas

Once you have selected a problem, the next step is to generate possible solutions and tests for the solutions. We can say very little about the best ways to generate ideas because we know so little about the process of "discovering" explanations. You may be unable to think of a possible solution while consciously attempting to solve the problem, but an idea may suddenly occur to you while you are engaged in some other activity. This phenomenon is akin to not being able to think of the name of an old friend while consciously trying to retrieve the name, and then having it "pop into awareness" a little later when you are otherwise occupied. It is very doubtful, however, that the name would have popped into awareness if a conscious search for it had not been made earlier. The same argument can be made about searching for a solution to a problem.

There is no way for an investigator to know beforehand whether his search will be successful. He may spend days, weeks, or even years in research before arriving at a solution. In some cases, it may not be possible to reach an acceptable solution. The investigator who is unable to generate a possible solution may decide to consider testing someone else's ideas. Investigators sometimes mention testable ideas in the discussion section of their articles. It is permissible to test someone else's ideas as long as that person is given credit. What is important is that good ideas get tested — not who originates the ideas or who tests them.

CRITERIA FOR EVALUATING IDEAS

Testability and Operational Definitions

It is important to evaluate ideas according to several criteria. Often an idea that initially appears to be good turns out to be either unimportant or untestable. Many ideas are untestable because they cannot be reduced to specific operations. If it is not clear what has to be done, then it is not possible to test the idea. A few examples should clarify these assertions.

An investigator interested in testing whether or not pornography has a deleterious effect on the moral fiber of youth is likely to encounter difficulty. First, it is difficult to decide what is pornographic and what is not. One person's pornography can be another person's art. Let us assume, however, that the investigator is able to find materials that most judges classify as hard-core pornography. One way to investigate the problem is to perform an experiment.

The crux of the experiment is to present the pornographic materials to one group of youths and to make sure that an "equivalent" group of youths does not see any such material. Then the only task is to measure whether the groups differ with respect to moral fiber. This is the second rub. It is not clear how one would go about measuring differences in moral fiber. Thus, the idea, as stated, is not testable. However, if the statement were made in terms of specific operations it could be tested. For example, one could investigate the influence of pornographic materials on the number of convictions for crimes involving sexual offenses. One would then have an *operational* definition of the idea previously expressed vaguely in the phrase "moral fiber." Although it would be difficult to obtain the necessary cooperation to do such a study, the idea is stated in such a way that, assuming agreement regarding what is pornographic, it could be tested.

The view that daily exercise will improve the mind is an unacceptable prediction because it is not clear what is meant by daily exercise or improving the mind. In contrast, the prediction that jogging two miles each day will result in higher scores on the Mednick Remote Associates Test (Mednick & Mednick, 1967) is acceptable because it is clear what operations have to be performed in order to test the prediction. (A phenomenon that has been defined in terms of the operations necessary in order to demonstrate it is said to be *operationally defined*.)

The assertion that the Freudian method of therapy is superior to other methods is meaningless unless a set of operations can be specified for each therapy and a single set of criteria for evaluating the different therapies can be agreed on. Unfortunately, it is difficult, if not impossible, to arrive at a single standard or set of evaluative criteria that would be acceptable to different therapists and to scientists. For the scientist, the standard would have to be stated in terms of observable, measurable behavior.

It is essential to avoid the use of vague language that leaves it unclear what operations should be performed to test the proposed view. There is one advantage to vaguely stated notions: it is not possible to refute them. By the same token, however, the vague language prevents the ideas from ever being supported by empirical evidence, and thus accepted by the scientific community.

Testability and Refutability

A testable idea is one that can be refuted. If a theory is so general that it can explain any possible outcome it is not testable. Many theories are not refutable because explanation is made after the fact. One example is the Freudian view of personality structure. The id, ego, and superego vie for control, but the decision as to what structure has control tends to be made after the fact. It is possible to describe behavior after the fact in terms of the interplay of the id, ego, and superego, but it is quite another matter to arrange a set of operations that would demonstrate that the notions about the id, ego, and superego are incorrect. A theory that cannot be refuted is of little use to the scientific community; there is no way to build a body of knowledge unless incorrect ideas can be rejected. By gradually rejecting what is wrong, we gain a more accurate picture of the true state of affairs.

Please do not conclude that vaguely stated theories are necessarily "bad." It is just that they are of no help to the investigator who is interested in empirically testing ideas in order to advance the knowledge of a field. If a vaguely stated, untestable theory is an aid to a practitioner in his efforts to help people solve their problems, then it is obviously of some worth. The interesting applied problem is whether the theory per se does prove to be a beneficial addition to the therapeutic process. Unfortunately, it is difficult to evaluate most personality theories since the criteria (the goals of therapy that follow from the theories) differ as a function of the theory considered. This brings us to another aspect of evaluating ideas.

Testability and Comparability

Many ideas are untestable because they involve a comparison of processes, events, or things that are simply not comparable. For instance, we cannot compare the effectiveness of two therapies if the criteria for evaluating a "cure" differ for the two therapies. To take another example, you may be concerned with the effects of marijuana and alcohol. For personal reasons, you would like to demonstrate that the effects of marijuana are at least no worse than the effects of alcohol. The problem is that comparing marijuana and alcohol is like comparing apples and oranges. Is one apple equal to one orange? How much marijuana is equal to a six-pack of beer?

It should be clear that we cannot assess the "true" relative effects of marijuana and alcohol. However, we can equate the two on dollar value and assess the relative effects. Thus, we might be able to conclude that the behavioral effects of smoking two dollars' worth of marijuana are no worse than the effects of drinking two dollars' worth of beer. Yet since many factors determine price (supply and demand, taxes, greed), it is unlikely that many people would be impressed by this demonstration. Except for the propaganda value of such an investigation, the knowledge obtained could hardly be described as more than trivial. However, the methodological point is that, if an investigator is comparing treatments, organisms, or whatever, he must be aware of the danger of making apples-and-oranges comparisons.

The apples-and-oranges problem may appear in many different disguises. Consider the problem of studying cognitive development by devising tasks appropriate for various age levels. Or consider preparing tasks appropriate for mentally retarded and normal individuals, for males and females, or for primates and humans. The difficulty is that there is no way to determine whether the differences obtained should be attributed to the use of different subject populations or to the different tasks involved.

Testability and Practical Considerations

Many ideas are testable in theory but not in practice because of ethical, financial, or other considerations. There may be many reasons why a particular study should not be conducted. Perhaps the investigator lacks facilities, animal or human subjects, or money for supplies. If an investigator believes her ideas are worth testing in spite of the large costs involved in collecting the relevant data, she can request support from federal, state, or private granting agencies. One should be reluctant to conclude that a study cannot be conducted if the only difficulty is lack of resources. However, if the difficulty is ethical, one should seriously consider not conducting the experiment.

Testability and Ethical Considerations

Ethics and the Use of Animals. Concern for the proper care and treatment of animals used in research is great. Researchers who use animals must be aware of the laws and guidelines for their care and handling. An investigator who plans to use animals should contact the local humane society and the American Humane Association, P.O. Box 1266, Denver, Colorado, 80201. The animal health regulations for each state can be obtained from the state public health office or state veterinarian. Another essential publication, available from the United States Department of Health, Education, and Welfare, is entitled *Guide for Laboratory Animal Facilities and Care.* Or, the investigator can write to the American Psychological Association, Office of Scientific Affairs, 1200 Seventeenth Street, N.W., Washington, D.C., 20036, for the manual on the care of animals.

Additional regulations must be followed when laboratory animals are used by people not trained in their care and treatment. The American Psychological Association Committee on Precautions and Standards in Animal Experimentation has prepared guidelines on the use of animals in school science behavior projects. These are published in the *American Psychologist,* 1972, Volume 27, page 337. Although they were intended primarily for students in intermediate and secondary schools, they are also applicable to the use of animals by students in colleges and universities. The guidelines are briefly considered here, to give the reader an appreciation of the steps used to safeguard the welfare of animals.

The first four guidelines cover the proper planning and supervision of each project, the adherence to the laws of each state and to the recommendations of humane societies, and the use of small animals that are easy to maintain or of invertebrates whenever possible. The fifth guideline is, "No student shall undertake an experiment which includes the use of drugs, surgical procedures, noxious or painful stimuli such as electric shock, extreme temperature, starvation, malnutrition, ionizing radiation, etc. except under extremely close and rigorous supervision of a researcher qualified in the specific area of study." The purpose of this restriction is, of course, to ensure that there are sound reasons for any unusual treatment of animals. The sixth guideline directs researchers to make certain the animals receive proper housing, food, water, exercise, gentle handling, and so forth. It is crucial that arrangements be made for the care of the animals over vacation periods.

The seventh guideline concerns the disposition of animals at the conclusion of the experiment. Sometimes the animals are maintained as pets. In some cases they are selected so that their normal life span corresponds to the duration of the experiment. In other cases it is necessary to perform euthanasia, which should be carried out only by a trained person. In such cases, remember that most of the animals used in experiments are bred solely for the purpose of research; they would not exist otherwise.

Ethics and the Use of Human Subjects. The task of determining ethical standards governing the use of human subjects is an immense undertaking. There are so many kinds of research projects involving human subjects and so many opinions on how the rights of these subjects should be protected that it is difficult to arrive at a set of principles to which all researchers can subscribe. In spite of the difficulty, the American Psychological Association appointed a Committee on Ethical Standards in Psychological Research to revise the association's 1953 code of ethics for research using human subjects. The committee worked approximately three years. They polled thousands of researchers, held numerous discussions at professional meetings, reviewed earlier ethical standards, and invited members of the American

Psychological Association to criticize each of the two drafts. The first draft appeared in July, 1971, the second in May, 1972. The adopted standards were published in the January, 1973, issue of the *American Psychologist* (p. 79). This list of ethical principles is as follows:

The Ethical Principles in the Conduct of Research with Human Participants*

1. In planning a study the investigator has the personal responsibility to make a careful evaluation of its ethical acceptability, taking into account these Principles for research with human beings. To the extent that this appraisal, weighing scientific and humane values, suggests a deviation from any Principle, the investigator incurs an increasingly serious obligation to seek ethical advice and to observe more stringent safeguards to protect the rights of the human research participant.

2. Responsibility for the establishment and maintenance of acceptable ethical practice in research always remains with the individual investigator. The investigator is also responsible for the ethical treatment of research participants by collaborators, assistants, students and employees, all of whom however, incur parallel obligations.

3. Ethical practice requires the investigator to inform the participant of all features of the research that reasonably might be expected to influence willingness to participate, and to explain all other aspects of the research about which the participant inquires. Failure to make full disclosure increases the investigator's responsibility to maintain confidentiality, and to protect the welfare and dignity of the research participant.

4. Openness and honesty are essential characteristics of the relationship between investigator and research participant. When the methodological requirements of a study necessitate concealment or deception, the investigator is required to ensure the participant's understanding of the reasons for his action and to restore the quality of the relationship with the investigator.

5. Ethical research practice requires the investigator to respect the individual's freedom to decline to participate in research or to discontinue participation at any time. The obligation to protect this freedom requires special vigilance when the investigator is in a position of power over the participant. The decision to limit this freedom increases the investigator's responsibility to protect the participant's dignity and welfare.

6. Ethically acceptable research begins with the establishment of a clear and fair agreement between the investigator and the research participant that

---

* The principles shown above were written by the Committee on Ethical Standards in Psychological Research. Copyright 1973 by the American Psychological Association, reprinted by permission.

The final version of the committee report, entitled *Ethical Principles in the Conduct of Research with Human Participants,* has been published by the American Psychological Association (1200 Seventeenth Street, N.W., Washington, D.C. 20036) in booklet form. Except for a slight wording change in Principle 3, the principles presented here are identical to those in the final report. The booklet offers a detailed discussion of each principle, to help the reader place the issues in context. I would encourage all who plan to use human subjects in research to obtain a copy of this report.

clarifies the responsibilities of each. The investigator has the obligation to honor all promises and commitments included in that agreement.

7. The ethical investigator protects participants from physical and mental discomfort, harm and danger. If the risk of such consequences exists, the investigator is required to inform the participant of that fact, to secure consent before proceeding, and to take all possible measures to minimize distress. A research procedure may not be used if it is likely to cause serious and lasting harm to participants.

8. After the data are collected, ethical practice requires the investigator to provide the participant with a full clarification of the nature of the study and to remove any misconceptions that may have arisen. Where scientific or humane values justify delaying or withholding information, the investigator acquires a special responsibility to assure that there are no damaging consequences for the participant.

9. Where research procedures may result in undesirable consequences for the participant, the investigator has the responsibility to detect and remove or correct these consequences, including, where relevant, long-term aftereffects.

10. Information obtained about the research participants during the course of an investigation is confidential. When the possibility exists that others may obtain access to such information, ethical research practice requires that this possibility, together with the plans for protecting confidentiality, be explained to the participants as a part of the procedure for obtaining informed consent.

Note that informed consent is the basic notion embodied in these ethical principles. That is, the investigator has an obligation to inform the potential subject of all the features of the experiment that can reasonably be expected to influence the subject's willingness to participate. If this is impossible, then the investigator must take additional steps to ensure that the rights of the subject are not violated.

The Stuart W. Cook Committee, the group responsible for drafting the ethical principles, invited thousands of researchers to list incidents of research involving ethical issues. Some of the incidents were reported in the special issue of *The Monitor* (May, 1972) in which the second draft of the standards was presented and discussed. To give you an appreciation of some of the ethical problems researchers may confront, a number of these incidents have been paraphrased in the list that follows:

*Examples of Research Involving Ethical Issues**

1. An investigator is interested in the effect of manipulating the level of initial self-esteem. The proposed research would involve having two people compete for the attention of a member of the opposite sex. The experimenter would arrange the situation in such a way that one competitor would experi-

---

* Selected and adapted from the Special Issue of The American Psychological Association *Monitor* (May, 1972).

ence an embarrassing defeat while the other would be victorious. In this case there is no way to inform the subjects about the factors that may influence their willingness to participate and still make the desired manipulation. Is it possible to do this research without violating the ethical standards?

2. An investigator observes people in situations in which they do not know they are being observed. A cost-benefit rationale is offered for the invasion of privacy. The value of the findings is weighed against the possible harm to the subjects (e.g., the extent to which their privacy is violated). In cases in which the investigator has any misgivings about the ethical issue, a decision is made not to conduct the research. Furthermore, the investigator consults his colleagues before starting any research of this nature and weighs their views in arriving at a decision. The plan is to inform the subjects in full about the nature of the experiment after it is completed. If the subjects object to the study or to aspects of it, the investigator would not publish the results. Is research of this nature ethical? Are there some situations in which it would be ethical and others in which it would be unethical?

3. An investigator who was studying procedures for reducing fear of snakes had his graduate students telephone undergraduates to determine their willingness to participate. The investigator was unaware that the graduate students told the undergraduates they had to participate. What standards are violated?

4. The subjects were informed correctly regarding the basic procedures that would be used, but they were misinformed about the purpose of the experiment. They were told the experiment was designed to test the speed of the visual system. Actually, the experimenter was interested in testing long-term memory. The subjects were not told the real purpose because the investigator was afraid this knowledge would influence their performance. The experimenter reasoned that a subject who would participate for the stated reason would also participate for the real reason. Is this an acceptable procedure?

5. A doctoral student was interested in factors influencing cheating. The doctoral student administered an examination, collected the papers, and then photographed each one. The students were not informed about the photographing. The papers were returned unscored and the students were given the opportunity to cheat while scoring their papers. The papers were collected again and were compared with the photographs. Is this an ethical procedure?

6. A professor of psychology worked on the production line in a factory for one semester. He did not reveal his identity to his coworkers or his reasons for being there. His purpose was to study the interactions of his coworkers. The findings proved to be useful in his subsequent teaching and research. His coworkers, some of whom he became very close to, were not informed of his purpose until the observation session was completed. Is this type of data collection ethical?

7. An experimenter returned fake test scores to male college students in order to assess the effects of success and failure on a second task. The subjects were told that the test scores were related to IQ and grade point average. After the second test, the subjects were told that the scores were faked

and why the false information was given. The entire experiment was executed in a single session so that any fears the subjects had could be quickly alleviated. Is this an acceptable procedure?

8. A kidney patient and his nearest relative were asked to consent to having the patient take some tests to determine cognitive functioning before and after hemodialysis. The investigators were interested in the effects of uremia on cognitive functioning. In this case there is some question whether the patient was coerced into participating since his life depended on his remaining in the program. Did the patient have a real choice? Is the procedure ethical?

9. An experiment was conducted to assess driver reaction to a stressful situation. The subject was asked to drive a car past a construction site. The experimenter rigged a human-looking dummy in such a way that it would be propelled in front of the car making it impossible for the subject to avoid it. The subjects reacted as one would expect. And, when they learned that the situation was rigged, they informed the experimenter of their displeasure. Despite their complaints, the experimenter continued testing subjects. Is this procedure ethical?

10. An investigator was interested in how children would perform a task after watching another child being punished for low performance in the task. The question of interest was whether observing a punishment scene would raise or lower the children's subsequent performance relative to children who did not observe punishment. The children were tested in pairs. The first member of each pair received a scolding for low performance. The child's task was to drop marbles through holes. Even though the children were doing their best, they were scolded for low performance for approximately three minutes of the six-minute session. It was clear to the experimenter that most of the children were very anxious. After the session was over, the experimenter explained that he was only fooling and praised each child extensively. Most of the children seemed to understand. Is it ethical to use psychological torment in research?

11. An investigator, who was using Galvanic Skin Responding procedures, had a subject become extremely upset during a testing session. The eight-year-old subject discontinued the experiment and went home. The experimenter was unaware of the subject's reason for leaving. Later, it was determined that the subject thought that blood was being extracted from his body since the electrode wires had a red plastic covering and red ink was used in the recording pens. Was the experimenter's behavior unethical?

12. The respondents to a mailed questionnaire were told that they would not be identified with their responses. A self-addressed return envelope was included for the "convenience" of the responder. The type and location of the stamp were such that the investigator could identify 100 of the respondents to the questionnaire. In this procedure unethical?

13. An investigator conducted a series of interviews with patients in a state mental institution. The investigator assured each patient that the taped interviews would not be heard by anyone but the other member of the research team. Under these circumstances many of the patients gave extremely candid responses. For the purpose of discussion, assume that one patient

indicated a strong desire to escape from the institution for the purpose of committing sexual offenses on young children. What would you do if you were the investigator?

You can decide whether or not each of the above incidents violates the adopted standards presented in the ethical principles list. It should be kept in mind that researchers were specifically asked to provide examples of research involving ethical questions. The incidents presented are not representative of the research problems encountered by the "typical" investigator. You may want to have additional information before evaluating some of the incidents. Indeed, an important aspect of evaluation is deciding what additional information, if any, is needed.

A consideration of the list of ethical principles and the list of examples of ethical issues should provide you with an awareness of some of the ethical problems that may be raised by research. If a proposed project is in violation of these ethical standards, the investigator must either abandon the project or change it to eliminate unethical procedures. In some cases there is likely to be disagreement about whether a research project is in violation of the standards. For instance, there will probably be disagreement regarding whether some of the incidents described in the examples of ethical issues list should be placed in the unethical or ethical category. In some of these cases it is likely that procedural changes could be made which would eliminate the ethical problem.

If there is considerable difference of opinion about whether a particular procedure is in violation of the ethical standards and there is no change that can be made to eliminate the ethical problem, then the investigator is well advised to abandon the project. Fortunately, the vast majority of research projects do not pose serious ethical problems. Of course, this does not mean that ethical considerations can be taken lightly. Every investigator should evaluate his procedures carefully to determine whether they conform to the ethical standards.

The Importance of Ideas

Many people usually participate in judging the contribution that a particular finding makes to knowledge. The investigator assesses the value of his work at various stages in the investigation, particularly the planning stage, and usually asks a colleague to participate in this evaluation. If the results are submitted for publication, the work is usually evaluated by specialists in the same area. Most journal editors insist that research findings pass a contribution-to-knowledge test as one step in determining whether the findings should be published.

At this point the student does not have to be concerned about the importance of his research problem. He can test an idea of personal interest regardless of the potential importance of the results. The beginning researcher or one-time researcher can allow himself the luxury of testing an idea that may not be of particular interest to others but that serves as his vehicle for learning more about research methodology.

MEASUREMENT

The Importance of Measurement

Measurement is the use of rules to assign numbers to objects or events (Stevens, 1951). The particular rules used determine the level of measurement that is obtained and, consequently, the operations that can be performed on the numbers. For example, we can assign numbers to ten people on the basis of their height, assigning number 1 to the shortest person, number 2 to the next shortest, and so on. Or, we could measure each individual in inches and assign the appropriate number to each individual. A person who is 71 inches tall would be assigned the number 71. In both cases we are using rules to assign numbers to people, but the rules differ. (The consequences of using different rules is discussed in Chapter 8.)

The advantages of measurement are objectivity, comparability, and ease of communication. There is usually neither a problem of agreement nor a problem of communication when performance is described in terms of a score (i.e., a number) on some task or test. For example, if intelligence is defined in terms of performance on the Stanford-Binet Intelligence Test, there is no misunderstanding about what the investigator means by intelligence. And, it is easy to compare individuals on intelligence. We can be objective because the procedure for determining the number is specified. In the final analysis, however, the advantage of a specific measurement depends on the rule that is used to assign numbers to objects or events. Some rules may help an investigator understand a phenomenon and some may not. The usefulness of a rule for assigning numbers to objects or events depends on the *reliability* and *validity* of the measuring instrument (i.e., the procedures or rules used to assign the numbers).

Reliability

One way to view reliability is in terms of consistent measurement. We want to know whether or not repeated measures will give consistent results. Let us assume that an investigator is interested in predicting success in medical school. She believes that stress tolerance is an important consideration, so she administers a stress tolerance test to 100 medical school students. The plan is to determine how the score on the test is related to success in medical school. In order to make sure that she has obtained a good estimate of each student's stress tolerance, she administers another test to each student two weeks after the first test. Let us assume that the two tests of stress tolerance are equivalent. (In some cases it is possible to assess reliability by using the same test at two points in time provided there are no carry-over effects from the first to the second testing.) The dismayed experimenter finds that there is little relationship between the scores of each student on the two tests. Some of the students who scored high on the first test scored high on the second test, but just as many others who scored high on the first scored low on the second. It should be clear that stress tolerance, at least as it is defined by these tests, is an *unreliable* phenomenon. Obviously, if it is not possible to obtain a consistent (reliable) measure of stress tolerance, it is difficult to make any statement about the relationship between amount of stress tolerance and performance in medical school. Thus, in most cases, obtaining a reliable measure is a prerequisite to investigating the relationship between two or more measures.

Another way to view reliability is in terms of the accuracy of measurement. When considering reliability in terms of accuracy or precision, we can view each individual's score as having two components, a *true score* and an *error score*. Please keep in mind that we *cannot* take a particular score and divide it into a true score component and an error score component. Nevertheless, we can *theorize* that there is a true score component and an error score component. Further, we can assume that the true score component taps stable characteristics of the individual. This component does not change over time unless there has been a basic change in the individual. The error component, on the other hand, does change over time. This component represents all the chance factors that are likely to influence performance at any one time. Chance factors can increase or decrease the true score, or leave it unchanged. Reliability is determined by the relative magnitudes of the true score and error score components. If the error score component is much smaller than the true score component then chance fluctuations over time are small and, as a result, the total score on each testing occasion will be determined primarily by the true score component. In this case successive measurements will be accurate (close to the true score) and consistent (they will yield about the same score) because scores will be determined largely by the subject's stable characteristics. If, on the other hand, there is a large error score component, scores for repeated testings of the same individual are likely to vary widely. The scores for each subject are likely to be inaccurate and inconsistent because performance is determined primarily by chance.

On the surface there seems to be little reason to include accuracy in our definition of reliability. Scores are either consistent over successive testings or they are not. Why theorize about a true score component and an error score component? The reason for using accuracy as well as consistency to define reliability is that accuracy is more useful in research methodology and psychological testing. We will define reliability in terms of accuracy when considering quasi-experimental designs (Chapter 6). Students who take courses in psychological testing will find that the accuracy view of reliability suggests procedures for increasing the reliability of psychological tests. That is, there are statistical principles that can be applied to test construction that probably would not have been discovered if investigators had restricted themselves to a consistency definition. It is important to increase the reliability of psychological tests, of course, because accurate measurement is a precondition for determining the relationship among events. It is difficult, if not impossible, to assess relationships accurately if performance scores have a large error score component.

Validity of Measurement

Reliability is a necessary but not sufficient condition for obtaining useful research findings. Because psychologists often use indirect procedures to measure characteristics of individuals (e.g., creativity, intelligence, authoritarianism, altruism) it is reasonable to ask whether the measurement instrument measures what it is intended to measure. If it does we can say that it is *valid*. There are three types of *validity* for measurement instruments: content, predictive, and construct.

Content Validity. Content validity is the representativeness of the items of the measuring instrument. Content validity is extremely important to instructors because they realize that their examinations should assess the student's mastery of the assigned material. Let us assume, for example, that your instructor assigns the first seven chapters of this text and then prepares a midterm examination to test you on their content. There are several ways that the midterm could be prepared. In two extreme cases, the test questions could be based on material taken from one chapter, or the questions could be based on material from all of the assigned chapters. If the quality of the items is about the same, the first test would have lower content validity than the second because the test questions for the first test would be less representative of the assigned material.

Content validity is difficult to determine because rating the representativeness of items is a subjective matter. In order to increase objectivity, one might have a number of judges independently rate the representativeness of the test items and then compare the judges' ratings to screen out poor items. The ease of determining content validity is related to the specificity of the content to be mastered; it is easier to attain if objectives are clearly stated. That is, content validity should be less of a problem if it is possible to specify what students are expected to know.

Predictive Validity. Predictive validity is similar to content validity; both tell us whether the test measures what it is supposed to measure. They are determined by different procedures, however. Predictive validity is determined by comparing the results of a test with an external *criterion* or standard. For this reason predictive validity is sometimes called criterion-related validity.

Let us assume that you are interested in assessing altruism. You construct a test and demonstrate that it is reliable; you call it the Altruism Test. But a friend objects because she does not think the test measures *true* altruism. She decides to make her point by constructing her own test, which she demonstrates to be reliable and calls the True Altruism Test. You object because you believe your test is every bit as good a measure of true altruism as hers. You and your friend have 100 people take both tests and you find that scores on one test are unrelated to scores on the other. That is, a person who scores high on one test does not necessarily score high on the other test. Since the two tests are unrelated it is apparent that they are measuring different things. Who, then, is measuring true altruism? In reality, there is little to be gained by arguing for such entities as true altruism, true anxiety, true intelligence, and so forth. Your test would have been more useful had you used stable behaviors to predict other behaviors instead of concentrating on a vaguely defined characteristic.

In fact, one way to determine the usefulness of a test, assuming it is reliable, is to determine whether the results can be used to predict other behaviors. In this case it is necessary to establish a criterion for altruism (such as donating blood or helping the poor) in order to assess the predictive validity of the test. We want to discover whether the score on the *test* predicts performance on the *criterion* (whether the person whose test score indicates a high degree of altruism will in fact donate blood or help the poor). Many needless disputes arise because people do not other to specify the criteria they use to evaluate success. For example, the problem of assessing the quality of instruction is complicated by the failure of many individuals to specify their criteria for evaluating instruction. A difficult problem encountered in assessing validity is establishing an acceptable criterion.

Construct Validity. A construct is a concept that has been invented to account for individual differences in behavior, or why people differ in performance. Investigators interested in construct validation assume that individuals possess stable characteristics that can be measured and used to account for performance in a number of situations. Testing a theory and validating a construct are the same except that construct validation involves testing a particular kind of theory, a theory about why individuals behave differently. Some theories do not make predictions about individual differences. For example, an investigator interested in testing a new instructional technique can determine whether the new technique increases overall performance. She may not be interested in explaining individual differences in classroom performance. On the other hand, an investigator interested in the relationship between anxiety and classroom performance (e.g., performance on a final examination) is likely to be interested in construct validation. Does anxiety, a construct, account for individual differences in performance? At one time it was common for investigators to be interested in individual differences or the effect of treatment manipulations (i.e., comparing an old and new technique) but not both. Today, many investigators combine the study of treatment effects with the

26 Introduction

study of individual differences (see Cronbach, 1975; Underwood, 1975). Since both approaches are designed to test theories of behavior and mental activity, it makes a great deal of sense to combine them, as we will do in this text. The student who prefers a more detailed discussion of reliability and validity can refer to Cronbach's *Essentials of Psychological Testing* (1970).

Validity of Experiments

The term validity is also used in reference to experiments. Because experiments are measurement instruments, in that they assess treatment effects, the uses of the term do not differ very much. In all cases we are concerned with the validity of a measuring instrument.

Campbell (1957) distinguishes between two kinds of validity for experiments. An experiment has *internal validity* if the treatment has an effect in or on an inherent experimental condition or activity (e.g., behavior in the laboratory). It has *external validity* if the treatment effect can be generalized beyond the specific experimental conditions or activities. Thus, a treatment effect that can be obtained in the real world (i.e., in different settings, with different populations of subjects, and so forth) has external validity.

SUMMARY

The reader who learns how research is conducted in the social sciences is in a good position to evaluate the reports of research findings and the claims of investigators and so-called experts. A knowledge of research methodology can have an important influence on how you evaluate ideas, what you consider interesting and important, and what you learn from experience. Psychology majors in particular should understand how knowledge is obtained in their discipline.

The assumptions of the scientific approach are *order, determinism, parsimony,* and *empiricism*. Scientists assume that events are ordered (follow each other in regular sequences) and that they are determined (have detectable antecedents). Parsimony refers to the preference for simple over complex explanation, and for general theories over specific theories. Empiricism is the scientific practice of subjecting ideas to systematic, controlled, tests, using observation and experiment.

The basic goal of science is to understand natural phenomena. We can compare two or more theories of a phenomenon by making predictions about observable events. *Theories* are tentative explanations that must be testable in order to be of any use to scientists. They guide research and serve as a basis for organizing knowledge. It is necessary to test them because the "natural" process of selecting good solutions is typically crude, slow, and subject to considerable error. The important questions to consider when evaluating ideas are: Is the idea important? Is it refutable? Is it possible to specify the operations that should be performed to test the idea? Are the processes or events to be compared actually comparable? Are the procedures used to test the idea practical and ethical? The ethical considerations involved in doing research are great regardless of whether animals or humans are tested.

Measurement is the use of rules to assign numbers to objects or events. The rules used determine the level of measurement and the operations that can be performed on the numbers. *Reliability* and *validity* are the two major factors determining the usefulness of a measuring instrument. Reliability refers to the consistency, or accuracy, of measurement. *Content validity* is the representativeness of the items of the measuring instrument. *Predictive validity* is determined by comparing performance on a measurement instrument to an external criterion. The goal of *construct validation* is to determine whether constructs (concepts invented for scientific purposes) can account for individual differences in behavior. *Internal validity* refers to whether the treatment has an effect in a given experimental instance. *External validity* refers to whether a treatment effect can be generalized.

QUESTIONS

1. Examine a recent issue of a newpaper for articles in which claims are made for a particular product, technique, or course of action. Select one of the claims not accompanied by supporting evidence and indicate how support for the claim could be obtained.
2. How does the scientific approach differ from a "common sense" approach to problem solving?
3. Defend or refute the parsimony assumption for the scientific approach.
4. Assume that there are three opposing theories to account for the relationship between frustration and anxiety. How might you decide which theory is best? That is, what criteria would you use to evaluate the three theories?
5. Define frustration and anxiety operationally.
6. Why are only testable ideas of worth to the scientific community? Give an example, other than those mentioned in the text, of one testable and one nontestable idea.
7. Evaluate each of the examples of ethical issues on page 18 in terms of the ethical principles listed on page 17.
8. A social psychologist is interested in bystander apathy. Her research plan involves having confederates fake heart attacks in different locations (e.g., classroom, subway, street, church) while wearing different "disguises" (e.g., well dressed, poorly dressed). She wants to measure the likelihood that bystanders will come to the aid of the "victim." What are the ethical considerations? Can research of this nature be performed without violating the ethical standards?
9. What is the relationship, if any, between operational definitions and measurement?

10. Distinguish between the consistency and accuracy views of reliability. Are these two views compatible?
11. Compare the three types of validity for measuring instruments.
12. Distinguish between internal and external validity.
13. Assume that you have developed a test to evaluate classroom instruction. Make a list of potential criteria that could be used to establish the predictive validity of the test.
14. Let us assume that you want to measure creativity. What kind of items should you use? How would you determine the reliability and validity of your test?

methods of research 2

To understand and evaluate research findings we need a good grasp of research methods. Casual reading in psychological journals may lead us to conclude that learning the methodology is a gigantic task. Fortunately, however, social scientist primarily use only four basic methods to conduct their thousands of investigations of behavior and mental activity. The conclusions that can be drawn from research findings depend on the method used. A knowledge of these four approaches — observation, correlation, experimentation, and quasi-experimentation — provides a good foundation for understanding and evaluating research.

THE OBSERVATIONAL APPROACH

Although observation is fundamental to all four approaches, the goal of the scientist using the observational approach is solely to describe the phenomenon. Initially a researcher might attempt to record as much of the organism's behavior as possible with no preconception about what behaviors are important. It is difficult to overemphasize the value of such broad observation, particularly in the early stages of an investigation. Investigators are often too quick to use controlled observations or experiments to test their views, thereby taking the risk of failing to see the forest for the trees. The researcher who takes the time to view the organism in several situations gains a better overall picture of the interrelations among the behaviors. A particular behavior may be understandable only in terms of other behaviors. The importance of unrestricted observation is not limited to the study of animals in their natural habitat, of course. It can be valuable in all areas of psychology with the possible exception of physiological psychology.

Restricted observations are made after the investigator has selected a particular phenomenon for study. Observations are then confined to those behaviors that are relevant for understanding the phenomenon. Usually this means that the investigator makes systematic observations and records them in detail. For example, if he is interested in territorial behavior, he may note the extent to which an animal will defend and mark its territory (e.g., urinating on the boundaries of its territory), and also the relationship between territorial and breeding behaviors. He may record the number of times an animal engages in each activity during a specified period such as one hour each day for a month.

The Observer

The function of the observer is, of course, to record in some way the behavior that actually occurred. This, it turns out, is not an easy task. One danger is that the observer will introduce bias by reporting more than is observed. For example, you may see a rabbit eating dandelions and record that the hungry rabbit ate dandelions. However, it is not clear that the animal was hungry; perhaps it was eating because of boredom, anxiety, or an unresolved oral fixation. Another danger is that the observer may not be equipped to make the relevant observations. For example, someone interested in the speech sounds of infancy may not be able to recognize the wide variety of sounds emitted by infants and therefore may fail to record the relevant behaviors. Obviously, in some cases it is best to use mechanical recording equipment instead of, or in addition to, a human observer. One must analyze the situation to determine what kind of observation (e.g., tape recorder, movie camera, human observer) and what level of observation (e.g., behavioral or physiological) will be most useful.

The advantage of the human observer is that humans, unlike tape recorders or television cameras, can evaluate what they observe. Thus humans can select only those behaviors bearing on the research problem. For example, an investigator interested in creativity in young children can train observers to pay attention to creative behaviors only. A tape recorder, television camera, or computer cannot be programmed to record only creative behaviors. However, a human observer may make recording errors.

There is ample reason to believe that human observers must be trained in order to minimize the number of recording errors. Untrained observers of the same event often disagree about what happened. Try staging an argument in front of a group of unsuspecting students. After the argument, ask the students to record what happened. If the staged event is complicated, the students are likely to disagree. We tend to be rather unobservant. (Can you recall the color of the outfit your companion was wearing yesterday?) Fortunately, it is possible to obtain reliable observations by deciding in advance what behaviors are to be observed and by training observers to respond to the appropriate features of the situation.

The reliability of observations can be checked by having observers independently record the same event. If they agree, the problem of reliability has been solved. The difficulty of obtaining agreement about the important aspects of a situation is not unique to the social sciences. It is well known, for example, that sports fans do not always agree about the occurrence of a rule infraction even though, presumably, they all have the same information.

Several different techniques can be used to observe behavior; they vary according to the nature of the situation and the relationship of the observer to the observee. For convenience in exposition, the observational techniques have been classified as reactive measures, nonreactive measures without intervention, and nonreactive measures with intervention.

Reactive Measures

The Nature of Reactive Measures. If an investigator observes the behavior of an animal and the animal detects his presence, a reactive measure will be obtained. That is, the animal may react to the presence of the investigator, and its reaction will be a part of the record. Similarly, if an animal is removed from its natural environment and placed in a new one for the purpose of observation, a reactive measure will result. The animal may react to the new situation. Ethologists and comparative psychologists have long realized that the behavior of an animal in its natural habitat can be markedly different from its behavior in an unnatural situation. They have also realized that it is important to remain unobstrusive when observing animals in their natural habitat.

Again, if a human knows that he is being observed, the result will be a reactive measure. For example (ethical questions aside), if a listening device placed in an apartment is detected, the behavior of the occupants will reflect the fact that they know they are being overheard. Many of the measures that psychologists obtain are reactive, including personality tests, intelligence tests, interviews, surveys, and questionnaires.

Psychologists are aware that their measures may be influenced by lack of candor in subjects who know they are being tested. For example, an individual taking a personality test may exaggerate in an effort to make a good impression. There is a lie scale for the Minnesota Multiphasic Personality Inventory that can be used to assess willingness to exaggerate. Those who respond that they never put off until tomorrow what they can do today are probably stretching the truth somewhat, as are those who indicate that they never do anything in private that they would not do in public. Items of this nature allow psychologists to estimate the veracity of the responses. Obviously, a reactive measure may be little value if the testee's responses are not candid. About all that can be concluded is that he would like to make a good impression. Sometimes the real purpose of a test is disguised in order to prevent biasing of the results. And, although some reactive measures may have little value, others can be very useful.

The Usefulness of Reactive Measures. Reactive measures have considerable usefulness because it is often necessary to assess performance with the full cooperation of the person being assessed. Achievement tests, intelligence tests, some personality tests, most skill tests, and most interviews are based on the assumption that very useful information can be obtained when the individual is fully aware that he is being evaluated. For example, if there are many applicants but only a few open positions, it may be desirable to use a reactive measure to determine the "best" applicants. Such a measure can ensure that each applicant will give his best effort.

Some applicants may not perform at the highest level of their capabilities because of emotional considerations; still, a reactive measure usually provides a better assessment of achievement and intelligence than a nonreactive measure. The relative usefulness of the two approaches can be determined, of course, by comparing their reliability and validity. A nonreactive measure is preferable in some situations.

Nonreactive Measures without Intervention

A man is driving his car on a four-lane interstate highway. The driving conditions are excellent: traffic is light, the road is dry, visibility is good. He checks the speedometer and notices that he is going slightly over the 70 mile per hour limit. He is unconcerned. He sees a police car ahead and slows down to 70. After passing the police car he gradually increases his speed over the speed limit. After about twenty minutes of driving, he sees two police cars with their warning lights flashing. The officers are slowing all traffic and requiring some drivers to pull their cars to the side of the road. Our driver was clocked by a helicopter going 81.12 miles per hour in a 70 mile per hour zone, so he received a ticket for speeding. (The example is true; my fine was twenty-one dollars.) The point is, of course, that our behavior when we know we are under observation may differ considerably from our behavior when we do not know. Law enforcement agencies recognize this fact and, therefore, use nonreactive measures as an additional means to apprehend lawbreakers.

This particular approach may produce an undesirable result, however, if motorists, in an effort to outwit lawofficers, spend more time looking up in the air for helicopters than watching the road. That is, a nonreactive technique may become ineffective with continued use. It is probable, for example, that the use of one-way mirrors is no longer an effective way to obtain a nonreactive measure of adult human behavior. Many students who serve in psychological experiments are aware that there could be someone watching them from behind the "mirror." Yet for many other nonreactive measures, there is little or no danger of discovery.

An investigator may conclude that reactive measures are unsatisfactory for his purpose because the behaviors that occur in a structured situation are much different from ones that occur naturally. If the natural behavior is of interest, then nonreactive measures should be used. Observing animals in their natural habitat is one way to obtain nonreactive measures without intervention. In order not to influence the behavior being observed the investigator should refrain from making changes in the animal's habitat, and should try to remain undetected.

A good source of information on nonreactive measures is an entertaining book by Webb, Campbell, Schwartz, and Sechrest (1966). It contains numerous examples of how such measures can be used for research in the social sciences. For example, alcohol consumption can be measured by counting the number of alcohol bottles in the garbage. Obviously, any form of bugging device, if undetected, would provide a nonreactive measure.

Public and private records may also provide useful nonreactive measures. An investigator may be interested in studying, say, the effect of a national disaster such as an earthquake in California on human migration to and from that state. If she contacts the major moving companies and obtains their records of moves in and out of California for the year preceding and the year following the earthquake, she can estimate its effect on migration. If there is "considerably more" movement out of California after the earthquake than there was before, *and* if the exodus is not attributable to other factors (e.g., industry moving out of California, weakness in the aerospace industry), then there is support for the view that the earthquake resulted in the exodus. Nonreactive measures can thus provide useful information, particularly if they are obtained at different times. If a particular event is *followed* by a marked change in the nonreactive measure, then there is some support for the view that the event caused the change. The weakness of this approach is that it is difficult to rule out other possible causes.

Nonreactive Measures with Intervention

The use of nonreactive measures without intervention may not be the most appropriate way to investigate a particular phenomenon because one may have to wait too long for it to occur. It may be necessary to modify the situation to produce the desired phenomenon. If so, the modification must be unsuspected. If the observee detects the intervention then, of course, the measure obtained will be reactive instead of nonreactive.

The observation that weaver finches build their nests after a rainfall may lead an investigator to conclude that rainfall is a necessary condition for nest building. Once this notion is formulated, it is then possible to intervene to assess its accuracy. Marshall and Disney (1957) showed that if green grass is made available to weaver finches, they will start to build nests in the absence of a preceding rainfall. Thus, the notion that rainfall is a necessary precondition is discounted. The intervention enabled the investigators to test their idea. If they had not intervened, it might have been a long time before an observer, a weaver finch, green grass, and dry weather occurred in such a way as to demonstrate that green grass and not rainfall is the necessary condition.

Intervention is also useful for studying human responses. For example, a social psychologist who wants to observe reactions to a person in distress may have a confederate fake a heart attack on a crowed subway. Since the "victim" is a confederate of the investigator, the procedure involves intervention. Or several confederates could stage a fight in order to determine how bystanders will respond.

One could argue that there is little need to go to the trouble of staging a fight or faking a heart attack. To find out how people will react in a particular situation, all you have to do is ask them. In some cases this is probably true. Some people who claim that they would intervene would in fact do so. However, in other cases, the self-report procedure (reactive measure) would yield misleading results. There are discrepancies between reactive and nonreactive measures. The usefulness of each is likely to depend on the problem investigated.

Observational techniques are useful for describing behaviors and — if the observer is more than a passive recorder of events — for suggesting ideas. For example, many therapists modify their methods as a result of observations made during therapy sessions. Yet in order to test adequately the ideas generated during simple observation, the therapist usually needs to go beyond it. Some sort of intervention may be required, or it may be necessary to use the correlational, quasi-experimental, or experimental method.

You should not conclude that only investigators in the social sciences use observational techniques. All sciences and many service professions use them extensively. The epidemiologist, for instance, frequently compares a current set of observations with an earlier set. It is possible to determine whether there is an epidemic of a particular disease by comparing the present incidence of the disease per 100,000 population with earlier observations of the incidence per 100,000. Or, the epidemiologist can evaluate the alleged side effects of a drug by comparing sets of observations. He can, for example, determine whether or not the number of deaths due to blood clotting per 100,000 is greater for women taking birth control pills than for women not taking them. Observational techniques are useful in so many areas partly because of the sheer number and kinds of observations already recorded. Information that is already a matter of public record can be used to answer many questions.

In summary, the three observational techniques differ with respect to whether the observer remains undetected and whether he intervenes.

THE CORRELATIONAL APPROACH

The Nature of Correlation

A *variable* is a thing or event that can be measured or manipulated. Once an experimenter through repeated observations has obtained information on several variables, the next logical step is to examine the relationships among these variables. Correlational methods can be used to specify the degree of relationship between variables. For two of the three correlational methods considered in this text, the basic task is to determine the tendency of a person who has a high, medium, or low score on one measure to have a high, medium, or low score on a second measure. For example, if there is a high positive correlation between the rate of pupil dilation and problem-solving ability, then people with rapid dilation should tend to be good problem solvers (e.g., solve many problems in a twenty-minute period), and people with slow dilation should tend to be poor problem solvers (e.g., solve few problems in a twenty-minute period). If there is a high negative correlation between the two measures, then those with rapid dilation should be poor problem solvers and those with slow dilation good problem solvers. Or, there may be little or no correlation between the two variables. The magnitude of a correlation can be any value from -1.00 to $+1.00$.

You should be careful not to misinterpret the adjectives *positive* and *negative* as used to modify *correlation*. They do not indicate a value judgment; a positive correlation is not better than a negative one. A positive correlation means only that high scores on one measure tend to go with high scores on the other, middle scores tend to go with middle scores, and low scores with low. A negative correlation means that high scores on one measure tend to go with low scores on the other, and middle scores with middle scores. The investigator often determines whether the obtained correlation is positive or negative by using a particular measuring procedure.

Let us assume that our investigator is interested in the relationship between the aggressiveness of adult male seals and the number of seals in their harems. She and another investigator observe a group of twelve adult males for a month and independently rank them by aggressiveness. The observers are in exact agreement regarding the rankings. The most aggressive seal is given the rank of one, the next most aggressive the rank of two, and so on. Then the animals are observed during the mating season and the size of the harem of each adult male is determined. Our investigator computes a correlation between the aggressiveness rankings and the size of harem measure and obtains a high negative correlation. This means that the seals with low numbers on the aggressiveness scale (i.e., the more aggressive seals) have larger harems. The investigator could have made the correlation positive, without changing its magnitude (or its meaning), by assigning the rank of twelve to the most aggressive male, eleven to the next most aggressive, and so on.

Correlation and Prediction

Prediction. One of the advantages to being able to specify the degree of relationship between two variables is that prediction is made possible. Predictions can be made about past as well as future events. Scientists can predict future events, and they can predict events that have already occurred if they do not know the outcome before making the prediction. For example, an investigator interested in testing an "environmental" theory of suicide may obtain a partial test of the theory by examining weather and suicide rates for the last several years. The weather information can be used to predict suicide rates for various areas of the country. After the predictions are made the investigator can examine the actual suicide rates to check the predictions. Of course, the predictions must be made before examining the suicide rates. There is no test of our *understanding* if we know the facts before making the predictions. If we use a theory to predict what will happen under certain experimental conditions we are making predictions for theoretical purposes; we want to evaluate our understanding (theory) of a phenomenon. On the other hand, predictions can be made for purely applied situations; such predictions are usually based on correlations.

Using Correlations to Make Predictions. The accuracy of prediction increases as the magnitude of the correlation increases. Thus, if two variables are correlated and we know an individual's performance on one of the variables, we can accurately predict performance on the second. In many applied situations it is important to be able to predict an individual's performance. For example, it is possible to predict harem size for seals accurately by assessing aggressiveness or vice versa. Or, if there is a high correlation between success in graduate school and performance on a particular test, the test can be used to predict success. If there are more applicants than can be accepted, it can be used to select the ones to be admitted. Whether or not such a selection procedure is justified would depend in part on the degree of relationship between the variables. In this case, success in graduate school would be the *criterion* on which to judge how well the test predicts.

If the correlation between the test and the criterion is perfect — i.e., if the person who gets the highest score is the best graduate student, the one who gets the second highest score is the second best, and so on — then we can justify using the test to screen applicants. However, if the correlation is not close to +1.00 or −1.00, it is more difficult to justify the procedure because the abilities that produce a high score on the test are not necessarily those that lead to academic success. If the actual correlation is .50, a person who does well on the test has a higher probability of doing well in graduate studies than one who does poorly on the test; however, some people who do well on the test will fail in graduate school and vice versa. In this case of an imperfect correlation between the test and the criterion, a person's decision as to whether the use of the test as a screening device is justified might well depend on his of her ability to perform well on written tests. An admissions office would, with reason, most likely be willing to accept the screening device in spite of its limitations, so long as the tests do predict academic success for a significant number of applicants.

Correlation and Causality

Interpreting a Correlation. Another advantage of correlation is that it can help support or refute notions about behavior. You have probably been warned not to infer a causal relationship from a correlation. This is good advice because inferring causality is, at best, very risky. Reservations of philosophers aside, the four criteria for causality accepted by most scientists are *association, time priority, nonspurious relation,* and *rationale* (Labovitz & Hagedorn, 1971). Association is the relationship between variables, frequently assessed by using correlational techniques. Time priority refers to which variable occurred first. (If smoking causes lung cancer, smoking should occur *before* lung cancer develops.) *Nonspurious relation* refers to the fact that no third variable accounts for the observed relationship between two variables. Rationale is the logic or explanation for the observed relationship. Is there a theoretical justification for the observed relationship? Does the observed relationship fit in with our understanding of similar phenomena?

Two variables can be related without being causally related. For example, although there may be a high correlation between the consumption of alcohol and the birth rate in the United States for the years 1947 to 1962, we would not want to conclude, necessarily, that the increased consumption of alcohol was responsible for the increased birth rate. We would need to determine the temporal relationship of the variables and whether one or more third variables could account for the obtained relationship, and evaluate any theory that was offered to account for the observed relationship. Similarly, there may be a high correlation between height and weight, but it does not follow that the relationship is causal.

Sometimes, however, highly correlated variables will be causally related. Many people are willing to conclude, for example, that smoking can cause lung cancer even though the evidence is almost entirely correlational. If it is necessary to make a decision about whether to stop smoking, it is reasonable to interpret the high correlation between smoking and lung cancer obtained in many studies as evidence of a causal relationship. Although this interpretation may not be correct, one can hardly question the smoker's right to make it. After all, the concern is with his lungs! Besides, temporal priority, spuriousness, and rationale all support a causal interpretation. There does not seem to be any reasonable alternative explanation, at least at the present time, for this high correlation.

The heated arguments over how to interpret a correlation generally occur when a causal interpretation is likely to have public influence *and* when there are other credible interpretations. For example, there is a positive correlation between the number of handguns and the number of homicides involving the use of handguns. In areas where there are many handguns, there are many homicides. If one interprets this correlation as indicating a casual relationship, one is likely to favor the outlawing of handguns. Yet, it is also possible that a high incidence of violence may cause people to buy handguns in order to protect themselves, rather than the other way around. One is free to argue for either position because correlational evidence may or may not reflect an underlying causal relationship. And, even when causality *is* involved, knowledge of the correlation does not by itself tell you which variable is the cause of the other. There is a correlational technique that makes it possible to reach cause-effect conclusions about variables but a consideration of this approach is beyond the score of this text (see Crano, Kenny, & Campbell, 1972).

Multiple Correlations and Causality. If a particular problem cannot be investigated by other methods, an investigator may decide to use the correlational approach extensively to get "close" to a causal statement. The basic difficulty with this approach is that some variable other than the one being considered may be responsible for the obtained correlation. Let us assume, for instance, that an investigator is interested in the factors that contribute to a successful marriage. She decides to correlate the degree of childhood happiness and marital happiness and obtains a high positive correlation. A critic points out that childhood happiness may not be the important variable. He believes, rather, that the important variable may be the number of siblings of each marital partner, and that the number of siblings is related both to happiness in childhood and to marital success. Thus, there are two plausible rival hypotheses for the relationship between childhood and marital success. If the number of siblings is the important variable then the relationship between childhood and marital success is spurious.

To test this notion our investigator can compute correlations separately for all subjects having the same number of siblings. That is, she can compute the correlation between childhood happiness and marital success for people having no siblings, then for people having one sibling, and so on. If she still obtains high correlations regardless of the number of siblings, then she can discount the critic's position. There is more reason to believe that the relationship between childhood and marital success is nonspurious. Other explanations can be tested by the same process. If the relationship cannot be accounted for by other variables (i.e., other rival hypotheses can be eliminated), then it is reasonable to place more confidence in the initial interpretation. It does not follow necessarily that there is a causal relationship between happiness in childhood and success in marriage, but this is a good possibility. A good theoretical justification for the relationship would make it even a better possibility.

The person who is selecting a mate may decide not to consider people who had unhappy childhoods. There is little reason to ignore the correlational evidence when making a decision because the correlation may, in fact, be due to a causal relationship between the two variables. Even if a third variable is responsible, it is still possible to use the correlation to predict marital success. Although it is important theoretically to determine whether two highly correlated variables are causally related, it may not make any practical difference.

Correlation and Discovery. Correlation, like observation, can lead to the discovery of possible causal relationships, which may then become the subject of experimental investigation. The correlational technique is somewhat better than the observational in that it specifies the degree of the relationship.

One should consider a variable's effect on behavior when selecting variables for experimental investigation. For example, if correlations of fifty different variables with the incidence of lung cancer lead to the discovery that some variables have high correlations with lung cancer whereas others have very low or zero correlations, then the investigator who wants to select some variables and manipulate them experimentally to assess whether they *cause* lung cancer would be well advised to select those with high correlations.

THE EXPERIMENTAL METHOD: BASIC PROPERTIES

Independent and Dependent Variables

As we said in our discussion of correlation, a *variable* is a thing or event that can be measured or manipulated. The manipulation can be qualitative (e.g., two or more instructional techniques) or quantitative (e.g., the amount of protein in a diet). It can involve comparing the presence of a thing or event with its absence (instruction versus no instruction, or protein versus no protein). Whatever can be manipulated can be used as an *independent variable*. For example, if a farmer varies systematically the amount of fertilizer that he uses on each of four plots, the amount of fertilizer is an independent variable. Independent and manipulated are synonymous terms in this case. Some investigators prefer to call these things or events *manipulated* variables rather than independent variables. The yield from the four plots (i.e., the number of bushels of corn) is also a variable, but it is not manipulated by the farmer. The number of bushels of corn is measured to assess the effect of the fertilizer manipulation. Variables used to assess the effect of manipulated (independent) variables are called *dependent* variables. The crux of experimentation is to manipulate independent variables and assess the effect of the manipulation by measuring dependent variables. That is, one conducts experiments to determine whether performance on a dependent measure (e.g., a behavior) does, in fact, depend on the level of the independent variable. The independent variable is what is manipulated; the dependent variable is what is measured.

Examples of Independent and Dependent Variables. A particular variable may be used as either an independent or a dependent variable, according to whether it is *controlled* by the experimenter or measured by the experimenter.

Let us assume that you are interested in the effect of the amount of rainfall on wheat production. You decide to manipulate the "rainfall" by varying the amount of time that you turn on a sprinkling system in an experimental wheat field, protected from natural rainfall. In this case the amount of rainfall is the independent variable because you have control over the sprinkling system. Yet rainfall can also be used as the dependent variable. You could conduct an experiment to assess whether salting the clouds or doing a rain dance results in greater rainfall than normally occurs. First, divide the thirty days of September randomly into three groups of ten days each. The rain dance is done for one set of ten days; the clouds are salted on the second set; and nothing is done for the third set. The effect of the independent variable (rain dance, salting clouds, nothing) is assessed by measuring the amount of rainfall for each of the three sets of days. In this case rainfall is the dependent variable. The rain dance and salting clouds are called the experimental conditions. The "nothing" period of time is the control condition. In this case, a period of ten days corresponds to a group of subjects or a plot of land.

In some cases the same thing can be used as an independent and dependent variable in the same experiment. One can manipulate the level of punishment given to subjects and then give them the opportunity to punish others. The amount of punishment they receive is the independent variable, the amount they administer is the dependent variable. Or, if an investigator is interested in the social effects of laughing, she can use the amount of laughing as both an independent and dependent variable. She can have a confederate remain quiet, giggle slightly, or give a hearty belly laugh according to a prearranged sequence. This is, of course, the independent variable. Then the effect of the confederate's laughter on the laughter of the subjects can be assessed. The laughing behavior of the subjects is the dependent variable.

Experimental and Control Groups. The labels experimental and control can be used to distinguish groups when the independent variable involves comparing the presence of a thing or event with its absence. The groups that receive the thing or event are called *experimental groups*. The group that does not receive the thing or event is called the *control group*. Thus, a farmer may vary systematically the amount of fertilizer that he uses on each of four plots and not apply any fertilizer to a fifth plot. In this case the four plots that received fertilizer are the experimental plots; the fifth plot, which did not receive any fertilizer, is the control plot.

The Logic of the Experimental Method

The experimental method differs from the observational and correlational approaches in that the experimenter manipulates one or more independent variables in an attempt to influence the behavior of the subjects. The logic of the method is straightforward. If two groups of "equivalent" subjects are treated identically in all respects except one *and* if the performance of the two groups differs, it follows that the one respect in which the groups varied (i.e., the independent variable) is the cause of the performance difference.

The proper use of the experimental method makes it possible to assess the association between variables (i.e., to determine the effect of the manipulated variable on behavior), to control time priority between variables (i.e., to make the manipulation *before* measuring behavior), and to assess nonspurious relationships, because groups are equivalent on all but manipulated variables. Thus all differences in behavior can be attributed to the planned manipulations.

A few words need to be said about the special meaning of *equivalent groups* in psychological research. Equivalent groups are not identical or equal in an absolute sense; rather, they are groups whose differences in performance can be attributed solely to chance fluctuations. The subjects in two groups can differ somewhat in performance and still be equivalent in this sense. Chance fluctuations are always present. A central question in analyzing the results of experiments is whether the performance differences between groups are due solely to chance or to chance *plus* the effect of the independent variable. Equivalent groups are formed when the procedures used for selecting and assigning subjects ensure that any differences between groups are due solely to chance.

SUBJECT VARIABLES AND THE EXPERIMENTAL METHOD

Definition of a Subject Variable

A *subject* variable is a characteristic of the subject that can be measured. Height, weight, age, intelligence, anxiety level, number of siblings, beauty, hostility, and self-esteem are all subject variables. Research in which such variables are varied requires special attention because these "'manipulations" do not fit neatly into either the correlational or experimental category. It is not possible to manipulate a subject variable in the same way as a nonsubject variable, such as instructional technique or incentive.

When a *nonsubject variable* is manipulated, the experimenter is free to determine what level of the independent variable each subject will receive; however, when a subject variable is used as the independent variable, its level has already been determined for each subject. The experimenter can only *select* subjects who have particular characteristics and compare them. For example, she can select some who are tall and some who are short and compare them on a dependent measure (e.g., strength), but she cannot decide who will be tall and who will be short. A subject variable can be manipulated only in the sense that the experimenter is free to *select* and compare subjects who differ on a characteristic of interest.

This distinction is an important methodological consideration. With a nonsubject variable manipulation it is possible to arrive at a cause-effect conclusion; however, with a subject variable, it is extremely difficult, if not impossible, to do so. "Manipulating" a subject variable is, for interpretational purposes, the same as correlating it with the dependent variable. One has to be careful *not* to conclude that a subject variable is the *cause* of group differences in performance on the dependent measure.

Subject Variables and Causality

The Correlation of Subject Variables. An investigator is interested in the relationship between intelligence, a subject variable, and classroom performance. One approach is to obtain an IQ score and a classroom performance score for each subject and then compute a correlation between the two sets of scores. The correlation would provide an index of the extent to which high IQ scores go with high classroom performance scores, middle scores go with middle scores, and low scores with low. Even if a high positive correlation were obtained, the investigator would still be unwilling to conclude that intelligence was the cause of classroom performance, because he would realize that other subject variables might be responsible. For example, people with high IQs may be more highly motivated to do well. Perhaps motivation is the important variable.

The Experimental Manipulation of Subject Variables. The fact that one should be reluctant to infer causality from correlational data but not from experimental data may lead the investigator to convert his correlational study into an "experimental" study. Instead of correlating intelligence with classroom performance he decides to form two groups, one of high IQ subjects and one of low IQ subjects, and to assess their classroom performance. The IQ manipulation (i.e., the *selection* of subjects who differ on IQ) is the independent variable and classroom performance is the dependent variable.

Now, in this experimental version of the study, if the high IQ group does better than the low IQ group, is it possible to conclude that intelligence caused the difference in performance? No. The "experimental" manipulation of a subject variable does not allow the investigator to arrive at a cause-effect conclusion. Performance and intelligence are related, but not necessarily causally related. High and low intelligence groups are likely to differ in more ways than intelligence; therefore, it is not possible to manipulate only intelligence through selection of subjects. The experiment is *confounded* in that some correlate of intelligence (e.g., motivation level) may have been responsible for the difference in performance. An experiment is said to be *confounded* when two or more variables could be responsible for the obtained difference in performance of two groups.

Suppose an investigator wants to test a prediction that blonde college girls are likely to have more dates. The procedure could be very simple. The investigator *selects* thirty natural blondes and thirty natural redheads and tabulates the number of dates each girl has for a given period. Let us assume that blondes had significantly more dates. Can this difference be attributed to hair color? No. All one can say is that the blondes had more dates. It is unreasonable to conclude that hair color was the reason; other factors such as aggressiveness, beauty, or intelligence may have been responsible. One can only conclude that hair color is related to having dates, *not* that the relationship is causal.

Subject Variables and Equivalent Groups. The selection of subjects according to hair color in the foregoing example is a subject variable manipulation. All experiments in which subject variables are manipulated are confounded since it is not possible to form equivalent groups and then introduce the independent variable. This point is very important and bears repeating. For nonsubject variable manipulations it is possible to establish equivalent groups. After such groups have been formed, the independent variable can be introduced. This makes it possible to ensure that the independent variable is the *only* one that is systematically varied so that differences in performance between groups can be attributed to it. It is reasonable to conclude that the *nonsubject* variable is the *cause* of the difference in performance on the dependent measure.

However, when a subject variable manipulation is made one cannot form equivalent groups because the characteristics of the subject determine the group in which the subject will be placed. If it is not possible to form equivalent groups before the independent variable is introduced, then there is no way to assess its effect accurately because there is no way to manipulate just *one* independent variable. It is unreasonable to reach a cause-effect conclusion when a subject variable is manipulated. Again, correlational studies and subject variable manipulations are similar in that it is only possible to assess whether the variables are related, not whether they are causally related.

Classification of Subject Variable Manipulations

The fact that subject variable manipulations are similar to correlational studies with regard to causality statements, and similar to the experimental method with regard to *some* procedures, makes it difficult to arrive at a simple, completely satisfactory classification. Some investigators classify subject variable manipulation as an instance of the experimental method. The subject variable is treated as the independent variable and the performance measure as the dependent variable. There is no harm in doing this as long as one remembers that the results of such experiments should not be interpreted in cause-effect terms. In this text, we will treat subject variable manipulation as a special case of the experimental method, applying the label of independent variable to subject variables as well as to nonsubject variables. By doing so, we can combine subject variable and nonsubject variable manipulations in the same experiment.

THE QUASI-EXPERIMENTAL APPROACH

The three approaches considered so far — observation, correlation, and experiment — are used extensively in research. A fourth approach, called quasi-experimental because of its similarity to the experimental method, is used when it is possible to utilize some but not all aspects of the experimental method (Campbell & Stanley, 1963). Quasi-experimental designs will be discussed in more detail in Chapter 6; our present goal is to distinguish between experimental and quasi-experimental methods. To do so we first need to reconsider the subject variable–nonsubject variable distinction.

We said that subject variables are characteristics of the subject that cannot be manipulated by the experimenter, such as age, sex, or intelligence. Experimenters can only *select* subjects according to their characteristics; they cannot change those characteristics. This is a crucial distinction for methodological considerations because the conclusions that can be made from an experiment depend on whether the experimenter can manipulate the independent variable. There are also some instances in which investigators are not able to manipulate *nonsubject* variables because they are limited by ethical, practical, political, or other constraints. If they have been given no constraints, investigators could, of course, manipulate virtually all nonsubject variables. Quasi-experimental designs introduce something like experimental control to data collection even though it is not possible to determine who gets the experimental treatment and who does not. They are used to investigate *nonsubject* variables.

Let us assume that you are interested in the effect of a new therapy for stuttering. For practical reasons you cannot manipulate who receives the new therapy and who does not. You are required to give the new therapy to all the available stutterers in order to get the cooperation required. Although you are not able to use the preferred method for testing (the experimental method), you may be able to use a quasi-experimental design. For example, you could perform a time-series experiment (Campbell & Stanley, 1963) in which you observe the incidence of stuttering in each participant at various intervals before and after introducing the therapy. Or you might try to find another group of stutterers, not available for therapy, who can serve as a comparison group. You could test both groups of stutterers at the same time (for example, in January), administer your therapy to the treatment group, and then test both groups at a second time (say, December).

Experimental versus Quasi-Experimental Method

The experimental method is certainly not the only acceptable way to evaluate the effects of a nonsubject variable. But if the investigator can systematically manipulate the variable of interest, there is no question that the experimental method is the best way to assess whether the variable influences behavior or mental activity. Although quasi-experimental procedures *can* provide evidence regarding the effect of a nonsubject variable, the number of rival explanations for quasi-experimental outcomes is typically greater than for experimental designs.

In terms of the distinction between internal and external validity discussed in Chapter 1, the experimental method is best for establishing internal validity but typically not as good as the quasi-experimental method for establishing external validity. Quasi-experimental techniques are useful for establishing external validity because they can frequently be used in natural settings. In other words, there is usually a trade-off between external and internal validity. It is difficult to have both external and internal validity for a single experiment because there is usually no good way to make treatment manipulations in natural settings without destroying the "naturalness" of the situation. Because the problem of generality (external validity or the parsimony assumption) varies for the different areas of psychology and the social sciences, some investigators (such as researchers interested in physiological or basic information-processing phenomena) hardly ever use quasi-experimental designs. Others (such as social psychologists, educational psychologists, and sociologists) may use quasi-experimental designs in addition to the three other methods.

CLASSIFYING RESEARCH ACCORDING TO METHOD

In the beginning of this chapter we noted that social scientists use four basic methods to accumulate knowledge: observation, correlation, experiment, and quasi-experiment. It is important to be able to classify research according to method because the method employed determines, in large part, what conclusions are justified. The following examples will give you some practice in classification. Try to classify each example before reading the discussion of it. (The label for each example is the title of the article discussed.)

Example 1 — Children's Reactions to Second-hand Smoke

A study was conducted (Cameron, 1972) in which 2365 children between the ages of seven and fifteen were interviewed to determine their reaction to smoking by others. The general finding was that the children did not like being exposed to tobacco smoke. Most of them disapproved of their parents' smoking and indicated some loss of respect for their parents because they smoked.

Discussion. It should be clear that the above study is an example of the use of an observational technique. A reactive measure was obtained. The children's responses might have been influenced by the fact that they knew the investigator was interested in their reaction to smoking. For example, a child who wanted to please may have concluded that the interviewer had a negative attitude toward smoking and may have responded accordingly. There is usually some danger that the results obtained with a reactive measure may be influenced by the subject's awareness of the evaluation. The investigator's task is to determine whether the advantages of the method outweight the bias that may result if some subjects modify their responses in an effort to please or displease her.

Example 2 — Marital Agreement as a Function of Status-related Agreement

Married couples of higher social status tend to agree with each other more than married couples of lower social status. The investigator (Bennett, 1971) interviewed ninety-six couples to assess whether the differences in agreement were due to marital interaction or to status. The spouses were interviewed separately to measure their attitude toward radioactive-fallout shelters. The degree of agreement of each couple was found to be directly related to status; the high status couples agreed more than the lower status couples. Yet, if individuals were artificially paired (i.e., couples were re-paired), the pairs of high status still agreed more than the pairs of lower status. The results suggest that status and not marital interaction is responsible for the differences in agreement.

Discussion. The above study shows that more than one method can be used in a single study. An observational technique is used in virtually every study because a performance measure is needed in order to use the correlational, experimental, or quasi-experimental method. Usually a reactive measure is obtained, because the subjects are aware that their performance is being assessed. In this study a reactive measure was used to assess each subject's attitude toward radioactive-fallout shelters, but subjects did not know that the investigator's principal interest was in the degree of marital agreement and its relation to social status. The investigator also used the correlational approach. The issue was whether high scores on the social status variable would go with high scores on the agreement variable.

Example 3 — Racial Discrimination in Apartment Rentals

The investigators (Johnson, Porter, & Marteljan, 1971) performed a study in southern California to determine whether minority groups were discriminated against by apartment landlords. The investigators had Mexican-American, black, and white male-female couples visit twenty-five apartment houses. Each couple inquired about the availability of an apartment and about rent and other fees. The results revealed that Mexican-Americans were discriminated against more than whites and blacks more than either of the others.

Discussion. This study is an example of the experimental method. The independent variable is the race of the potential tenants, and the dependent variables are the information on availability, on rent, and on miscellaneous fees provided by the landlords. This is a nonsubject variable manipulation, because the race of the potential tenants, and not some characteristic of the landlords, was manipulated. The subjects in this experiment were the twenty-five landlords. Subject variable manipulations are made by assigning subjects to groups on the basis of a particular characteristic; there was no such assignment in this experiment. The only variable manipulated was the characteristics of the potential tenants, so it is possible to conclude that these characteristics were responsible for the differences in the information obtained.

Some readers may prefer to consider the independent variable to be any differences between the potential tenants and not just race differences. That is, although it is probable that the race of the potential tenants were responsible for the differences in the information provided by the landlords, it is also possible that other characteristics, such as differences among the couples in dress or manner, were responsible. In some cases, there may be disagreement regarding the exact nature of the independent variable.

Example 4 — Effects of Early Social Deprivation on Emotionality in Rats

The investigators (Koch & Arnold, 1972) assigned ninety-five newborn rats to four different rearing conditions to assess the effect of social deprivation on emotionality. One group was reared with mother and peers, a second group with mother but without peers; a third group was reared in incubators with peers; a fourth group in incubators in isolation. Several measures of emotionality (e.g., heart rate, frequency of urination) were obtained when the rats were 65 and 113 days old. The general finding was that maternally deprived rats showed higher emotionality.

Discussion. This study is an example of the use of the experimental method. The assignment of subjects to groups was such that the investigators could be confident that the groups were equivalent before introducing the independent variable. The independent variable was the type of early social experience, a nonsubject variable. Although early social experience is a characteristic of the subject, this is not a subject variable manipulation in the sense used in this text, because the manipulation is under the control of the experimenter. He decides which rat gets a particular early experience and which does not. Thus it is possible to manipulate just one "subject" variable — not merely to *select,* as in a typical subject variable case. It is reasonable, therefore, to conclude from this experiment that the maternal deprivation *caused* the higher emotionality.

Example 5 — Sex, Setting, and Reactions to Crowding on Sidewalks

The investigator (Dabbs, 1972) studied people's reactions to having someone stand very close to them at stoplights and bus stops. The basic procedure consisted of having a male or female confederate of the investigator approach and stand very close to a pedestrian waiting for a bus or for a traffic light to change. There were 643 pedestrians, both males and females. The extent to which each pedestrian moved away from the confederate was recorded. One finding was that male confederates induced more movement than female confederates, and female pedestrians tended to move more than male pedestrians.

Discussion. The above study can be classified as an example of an observational technique. A nonreactive measure was obtained in that the pedestrians were not given any reason to suspect that their movement, relative to a confederate, was being recorded. The intervention is, of course, the presence of the confederate. It is likely that the investigator would have had to wait a long time to determine how pedestrians react to crowding if he had waited for the crowding to occur naturally. By using confederates, he could arrange the situation of interest and then observe subjects' reactions.

Some readers may object to the above classification because they believe the study is more accurately classified as experimental or quasi-experimental, with sex of the confederate, sex of the pedestrian, and location of the encounter (bus stop or stoplight) as the three independent variables. Sometimes it is possible to make a case for more than one classification, because the study has the properties of more than one method. Nonreactive measures with intervention and the quasi-experimental method are especially likely to overlap. It is frequently possible to decide between these two classifications and the experimental method by considering how the subjects were assigned to conditions. If no attempt is made to ensure that the subjects tested in each condition are equivalent before obtaining the dependent measure, it is usually more appropriate to view the research as an instance of an observational technique or a quasi-experimental design. If an effort *is* made to ensure such equivalence then the study may be regarded as an example of the experimental method. If the investigator had used a procedure to ensure that the pedestrians approached by male confederates were equivalent to the pedestrians approached by female confederates this study would have been a good example of the experimental method — if the sex of the confederate was the only variable manipulated. The major weakness of all studies in which procedures are not used to obtain equivalent groups before the manipulation is that it is difficult to know whether any obtained differences between conditions is due to the treatment or is simply a result of the "selection" of better or poorer subjects for the treatment than nontreatment conditions.

Example 6 — The Physical Attractiveness of Dating versus Married Couples

The investigators (Cavior & Boblett, 1972) were interested in whether there is a higher correlation between the physical attractiveness of married partners or of dating partners. The correlations were obtained by having judges independently rate each person on physical attractiveness. The subjects were unaware that they were being so rated. Then a correlation was computed to assess the extent to which people with high scores on physical attractiveness marry people with high scores, middle scores go with middle scores, and low scores with low. A similar procedure was used for the people who were dating partners. The major finding was that the correlation was considerably higher for married partners than for dating partners.

Discussion. It should be clear that this study involved obtaining a nonreactive measure without intervention and then the correlational approach. The measure was nonreactive in that the subjects were not given any reason to believe they were being judged on their physical attractiveness. There are some obvious ethical problems in obtaining nonreactive measures on human subjects. However, there would be numerous methodological difficulties to overcome if a study of this type were performed by obtaining reactive measures. The partners who would give their informed consent to participate in a study on physical attractiveness might not be representative of married or dating partners. For example, consider the likelihood of a couple giving their informed consent if both members were physically attractive. Now consider the likelihood if one member were attractive and the other unattractive.

Example 7 — Ads without Answers Make the Brain Itch

Chance (1975) reported the results of a project in Kentucky under the direction of Martin Sundel, a psychologist. The purpose of the project was to evaluate whether ads with solutions or without solutions would be more effective in getting people to evaluate their life problems. Some of the ads offered solutions to problems and some did not. For example, in one solution ad the husband was told he should listen and try to understand why his wife nagged. One of the nonsolution ads about alcohol and drug abuse ended with questions like, "How many drinks are required to bring back love?" The ads appeared on seventeen radio stations, five television stations, and in eighteen newspapers over a sixty-week period. The effectiveness of the ads was evaluated by surveys and the number of calls to a crisis and information center about problems mentioned in the ads. The results suggest that ads without answers are better for getting people to consider their life problems.

Discussion. Several methods are used in this case. The surveys used to evaluate the ads can be classified as reactive measures. The number of phone calls to the crisis and information center, on the other hand, is a nonreactive measure obtained with intervention (the ads). Thus, two observational techniques were used. The type of ad manipulation is probably best classified as quasi-experimental. It is not fully experimental because there is no good way to know whether the people who saw the solution ads were equivalent to the people who saw the ads without solutions. Yet the fact that the ads were presented several times over the sixty weeks increases the likelihood that the different responses to the ads are attributable to the nature of the ads and not to other considerations. If the same results are obtained a number of times there is more reason to believe that the treatment has an effect. A quasi-experimental approach can be used to come close to the control obtained when using the experimental method.

The reader should now have an understanding of the four basic methods used in accumulating knowledge in the social sciences. It should be clear from the examples that many investigators used a combination of research techniques in a single study. They may also study the effect of more than one independent variable in a single study. It is frequently necessary to do so because the effect of one independent variable may be influenced by the level of a second. Although the previous discussion should have given you a general understanding of the scope of the four methods, we now need to consider the experimental method in greater detail.

THE EXPERIMENTAL METHOD: ADDITIONAL PROPERTIES

Experiments with One Independent Variable

We wish to consider how experiments with two independent variables differ from experiments with one independent variable. To provide a base for the discussion of experiments with two independent variables we must first consider some points about experiments with one independent variable. To simplify the task, let us assume that all subjects who receive a particular treatment attain the same level of performance on the dependent variable. That is, we will assume that all subjects have identical ability. Any difference between groups can be attributed to the effect of the treatment manipulation because we are assuming that there are no chance fluctuations.

Example 1 — Independent Variable Affects Dependent Variable. Assume that a two-group experiment is conducted to assess the effect of the volume at which music is played on the rating of the music. Each subject is asked to rate the same classical piece on a scale from 1 to 30. A score of 30 is the most favorable rating. Ten subjects rate the piece when it is played at high volume, and ten others rate it at low volume. This is a nonsubject variable manipulation; it is possible to form equivalent groups before introducing the independent variable.

The results are clear. All subjects who hear the piece at low volume give it a rating of 20, and all who hear it at high volume give it a 25. Thus, the volume manipulation had an effect of five units, since all subjects in the high volume condition rated the piece five units higher than all subjects in the low volume condition. The *effect* of the independent variable is assessed by comparing the average score on the dependent measure for the subjects in the two conditions. In this case there are only two conditions; there is one independent variable (volume setting) and two *levels* of the independent variable, low volume and high volume. The *levels* of an independent variable are determined by the experimenter. One could, for example, have three levels of the independent variable: low, medium, and high volume. The *effect* of an independent variable, on the other hand, is determined by performance on the dependent measure. The experimenter does not control the effect of an independent variable; he or she measures or assesses the effect of an independent variable by comparing the performance on the dependent measure of subjects who receive different levels of the independent variable. The ability to distinguish between levels and effects is crucial.

Example 2 — Independent Variable has no Effect on Dependent Variable. Let us assume that the same two-group experiment is conducted to assess the effect of volume on music enjoyment. In this case, however, the subjects rate a ballad instead of a classical piece. Ten subjects rate the ballad at high volume and ten others rate it at low volume. Thus, we again have two levels of the independent variable, volume setting. The dependent measure is the rating each subject gives the ballad.

The results are clear. All subjects who hear the piece at low volume give it a rating of 20, and all who hear it at high volume give it a rating of 20. Since the rating that the piece receives is not influenced by the volume setting, we say that the independent variable has *no effect*. Performance on the dependent measure determines whether the independent variable has an effect.

Experiments with Two Independent Variables

Experiments can be conducted in which equivalent groups are formed and two independent variables are then introduced. The independent variables can be two subject variables, one subject variable and one nonsubject variable, or two nonsubject variables. Let us consider an experiment in which two nonsubject variables are manipulated.

Example 3 — Interacting Variables. Assume that a 2 by 2 factorial design is used. This means that there are two independent variables and two levels of each. The two independent variables are type of music and volume setting. A classical piece is played at low and high volume and a rock piece is played at low and high volume. Thus, there are four conditions: classical at high volume, classical at low volume, rock at high volume, rock at low volume.

52 *Methods of Research*

Once again, each subject is asked to rate a piece on a scale from 1 to 30, and there are ten subjects in each condition. Because both independent variables are nonsubject variables it is possible to form equivalent groups before introducing them. The results of the experiment are presented in Table 2-1. The letter X refers to any score. The symbol $\bar{X}$ (called x-bar) is a label for the mean. The scores in each condition are the ratings of the ten subjects, one score per subject.

A consideration of the results presented in Table 2-1 is fairly straightforward if we try to do only one thing at a time. We want to know whether the independent variables influenced performance on the dependent measure (music enjoyment rating), so we compare the performance of subjects on the dependent measure. We can only consider one independent variable at a time. Let us consider the type of music manipulation (rock versus classical) first. How do we determine whether the type of music manipulation influenced

TABLE 2-1

The Rating of Each of Forty Subjects as a Function of the Type of Music Presented and the Volume of the Music in Example 3 (fictitious data)

Volume setting	Type of music — Rock		Type of music — Classical		Row mean
Low	10 10 10 10 10 10 10 10 10 10	$\bar{X} = 10$	20 20 20 20 20 20 20 20 20 20	$\bar{X} = 20$	15
High	25 25 25 25 25 25 25 25 25 25	$\bar{X} = 25$	25 25 25 25 25 25 25 25 25 25	$\bar{X} = 25$	25
Column mean	17.5		22.5		

performance on the dependent measure? All we need is a little imagination. Because we are concerned only with the comparison between rock and classical music (at this time we do not have any interest in the volume setting) we can pretend that the experiment was a two-group instead of a four-group experiment. Twenty subjects rated the rock piece and twenty rated the classical piece. We want to compare the performance of these *two* groups. We can ignore the volume setting manipulation because volume setting cannot be used to account for any obtained difference between the two groups of subjects. A mean score for each group is obtained by adding all the scores for the group and dividing the sum by the number of scores. The mean for the rock music condition (ignoring volume) is 17.5. The mean for the classical music condition is 22.5 Because there is a difference between the two conditions there is an effect due to the type of music manipulation; this effect is 5.

We can use a similar procedure to assess the effect of the volume setting. Once again we pretend that the experiment was a two-group instead of a four-group experiment. This time one group consists of all the subjects who received low volume settings; the other group consists of all the subjects who received high volume settings. The mean for the low volume subjects is 15. The mean for the high volume subjects is 25. A comparison of the two means reveals that the effect of the volume setting manipulation is 10. We have determined that both manipulations — of the type of music (effect = 5) and of the volume setting (effect = 10) — influenced performance on the dependent measure. Because all the data were used to obtain these two effects they are frequently called *main* or overall effects. Manipulating the type of music produced a main effect, and manipulating the volume setting produced another *main effect*. Moreover, there was an *interaction* between the type of music and the volume setting.

Two independent variables interact if the *effect* of one is influenced by the *level* of the other. In the present example, the effect of the volume setting can be assessed separately for classical and rock music; for classical music it is five units (25, the mean for high volume classical music, minus 20, the mean for low volume classical music) and for rock music it is fifteen (25, the mean for high volume rock music, minus 10, the mean for low volume rock music). Because the effect is different for classical music than for rock, the two variables interact. Notice that it is the independent variables themselves that interact and *not* the levels of the variables. It is incorrect to say that low volume interacts with type of music or that rock music interacts with the volume setting. The two independent variables, type of music and volume setting interact, not the levels of each.

Thus, *interaction* has a special meaning when used to describe the relationship between independent variables. It means that the *effect* of one independent variable is influenced by the level of another. To appreciate this fact we can imagine that the investigator studied the effect of volume setting on musical enjoyment with only the rock piece or only the classical piece. That is, we can imagine that two separate experiments were performed to assess the effect of volume setting, one with rock music and one with classical music. We want to know whether the two experiments yield the same results. Is the effect of volume setting the same regardless of the type of music considered? If the conclusion we reach about volume setting depends on the type of music we consider, then the two variables (volume setting and type of music) interact.

Example 4 — Noninteracting Independent Variables. Assume now that a similar experiment was conducted in which the two types of music were rock and march. These results are presented in Table 2-2. Once again, we assess the effects of the independent variables one at a time. To determine the effect of the type of music manipulation we compare the twenty subjects who rated the march piece with the twenty subjects who rated the rock piece.

TABLE 2-2

The Rating of Each of Forty Subjects as a Function of the Type of Music Presented and the Volume of Music in Example 4 (fictitious data)

Volume setting	Type of music — Rock	Type of music — March	Row mean
Low	10, 10, 10, 10, 10, 10, 10, 10, 10, 10 $\bar{X} = 10$	5, 5, 5, 5, 5, 5, 5, 5, 5, 5 $\bar{X} = 5$	7.5
High	25, 25, 25, 25, 25, 25, 25, 25, 25, 25 $\bar{X} = 25$	20, 20, 20, 20, 20, 20, 20, 20, 20, 20 $\bar{X} = 20$	22.5
Column mean	17.5	12.5	

The type of music manipulation had an effect of 5. A comparison of the twenty subjects who heard the music at low volume with the subjects who heard it at high volume reveals that the effect of the volume setting was 15. Thus, there was a *main effect* of type of music and a *main effect* of volume setting. Note, however, that there was no interaction between type of music and volume setting. The effect of volume setting was the same for rock music (25, the mean for high volume rock music minus 10, the mean for low volume rock music) as for march music (20, the mean for high volume march music minus 5, the mean for the low volume march music). The effect of the volume setting did not depend on the type of music considered. Type of music and volume setting do *not* interact.

The use of concrete examples, especially your own examples, can help you to grasp the concept of interaction. With a little effort you should be able to think of variables that can be expected to interact. There is no good substitute for generating your own examples and considering all possible outcomes. If you do this you should be able to demonstrate that two variables can interact even when neither has an effect on overall performance.

Experiments with two or more independent variables are useful because they allow investigators to determine the *main effects* and *interactions* between independent variables. The study of interactions between variables is extremely important. It would, of course, be much easier to understand behavior if the effect of each independent variable was the same regardless of the level of the other independent variables. However, it is abundantly clear that this is frequently not the case. Variables can interact, so understanding the effect of a particular independent variable also involves knowing what other variables, if any, interact with it. Let us consider a final example to demonstrate the importance of interactions.

Example 5 — Subject Variable and Nonsubject Variable Manipulations. Assume that an investigator has developed a new method of instruction to motivate students academically. She believes the method will increase academic performance as assessed by grades. She wants to establish whether the method is successful and whether its success depends on the characteristics of the students. To accomplish this end, forty natural science students and forty social science students are recruited for the experiment. The subject variable is the type of student, natural science or social science. The investigator is not interested in comparing the performance of the two types of students; she wants to know how effective the new method will be with each type.

The next step is to divide the social science students into two equivalent groups of twenty each, and the natural science students in the same way. The investigator then gives the new method to one group of natural science and one group of social science students. The other two groups are treated identically except that they are not given the new method. Thus, if there is a large difference in the performance of the two groups of social science students after the method manipulation, the difference can be attributed to the method because the two social science groups were previously equivalent. The same thing is true for the natural science students.

Let us assume that the method facilitated the academic performance of the social science students but not of the natural science students. Specifically, the social science students who received the method were far superior academically to the social science students who did not receive it for two successive school terms following its introduction. Yet, the two natural science groups did not differ during the same period. A comparison of the performance of the social science students to that of the natural science students is of little interest, because these subjects differ in many respects. The important point is that the method was effective for the social science students only. If the investigator had used only natural science students in the experiment, she would have concluded that the method does not have any effect. If she had used only social science students, she would have concluded that it does have an effect but would perhaps have remained unaware of its limitations. In short, the combination of subject variables and nonsubject variables in a single experiment can be a very useful way to study behavior. We can assess whether the effect of a particular treatment, such as a drug, instructional technique, therapy, or advertisement, depends on the type of person receiving the treatment.

The results presented in Tables 2-1 and 2-2 may seem very artificial because all subjects given the same treatment had the same score. For the present, however, there is no harm in assuming that all subjects are of identical ability, and such an assumption should make it easier to understand how the effects of independent variables and interactions are assessed. They are assessed in basically the same way when subjects differ in ability, but then one has to be careful about concluding that an obtained difference between conditions is a result of the treatment manipulation. A difference may be due solely to the chance fluctuations that are always present. The problem of deciding when to attribute differences to the independent variable(s) plus chance, and when to attribute them solely to chance, will be considered in detail in subsequent chapters.

SUMMARY

The function of the observer is to record the behavior of interest. This task is not easy because the observer may bias the observations, lack the proper skills or equipment to record the relevant behavior, or fail to agree with other observers.

The observational techniques fall into three classes: reactive measures, nonreactive measures without intervention, and nonreactive measures with intervention. A reactive measure is obtained whenever the observee is aware that his behavior is being recorded, or whenever he is placed in a new environment for observation. His behavior may be influenced by his awareness of the investigator or the investigator's equipment. Nonreactive measures without intervention are obtained whenever the observee is unaware that his behavior is being recorded and no changes are made in his situation. The behavior that occurs is natural. Nonreactive measures with intervention are obtained without the observee's knowledge, but with the investigator intervening to ensure that the appropriate circumstances exist.

Correlational techniques allow investigators to specify the degree of relationship between variables. Correlation can be used to predict; the accuracy of the prediction will depend on the magnitude of the correlation. Although most correlational techniques do not permit one to infer a causal relationship the correlation may, in fact, be due to a cause-effect connection between the variables. If such a connection does exist, then the variables will be correlated. The reverse is not true however. Thus, correlational techniques can be used to "discover" causal relationships in that two highly correlated variables may prove to be causally related when subjected to experimentation.

The experimental method differs from the other approaches in that the experimenter manipulates one or more independent variables and assesses the effect of the manipulations on one or more dependent measures. The independent variable is what the investigator manipulates, i.e., the treatment. The dependent variable is what he measures to assess the effect of the independent variable. The logic of the method is to treat equivalent groups identically in all respects except one. If the groups differ in performance following the introduction of the treatment, then the difference can be attributed to the effect of the treatment.

A subject variable is a characteristic of the subject that can be measured. If a subject variable is used as an independent variable, it is essentially impossible to form equivalent groups prior to its introduction, since it is not possible to ensure that any between-group differences are due solely to chance. The nature of the subject variable dictates the composition of the groups. Therefore, it is extremely difficult, if not impossible, to study just one subject variable and thus to arrive at a cause-effect statement.

The use of the experimental method is not limited to situations in which only one independent variable is manipulated. Experiments can be conducted in which the independent variables are all nonsubject variable manipulations, in which some are subject variables and others are nonsubject variables, and in which all are subject variables. If two or more independent variables are manipulated in the same experiment, it is possible to assess whether they interact.

Independent variables interact; dependent variables do not. Dependent variables are used to assess the effect of independent variables. If the effect of one independent variable is influenced by the level of another, they are said to interact.

Quasi-experimental designs are procedures for introducing something like

58 *Methods of Research*

experimental control in data collection operations even though it is not possible to determine who gets the experimental treatment and who does not. They are needed when investigators are not able to manipulate *nonsubject* variables because they are limited by ethical, practical, political, or other constraints. These techniques are useful for establishing external validity because they can frequently be used in natural settings.

QUESTIONS

1. What are the advantages and disadvantages of each of the three observational techniques? Give an example of how each of these techniques might be used.
2. Support or refute the view that it is impossible to demonstrate causality from correlational evidence.
3. What determines whether a positive or negative correlation is obtained? Are positive correlations better than negative ones?
4. What points should be considered before using a test to determine who should be admitted to medical school?
5. How can correlational techniques be used to "discover" causal relationships?
6. What are the advantages and disadvantages of the correlational and experimental methods?
7. Distinguish between independent and dependent variables, and give an example of each.
8. Distinguish between subject and nonsubject variables, and indicate the procedures used to manipulate each kind. That is, how do the procedures used for manipulating a subject variable differ from those for a nonsubject variable?
9. Why should an investigator who makes a subject variable manipulation avoid reaching cause-effect conclusions?
10. What does it mean to say that two variables interact? Give an example of two that can be expected to interact and indicate why your expectation is reasonable.
11. What is the advantage of manipulating a subject variable and a nonsubject variable in the same experiment?
12. An investigation was conducted by Norris (1971) in which the crying and laughing behavior of ninety severely retarded children who were living at home was compared with that of fifteen such children who were living in an institution. The children living at home attended a training center. Those in the institution attended the institution school. The investigator observed the children for ten consecutive school days. He concluded that those who lived at home laughed more than those in the institution, but that there was no difference in crying behavior between the two groups. Describe the method used by the investigator. Be specific. For example, if the experimental method was used, indicate the independent and dependent variables. Can the differences observed be attributed to where the children lived? Why or why not?
13. Cohen, Liebson, and Faillace (1972) performed a study in which alcoholics

were tested under two different conditions. Each alcoholic was allowed to drink ten ounces of alcohol each day for the duration of the five week study. Each was tested under Condition A for the first, third, and fifth weeks, and Condition B for the second and fourth weeks. In Condition A the subject was given special privileges for drinking five or less ounces of alcohol each day. In Condition B no such special privileges were given. The major finding was that subjects drank less per day under Condition A than Condition B. What method was used in this study? Be specific. Can the differences in drinking be attributed to the special privileges manipulation? Why or why not?

14. Schusterman and Gentry (1971) studied four captive male sea lions, noting their annual weight fluctuation, food consumption, and territorial behaviors. They found that the annual weight fluctuation was related to the reproductive season. Seasonal fattening, which started at five years of age, was associated with increased signs of territoriality. What method(s) did the investigators use?

15. Imagine that an investigator was interested in the effects of alcohol and sleep deprivation on vigilance. The vigilance task involved responding (pressing a key) every time a barely audible stimulus was presented. The number of correct detections in a four-hour period was the dependent measure. There were two levels of alcohol (4 ounces versus none) and two levels of sleep deprivation (36 hours versus none). Indicate a set of fictitious results that would lead the investigator to conclude that there was (were):
    a. a main effect of alcohol only
    b. a main effect of sleep deprivation only
    c. an alcohol by sleep deprivation interaction only
    d. two main effects and an interaction

estimation and hypothesis testing 3

Social scientists are interested in hypothesis testing and estimation. The first step, which we discussed in Chapter 1, is to select a suitable problem and generate hypotheses that can be tested. As we know, the nature of the problem selected and the quality of the hypothesis are crucial. No methodological or statistical procedure can salvage a poor idea. It is impossible to separate the quality of the idea from the quality of the predictions that follow from it because only testable ideas are of worth to the scientific community.

After a tentative solution has been generated, it is necessary to prepare a test of it. In order to do so, of course, the problem has to be stated in a way that allows predictions about observable events. The investigator can use the observational, correlational, quasi-experimental, or experimental method to test the proposed solution. In this chapter we will mainly examine the use of the experimental method. The other methods are also important, both for hypothesis testing and estimation, but we will consider the experimental method first because an understanding of this method should help us to understand the others. The experimental method is an extremely useful and powerful way to test explanations of phenomena.

Estimation is used to make inferences about quantities that cannot, usually for practical reasons, be tested directly. For example, it would be much easier to select a sample of 100 students for study from all the students at the University of Wisconsin than to include all the students in the study. It would be difficult, if not impossible, to test the entire population of interest in any study. The best we can do is select a portion of the available people, objects, or events, obtain the desired information, and then estimate the value for the rest. Two topics have to be considered to lay the groundwork for the further discussion of estimation and hypothesis testing: randomization and probability.

RANDOMIZATION

Random Sampling

The purpose of random sampling is to obtain a sample that is representative of the population being studied. The sample is usually a small portion of the subjects who could have been selected; the larger group of potential subjects is called the *population*. For example, fifty students could be selected randomly from all the undergraduates at the University of Texas at Austin. The fifty students would be the sample; all the undergraduates would be the population. The population can be defined as the total number of potential units for observation. It can have relatively few units (e.g., all the redheads at the University of Oregon), a large number of units (e.g., all humans in North America), or infinite number of units (e.g., the possible outcomes obtained by tossing a coin an infinite number of times).

For a sample to be completely random, each subject in the population being considered should have an equal chance of being selected and the selection of one subject should not influence the selection or nonselection of another; all conceivable samples should be equally likely.

Sometimes it is necessary to place restrictions on random sampling in order to obtain a sample with certain characteristics. For example, if a random sample of 1000 subjects were selected from the United States population, it might not contain any blacks. Such a sample is extremely unlikely, but it is possible. If it is important to include representatives of minority groups, then the sample can be randomly selected with the restriction that its minority group composition match that of the general population.

Random Sampling Example. Let us assume that you want to select a random sample of 50 students from a college having an enrollment of 980. One way of selecting them would be to print each student's name on a piece of paper, throw all the pieces into a large basket, mix them up, and then draw out fifty pieces of paper while you are blindfolded. You would obtain a random sample because each student, and any combination of fifty students, could be selected. However, this procedure would be very time-consuming if a sample is being selected from a large population.

Instead of printing all the names on separate pieces of paper you may decide to use the student directory, which provides an alphabetical listing of the 980 students. You assign a number to each student from 1 to 980 by using the alphabetical listing. That is, the first student in the listing receives the number 1 and the last student in the listing receives the number 980. Then you turn to Appendix C-11 to select fifty numbers from 1 to 980 from the table of random numbers. To select the fifty numbers you first select a starting number in a haphazard manner and then block off successive digits in groups of three (i.e., you want numbers between 1 and 980). Once you select your three-digit starting number you simply continue to select successive *three-digit* numbers by going either vertically or horizontally (but not both) in the table. For example, if your haphazard method for entering the table gave you the 21th row and the 27th column on page 352 as a starting point, your starting digit is zero. Going across (i.e., we will finish the 21th row before starting the 22th row) the first three digit number is 002. The next ten, three-digit numbers would be 035, 553, 151, 510, 083, 632, 255, 407, 666, and 268. You continue until you have obtained fifty different numbers from 1 to 980. The students who have numbers corresponding to the fifty numbers selected from the table constitute a random sample. Each student and any combination of students had an equal chance of being selected for the sample.

Random Assignment

It is important to distinguish between random sampling and random assignment. The purpose of random sampling is to obtain a sample that is representative of a larger population so that the properties of the population can be estimated. The purpose of random assignment of subjects is to obtain equivalent groups before introducing the independent variable so that the effect of that variable can be estimated.

It is not unusual for investigators to place restrictions on their random assignment procedures. There are statistical and methodological advantages to randomly assigning the subjects to groups with the restriction that there be an equal number of subjects in each group. A simple way to ensure this is to use the table of random permutations of the first eight digits, found in Appendix C-1. The table contains 280 random sequences of the eight numbers.

Random Assignment Example. An investigator wants to assign sixty subjects to three conditions so that there are twenty subjects in each condition. He can do this by using twenty of the sequences of eight numbers in Appendix C-1. The first step is to select the starting sequence by some random procedure. Say that he puts each of the numbers from 0 to 8 on a piece of paper and puts the papers in a hat. For the first draw, it is only necessary to use the numbers from 0 to 2 (since there are only 280 sequences in the table). For the second draw, only use numbers 0 to 8. For the third draw, all ten numbers should be used (unless the second draw was an 8, in which case the starting sequence would have to be 280). After three draws the starting sequence would be selected. For example, if the numbers drawn were 1, 6, and 3, in that order, the starting sequence would be 163.

After the starting sequence is selected and located in the table, it is only necessary to note the ordering of the numbers 1, 2, and 3 in each sequence, because only three groups of subjects are needed; the other five numbers in each sequence are ignored. The order in the first sequence (i.e., sequence 163) is found to be 2, 3, 1, so the first subject is assigned to condition 2, the second to condition 3, and the third to condition 1. The same procedure is followed, using the next nineteen consecutive sequences to assign the other fifty-seven subjects to the three conditions. The next sequence (164) is used for the next set of three subjects, and so on. When twenty sequences have been used there will be twenty subjects in each condition. The subjects will be randomly assigned to the three conditions with the restriction that there be an equal number in each.

Although it is permissible to place some restrictions on the random assignment of subjects to groups, it is crucial that only chance determine the condition to which a particular subject is assigned. The random assignment of subjects to conditions enables the experimenter to be reasonably confident that the groups are equivalent before the experimental manipulation.

PROBABILITY

To make estimates and to test hypotheses we need to have some understanding of probability. After defining probability we will learn how to obtain frequency distributions and sampling distributions and how to use them to determine probability and chance fluctuations.

The Concept of Probability

The Common Sense View of Probability. Most people have what we call a common sense notion of probability. This notion usually consists of a subjective estimate of the likelihood that a particular event will occur (e.g., the probability of rain, the probability of winning a sporting event, the probability of getting married, the probability of passing a course). Because scientists have a penchant for quantification, however, they prefer a quantitative approach. Yet the subjective view of probability that many people have may also have a quantitative basis that is not articulated. For example, if you see dark clouds in the sky, you may predict that the chances of rain are about 90%. This prediction may be based on previous observations of similar weather conditions. Perhaps you have noticed that this particular weather condition occurred 100 times, and 90 times out of 100 rain followed within three hours. If you have this information, you can reasonably assert that the probability of rain is 90%. You expect that if this same weather condition occurs 100 more times, it will rain about 90 out of the 100 times.

Probability, Odds, and the Long Haul. You may be a little annoyed by the assertion that the probability of rain is 90%. After all, it either rains or it doesn't, so why assert that there is a 90% chance of rain? Many people would prefer simple rain-or-shine predictions. Why bother with probability statements? Does it really matter whether the probability of rain is 90% or 60%? In the long haul, it makes a great deal of difference; in making all-or-none predictions you can expect to be right 90% of the time in one set of circumstances and only 60% in the other. Or, the problem can be considered in terms of confidence in the prediction.

One way of assessing confidence is to vary the odds in a betting situation. If the probability of rain is 90% and you predict rain, it is reasonable for you to give 9 to 1 odds (i.e., you pay 9 if you lose and receive 1 if you win) and still come out about even over the long haul. That is, if you make the same prediction 100 times under similar circumstances, you should expect to lose about 10 times and win about 90 times. The winnings ($90 \times 1 = 90$) should be about equal to the losses ($10 \times 9 = 90$). If the probability of rain is only 60% you would be very foolish to give 9 to 1 odds. In short, an exact probability statement makes sense if you consider the long haul or the odds in a betting situation.

Definition of Probability. The probability of an event can be defined as the ratio of the number of favorable events to the total number of possible events. The only effect that is assumed to operate is *chance*. Therefore, there is the same likelihood that each event will occur. A few simple examples should help to clarify the notion of probability. Consider the probability of drawing the ace of spades from a standard deck of well-shuffled playing cards. Since there is only one favorable event, the ace of spades, and 52 possible events, the probability is one fifty-second or .019. If only chance is operating, then each card has the same probability of being drawn. Consider the probability of drawing any spade. In this case there are 13 favorable events (13 spades) and 52 cards in all, so the probability is thirteen fifty-seconds or .25.

The computation of the ratio of favorable events to total possible events to determine the probability of a particular event occurring is a simple procedure as long as one considers simple events, such as drawing a particular card, or rolling a seven with two dice. As the events become more complicated or the number of possible outcomes increases, it is no longer feasible to enumerate the number of favorable events and the total number of possible events. Examples of more complicated events and ways to compute the probability of their occurrence are presented in Appendix A-1. The student with even an elementary understanding of probability is better equipped to understand the risks involved in games of chance, such as roulette and lotteries, and games based partly on chance, such as poker.

Frequency Distributions

Types of Frequency Distributions. A distribution is a set of values or scores for a particular attribute or variable. There are many kinds of distributions. One could obtain a distribution of scores on a final examination, a distribution of annual salaries for all truck drivers in Texas, a distribution of the weights of all college professors in California, and so on. Let us consider a hypothetical distribution of scores on a final examination in a biology class

TABLE 3-1

The Frequency Distribution for the Forty Scores on the Biology Final Examination

Score	Frequency	Score	Frequency
83	2	57	2
75	1	56	5
72	1	54	2
68	1	53	4
66	1	52	1
65	2	51	2
64	1	48	1
61	2	43	2
59	4	42	3
58	2	38	1

of forty students. The scores are: 51, 56, 83, 42, 52, 54, 53, 58, 61, 42, 83, 53, 54, 53, 59, 48, 65, 72, 75, 59, 61, 68, 43, 38, 65, 56, 56, 57, 51, 53, 56, 57, 43, 58, 59, 56, 59, 64, 66, 42.

It is difficult to describe this set of scores as it presently stands. About all one can do is read the entire set. A frequency distribution can be obtained by simply arranging the scores in ascending or descending order and counting the number of times each occurs. That is, one determines the frequency of each score in the distribution. A frequency distribution for this set is presented in Table 3-1. A clearer description of the scores is arrived at when they are tabulated in frequency distribution form.

Usually an even clearer description is possible when the scores are grouped into categories as in Table 3-2. Although Table 3-2 is somewhat easier to read than Table 3-1, some information was lost in going from the frequency distribution to the grouped frequency distribution. It is not possible to deter-

TABLE 3-2

The Grouped Frequency Distribution for the Forty Scores on the Biology Final Examination

Scores	Frequency
76–85	2
66–75	4
56–65	18
46–55	10
36–45	6

66 *Estimation and Hypothesis Testing*

mine how many students received each score by referring to the grouped frequency distribution.

The grouped frequency distribution in Table 3-2 is presented in graphic form in Figure 3-1. When distributions are graphed, frequency in presented on the ordinate, or *y* axis (vertical axis), and the scores on the abscissa, or *x* axis (horizontal axis). For example, since there were eighteen scores in the 56 to 65 interval (labeled 60.5, the middle point in the category), the height of the bar is 18 units on the ordinate for this interval. The same information is given in the graph in Figure 3-1B except that the form is different and one category at each extreme has been added so that the line, which connects the dots indicating the frequency of each category, touches the abscissa.

Probability and Frequency Distributions. A graph can be used to depict the probability of particular outcomes. For example, consider the probability of selecting a student from the biology class with a score of 76 or over if only chance is operating. Since there are two students in the 76 and over category, there are two favorable events. There are forty students in all, so the probability is two-fortieths or .05. This means that if you made 100 selections and replaced your selection each time, you should expect to select a student with a score of 76 or more five times in the 100 attempts. Or, stated differently, the bar for the 76–85 category (labeled 80.5) in Figure 3-1A is 5% of all the bars. A percentage, of course, is simply another way of relating the number of favorable events to the total number of events.

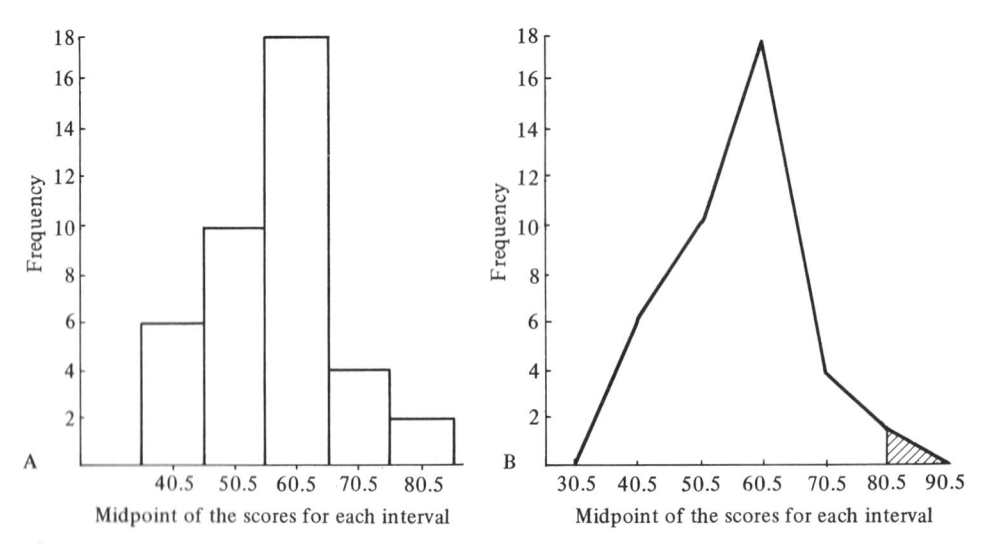

FIGURE 3-1

The grouped frequency distribution for the forty scores on the biology final examination. Figure A is a bar graph (histogram) and Figure B is a frequency polygon.

The graph in Figure 3-1B can also be used to indicate the probability of a particular outcome. The area underneath the curve can be used to represent the total number of events. If this is done, then there is no need to worry about the absolute frequency levels for any score or block of scores. The relative height of the curve can be used to indicate the relative frequency of particular outcomes. The principal concern in hypothesis testing is whether a particular outcome is a rare event, so our concern will be with the end parts or extremes of each curve. For example, one can consider the probability of selecting a student with a score of 76 or more if only chance is operating. To do this, one can divide the shaded area of the curve in Figure 3-1B by the total area under the curve.

Imagine that the area under the curve is a piece of pie, and consider what portion the shaded part is of the whole. Or, if you prefer, you can imagine that the piece of pie is a raisin pie and that there are 100 raisins equally distributed over the entire piece. If you select one raisin, what is the probability that it will come from the shaded portion if only chance is operating? Selecting a particular raisin is analogous to conducting an experiment. The task is to assess whether the outcome of the experiment is a rare event (i.e., is in the shaded portion of the curve) if only chance is operating. We must next consider how one makes such an assessment.

Sampling Distributions

Empirical Sampling Distributions. Let us assume that we are performing a pseudo-experiment in which random assignment is used to form two groups of ten subjects each. (The experiment is a pseudo-experiment in that no independent variable is manipulated.) The subjects in each group are a *sample* from a larger set of potential subjects. We call our groups Group 1 and Group 2. The groups are treated identically. After forming our groups we obtain a score on the dependent variable for each subject. Then a mean score is computed for each group, and the Group 2 mean is subtracted from the Group 1 mean to obtain the difference between the two group means. If this procedure were repeated until the pseudo-experiment had been conducted 100,000 times, the result would be 100,000 numbers. Each number would represent the difference between a Group 1 and a Group 2 mean.

A distribution using these 100,000 numbers could be made by plotting the frequency with which each mean difference was obtained. However, since this is a distribution of sample values, the difference between sample means, it is called a sampling distribution instead of a frequency distribution. Because an independent variable is *not* manipulated, the sampling distribution obtained must reflect *chance fluctuations.* Chance fluctuations are differences between scores which are due solely to chance, not to treatment effects. As we will see shortly, it is important to know how large a difference we can expect between two groups if only chance is operating.

The sampling distribution just considered is a sampling distribution of the difference between two means because we always subtracted one group mean from the other (obtained a difference score) for each of the scores represented in the sampling distribution. This is only one of many kinds of sampling distributions. We can obtain an empirical sampling distribution simply by taking a number of random samples of the same size from a population.

Let us assume that you are interested in determining the average weight of all female students at a large midwestern university. It would be too difficult to get this information for all the female students so you decide to select a *random sample* of 100 from the *population* of 15,000 female students at the university. You select your sample, obtain the weight of each person in the sample, and then compute the mean weight for the sample by adding all 100 weights and dividing by 100. If you have no information about the population mean (i.e., the mean weight for all 15,000 female students), the sample mean is the best estimate of the population mean. Because you used random sampling your sample is representative of the population. You do not have a sampling distribution, of course, because you selected only one sample. In order to obtain a sampling distribution you have to repeat the above procedure.

Although it is not practical to obtain empirical sampling distributions let us *imagine* that you repeat the above procedure until you have 500 samples of 100 female students. A student could be in more than one sample because the total population that you are sampling is only 15,000 students. You now have 500 sample means each based on 100 observations (female students). Do you think that all 500 sample means will be the same? On one hand we might expect them to all be about the same because each sample was chosen to be representative of the population. On the other hand we must expect chance fluctuations because it is likely that some samples will include more heavy or light female students than other samples. The sampling distribution for the 500 estimates will tell us how much chance fluctuation we can expect among the estimates.

The amount of chance fluctuation among sample means is related to the size of the sample. Imagine that you obtain two empirical sampling distributions for the population of 15,000 female students just considered. The first sampling distribution is obtained by selecting 500 samples of *3* students each. The second sampling distribution is obtained by selecting 500 samples of *150* students each. Thus, we have 500 estimates of the population mean based on 3 people in each sample, and we have 500 estimates of the population mean based on 150 people in each sample. Do you expect the 500 estimates based on 3 people in each sample to be the same? Do you expect the 500 estimates based on 150 people in each sample to be the same? In which case do you expect more chance fluctuation among the 500 estimates? You will probably see there will be more fluctuation among the sample means with the small samples than the large samples. This is because the probability of selecting 3 heavy or 3 light students is considerably greater than the probability of selecting 150 heavy or 150 light students, if only chance is operating. In any case the sampling distribution based on the 500 samples of 3 students will tell us how much fluctuation of the sample means we can expect for this sample size. And, the sampling distribution based on the 500 samples of 150 each will tell us how much chance fluctuation of the sample means we can expect for this sample size. Sampling distributions are important because they tell us how much fluctuation to expect between sample values (e.g., sample means) if only chance is operating, as is the case when randomization procedures are used and no independent variable is manipulated.

The above examples are all empirical sampling distributions of *means* because sample means or the differences between sample means were plotted to yield the distribution of sample values. There are other sampling distributions not based on sample means. For example, we could randomly select 100 students from a larger population of 20,000 students, determine the weight and height of each student, and then compute the correlation between weight and height for all 100 students. This procedure would yield one number, between −1.00 and +1.00, for the sample. We could repeat the procedure until we had 700 correlations and then plot their frequency. We would then have an empirical sampling distribution because each correlation is a *sample* value. We can expect the sample values to be *about* the same, since each sample correlation is an *estimate* of the correlation in the population (i.e., the correlation you would get if all 20,000 students were considered). Yet there would be some fluctuation among the values because only chance determines who is selected for each sample.

In sum, it is possible to obtain an empirical sampling distribution by taking a number of random samples of the same size from a population, determining a single value for each sample (e.g., mean or correlation), and then plotting the distribution of the sample values. There are numerous sampling distributions because the size of the samples selected and the sample value determined (e.g., mean or correlation) determine the properties of the sampling distribution. The crucial point is that sampling distributions obtained with random sampling procedures are useful because they tell us how much fluctuation to expect among sample values if only chance is operating. As we will see shortly, this information is important for estimation and hypothesis testing.

It would be too difficult to obtain sampling distributions empirically. The above examples were presented only to give you an understanding of the general nature and usefulness of sampling distributions. It is not necessary to obtain sampling distributions empirically because they can be obtained by using mathematics.

Mathematical Sampling Distributions. The sampling distributions obtained by using mathematics are essentially the same as empirical distributions if each empirical sampling distribution is based on an extremely large number of samples (e.g., 100,000). The mathematical sampling distributions are distributions that would be obtained if an *infinite* number of empirical samples were selected. Although the mathematical derivation of sampling distributions is beyond the scope of this text, you should remember that it is possible to use mathematics to obtain sampling distributions that indicate the amount of fluctuation we can expect if chance only is operating. The sampling distributions are available. Our concern will not be with how they were obtained but with how we can use them for estimation and hypothesis testing.

ESTIMATION

The goal of *estimation* is to determine characteristics of a population by determining the characteristics of a small portion of that population (a sample). The crucial step in this process is obtaining a representative sample. Values for the sample (e.g., the sample mean) are called *statistics*. Values for the population (e.g., the population mean) are called *parameters*. Thus, statistics describe samples, and parameters describe populations. If a representative (random) sample is selected, statistics can be obtained to estimate parameters. For example, if you select a random sample of twenty-five college students from a small liberal arts college, the population is all students at the college. The mean intelligence score for your sample (a statistic) could be used to estimate the mean for the population (a parameter).

Investigators interested in estimating population parameters from statistics are concerned with the properties of their estimators (i.e., statistics) and the different kinds of estimates that can be made. Sampling distributions are crucial for estimation because the characteristics of the appropriate sampling distribution determine the properties of the estimator. For example, sampling distributions allow investigators to indicate a margin of error for their predictions (i.e., the "accuracy" of their predictions).

HYPOTHESIS TESTING AND THE EXPERIMENTAL METHOD

Research and Null Hypotheses

It is necessary to distinguish between two kinds of hypotheses: research, and null. A *research hypothesis* is an assertion about a particular phenomenon that is, typically, derived from a theory. We develop theories for phenomena in order to make predictions about observable events. For example, we might assert that a particular independent variable will have an effect on a dependent measure. Our prediction is called the research hypothesis (usually indicated by the symbol H_1) because it will be of scientific interest, if it is supported by tests. The *null hypothesis* (usually indicated by the symbol H_0) is the statement that the treatment manipulation will *not* have any effect — that there is zero effect due to the independent variable. If the null hypothesis is true, then the observed differences in performance on the dependent measure are due solely to chance fluctuations. If the research hypothesis is true, then the differences are due to chance fluctuations *plus* the effect of the independent variable.

The major task is to determine whether the research hypothesis or the null hypothesis is true. The only one that can be tested is the null hypothesis; the research hypothesis cannot be tested directly. Therefore, the hypotheses must be formulated in such a way that they cannot both be correct. If the null hypothesis is false, then the research hypothesis must be correct, if the experiment is methodologically sound. The next step is to select an experimental design.

Experimental Designs

The experimental or quasi-experimental design is the plan used to test whether a manipulation has an effect. Experimental designs can be divided into two categories, between-subject designs and within-subject designs. In a between-subject design each subject gets only one level of each independent variable. For example, if a between-subject design is being used to test the effect of alcohol on motor performance, each subject would either receive alcohol or not receive it. He would not be tested under both alcoholic and nonalcoholic conditions. In a within-subject design each subject would get more than one level of the independent variable. When each gets more than one treatment it is frequently possible to evaluate the effect of the treatment manipulation within each subject's data.

The various experimental designs (but *not* quasi-experimental designs) can be viewed as different procedures for obtaining equivalent groups. There are two kinds of between-subject designs: *random-groups designs* and *matched-groups designs*. Random assignment of subjects is used to obtain equivalent groups in a random-groups design. In a matched-groups design, the groups are equated on the variables selected for matching. If a nonsubject variable is manipulated as an independent variable in a matched-groups design, then random assignment should be used along with matching so the investigator can be confident that the groups are equivalent. For a within-subject design, all subjects are tested at each level of the independent variable; this makes it possible to attribute differences in performance at the various levels solely to the effect of chance fluctuations or to chance fluctuations plus the independent variable, if there are no confounding variables. Chance fluctuations are always present regardless of the design used, but their magnitude is influenced by the type of design.

The word *subject* in the name of the two designs may lead you to conclude that experimental designs are appropriate for experiments using animal and human subjects only. This is not the case. The subjects may be either inanimate or animate. The subject is the object or organism that receives the treatment. The condition or performance of the subjects is compared to assess whether the difference in the way the subjects have been treated has had any effect. For example, an investigator interested in evaluating a new automobile paint could use automobiles as subjects and manipulate the kind of paint used for each as the independent variable. The dependent variable could be the amount of rust after a four-year period. If only one kind of paint is used for each automobile, the investigator has used a between-subject design; if several kinds of paint are used for each, he has used a within-subject design.

Performing and Analyzing the Experiment

The investigator tries to perform the experiment in a way that allows her to assess the effect of the independent variable(s). She must obtain equivalent groups before introducing the independent variable. Then it will be reasonable to attribute any obtained difference to chance plus the effect of the treatment. The basic problem is to ensure that the subjects in the various conditions are treated identically except for the intended manipulation. After collecting the data, she can analyze the subjects' performance on the dependent variable to assess the influence of the manipulation.

Differences believed to be due to chance *and* the independent variable are attributed to the effect of the independent variable. That is, the distinguishing feature is whether the independent variable has an effect. Chance fluctuations are not distinguishing because they are always present. If the obtained differences are attributed to chance fluctuations, then, of course, the null hypothesis is not rejected. To determine whether or not such differences should be attributed to chance, one must consider the likelihood of particular outcomes if only chance is operating. Section II of this text is largely devoted to procedures for deciding such questions.

The Relationship between Design and Analysis

Design and analysis are interrelated, so considering how an experiment will be analyzed can be useful in detecting flaws in design. It is a very common mistake to design an experiment without considering how the results will be analyzed. If the experimenter makes no mistakes in design the subsequent analysis should not cause any particular difficulty. Unfortunately, in some instances experimenters expect to be able to salvage a poorly designed experiment by performing a sophisticated statistical analysis — an unreasonable expectation. The time to think about the analysis is before collecting the data. Considering the analysis and some possible outcomes of the experiment is one way to check the adequacy of the design.

THE LOGIC BEHIND THE STATISTICAL
ANALYSIS OF EXPERIMENTS

Statistical Tests

To determine whether obtained differences are due to the effect of the independent variable or only to chance we need to perform statistical tests.

All the statistical tests to be considered in the second section of this text deal with the probability of a particular event occurring by chance. The essential question is whether the results obtained are a common or rare occurrence when only chance is operating. A statistical test can answer this question. The end result of the test is a single number, which is then compared with a number found by referring to the appropriate statistical table. Whether the experimental outcome is a rare or common event *when the null hypothesis is true* is determined by making this comparison. The statistical test is a procedure for evaluating the null hypothesis. If the experimental outcome is a rare event, assuming the null hypothesis is true, then the null hypothesis is rejected. If it is not rare, then the null hypothesis is not rejected.

Significant Differences. The obtained differences between groups are said to be *significant* if the results are unlikely to occur on the basis of chance. If a particular experimental outcome is a rare event when chance only is operating, it is reasonable to assert that *more than* chance is operating and to reject the null hypothesis and accept the research hypothesis. In this case the investigator asserts that the differences between the treatments were not due solely to chance fluctuations, but to chance *plus* the effect of the independent variable. If the results are such that the null hypothesis can be rejected, the obtained differences are said to be significant. Statistical tests are often called *significance tests* because they are designed to determine whether obtained differences are rare, and therefore a significant event, or common, and therefore insignificant.

Significance Level. The curious reader is probably wondering how rare an event must be to be called significant. That is, how rare does an experimental outcome have to be, assuming that chance only is operating, before the investigator will reject the null hypothesis and accept the research hypothesis? The actual level varies somewhat depending on the research area, but most investigators will accept an outcome that has a probability of .05 or less as a rare event. If the probability of an event occurring is .05, it can be expected to occur five times in every 100 if only chance is operating. The level used to define a rare event is called the *significance level*. The name follows from the fact that the obtained differences are significant, i.e., attributable to the effect of chance *plus* the effect of the independent variable, if the probability of the experimental outcome is less than the significance level.

The significance level that is adopted defines what is meant by a rare event *and* what is meant by equivalent groups. Groups are said to be equivalent if the probability of the obtained outcome is greater than the significance level, assuming that chance only is operating. If an investigator selects the .001 significance level, then the probability of rejecting the null hypothesis when the null hypothesis is true is 1 in 1000. In this case a rare event is defined as an event with a probability of .001 if only chance is operating. The probability of obtaining equivalent groups *before* the independent variable is introduced is .999 if chance only determines the assignment of subjects to groups.

The probability of a rare event and the probability of obtaining equivalent groups must sum to 1.00 because these are the only two possible events. If the .05 significance level is adopted and the null hypothesis is true, then the probability of a rare event is .05 and the probability of obtaining equivalent groups is .95. If the independent variable does not have any effect (i.e., the null hypothesis is true), the probability of obtaining equivalent groups *after* the introduction of the independent variable is the same as the probability of obtaining equivalent groups *before* its introduction. Thus, if chance only is operating then it is highly likely that "small" mean differences will be obtained on the dependent measure after the introduction of the independent variable, so the investigator will probably be unable to reject the null hypothesis. However, since it is possible to obtain "large" mean differences solely on the basis of chance, an investigator may occasionally reject the null hypothesis when the null hypothesis is true. Yet most of the time when the null hypothesis is rejected it will, in fact, be false. That is, in most cases "large" mean difference between groups are due to the effect of chance fluctuations *plus* the effect of the independent variable.

To summarize, the important point is that the significance level defines what is meant by a rare event and what is meant by equivalent groups. If the obtained differences are so large that the probability that the outcome is due solely to chance is equal to or less than the significance level adopted, the null hypothesis is rejected. A rare event has occurred if chance only is operating, and the group differences are said to be significant. If the obtained differences are such that the probability that the outcome is due solely to chance is greater than the significance level adopted, the null hypothesis cannot be rejected. A common event has occurred if chance only is operating and the groups are said to be equivalent.

It is important that you not misinterpret the information presented in the preceding paragraphs. It does not necessarily follow that it is a good idea to adopt a stringent significance level to increase the probability of obtaining equivalent groups. The reason this may not be a good idea will be discussed later in the chapter. It should also be emphasized that the significance level is selected *before* comparing the performance of the groups. It should not be changed after the performance is known. The selection of a significance level is usually not an important consideration since the investigator has little latitude in making the choice. Most investigators adopt the .05 level. One who wants to convince others that his research hypothesis is correct is unlikely to do so if a very lenient significance level (say, .15) is adopted. The reason why most investigators select the .05 level is also considered later in the chapter.

In short, the crucial consideration in performing a statistical test is whether the outcome of an experiment is rare or common if the null hypothesis is true. The likelihood of a particular outcome is determined by comparing the obtained outcome with the distribution of possible outcomes. The distribution of possible outcomes is obtained from sampling distributions.

Experimental Error and Rejecting the Null Hypothesis

Statistical tests are performed to assess whether obtained differences between conditions are rare or unlikely if the null hypothesis (H_0) is true. The investigator has some freedom to decide how "unlikely" the results have to be before they should be labeled significant. If he wants to be very careful and not claim that the manipulation has had an effect unless there is almost no question about it, he can accept a very stringent significance level such as .001. (This can be represented as $p < .001$; the p stands for probability.) If the obtained differences are so large that the results are significant at the .001 level, there is less than one chance in a thousand that the results are due to chance. If the investigator attributes the obtained differences to the effect of the independent variable, there is some possibility that he is wrong. Perhaps only chance is operating, that is, H_0 is true. The point is that the possibility of being wrong when rejecting the null hypothesis cannot be eliminated, but the probability can be controlled. The probability of being wrong is equal to the significance level adopted. In the present case it is one in a thousand.

Investigators attempt to reject the null hypothesis and, in general, are not interested in accepting it. If the null hypothesis is rejected then the research hypothesis can be accepted. However, if the null hypothesis is not rejected, then the research hypothesis should neither be accepted nor rejected. Investigators are free to accept the research hypothesis if they reject the null hypothesis because they know the probability of being wrong. The probability of being wrong if the null hypothesis is accepted cannot be determined.

Type 1 and Type 2 Errors. There are four possible situations that need to be considered in order to discuss the two kinds of errors an investigator can make when using the experimental method. These four situations are represented in Table 3-3. The investigator's task is to decide between the null hypothesis (H_0) and the research hypothesis (H_1) as labeled in the column heads (Columns go down the page; rows go across the page.). The state of nature is either that H_0 is true or H_1 is true. We do not know the true state of nature in an absolute sense, but we do experiments in an effort to reach conclusions about it. Sometimes our decisions are correct; sometimes they are incorrect. Let us look at the two kinds of incorrect decisions.

TABLE 3-3

The Four Outcomes When Evaluating an Independent Variable

		Investigator's decision	
		H_0 (Does not reject H_0)	H_1 (Rejects H_0)
State of nature	H_0 is true	Correct decision (Probability = $1 - \alpha$)	Type 1 error (Probability = α)
	H_1 is true	Type 2 error (Probability = β)	Correct decision (Probability = $1 - \beta$)

If we assert that the independent variable has an effect (we reject the null hypothesis and accept the research hypothesis) when in fact it does not, we commit an error. This is called a Type 1 error, and the probability of committing it is equal to the significance level (also called the alpha level) that we have adopted. However, we can make another kind of error. If we assert that the independent variable has no effect (we fail to reject the null hypothesis) when in fact it does have an effect (i.e., H_1 is true) we are committing a Type 2 error. The Greek letter beta (β) is used to indicate the probability of making a Type 2 error. The reason investigators are reluctant to conclude, when they fail to reject the null hypothesis (H_0), that the independent variable does not have an effect is that the probability of making a Type 2 error cannot be determined. The probability of making a Type 2 error is determined by the procedures used and the *real* effect of the independent variable. The probability decreases as the real effect of the independent variable increases, but that effect cannot be known. There is therefore no way to determine the probability of making a Type 2 error.

Sampling Distributions, Experimental Error, and Rejecting the Null Hypothesis

Another way to consider the question of experimental error and rejection of the null hypothesis is to imagine that we know the true state of affairs. That is, although we cannot determine mathematically what the sampling distribution would be when the research hypothesis is true, we can imagine several situations that could arise.

Null Hypothesis Is True. Assume that a simple two-group experiment was conducted in which one group (the experimental group) received a new drug

The Logic Behind the Statistical Analysis of Experiments   77

and a second group (the control group) did not. For the first situation, assume that the null hypothesis is true. The drug does not have any effect on behavior. Figure 3-2A represents this state of affairs. The curve represents the distribution of possible experimental outcomes if only chance is operating, i.e., H_0 is true. It is assumed that the control group mean is subtracted from the experimental group mean. The right portion of the curve represents the probability that the experimental group mean will be larger than the control group mean (i.e., a positive difference will be obtained). It can be seen that the probability of obtaining a large mean difference between the groups is

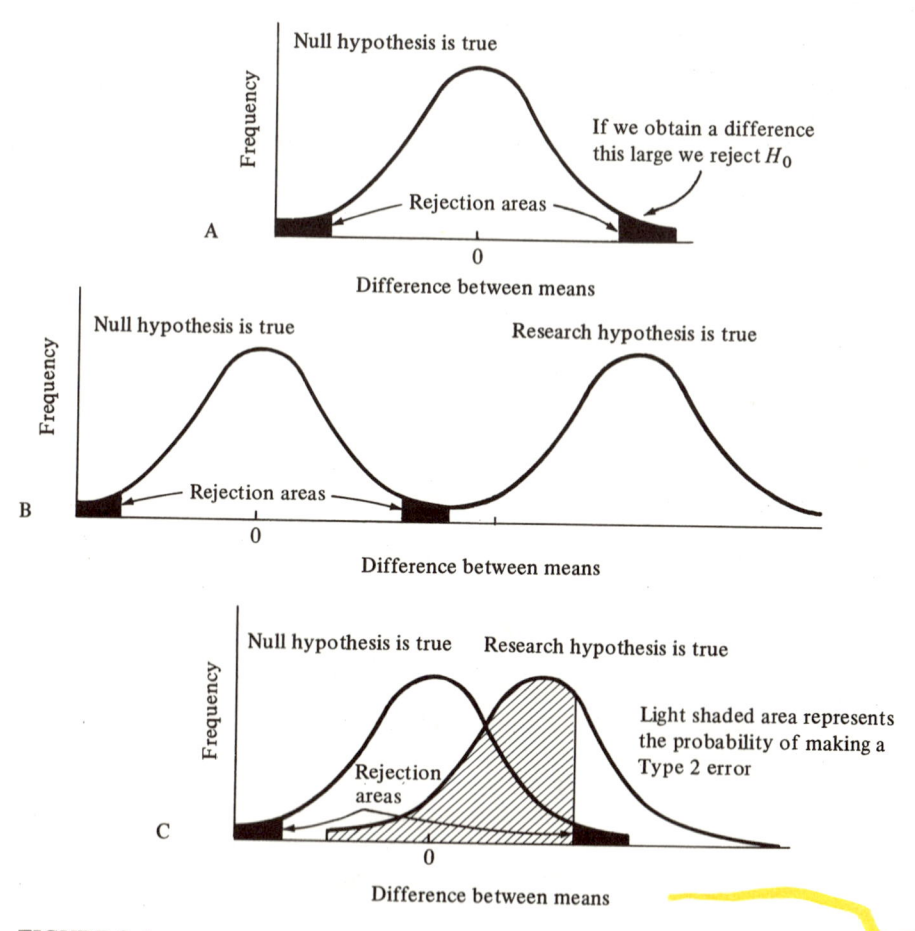

FIGURE 3-2

The null hypothesis sampling distribution and the "research hypothesis sampling distribution" for three possible situations. In A the independent variable has no effect. In B the independent variable has a large effect. In C the independent variable has a small effect.

78 *Estimation and Hypothesis Testing*

less than the probability of obtaining a small mean difference. The left portion of the curve represents the probability that a negative difference will be obtained. The mean of the null hypothesis sampling distribution is zero.

Only chance fluctuations should produce a difference between the two sample means because we have assumed that the null hypothesis is true. Thus, the probability of making a Type 1 error (concluding that the independent variable has an effect when in fact it does not) is equal to the significance level (say .05). The probability of making a correct decision (failing to reject the null hypothesis) is 1 minus alpha (α), or .95. There is no way to make a Type 2 error in this case because we are considering the situation in which the null hypothesis is true. It is only possible to make a Type 2 error when H_1 is true (see Table 3-3).

Independent Variable Has a Large Effect. Assume that the independent variable has a large effect. Figure 3-2B represents this state of affairs. In this case the research hypothesis sampling distribution indicates the true state of affairs, but the null hypothesis sampling distribution is used to assess the effect of the manipulation because there is no way to obtain the research hypothesis sampling distribution. The only distribution that is available is the null hypothesis sampling distribution. We use the null hypothesis sampling distribution in deciding to reject or fail to reject the null hypothesis. Although the research hypothesis sampling distribution is not available we can *imagine* what the distribution would be like if the independent variable had a large effect. In this case we are *assuming* that the drug increased the performance of the experimental group relative to the control group because large group differences are obtained between the two groups, that is, the drug has a large effect. The research hypothesis sampling distribution has almost no overlap with the null hypothesis sampling distribution.

The independent variable has a large effect, so a large mean difference between the samples is likely. That is, because the independent variable has a large influence on performance, it is likely that the mean difference between groups, which is based on the effect of the independent variable *plus* chance effects, will also be large. Since the obtained difference is evaluated according to the null hypothesis sampling distribution it is almost certain that the null hypothesis will be rejected.

The probability of making a Type 2 error (β) is very small because there is very little chance of obtaining a small difference between the two treatment means. Thus, the probability of making a correct decision, equal to 1 minus β, is very large. The probability of making a correct decision when H_1 is true is called the *power* of the test. The power is equal to 1 minus β.

Independent Variable Has a Small Effect. Assume that the independent variable (the drug) has a small positive effect on performance. Figure 3-2C represents this state of affairs. The probability of making a Type 2 error is quite large (see the lightly shaded area in the figure). The probability of making a Type 2 error increases as the overlap between the null hypothesis sampling distribution and the research hypothesis sampling distribution increases. The magnitude of the effect of the independent variable is one factor that influences the probability of making a Type 2 error. Since the real effect is unknown, it is not possible to calculate the probability of making a Type 2 error. Investigators are willing to reject the null hypothesis and accept the research hypothesis because they know the probability of making an error when they do this. They are reluctant to accept the null hypothesis (reject the research hypothesis) because they do not know the probability of making an error (Type 2 error) when they accept the null hypothesis.

Relationship between Type 1 and Type 2 Errors. The probability of making a Type 1 error is equal to the significance level that is adopted, so adopting a more stringent significance level decreases the probability of making a Type 1 error. If this were the only consideration it would be a good idea to adopt a very stringent significance level. However, investigators are also concerned about making Type 2 errors, and the probability of making a Type 2 error is also related to the significance level. Adopting a more stringent significance level increases the probability of making a Type 2 error. This fact can be appreciated by examining Figure 3-2C. The shaded area in the research hypothesis sampling distribution represents the probability of making a Type 2 error. If the rejection area under the null hypothesis sampling distribution is increased (i.e., a more lenient significance level is adopted), the probability of making a Type 2 error decreases (i.e., the shaded portion under the research hypothesis sampling distribution decreases). The reverse is true if a more stringent significance level is adopted, so the investigator who is more interested in avoiding Type 1 errors is likely to adopt a stringent significance level. The one who wants to avoid Type 2 errors is likely to adopt a lenient significance level. Most investigators are about equally interested in avoiding Type 1 and Type 2 errors so they take a middle position and select the .05 significance level.

One-tailed versus Two-tailed Tests

As we know, if the null hypothesis is true, the independent variable has no influence on the dependent measure, and if the research hypothesis is true, the independent variable does have an influence. Now in some cases an investigator may want to be more specific about the effect of the independent variable on the dependent variable. Instead of simply asserting that the independent variable has an effect he may want to specify the direction of the effect. For example, if a two-group experiment is conducted the investigator may predict that the experimental subjects will be better than control subjects. The research hypothesis is supported only if the experimental subjects are better. The null hypothesis is accepted if control subjects are better than experimental subjects regardless of the magnitude of the difference between the two conditions. The investigator who predicts the direction of the results makes a one-tailed test. The investigator who does not predict the direction of the results makes a two-tailed test.

Advantages of a One-tailed Test. The reason for the labels one-tailed and two-tailed can be appreciated by referring to the null hypothesis sampling distribution presented in Figure 3-2A. For this demonstration, assume that the control group mean is always subtracted from the experimental group mean. The investigator making a two-tailed test rejects the null hypothesis whenever there is a large difference between the two means regardless of whether the experimental mean is more or less than the control mean. He is interested in both tails, or extremes, of the sampling distribution curve. If the investigator selects the .05 significance level, 2.5% of the area under the curve at each tail is designated as the rejection area.

The "advantage" of making a one-tailed test is that 5% of the area under the curve at only one extreme is selected. If the 5% is selected at the right extreme only, then a smaller mean difference is needed to reject the null hypothesis if the results are in the predicted direction. Thus if the results are in the predicted direction, the probability of rejecting the null hypothesis is greater with a one-tailed than a two-tailed test. Unfortunately, some investigators misuse one-tailed tests.

Misuse of One-tailed Tests. An investigator predicts that the experimental subjects will be better than control subjects. Since a directional prediction is made, the investigator plans to use a one-tailed test. Assume that the investigator who adopts the .05 significance level can reject the null hypothesis if a mean difference of 4 or more is obtained, provided the results are in the predicted direction. Unfortunately, the results are in the opposite direction. The control group mean is 6 more than the experimental group mean. In this case the experimenter should not reject the null hypothesis. The prediction was in the wrong direction so he should not benefit from the fact that the obtained difference exceeded the difference needed for a one-tailed, or even a two-tailed, test of the prediction. If the experimenter switches to a two-tailed test after the results are obtained and reports the results as significant, then he has actually used a two-tailed test and accepted the .075 level of significance (5% at one tail and 2.5% at the other).

Selecting a One- or Two-tailed Test. To use a one-tailed test correctly it is necessary to make the prediction prior to collecting the data. If the results are in the opposite direction to that predicted, then the null hypothesis cannot be rejected even though large differences are obtained. An investigator who reports as significant results that are in the direction opposite to what he predicted is using a two-tailed test. Before deciding to use a one-tailed test you should ask yourself whether you are willing to accept the null hypothesis if the results are in the opposite direction and large differences are obtained. If you are not willing to do this, you should not use a one-tailed test. You would only be deceiving yourself about the significance level you have adopted. Most investigators always use the two-tailed test.

SUMMARY

Social scientists are interested in making inferences about quantities that cannot be tested directly and in testing hypotheses about behavior and mental activity. Randomization techniques are important for estimation and hypothesis testing. The purpose of random sampling is to obtain a sample that is representative of the larger population being studied so that sample values (statistics) can be used to estimate population values (parameters). The purpose of random assignment is to obtain equivalent groups prior to the introduction of the independent variable.

To make estimates and test hypotheses it is necessary to have some understanding of probability. The probability of an event can be defined as the ratio of the number of favorable events to the total number of possible events. The only factor that is assumed to operate is chance. Sampling distributions are important because they tell us how much fluctuation to expect among sample values if chance only is operating. We can determine the probability of a particular experimental outcome if we have the distribution of possible outcomes when chance only is operating.

The overall logic of hypothesis testing is rather simple. One starts with an idea that can be tested by making predictions about observable events. In many cases this means that an experimenter predicts that an independent variable will have an influence on performance. Such an assertion is called the research hypothesis. The null hypothesis is the assertion that the independent variable will not have an effect. The testing procedure usually involves obtaining groups that are likely to be equivalent and then introducing the independent variable. The effect of the independent variable is assessed by comparing the way the subjects in the various conditions perform on the dependent variable.

After the results are obtained the outcome is determined and compared with a distribution of possible outcomes based on the assumption that the null hypothesis is true. If the outcome is a rare event when compared with the appropriate null hypothesis sampling distribution, then the null hypothesis is rejected. The experimenter has reason to believe that the particular outcome is not a rare, chance event; instead, he attributes the obtained differences to the effect of the independent manipulation. Experimenters attempt to reject the null hypothesis and, in general, are not interested in accepting it. They know the probability of being wrong when they reject the null hypothesis but they do not know the probability of being wrong if they accept it.

QUESTIONS

1. Distinguish between the following terms:
    a. estimation and hypothesis testing

b. sample and population
   c. statistic and parameter
   d. random sampling and random assignment
   e. research hypothesis and null hypothesis
   f. frequency distributions and sampling distributions
   g. one-tailed and two-tailed tests
   h. Type 1 and Type 2 errors
2. How would you select a random sample of 50 students from your college or university? How would you select a random sample of 100 people from your state or province?
3. What procedure would you use to randomly assign the members of your class to five groups?
4. How do we determine the probability of any event's occurring if chance only is operating?
5. Consider the following proposition: The task is to draw an ace from a standard deck of playing cards. You pay a dime if you fail to draw an ace and receive a dollar if you succeed. The cards are shuffled after every draw. Would you accept this proposition? Why or why not? Would you accept the proposition if each draw cost only a nickel?
6. Consider the following proposition: A roulette wheel has nine slots numbered 0 through 8. You can pick any number or all the even numbers or all the odd numbers. If you select even numbers or odd numbers and win, you win the same amount that you bet. On this type of bet you lose, of course, if the little ball ends up in the zero hole. If you select any single number from 0 through 8 and win, you receive seven times what you bet. Assuming that you have a strong urge to gamble, would you pick a single number, odd numbers, or even numbers? Does it make any difference? Do you expect to win or lose?
7. What are sampling distributions and why are they important?
8. How are null hypothesis sampling distributions obtained?
9. Why is it important to state the research hypothesis in such a way that only either the null hypothesis or the research hypothesis is correct?
10. What are "equivalent groups"? How does the significance level you adopt affect the meaning of equivalent groups?
11. What determines the probability of making a Type 1 error? What determines the probability of making a Type 2 error?
12. What is the relationship between the significance level and the probability of making a Type 1 or Type 2 error? That is, what is the effect of decreasing the significance level (e.g., .01 instead of .05) on each of these errors?
13. Explain why investigators attempt to reject the null hypothesis and, in general, are not interested in accepting it.
14. Why is it better to use a two-tailed than a one-tailed test?

between-subject designs 4

THE LOGIC OF ANALYSIS OF VARIANCE

The Concept of Variance

There is a close relationship between the design and analysis of experiments. Once we understand the logic of analysis of variance we will be able to evaluate experimental designs and procedures more effectively.

The concept of variance is not as difficult as it at first seems. We want to measure the extent to which scores vary, and to do this it is convenient to have a reference point. The *mean* is that reference point. It is computed by adding all the scores and dividing the sum by the number of scores. For example, if we measured the heartbeat rate of five children we might obtain the following five scores: 83, 68, 65, 75, 74. To obtain the mean we add the five scores (total = 365) and divide by 5, the number of scores. This calculation gives us a mean of 73. We can then find the difference between each score and the mean, and add up the difference scores. That is, we can determine how much, if any, each score *deviates* from the mean by subtracting the score from the mean or the mean from the score. If this is done for each score and these deviations from the mean are added, the sum will be equal to zero. This computation is presented in Table 4-1.

The sum of the deviations from the mean is not a suitable measure of variability (i.e., the extent to which scores differ or fluctuate) because it will always be zero; the sum of the positive deviations is always equal to the sum of the negative deviations. The problem could be "solved" by ignoring the minus sign and adding all the deviations regardless of sign. Although this procedure would yield a measure of variability, there are statistical and

TABLE 4-1

The Heartbeat Rate for Five Children and the Computation of the Variance of These Scores. (The deviation scores are obtained by subtracting the mean from each score.)

Heartbeat score (X)	Deviation score $(X - \bar{X})$	Squared deviation score $(X - \bar{X})^2$
83	10	100
68	-5	25
65	-8	64
75	2	4
74	1	1
Sum = 365	Sum = 0	Sum = 194

$\bar{X} = 73$

$$\text{Variance} = \frac{\text{Sum of the squared deviation scores}}{\text{Number of scores minus 1}}$$

$$\text{Variance} = \frac{194}{4} = 48.50$$

practical reasons for using, instead, a measure obtained by squaring each deviation from the mean. The number obtained by taking the sum of the squared deviation scores and dividing by the number of scores minus one is called the *variance*.

You will probably remember that sample values can be used to estimate population values when the sample is selected randomly from the population. The sample values are called statistics, and the population values are called parameters. If the five children were selected randomly from a large population of children (e.g., all third-grade students in Peoria, Illinois) we could use the sample results to estimate the population values. The sample mean would be the best estimate of the population mean, and the sample variance would be the best estimate of the population variance. Sometimes all the scores for the population may be available. In this case there would be no need for estimation; the mean for the population would be computed by summing all the scores and dividing by the number of scores (i.e., the size of the population). The computation of variance, on the other hand, differs for populations and samples.

The variance of a population is the sum of the squared deviations from the mean divided by the number of scores. In computing the variance for a sample of less than thirty scores from a population, the sum of the squared deviations is divided by the number of scores minus one. The reason for this is to obtain a more accurate estimate of population variance. Over the long haul, the sum of the squared deviations divided by the number of scores minus one provides a better estimate than the sum of the squared deviations divided by the total number of scores. If there are more than thirty scores, however, the variance is not influenced very much by which divisor is used.

Some investigators divide by the number of scores if their sole concern is *describing* the scores, and they divide by the number of scores minus one if their concern is *estimating* population variance. Since variance is usually computed for small samples (i.e., fewer than thirty scores per group or sample) and not for the entire population, most investigators always divide by the number of scores minus one. That is, they do not bother to distinguish between a variance for description and one for estimation; the variance for estimation fulfills both functions. In this text, variance will always be computed by dividing by the number of scores minus one, regardless of the size of the sample. The symbol s^2 is usually used for sample variance.

You are encouraged to study the example in Table 4–1 until it is clear that variance is nothing more than a measure of the extent to which scores differ from the mean. Or you may wish to compute the variance for each of the following three sets of scores. Set A is 5, 5, 5, 5, 5, 5. Set B is 4, 6, 4, 6, 4, 6. Set C is 1, 9, 1, 9, 1, 9. By computing the three variances you will see that the variance provides a measure of the extent to which scores differ from a mean. If the variance is computed for a sample, the sample variance can be used to estimate population variance. The crux of the analysis of variance with a random-groups design is to obtain two independent estimates of population variance. The next task is to consider how two independent estimates can be obtained.

Obtaining Two Estimates of Population Variance

One estimate of population variance can be obtained by determining the variability in performance *within* each group. The variability in performance within each group provides an estimate, so there are as many estimates as there are groups. We need only one estimate based on fluctuations of scores within groups, so we take an average of the sample variances as the best within-group estimate of population variance. The other estimate of population variance is based on group means. If the null hypothesis is true, the group means can be regarded as a distribution of sample means from the same population. This distribution of sample means can be used to obtain another estimate of population variance. Because this second estimate is based on group means it is a between-group estimate of population variance. The first estimate of population variance is influenced by fluctuations within each group, and the second, which is based on differences between means, is influenced by differences between groups (between means). Examples should help us to clarify the point that two independent estimates of population variance can be obtained.

Example 1 — Large Treatment Effect. Let us assume that an investigator was interested in comparing the effects of two drugs on problem solving behavior. The dependent measure was the number of minutes required to solve the problem. The independent variable was the type of drug, A or B. The results of the experiment are presented in Table 4-2. Our task is to consider how two independent estimates of population variance can be obtained. Later we will consider how these estimates can be compared in order to make statements about the effects of treatments.

First we need to compute the variance for each group separately. Remember that this calculation is made by computing the mean for each group, subtracting the group mean from each score, squaring each deviation score, summing the squared deviation scores, and then dividing the sum of the squared deviation scores by the number of scores minue one. The letter n is used as a symbol for the number of scores in each condition. For the two conditions in the first example, the variance for the group receiving Drug A is .80 and the variance for Drug B is .80. The estimate of population variance based on within-group variance is also .80 because the two sample estimates are equal. We can obtain the within-group estimate of population variance by adding the individual estimates and dividing by the number of estimates. These computations are presented in Table 4-2.

We can also obtain an estimate of population variance by considering between-group fluctuations (the extent to which the group means differ). In this case we use means instead of individual scores. If we are going to determine the extent to which means fluctuate we need a reference point. The *overall mean* or grand mean will be our reference point. The overall mean is obtained by adding all the scores (sum = 72) and dividing by the number of scores, 12 in this case. The overall mean is 6 (i.e., 72/12 = 6). The estimate of population variance based on between-group fluctuation is obtained by substracting the overall mean from group mean, squaring the difference, summing the squared difference scores, multiplying by the number of scores in each condition, and then dividing by the number of groups minus 1. This computation is also presented in Table 4-2.

For the example just considered, the between-group and within-group estimates of population variance are markedly different (.80 for the within-group estimate and 48 for the between-group estimate). It is reasonable to ask, therefore, which estimate is the better estimate of population variance. The within-group estimate is better; it should reflect chance fluctuation only because all subjects within a group are treated the same. The between-group estimate should reflect chance fluctuations *plus* any effect of the independent variable; if the independent variable has an effect, the between-group estimate should be larger than the within-group estimate. If chance only is operating (i.e., there is no effect due to the independent variable) the two estimates

TABLE 4-2

The Results and Analysis of the Experiment Used as Example 1 (fictitious data)

Drug A	$(X - \bar{X})$	$(X - \bar{X})^2$	Drug B	$(X - \bar{X})$	$(X - \bar{X})^2$
3	-1	1	7	-1	1
4	0	0	8	0	0
5	1	1	9	1	1
3	-1	1	7	-1	1
4	0	0	8	0	0
5	1	1	9	1	1
Sum 24	0	4	Sum 48	0	4
$\bar{X} = 4$			$\bar{X} = 8$		

Computation of within-group variance

Variance (s^2) for Drug A condition

$$s^2 = \frac{\text{sum}(X - \bar{X})^2}{n - 1} = \frac{4}{5} = .80$$

where n = number of scores (subjects) in each group, in this case $n = 6$

Variance for Drug B condition

$$s^2 = \frac{\text{sum}(X - \bar{X})^2}{n - 1} = \frac{4}{5} = .80$$

Within-group estimate of population variance

$$\frac{\text{Sample 1 estimate} + \text{Sample 2 estimate}}{2} = \frac{.80 + .80}{2} = .80$$

▸ Computation of between-group variance

Drug A condition   Drug B condition

$\bar{X} = 4$ $\bar{X} = 8$ Overall mean = $\frac{24 + 48}{12} = 6$

$$\text{Between-group estimate} = \frac{n \, \text{sum}(\text{group mean} - \text{overall mean})^2}{k - 1}$$

where k = number of groups

$$\text{Between-group estimate} = \frac{6[(4 - 6)^2 + (8 - 6)^2]}{2 - 1}$$

$$\text{Between-group estimate} = \frac{6(8)}{1} = 48$$

should be about the same. We obtain two independent estimates of population variance so that we can compare the estimates to assess the effects of treatment manipulations.

We said that the between-group estimate should be larger than the within-group estimate if there is a treatment effect. If the independent variable does not have an effect, then the group means can be considered sample means, which are estimates of the same population mean. However, when it does have an effect the group means will not all be estimates of the same mean because the independent variable will result in an increase or decrease in one or more of the group means. In short, there should be greater fluctuations between the group means when the independent variable has an effect than when it does not. But there is no reason to expect within-group fluctuations to increase if the independent variable has an effect.

In sum, the crux of the analysis of variance test is to compare the between-group and within-group estimates of population variance. If the two estimates are about the same, there is no reason to reject the null hypothesis. If the between-group estimate is considerably larger than the within-group estimate, then the null hypothesis can be rejected. To conclude that the independent variable has an effect, the within-group fluctuations must be smaller than the between-group fluctuations.

Example 2 — No Treatment Effect. Let us assume that an investigator compared the effects of two drugs on problem solving behavior. The dependent variable was the number of minutes required to solve the problem. The independent variable was the type of drug, C or D. Assume that the results presented in Table 4-3 were obtained and that the investigator computed the two estimates of population variance, a between-group and a within-group estimate, as presented in Table 4-3. The procedure used to obtain the two estimates is identical to the procedure used for Example 1. The between-group and within-group estimates are identical in this case so there is no basis for rejecting the null hypothesis. To reject the null hypothesis the between-group estimate has to be *significantly* larger than the within-group estimate. We will consider procedures for determining whether the between-group estimate is significantly larger than the within-group estimate in later chapters. Here we want to demonstrate that two independent variance estimates can be obtained and then compared to evaluate whether a treatment (independent variable) influenced performance on the dependent measure.

The example in Table 4-3 is somewhat unusual in that the two estimates of population variance are identical. This can happen, of course, but it is more likely that the two estimates will vary somewhat even when there is no treatment effect. If chance only is operating, the between-group estimate can be smaller than, equal to, or larger than the within-group estimate. We reject the null hypothesis only when the between-group estimate is *significantly* larger than the within-group estimate.

TABLE 4-3

The Results and Analysis of the Experiment Used as Example 2 (fictitious data)

Drug C	$(X - \bar{X})$	$(X - \bar{X})^2$	Drug D	$(X - \bar{X})$	$(X - \bar{X})^2$
5	−9	81	15	−5	25
25	11	121	35	15	225
25	11	121	15	−5	25
10	−4	16	15	−5	25
5	−9	81	20	0	0
Sum 70	0	420	Sum 100	0	300
	$\bar{X} = 14$			$\bar{X} = 20$	

Computation of within-group variance

Variance for Drug C condition

$$s^2 = \frac{\text{sum } (X - \bar{X})^2}{n - 1} = \frac{420}{4} = 105$$

Variance for Drug D condition

$$s^2 = \frac{\text{sum } (X - \bar{X})^2}{n - 1} = \frac{300}{4} = 75$$

Within-group estimate of population variance

$$\frac{\text{Sample 1 estimate + Sample 2 estimate}}{2} = \frac{105 + 75}{2} = 90$$

Computation of between-group variance

Drug C condition   Drug D condition

$\bar{X} = 14$ $\bar{X} = 20$ Overall mean $= \dfrac{70 + 100}{10} = 17$

$$\text{Between-group estimate} = \frac{n \text{ sum(group mean − overall mean)}^2}{k = 1}$$

$$\text{Between-group estimate} = \frac{5[(14 - 17)^2 + (20 - 17)^2]}{2 - 1}$$

$$\text{Between-group estimate} = \frac{5(18)}{1} = 90$$

Analysis of Variance and Experimental Design

An understanding of the logic of analysis of variance is important for methodological as well as statistical purposes because design and procedural decisions can have a marked influence on the within-group and between-group estimates of population variance. The reader should remember that investigators are interested in rejecting the null hypothesis. There is little satisfaction in failing to do so. If an independent variable does have an effect on the dependent variable, the effect is more likely to be detected if the investigator is able to keep within-group fluctuations to a mimimum. It is important to know what effect a particular design or procedure has on these fluctuations.

THE RANDOM-GROUPS DESIGN

Properties of the Random-groups Design

In a between-subject design each subject receives only one level of each independent variable. For example, to assess the effects of reward on motor performance each subject would either receive the reward or not receive it. The treatment is between subjects in that the performance of different subjects is compared to assess the effect of the independent variable. If there is more than one independent variable each subject gets only one combination of levels. For example, if there were two levels of one independent variable (low and high incentive) and three levels of a second variable (drug A, B, C), each subject would receive either high or low incentive and drug A, B, or C. No subject would receive both high and low incentive or more than one drug. The second important characteristic of the random-groups design is that random assignment is used so that the investigator can be fairly confident that the groups are equivalent before introducing the independent variable.

The Logic of the Random-groups Design

The random assignment procedure is meant to ensure that between-group differences before the introduction of the independent variable will be due solely to chance fluctuations. If chance only determines the assignment of subjects to conditions, then the significance level that is adopted will determine the probability of obtaining equivalent groups before the introduction of the independent variable.

Assume that an investigator decides to use a random-groups design to assess the effects of a particular independent variable on heartbeat rate. Let us assume further that, unknown to the investigator, redheads have faster heartbeats than nonredheads. Will the random assignment procedure result in groups with approximately the same number of redheads so that group differences will not be attributable to having too many redheads in one group? If the .05 significance level is adopted, the investigator can be confident that random assignment will yield equivalent groups prior to the introduction of the independent variable approximately 95% of the time. Therefore, if significant differences between groups are found *after* the introduction of the independent variable, it is reasonable to assert that these differences are due to chance *plus* the effect of the independent variable, since the probability that they are due to chance alone is known to be small (i.e., .05). This probability is known to be small *because* the random assignment procedure was used to ensure that only chance determined the assignment of subjects to conditions.

Experiments with One Independent Variable

The random-groups design can be used whenever it is possible to randomly assign subjects to groups and then introduce the independent variable. It follows, therefore, that this design can be used to test essentially all independent variables except subject variables.

It is possible to assess, for instance, the effect of a new drug by using a random-groups design. The subjects are randomly assigned to either the experimental or control condition. Then the treatment is administered, and the effect of the treatment on some dependent variable is assessed. If the performance of the experimental subjects on the dependent variable differs significantly from that of the control subjects the difference can be attributed to the effect of the treatment. The control subjects should be treated the same as the experimental subjects except for the intended manipulation. To ensure that the use of the drug is the only manipulation the subjects must not be given any information about the treatment conditions. The control subjects are given a placebo; the experimental subjects are given the drug. Neither the subjects nor the person administering the treatments should know which treatment a subject receives. Experiments in which both the subjects and the person administering the treatments are kept unaware of the nature of the manipulation are frequently called *double-blind* experiments.

Although a two-group experiment can be used to assess the effect of a particular manipulation, investigators frequently prefer to use more than two levels for an independent variable. The use of additional levels of an independent variable allows them to answer additional questions. For example, an investigator interested in the effect of a new drug may manipulate the amount of the drug administered. In this case a three-group random-groups design could be used. One group would receive a high dose; a second group a low dose; and the third, a placebo. The investigator would be able to determine whether the drug has an effect *and* whether the dosage has an effect.

It is difficult to overstate the importance of the random-groups design because it is useful for a wide variety of research problems. It is an extremely powerful design because there are so many independent variables that can be introduced after subjects have been randomly assigned to conditions. Investigators interested in all areas of human information processing, development, and social behavior use this design extensively. Instructors frequently have their students perform experiments in which one independent variable is manipulated by using the random-groups design. The beginning student, in particular, should find it useful, because it is an excellent vehicle for learning about research methodology. An understanding of this design is the basis for more complicated experiments so it needs to be studied extensively. Let us consider another example.

Imagine that you are interested in the effect of diet on intellectual development; you believe that adequate protein is extremely important, particularly during the early years. For ethical, practical, and legal reasons you are not able to use human subjects in your experiment, so you use rhesus monkeys. Assume that a reliable and valid test of intellectual development is available and that the test can be administered to all subjects when they mature at four years of age. This test is the dependent measure; the diet of each subject is the manipulated variable. You give a high protein diet to one group and a low protein diet to the other. Because diet is a nonsubject variable you can evaluate its effect by using the random-groups design. That is, you can randomly assign each subject to one of the two groups and then introduce the diet manipulation. The diet manipulation must be the only variable that is manipulated systematically because you want to attribute any between-group differences (i.e., any significant differences) to the diet. It is extremely important, then, that the groups be treated alike.

If the groups are not treated alike except for the intended manipulation, the experiment would be *confounded*. An experiment is confounded when it is not clear whether the results are due to the independent variable manipulation or to some other unintended manipulation. For example, if the subjects receiving high protein diets were given more stimulation than subjects receiving low protein, there would not be any way to determine whether any obtained differences in intellectual performance were due to protein or stimulation.

The experiment can be criticized because it lacks a control group. One could argue that a normal diet group should have been used in addition to low and high protein groups. If the control condition had been included there would have been three levels of diet (low protein, normal protein, and high protein). Without a control group, even if you obtain a protein effect, you will not be able to determine whether or not low protein retards intellectual development or high protein facilitates it. You can indicate the difference between low and high protein but you cannot make any assertions about low and high protein relative to the normal diet. You must limit the conclusion to the levels of the independent variable used.

Some highly sophisticated designs allow one to make statements about levels of an independent variable other than the levels included in the experiment. Our discussion is limited to what are called *fixed effects models* — designs in which it is necessary to limit conclusions to the levels of the independent variable manipulated.

Experiments with Two Independent Variables

Experiments in which more than one independent variable is manipulated allow the investigator to determine the interaction of independent variables and the main effects of each independent variable. Since it is necessary to have a minimum of two levels of each independent variable, a minimum of four groups is required each time two independent variables are investigated with a random-groups design. We can, for example, randomly assign subjects (indicated by $S_1, S_2, \ldots S_{40}$ in Table 4-4) to four different groups and then introduce two independent variables, as demonstrated in Table 4-4. Each subject receives only one combination of levels so there are four independent groups in this experiment. No subject can be assigned to more than one group when a random-groups design is used.

Two examples should demonstrate the usefulness of the factorial random-groups design. For the first example, a 2 by 3 factorial design, assume that you are interested in ways to convince people to stop smoking. You obtain the cooperation of 150 smokers and randomly assign them to six groups so that you have 25 smokers in each group. You then introduce your two independent variables, incentive (five dollars versus nothing) and the type of antismoking campaign (emotional appeal, practical, control). This design is presented in Table 4-5. It is a 2 by 3 factorial design because there are two

TABLE 4-4

A 2 by 2 Factorial, Random-groups Design

		Independent variable 1	
		Level 1	Level 2
Independent variable 2	Level A	S_1 S_2 . . . S_{10}	S_{21} S_{22} . . . S_{30}
	Level B	S_{11} S_{12} . . . S_{20}	S_{31} S_{32} . . . S_{40}

TABLE 4-5

A 2 by 3 Factorial, Random-groups Design in Which Incentive and Antismoking Campaigns Are the Independent Variables Manipulated

		Type of antismoking campaign		
		Emotional appeal	Practical appeal	Control
Incentive	$5/day			
	Nothing			

levels of one independent variable and 3 levels of the other. For the incentive manipulation, subjects either get five dollars for every day they do not smoke or they get nothing. The antismoking campaigns differ in that some subjects (controls) are simply told to stop smoking, others (practical) are given specific procedures to use when they have the urge to smoke, and others (emotional appeal) are shown in graphic detail the misery and pain that can accompany lung cancer. The dependent measure is the average number of cigarettes each subject smokes per day.

The results of the above experiment should provide interesting information about the effects of incentive, type of antismoking campaign, and the interaction of these two independent variables. For example, the effect of the antismoking campaigns may depend on the level of incentive; there may be larger differences among the three levels of the antismoking manipulation when there is no incentive than when there is.

There are likely to be some problems with the above experiment because subjects given five dollars per day to stop smoking may not be as truthful about reporting their smoking behaviors as are subjects who are not paid to stop smoking. You would have to take steps to ensure that the reports were accurate before evaluating the incentive manipulation. And you would need to make sure that the smokers were treated identically except for the intended manipulations. Obviously, we would not want the emotional appeal to take twice as long to administer as the practical appeal because the amount of contact with the smoker, and not the content of the appeal, could be responsible for any change in smoking behavior. Similarly, you should spend as much time with the control subjects as the other subjects to make sure that any obtained differences are attributable to the content of the message (type of antismoking campaign) and not merely to the amount of social interaction between the investigator and the subjects.

You may want to consider different possible outcomes for the above experiment to increase your understanding of main effects and interactions. Factorial random-groups designs are useful in many research areas because it is frequently necessary to know how independent variables interact as well as what their main effects are. Social psychologists use factorial designs extensively because there is considerable evidence to suggest that the effects of many independent variables manipulated by social psychologists (e.g., credibility of the communicator, physical presence of others, content of the communication) depend on the social context in which they are investigated. Drug researchers also have considerable use for factorial, random-groups designs because it is well-known that drugs interact (Hussar, 1973). Drug interactions are obtained when the effect of one drug is influenced by the prior or concurrent administration of another drug. The effects of many drugs are influenced greatly by the amount of alcohol consumed by the patient so it is very important to know which drugs interact with alcohol and which do not. It is not enough simply to tell patients not to drink when they are taking medication, because many patients faced with a choice between taking their medication or drinking will decide not to take their medication. Some drugs given in combination can lead to overdose, which would not result if the drugs were administered singly. In short, there is ample reason to believe that factorial, random-groups designs will continue to play an important role in medical and psychological research.

Subject and Nonsubject Variable Experiments

It is common for investigators to use the random-groups design to assess the effects of two or more independent variables in the same experiment. It is also possible to combine the investigation of a subject variable with a nonsubject variable in the same experiment. The random-groups design can be used for the nonsubject variable manipulation but not for the subject variable manipulation.

Let us consider an experiment in which the two types of variables are investigated. Imagine that you are interested in the effect of programmed instruction on performance in introductory psychology courses. You decide to compare programmed instruction with the more traditional lecture-discussion approach. You are also concerned about the possible generality of any effect, so you decide to test your manipulation of instruction with different kinds of subjects — low achievers and high achievers. You *select* a group of low achievers and high achievers by examining grade point averages of all subjects available for the experiment. Thus, prior achievement is your subject variable. You randomly assign all the low achievers to the two instructional conditions, and you randomly assign all the high achievers to the two instructional conditions. You now have one subject variable (achievement level) and one nonsubject variable (type of instructional program). The design of this experiment is presented in Table 4-6.

You are not particularly interested in comparing the performance of low and high achievers. These subjects were not assigned randomly to the two

TABLE 4-6

A 2 by 2 Factorial Design in Which a Subject Variable and a Nonsubject Variable Are Investigated. The Subjects at Each Achievement Level Are Randomly Assigned to the Programmed or Lecture-discussion Conditions.

		Type of instructional program	
		Programmed instruction	Lecture-discussion
Achievement	Low		
	High		

achievement conditions, so there is no way of knowing what nonmanipulated variables may be responsible for performance differences. However, since you were able to use a random assignment procedure for the type of instructional program manipulation, you can attribute significant differences between the programmed approach and lecture-discussion to the manipulation. That is, because each low achiever was randomly assigned to one of the two instructional conditions, and each high achiever was randomly assigned to one of the two instructional conditions, you can be reasonably confident that the subjects in the programmed instruction and lecture-discussion conditions were equivalent before the independent variable was introduced.

The major reason for combining the manipulation of the nonsubject variable with the selection of different subjects is to assess whether the effect, if any, of the nonsubject variable depends on the type of subject. This knowledge can be valuable. If a variable such as instructional method has an influence on course performance it is important to determine the circumstances under which it has an effect. For example, if programmed instruction were better than the lecture-discussion approach for the low achievers but not for the high achievers, there would be no reason to advocate programmed instruction for high achievers. The combination of subject variables and nonsubject variables in factorial experiments is a useful way to determine whether the effectiveness of different manipulations (e.g., instructional techniques, therapies, advertising approaches) depend on characteristics of subjects (e.g., age, personality, intelligence).

MATCHED-GROUPS DESIGNS

A matched-groups design is a between-subject design in which the groups are equated on one or more matching variables (e.g., intelligence). Matching variables are subject variables. If a nonsubject variable is held constant for all conditions (i.e., the groups are equated on a nonsubject variable), it is said to be *controlled*. For example, if the experimental subjects and control subjects are given the same amount of time to complete their tasks, the time variable is controlled. Time is, of course, a nonsubject variable. In short, investigators *match* groups on subject variables and *control* nonsubject variables. The reasons for matching and the procedures used depend on whether the independent variable is a subject or nonsubject variable.

Matched-groups Designs and Subject Variables

The reason for using a matched-groups design for a subject variable manipulation is readily understood. In a subject variable manipulation, as we have seen before, it is not possible to equate the groups before introducing the independent variable because the nature of the independent variable determines the composition of the groups. For example, assume an investigator devises a test to identify people with high levels of anxiety and people with low levels, and then compares them on a learning task. If the two groups differ it is not reasonable to conclude that the differences in anxiety level were responsible for the learning differences because people who differ in anxiety level may also differ in many other ways. High anxiety subjects may be more motivated, intelligent, submissive, or authoritarian than low anxiety subjects.

Now let us assume that the investigator is aware that other subject variables may be responsible for the learning differences. To circumvent this problem she decides to use a matched-groups design. She gives 3000 subjects a number of tests and obtains biographical information on each subject. She then uses the results of the anxiety test to obtain a pool of 500 high anxiety subjects and 500 low anxiety subjects. Then the results of the other tests and the biographical information are used to select two groups of 50 high anxiety and 50 low anxiety subjects who are equal on a number of other characteristics, such as intelligence, achievement motivation, number of siblings, past achievement, and intelligence of parents. The investigator compares the learning scores of the two groups and obtains a significant difference. Should she conclude that the differences in anxiety were responsible for the differences in learning?

Researchers are likely to disagree somewhat on the answer to this question. Most would probably argue that the evidence for a causal relationship is less than overwhelming. Many would reject the evidence because a particular variable (e.g., ability to create images) was not used as a matching variable. Yet if given a choice between this procedure and the manipulation of a subject variable without matching, most would prefer the matching procedure if the variables that are known to influence learning were matched.

If the use of the matching procedure is the best method available for studying the effects of a particular subject variable, there is little choice but to use it. Note that this use of a matched-groups design is essentially the same as computing a correlation between two variables while holding other variables constant. You will recall that the manipulation of a subject variable is similar to the use of a correlational technique in that cause-effect conclusions are, from a theoretical point of view, almost never warranted.

Matched-groups Designs and Nonsubject Variables

The investigator who makes a nonsubject variable manipulation can use random assignment to obtain equivalent groups before introducing the independent variable (i.e., the random-groups design is appropriate). The decision to use a matched-groups design instead is frequently difficult to make because this design has both advantages and disadvantages. The advantages are methodological or theoretical; the disadvantages are all practical. In principle, matching can never be worse than solely relying on random assignment.

Prerequisite for Matching. The investigator who is contemplating whether or not to use a matched-groups design should first consider whether there is a suitable matching variable. A suitable matching variable is a subject variable that is correlated with performance on the dependent measure. Subject variables that have a high correlation with the dependent measure are more suitable than ones that have a low correlation. For example, if an experiment is to be performed to assess the effects of transcendental meditation training on motor performance, motor performance would be the dependent measure. Assume that the correlation between the motor performance test and intelligence is .05, whereas the correlation between a dexterity test and motor performance is .85. In this case the dexterity test would be a far better matching variable than the intelligence test.

There is no reason for matching unless the matching variable is related to the *dependent* measure. Matched-groups designs are used to exert some control over the subjects' performance on the dependent measure. If the matching variable is unrelated to the dependent variable, then matching will have no effect. This fact is important but it frequently escapes the beginning researcher, as evidenced by the many studies in which the matching variable was unrelated to the dependent variable. For example, several decades ago most investigators routinely matched on intelligence. Apparently they believed that intelligence is related to just about every conceivable dependent variable. It isn't. Having a subject variable that correlates with the dependent measure is a *prerequisite* for using a matched-groups design.

If there is a subject variable that highly correlates with the dependent variable you can then consider whether it is feasible to match on this variable — that is, whether the advantages to be gained are great enough to justify the time and effort needed for matching. In many cases the advantages are too slight to justify the use of the matched-groups design. In many other cases no subject variable is known to highly correlate with the dependent measure.

Reasons for Matching. There are two major reasons for using a matched-groups design with a nonsubject variable manipulation. The first is to provide greater assurance that the groups are equivalent before introducing the independent variable. For example, let us assume that hair color is highly related to performance on the dependent measure. Redheads perform better than nonredheads. The investigator who is aware of this may elect to match the groups on hair color by having the same number of redheads and nonredheads in each group. Of course, he must randomly assign subjects to conditions except for the limitation that the matching restriction places on random assignment; he must not decide which redheads and nonredheads will be in each group. The procedure used in matching will determine whether the matched-groups design will influence anything besides the equivalence of groups prior to the introduction of the independent variable.

The second major reason for matching is to reduce within-group variance. The within-group variance, as we know, is a measure of the extent to which subjects in the same group perform alike. If the within-group fluctuations can be reduced by matching, there is greater likelihood of detecting the effect of the independent variable. Remember that the effect of an independent variable is assessed by comparing a between-group estimate of population variance with a within-group estimate. If the within-group estimate is considerably smaller than the between-group estimate, the null hypothesis can be rejected. The probability of detecting the real effect of an independent variable increases as the within-group fluctuations decrease. The influence of a matched-groups design on the detection of such an effect depends on the procedure used in matching.

Matching Procedures and Nonsubject Variables

Matching that Reduces Within-group Variance. Let us assume that intelligence correlates highly with the dependent measure. People with high IQs get high scores on the dependent measure, and people with low IQs get low scores. If the investigator uses the random-groups design and subjects who vary considerably in IQ, there will be considerable within-group fluctuation in the scores on the dependent measure. The subjects of high intelligence will get high scores and those of low intelligence will get low scores.

If the independent variable does not have an effect the two estimates of population variance will usually be about the same, as in the example presented in Table 4-3. The between-group and within-group estimates of population variance are both equal to 90. If the between-group estimate is divided by the within-group estimate, the quotient is one. Since a quotient of one is likely to occur on the basis of chance, the null hypothesis cannot be rejected. Remember that the two estimates probably will *not* be *exactly* the same if the null hypothesis is true. For this example, however, there is no harm in assuming that they are the same.

The random-groups design was used in the above example but a matched-groups design could have been used. The investigator could have matched on intelligence in such a way as to reduce both variance estimates by using only subjects who had, say, an IQ of 110. Such a selection would have reduced within-group variance because in this case we assumed that IQ correlated highly with the dependent measure. It would also have reduced between-group variance because the groups were equated on IQ; therefore, the mean performance of each group on the dependent measure would more likely be the same if matching were used than if not. These two variance estimates from a matched-groups design, then, will be smaller than the corresponding pair from the random-groups design.

Assume that the within-group variance estimate is equal to 10 and the between-group estimate is equal to 10. Now, if we assume that the effect of the independent variable increases the *between-group* estimate by 60, we can demonstrate the advantage of using a matched-groups design over the random-groups design. For the random groups design, the between-group estimate of population variance would be 150 (i.e., 90 + 60) and the within-group estimate would be 90. If the between-group estimate is divided by the within-group estimate, the quotient is 1.67. For the matched-groups design example, the between-group estimate would be 70 (i.e., 60 + 10) and the within-group estimate would be 10. The quotient obtained by dividing the between-group estimate of population variance by the within-group estimate would be 7.00. There would be a greater likelihood of rejecting the null hypothesis with a matched-groups design than with the random-groups design if the independent variable had an effect.

We have assumed that the effect of the independent variable is the same whether the subjects vary considerably in IQ or not. For the purpose of our example there is no harm in making this assumption. However, selecting subjects on the basis of their performance on a matching variable can reduce the generality of the finding. For example, if all the subjects have an IQ of 110, some investigators would argue that there is little reason to believe that the same finding would be obtained with subjects with markedly higher or lower IQs. If IQ and the independent variable are both used as independent variables, the two may interact.

The numbers used in the above examples were for illustration only. The use of a matched-groups design may not decrease the within-group estimate of population variance by so much. The important point is not the magnitude of the reduction but the fact that a reduction in within-group variance increases the likelihood of rejecting the null hypothesis if the independent variable has an effect.

The way the matching is carried out will determine its effect. In the previous example, the within-group and between-group estimates of population variance were decreased by the matching procedure, so the procedure had a desirable effect. The important point here is that *within-group* variance was reduced. The reduction of between-group variance is not necessarily desirable. Unless the matching procedure reduces within-group variance, matching is a questionable practice.

Matching that Reduces Between-group Variance. If the sole purpose of matching is to provide further assurance that the groups are equivalent prior to the introduction of the independent variable, then matching may not be justified.

Assume once again that intelligence correlates highly with performance on the dependent measure. If a random-groups design is used, the between-group and within-group estimates of population variance will be about the same if the independent variable has no effect. If a matched-groups design is used to increase the likelihood that the groups are equivalent before the independent variable is introduced, the matching procedure *could* result in the reduction of the between-group estimate of population variance without having much of an effect on the within-group estimate. Suppose that the investigator matches on intelligence by making sure each group has the same mean and variance on the intelligence variable. Unless he excludes subjects with extreme scores on the matching variable, the procedure will have little effect on the within-group estimate of population variance. Equating the means will reduce only the between-group variance. There is not much advantage to reducing between-group variance unless within-group variance is also reduced.

The likelihood of making a Type 1 error decreases when a matching procedure reduces differences between groups but does not affect within-group fluctuations. Yet it is highly unlikely that the slight reduction in the probability of making such an error is worth the extra effort involved in matching. The goal of decreasing the probability of making a Type 1 error can be accomplished more easily by adopting a more stringent significance level, say .01 instead of .05.

Subject by Subject Matching. Matching that is done by obtaining pairs or sets of subjects who are equal on the matching variable makes it possible to use a within-subject instead of a between-subject analysis. For example, assume that an investigator wants to match the groups on weight before investigating the effectiveness of three dieting programs. There are two treatment conditions and one control condition. He recruits three people who weigh the same and randomly assigns one subject to each condition. This is repeated for successive sets of three people. The use of this procedure will allow the investigator to analyze the results so that fluctuations due to initial weight will not be included when the size of the chance fluctuations is determined. If the matching is carried out in this way, the design is similar to the within-subject designs discussed in the next chapter.

SUMMARY

The crux of analysis of variance with a random-groups design is to obtain two independent estimates of population variance. One estimate can be obtained by determining within-group variance, which is a measure of the extent to which subjects in the same treatment condition perform alike on the dependent measure. The other estimate is the between-group variance, based on group means. The two estimates of population variance tend to be about the same if the null hypothesis is true. If the independent variable has an effect, the between-group estimate tends to be larger than the within-group estimate. To maximize the likelihood of rejecting the null hypothesis when the independent variable has an effect it is necessary to keep within-group fluctuations as small as possible.

In a between-subject design each subject receives only one level of each independent variable. The random-groups design is a between-subject design in which random assignment is used in an effort to ensure that the groups are equivalent before the independent variable is introduced. Equivalence of groups permits subsequent differences in performance to be attributed to the effect of the independent variable. The random-groups design can be used whenever it is possible to randomly assign subjects to groups before introducing the independent variable.

A matched-groups design is a between-subject design in which the groups are equated on one or more matching variables. Matching variables are subject variables. Investigators *match* groups on subject variables and *control* nonsubject-variables. Matched-groups designs are used with subject variable manipulations in an attempt to equate the groups on the relevant subject variables that are not being investigated. When the investigator is able to match on these nonmanipulated subject variables there is more reason to attribute any obtained differences between groups to the subject variable that was varied.

Several considerations are involved in the question of whether to use a matched-groups design when a nonsubject variable manipulation is made. There is absolutely no reason to consider matching unless the variable to be matched is related to the dependent measure. One reason for matching is to provide greater likelihood of equivalent groups. Another reason is to reduce within-group variance. If the matching procedure does not reduce within-group variance or does not allow the investigator to use a within-subject instead of between-subject statistical analysis, then the use of a matched-groups design is a questionable practice.

QUESTIONS

1. Assume that the following results were obtained in an experiment investigating the effects of incentive on motor performance. The dependent measure was the number of errors. Calculate the within-group and between-group estimates of population variance.

Incentive group	Control group
4	10
5	8
6	9
6	10
4	9
5	8

2. What is the logic of analysis of variance — that is, why is it important to obtain two independent estimates of population variance?
3. A biochemist claims to have developed a pill that will increase IQ by five points for every pill administered. To test this claim you do an experiment in which you randomly assign subjects to a 0, 1, 2, or 4 pills condition. All subjects in one group get no pills; all subjects in another get one pill, and so on. What will be the effect of the independent variable on within-group and between-group fluctuations if the biochemist is correct?
4. What is the logic of the random-groups design? Does the random assignment of subjects to conditions guarantee that the groups are equivalent prior to the introduction of the independent variable? Why?
5. When can you use the random-groups design?
6. What is the advantage of manipulating a subject variable and a nonsubject variable in the same experiment?
7. Why are matched-groups designs used when a subject variable manipulation is made? How is this design useful for evaluating subject variables?
8. What are the advantages and disadvantages of using a matched-groups design when assessing the effect of a nonsubject variable?
9. Explain why reducing within-group variance increases the likelihood of rejecting the null hypothesis if the independent variable has an effect.
10. An investigator used a matched-groups design in which intelligence was the matching variable. The groups were matched on intelligence by equating the group means and variances. That is, each group had the same mean IQ score and the same variance for their IQ scores. What factors should be considered when evaluating this procedure?
11. What factors should an investigator consider when deciding whether to use the random-groups or a matched-groups design?

within-subject designs 5

The fact that between-subject designs can be used for so many different research problems may lead the student to conclude that there is little need for additional designs. But although the between-subject designs are very broad in scope, research problems frequently arise for which the use of these designs is difficult, impractical, or impossible. The relative importance of between- and within-subject designs varies greatly from problem area to problem area and from investigator to investigator. In some areas the research methodology is based almost entirely on one of the two designs. Yet in other areas investigators switch back and forth between the two, depending on the hypothesis under investigation. This chapter should give you a better understanding of why investigators use the designs they do and will help you determine the relative usefulness of between- and within-subject designs for your area of personal interest.

PROPERTIES OF WITHIN-SUBJECT DESIGNS

Within-subject Manipulations

The label *within-subject* is appropriate in that sometimes one can obtain a good estimate of the effectiveness of the independent variable from the data of a single subject. For example, to use a within-subject design to compare the effectiveness of two brands of car paint, you would paint your car with both paints by alternating strips of Paint A and Paint B. Then you could evaluate the paints at a later date. The appearance of the paint would be the dependent measure. The single subject in this case is, of course, your car.

By comparing the appearance of Paint A strips with that of Paint B strips, you can assess the effectiveness of the two paints within a single subject. For a between-subject design it would be necessary to compare different subjects (i.e., different cars) to assess the effect of the independent variable (i.e., type of paint).

The major distinguishing feature of a within-subject design is that each subject gets more than one level of each independent variable. In all the examples of within-subject designs in this text each subject receives all levels of each independent variable, as illustrated in Table 5-1. The table suggests that fewer subjects are needed to evaluate the effect of an independent variable if a within-subject design is used than if a between-subject design is used. This is usually the case. In fact, since each subject can provide information about the effect of the independent variable when a within-subject design is used you may be willing to conclude that, except for the problem of the generality of the finding, one subject is all that is needed to make the evaluation. In rare instances this is true, but usually it is necessary to obtain data from more than one subject. The label *within-subject* should not be interpreted to mean that one subject is enough.

Nonsubject Variable Manipulations

Within-subject designs can be used to evaluate the effectiveness of nonsubject variables only. It is, of course, impossible to manipulate subject variable characteristics such as age, intelligence, or number of siblings in a within-subject design. Yet, as is true with between-subject designs, it is possible to study a subject variable and nonsubject variable manipulation in

TABLE 5-1

An Example to Demonstrate the Distinguishing Feature of Between- and Within-subject Designs

\multicolumn{4}{c}{*Type of design*}
\multicolumn{2}{c}{*Between-subject*}	\multicolumn{2}{c}{*Within-subject*}
Condition A	Condition B	Condition A	Condition B
Fred	Larry	Harry	Harry
Sam	Joel	Pete	Pete
Bob	Jack	Joan	Joan
Helen	Bert	Mary	Mary
Gary	Tom	Mark	Mark
Glenn	Jim	Rose	Rose
Ray	Stan	Lauren	Lauren

the same experiment. A within-subject design can be used for the nonsubject variable manipulation, allowing us to assess whether the effect of the manipulation depends on the type of subject tested. If a between-subject variable (e.g., a subject variable) and a within-subject manipulation are studied in the same experiment, the design is mixed. That is, since both types of design are used in the same experiment the design for the entire experiment is called a *mixed* design.

Unfortunately, it is not possible to specify the exact conditions under which a particular design should be chosen. Within-subject designs can be used for many of the same purposes as between-subject designs. Although it is frequently *possible* to use either one, a thorough analysis of methodological, practical, and statistical considerations should lead the investigator to conclude that one design is better than another for the intended purpose. To make a thorough analysis one must be aware of the advantages and limitations of within-subject designs.

ADVANTAGES OF WITHIN-SUBJECT DESIGNS

Number of Subjects

Fewer subjects are needed to evaluate the effectiveness of an independent variable in a within-subject than in a between-subject design. In the former, each subject is tested at every level of the independent variable; thus, more information is obtained from each. The number of subjects needed depends on several factors. One is the number of times each subject is tested in each condition. For example, an investigator interested in the effect of three levels of illumination on visual acuity may test the same subject hundreds of times under each level. A considerable amount of information can be obtained from a single subject when such repeated observations are made. Yet for many experiments it is only possible to test each subject once in each condition. All things being equal, the number of subjects needed will decrease as the number of times a subject is tested in each condition increases.

Other factors in determining the number of subjects needed are the number of levels of the independent variable used, and the magnitude and consistency of the effect. Usually the number of subjects needed increases as the number of levels of the independent variable increases because more subjects are required to balance out the effects of nonmanipulated variables. The task is to distribute any time-related effects (e.g., practice, fatigue) equally across the conditions being tested. The number of subjects needed to distribute the effects usually increases as the number of levels of the independent variable increases, but the number of subjects needed tends to decrease as the magnitude and consistency of the effect of the independent variable increases. For example, if five subjects are tested and the same effect is obtained for each, most investigators would probably accept the finding as being reliable, particularly if a large effect were obtained. However, if five subjects are tested and the manipulation has one effect for four subjects and the opposite effect for one subject, then most investigators would probably prefer more information before deciding whether to accept or reject the finding.

Efficiency of Within-subject Designs

A within-subject design is a very powerful way to assess whether an independent variable has an effect. The power or efficiency of a design is analogous to the power of a microscope or telescope. Increasing the power of a microscope enables the observer to see smaller objects. Similarly, the use of a within-subject design sometimes allows the investigator to detect effects that cannot be detected with a between-subject design. It allows him to determine whether the mean differences in treatments are greater than might be expected on the basis of chance fluctuations within individuals. Chance fluctuations within individuals tend to be smaller than those between individuals. That is, the performance of the same person at two different times tends to be more alike than the performance of two different people at the same time when some subject variable, known or unknown, is correlated with the performance measure.

You will remember that a matched-groups design can be used to reduce within-group variance if the matching subject variable correlates highly with the dependent measure. It is possible, for example, to reduce within-group variance by using only subjects who have an IQ of 110 if intelligence correlates highly with the dependent measure. When within-group variance is decreased the probability of rejecting the null hypothesis is increased if the independent variable has an effect.

The use of a within-subject design carries the matching procedure to the extreme in that using this design is functionally the same as matching the groups on *all* subject variables. If the same subjects are used in all treatment conditions then, of course, the treatment conditions are matched on all subject variables. When a within-group design is used the chance fluctuations in performance within *individuals, not* the fluctuations within *groups,* are used to assess the effect of the independent variable. Thus, a different statistical analysis is required for within-subject than for between-subject designs — because chance fluctuations in the performance of one person at two points in time tend to be smaller than the fluctuations of two people at the same point in time because all the subject variables are matched in one case but not in the other.

Let us assume that an investigator has developed two tasks, A and B, of *identical* difficulty. You are tested on Task A and then on Task B, with ample time for rest between the two sessions. Two other people are randomly selected and then tested on Task A only. The question is whether your two scores will be more alike than the two scores obtained by the other two subjects. That is, do within-subject chance fluctuations tend to be greater or smaller than between-subject chance fluctuations? The answer depends on whether any subject variables are correlated with performance on the tasks. For example, if intelligence correlates highly with task performance then your scores should be more alike than the two scores of the other subjects since you have, presumably, the same IQ when you perform Task A as when you perform Task B. It is unlikely that two people selected at random would be of equal intelligence, so their scores would be more likely to vary. The same argument can be made for any other subject variable. Within-subject chance fluctuations will tend to be the smaller since there are usually some subject variables that correlate with performance on the dependent measure.

Efficiency is defined in terms of the size of the chance fluctuations used to evaluate the effect of the independent variable (i.e., the variance of the null hypothesis sampling distribution). The smaller the chance fluctuations the greater the efficiency. Because the chance fluctuations within subjects tend to be smaller than those between subjects, within-subject designs are usually more efficient than between-subject designs. The likelihood of rejecting the null hypothesis tends to be greater, all things being equal, for a within-subject design if the independent variable has an effect.

In some cases it is an understatement to say that there is a statistical advantage to using a within-subject design. The advantage of such a design is so marked under some conditions that there is little or no need for statistics. If it is possible to obtain a stable rate of responding, introduce the independent variable, and obtain a change in responding there may be no need for statistical techniques. This is particularly true if it is possible to modify the level of responding at will by alternating the presence and absence of the treatment manipulation, as in many operant conditioning experiments.

LIMITATIONS OF WITHIN-SUBJECT DESIGNS

Inappropriateness of the Design for Some Problems

The use of a within-subject design is not appropriate for some experiments because it is neither possible nor feasible to administer all the treatments to a single subject. For example, an investigator interested in the effect of a particular training technique should not test subjects in both the trained and nontrained condition because the use of one treatment precludes the use of the other. Once a subject is trained it is not possible to untrain him. Testing all the subjects in the untrained condition first is not an acceptable solution because any obtained differences may be due to either the ordering of the treatments or their nature.

The within-subject design may be inappropriate because of practical considerations involved in obtaining the data. If it takes four hours to test each subject when using a within-subject design and thirty minutes when using a between-subject design, then practicality may dictate the use of the latter.

Demand Characteristics

Another limitation of within-subject designs is that demand characteristics are likely to be a bigger problem than with a between-subject design. Demand characteristics are those aspects of the experiment that allow a subject to make a good guess about what the experimenter "wants." The results of the experiment may be drastically influenced if a subject can determine what it is all about or how the experimenter would like him to respond. He may attempt to please the experimenter and provide what he believes to be the desired results. Human subjects are more likely to be able to figure out the experimenter's expectations when a within-subject design is used because they experience all the levels of the independent variable.

Controlling Nonmanipulated Variables

The problem of controlling nonmanipulated variables tends to be greater with within-subject designs because the subjects are always tested at two or more points in time. Therefore, the experimenter has to take steps to ensure that time-related variables such as the ordering of the treatments or practice and fatigue effects are not responsible for any obtained differences between the treatment conditions. Time-related variables may limit the use of within-subject designs because it is sometimes difficult or impossible to control these effects.

METHODOLOGICAL AND INTERPRETATIONAL CONSIDERATIONS

Counterbalancing

Nature and Purpose of Counterbalancing. Counterbalancing refers to the use of procedures that distribute the effects of nonmanipulated variables over the treatment conditions so that obtained differences can be attributed to chance and the treatment manipulation and not to the nonmanipulated variables. (It is *not* used to eliminate chance fluctuations.) Counterbalancing is accomplished by varying the order of treatments within or between subjects. It is important to control the effects of ordering because a subject may become practiced or fatigued as the experiment progresses. If each subject gets each treatment a number of times then it is possible to balance out the effects of time-related variables by presenting the treatments in a random order. If each subject receives each treatment only once, then more than one subject is needed to balance out time-related variables. For example, when there are two treatments, A and B, and all subjects receive Treatment A followed

110 Within-subject Designs

by Treatment B, it is not possible to attribute any obtained differences to the effect of the treatment; perhaps the ordering of the two treatments was the important consideration. But if half the subjects receive Treatment B followed by Treatment A, the results obtained from all subjects can be combined to balance out the effect of the order of presentation (if there is equal transfer from A to B and B to A, a point that will be considered in detail later). Table 5-2 shows an experiment with and without counterbalancing; the order of treatments was balanced in one case but not the other. In both cases we can compare the A and B treatments by obtaining a mean score on the dependent measure for each of the treatments. The two procedures differ in that differences between the two treatments are interpretable with counterbalancing but not without counterbalancing. If all subjects are given Treatment A and then Treatment B there is no way to determine whether any obtained difference is due to the actual treatment or to time-related effects (e.g., practice, fatigue). Thus, without counterbalancing the experiment is confounded.

The purpose of counterbalancing is to compensate for the effects of time-related variables. The procedures used depend on the number of subjects available and the number of treatment conditions. When complete counterbalancing is used, every treatment is presented in each position an equal number of times and every treatment follows every other an equal number of times. Let us look at an example.

Complete Counterbalancing. An experiment is conducted to assess the effect of four different kinds of print (pica, elite, script, great primer) on speed of oral reading. For convenience in exposition, the four kinds of print can be identified as A, B, C, and D. All subjects read the same four passages in

TABLE 5-2

An Experiment with and without Counterbalancing

| **With counterbalancing** || **Without counterbalancing** ||
Subject	Order of treatments	Subject	Order of treatments
1	A B	1	A B
2	B A	2	A B
3	A B	3	A B
4	A B	4	A B
5	B A	5	A B
6	B A	6	A B
7	A B	7	A B
8	B A	8	A B
9	A B	9	A B
10	B A	10	A B

the same order, but the print for each passage is varied. The independent variable is kind of print (A, B, C, D); the dependent variable is speed of reading. To conclude that differences in the speed of reading are due to kind of print and not to other factors it is necessary to counterbalance the presentation order of the four kinds of print.

To completely counterbalance the order of the treatments (A, B, C, D) it would be necessary to have twenty-four subjects each getting one of the twenty-four different orders of the four treatments. The twenty-four possible orders are presented in Table 5-3; note that each treatment is presented in each sequential position six times. Each subject is randomly assigned one sequence from 1 to 24; the sequences are not used in the same order in which they are presented in the table. Only chance determines which sequence each subject receives.

Let us assume that the twenty-four subjects are randomly assigned to the twenty-four possible sequences with the restriction that each sequence be used only once. The subjects are tested and the results analyzed. The analysis reveals that the kind of print influences the speed of reading. That is, there are significant differences in speed of reading among the four treatment conditions. It is not reasonable to attribute the results to the order in which the treatments were presented because all possible orders were used.

Partial Counterbalancing. When many treatments are given it is no longer feasible to use complete counterbalancing because there are so many different possible orderings of the conditions. For example, there are 120 different presentation orders of five conditions, thereby requiring 120 subjects. With a large number of treatments or a limited number of subjects, it is necessary to use partial counterbalancing.

TABLE 5-3

The Twenty-four Possible Sequences of Treatments for the Experiment Investigating the Effect of Kind of Print on Speed of Reading

Sequence number	Order of treatment	Sequence number	Order of treatment
1	A B C D	13	C A B D
2	A B D C	14	C A D B
3	A C B D	15	C B A D
4	A C D B	16	C B D A
5	A D B C	17	C D A B
6	A D C B	18	C D B A
7	B A C D	19	D A B C
8	B A D C	20	D A C B
9	B C A D	21	D B A C
10	B C D A	22	D B C A
11	B D A C	23	D C A B
12	B D C A	24	D C B A

112 Within-subject Designs

Let us assume that only twelve subjects are available instead of twenty-four. The twelve subjects are randomly assigned to twelve of the twenty-four sequences such that each treatment (A, B, C, D) is presented in each position three times. Most investigators would probably accept this counterbalancing procedure and not be concerned about any confounding effects due to treatments and presentation order even though each treatment did not precede and follow every other treatment an equal number of times. Evaluation of the adequacy of a counterbalancing procedure comes down to a question of belief. Do other investigators believe the controls are adequate? It is unlikely that many investigators would accept the counterbalancing procedures if, say, only two sequences were randomly selected and six subjects were tested in one sequence and six in the other. But as the number of different sequences used is increased, the likelihood of adequately controlling for possible confounding effects is also increased.

There is no absolute point at which one can say the counterbalancing is adequate (e.g., seven or more sequences) because some investigators will be more concerned about the adequacy than others. You should do the best job that conditions allow. If you can obtain twenty-four subjects, there is little reason not to use complete counterbalancing. If you can only obtain twelve subjects, you have to settle for a less than complete procedure, but using each kind of print in each position in the presentation sequence an equal number of times would still convince most investigators that you had counterbalanced adequately. Obviously, if conditions are too unfavorable (e.g., you only have a few subjects), you should not do an experiment that requires extensive counterbalancing between subjects in order to control the effects of time-related variables.

Similar procedures can be used if each subject receives each condition more than once. For example, if there are two conditions, A and B, and each subject is to receive each condition twice, then half the subjects could receive an ABBA, ABBA sequence, and the other half could receive a BAAB, BAAB sequence.

Differential Transfer

Counterbalancing the order in which treatments are presented is a very useful way to control for ordering effects — but it does not always work. It may not balance out presentation order effects if there are differential carry-over effects from one treatment condition to the next. If the results obtained with Condition B are different when C precedes B than when A precedes B, there is differential transfer. When there are such transfer effects, it may be impossible to counterbalance the order of treatments to control position effects.

To illustrate what is meant by differential transfer, let us assume that you are concerned with investigating the effects of alcohol on motor performance.

You assess motor performance by using a pursuit rotor, an instrument that has a moving disk, much like a phonograph record, with a small target on the disk. The subject's task is to keep a stylus on the target while the disk is moving. The difficulty of the task can be varied by increasing or decreasing the speed of the disk. A clock can be hooked up with the pursuit rotor so that the time on target is recorded. The amount of time a subject is on target in ten test trials of one minute each is the dependent measure. The independent variable is whether subjects have two ounces of alcohol, four ounces of alcohol, or no alcohol (control) one half hour before being tested. You would, of course, administer the alcohol in such a way (e.g., in a very large glass of orange juice) that the subjects would not be fully aware of their treatment condition. A question of some importance is whether a within-subject design could be used.

The motor performance of subjects when given no alcohol is likely to be influenced greatly depending on whether the no alcohol treatment precedes or follows the other two alcohol conditions. Imagine a subject given the sequence of two ounces of alcohol, thirty minutes of rest, pursuit rotor test, four ounces of alcohol, thirty minutes of rest, pursuit rotor test, no alcohol, thirty minutes of rest, pursuit rotor test. It would be unreasonable to argue that the last test was actually under a no alcohol condition. The effect of the no alcohol manipulation in this sequence of treatments is apt to be vastly different than in the sequence in which no alcohol is given as the first treatment. Since carry-over effects from prior treatments are probable, it is only possible to assess the effect of the first treatment administered. In this case, it is more reasonable to use a between-subject design and randomly assign subjects to groups. Or you could counterbalance the three treatment conditions, use a within-subject design, and administer one treatment each day for three consecutive days.

The above example is an obvious case of differential transfer. The carry-over effects between the alcohol and no alcohol treatments depend on the ordering of the treatment. Often, however, it is not clear that differential transfer effects will be obtained. For example, if the independent variable is task difficulty, performance on the easy task may be quite different when preceded by a difficult task than when preceded by another easy task. If there is reason to suspect that carry-over effects will make it difficult to interpret the treatment manipulation, it is a good idea to opt for the random-groups design.

Generality of Research Findings

Interest in Establishing Generalities. It is possible to manipulate subject and nonsubject variables in the same experiment regardless of whether a between- or within-subject design is used to assess the effect of the nonsubject variable manipulation. Manipulating both kinds of variables enables the experimenter to determine whether the effect of the nonsubject variable manipulation depends on the type of subject being used. If it does not, then the finding can be said to have greater generality.

Investigators differ considerably about their interest in demonstrating the generality of a finding. Some of them assume that it is unnecessary because they believe in the generality of behavioral laws. They believe one should not worry about a separate set of laws for each type of subject. It follows from this view that a manipulation that is effective with one subject should be effective with others; some investigators will accept a finding that has been obtained by testing one subject in a within-subject design.

On the other hand, some investigators are unwilling to generalize such evidence much beyond the one or two subjects tested. If the effect of a nonsubject variable manipulation *does* depend on the characteristics of subjects, and if only one or two subjects are used the experimenter may have happened to use only the type of subject who shows the desired effect. Some investigators place less weight on the evidence obtained in this way because a generalization of such results tends to deny the importance of subject variables.

There is something to be said for both points of view. Obviously, we need to know when subject variables are important and when they are not. If subject variables are relatively unimportant for many nonsubject variable manipulations, then much time and effort can be wasted in the attempt to demonstrate the generality of particular findings. There can be little question that the generality of very important findings should be determined by such methods as using different types of subjects. However, it seems unreasonable to insist that each experiment contain a large sample of subjects so that the pervasiveness of an effect can be determined; it is simply more economical to determine, first, whether the effect exists.

Design and Generality. You may wonder what the relationship is between design and generality. Specifically, which of the two basic designs yields findings of greater generality? There is no clear answer to this question because each design has an advantage and a disadvantage. The advantage of a between-subject design is that more subjects are tested. The greater the number of subjects tested, all things being equal, the greater the generality of the results. The disadvantage of this design is that the effect of the independent variable cannot be assessed for each subject but only for the group. However, if the effect is very large (e.g., if the worst subject in the experimental condition is better than the best subject in the control condition), it is probably fair to conclude that the independent variable influenced every experimental subject.

The situation is reversed in a within-subject design. Usually fewer subjects are used, but it is frequently possible to assess the effect of the independent variable for each. If all subjects tested demonstrate the same effect and many subjects are tested, then most investigators would be very willing to generalize the finding. Usually, however, the number of subjects tested is quite small when the effect of the independent variable can be assessed for each. In sum, the generality of a research finding tends to be independent of the type of design used. Findings of little and of considerable generality can be obtained with each type.

SELECTING A WITHIN-SUBJECT DESIGN

We have now reached the point where it is possible to discuss generally the selection of a within-subject design. The task for the investigator is to weigh the advantages and disadvantages of each type of design and then select the one that will provide the best test of the effectiveness of the independent variable.

The major factors to consider are the nature of the independent variable, the number of subjects available, the resources available, and the statistical advantages. The most important consideration is the independent variable because its nature will frequently dictate the type of design. In some cases within-subject designs are ruled out because testing each subject in more than one treatment condition would be impossible, or would result in differential transfer, destroy the intended manipulation, or alert subjects to the "real" purpose of the experiment. Yet when a limited number of subjects are available, or when subjects can be tested in all treatment conditions, the investigator should give serious consideration to the within-subject design. Methodological and practical considerations may suggest the use of one type of design over the other; if not, the decision can be based on statistical considerations. Since the within-subject design is the more efficient, it is preferred.

In sum, there is no list of rules that an investigator can apply when selecting a design. In general, however, within-subject designs should be seriously considered whenever a small number of subjects are available, extensive training or testing is required, differential transfer does not loom as a confounding variable, or the magnitude of the effect of the independent variable is believed to be small — that is, when an efficient design is needed.

USES OF WITHIN-SUBJECT DESIGNS

Most investigators who study nonsubject variables use within-subject designs at one time or another. Investigators in some areas, such as perception and operant conditioning, rarely use anything else. Moreover, within-subject designs are being used to investigate an increasing number of problems in applied research. Although both between- and within-subject designs have been used in applied research for a number of years, the use of the latter with a small number of subjects is more recent.

Research with One Subject

The basic task in using the experimental method is the same regardless of the number of subjects tested; it is to determine whether the treatment manipulation influences behavior. When only one subject is used and it is impossible to repeat the manipulation numerous times, it is necessary to obtain fairly stable behavior in order to do research.

Let us assume that an investigator wants to assess the effect of the withdrawal of attention on the temper tantrums of a four-year-old boy. It is necessary to establish how many times a day the child has a temper tantrum under "normal" conditions. Say that he has had seven to ten tantrums per day during the two weeks before the treatment manipulation. The treatment is to ignore the boy every time he has a tantrum. In all other respects, the investigator maintains the same relationship with him. If there is a sharp drop in the number of tantrums (i.e., to zero or one per day for the second week of treatment), it is reasonable to conclude that withdrawal of attention was responsible for the change in behavior (which is also to say that attention *reinforced* the tantrums).

Should the investigator want to be even more convinced that the manipulation was effective he could reinstate the "normal" conditions (i.e., pay attention to the child during a tantrum) to see if the child will resume the tantrum behavior. Let us assume that over the period of one week the child gradually returns to having seven to ten temper tantrums per day. If the withdrawal of reinforcement treatment is reinstated and the tantrum behavior quickly drops to zero again there can be little doubt that the manipulation was effective (see Wolf & Risley, 1971).

You should not conclude from this example that there are few, if any, problems in doing applied research with a small number of subjects. An interesting and informative account of some of the problems involved in such research is given by Wolf and Risley (1971). These authors emphasize the fact that it may be necessary to introduce the treatment manipulation more than once to make sure that the results are not due to a confounding variable. In the above experiment, for example, the investigator attributed the reduction in tantrum behavior to the manipulation. Yet it is possible that the little boy stopped having tantrums for other reasons. Perhaps the little girl next door gave him a long, wet kiss as a means of providing consolation. The boy, a keen observer of behavioral contingencies, noted the tantrum/kissing contingency and decided to discontinue tantrums. This alternative explanation can be rejected if the investigator withdraws reinforcement on a number of occasions and obtains a marked reduction in tantrums each time.

Research with Established Baselines

The use of within-subject designs with a small number of subjects is likely to be effective only if the experimenter has enough control over the situation to obtain a stable rate of responding or a stable response (as in some studies of sensation and perception). Or, in some cases, he can make use of the fact that a stable rate of responding exists even though he has little control. For example, a drug addict or alcoholic may have a stable rate of using drugs or drinking. It may, therefore, be possible to assess the effects of different treatments and still avoid the ethical problems involved in using a control group. In order to use the random-groups design to assess the effectiveness of a particular treatment for alcoholism or drug addiction one must assign the subjects to treatment and no treatment conditions. Many investigators and practitioners are unwilling to do this because they believe it is unethical to deny treatment to anyone. This difficulty can be avoided with a within-subject design because in such a design it is possible to treat everyone and compare the level of response before and after treatment. Although this approach has advantages it has a few disadvantages too. One particularly troublesome difficulty is demand characteristics. The fact that subjects and patients try, in general, to do what experimenters and therapists want them to do makes it difficult to isolate the effects attributable to the treatment.

SUMMARY

The major distinguishing feature of a within-subject design is that each subject gets more than one level of each independent variable. In a between-subject design each subject receives only one level of each independent variable. Within-subject designs can be used to evaluate nonsubject variables only. Since the two types of designs can be used for many of the same purposes it is frequently possible to use either one to investigate a particular effect.

The advantages of the within-subject design are that fewer subjects are needed and the design is usually more efficient than a between-subject design because the independent variable is assessed in terms of chance fluctuations within subjects. Chance fluctuations within subjects are smaller than those between subjects because all subject variables are matched in the one case but not in the other.

Within-subject designs are simply not appropriate for some experiments. It is not always possible or feasible to administer all the treatments to a single subject. Demand characteristics are likely to be a bigger problem in these designs because the subject has a better chance of determining what the experimenter wants in the way of results if he is tested in all treatment conditions. Also, it is necessary to control time-related variables because subjects are tested at two or more points in time.

The major methodological problems involved in within-subject designs are counterbalancing the effects of time-related variables and determining whether there is differential transfer between the various treatment conditions. The problem of the generality of the research findings does not appear to be any greater than it is in between-subject designs.

The nature of the independent variable, the availability of subjects and resources, and statistical considerations are the principal factors to consider when selecting a design. The nature of the independent variable is the most

118 Within-subject Designs

important consideration because its manipulation will frequently dictate the choice of the design. Within-subject designs are useful in a wide variety of areas. They are especially useful in applied research because the effectiveness of treatment manipulations can be assessed with one subject, allowing the investigator to give the treatment to all subjects.

QUESTIONS

1. Distinguish between within- and between-subject designs and give an example of each.
2. What is the purpose of counterbalancing? Why is counterbalancing used extensively when within-subject designs are used?
3. How would you counterbalance if you had three treatments, a within-subject design, and twelve subjects?
4. What is differential transfer? Give an example of an independent variable that you believe would produce differential transfer effects. Give an example of one that you believe would not produce such effects. How would you determine whether or not you were correct in your judgments?
5. What are the advantages and limitations of within-subject designs?
6. Explain why a within-subject design is likely to be more efficient than a between-subject design. How is efficiency defined in this regard?
7. Assume that an investigator is interested in the effect of a physical disability on inducing compliance behavior. The independent variable is whether the experimenter's confederate wears an eye patch or not. The dependent variable is the number of letters, if any, that the subject agrees to write to aid the confederate's "Help Save the Redwoods" campaign. Each subject is led to believe that the confederate is another subject serving in the same experiment. The experiment is actually conducted while both "subjects" are supposedly waiting for the investigator. What type of research design should be used? Why?
8. Assume that you are given the responsibility for evaluating the effect of a new rehabilitation program in a state prison system on the rate of recidivism. You have the authority to decide whether a prisoner is assigned to the new or old program, or both. What type of design would you use? Why?
9. Assume that a new drug has been developed to reduce hypertension. The independent variable is whether the drug or a placebo is administered to the subjects. The dependent measure is blood pressure. What type of design would you use? Why?
10. Assume that you have been hired by the state to evaluate the claims made by the advocates of a speed reading course. You have the cooperation of the people who conduct the course. What type of design would you use to evaluate it? Why? What would you use as the dependent measure?
11. Let us assume that you want to test the view that the ability to discriminate among fine wines is developed as a result of experience — that people who have consumed a number of fine wines develop their powers of discrimination. Assume that large quantities of wine and time are available. What

type of design would you use to test the view that there is a causal relationship between consumption and the ability to discriminate among wines? Why? What treatment conditions would you use? Would you use a double-blind procedure for the testing stage?
12. How would you evaluate the effectiveness of heroin substitutes such as methadone for reducing drug addiction?
13. How would you evaluate the effectiveness of two different fabric softeners, hand lotions, soaps, lipsticks, coffeepots, paints, or fertilizers?

nonexperimental and quasi-experimental designs 6

In this chapter we will consider nonexperimental and quasi-experimental designs. Quasi-experimental designs are discussed because they can be very useful for studying problems when experimental designs are not suitable. Nonexperimental designs are considered because they are *not* useful. We need to know why they are not useful so that we will avoid them.

NONEXPERIMENTAL DESIGNS

Examples of Nonexperimental Designs

Single Group Observed Once. Often a treatment is introduced to a single group and then a performance measure is obtained. There is no control or comparison group and there is no comparison of performance before and after treatment. For example, one could evaluate the effect of a therapy by interviewing patients after such therapy. Should we accept at face value the patient's claim that the therapy was successful? Assume that we evaluate the effectiveness of individualized instruction by giving all students individualized instruction and then considering their performance on the final examination. Will this procedure allow us to reach conclusions about the effectiveness of individualized instruction? We could generate many similar examples in which a single group is observed once in a nonexperimental design. We could "evaluate" the effectiveness of a treatment (e.g., therapy, drug, training program, new product) by administering the treatment to all available subjects and obtaining some performance measure. This approach has been called the one-shot case study (Campbell, 1957). As we will see shortly, there are very serious problems with such a design.

Single Group, Pretest-Posttest Design. The major problem with the single group observed once design is that there is no way to evaluate whether the treatment is related to performance on the dependent measure. We need a way to assess whether the introduction of a treatment produces a *change* in performance. Thus, one might argue that it is necessary to have two performance measures, one taken before administering the treatment and one following treatment. Then the two performance measures can be compared to evaluate the treatment. If there is a significant difference between the pretest and posttest scores it is tempting to conclude that the treatment was responsible for the change.

The single group, pretest-posttest design has been used extensively because, on the surface at least, it appears to be a good design. One measures behavior, administers a treatment, and then measures behavior again. If there is a change, such change must be a result of the treatment. There *appears* to be little reason to bother with a control group when it is possible to measure the behavior of interest immediately before and after treatment. The design is attractive for another reason; one is able to select subjects on the basis of the pretest. Thus it is only necessary to administer the treatment to subjects who can be expected to benefit from it.

Let us assume that you are interested in evaluating a therapy for reducing anxiety. You prefer to treat subjects who are anxious; nonanxious people do not need the therapy. To find anxious people you administer an anxiety test to a large class of introductory psychology students ($n = 600$). You use the results of the pretest to select the twenty-five most anxious students, then you administer the therapy to them (assume they cooperate) and then give them an anxiety posttest, that is equivalent to the pretest to determine whether the treatment had any effect. If there is a significant decrease in the anxiety scores from the pretest to the posttest can the difference be attributed to the therapy?

For a second example, let us assume that you teach remedial reading. You would like to evaluate a new remedial reading program, so you administer a reading test to a large number of third-grade students in a large metropolitan elementary school. You select the fifty students who have the lowest reading scores for your remedial reading program. After they complete the eight-week-reading program they are retested to assess the effects of the reading program. If there is a significant increase in the scores from pretest to posttest, should you attribute this change to the effect of the reading program?

A single group, pretest-posttest design is preferred over the single group observed once design, but there are serious problems with both designs. They are rarely used because most investigators are aware of their limitations, which will be considered later in this chapter.

The Static-groups Design. In the static-groups design two or more groups are compared. One group receives the treatment and the other group does not. The groups are intact (static); the investigator does not assign subjects to groups. There is no way to know whether the groups are equivalent before the treatment is introduced (see Campbell & Stanley, 1963).

There are several ways to use the static-groups design. If we compare the annual salaries of people in the forty to fifty age bracket we are likely to find that the annual salary of college graduates is considerably higher than for nongraduates. Is it reasonable to conclude that the "treatment" (graduating from college) is responsible for the difference in mean salary? We can compare elementary schools that require their teachers to obtain graduate degrees with those schools that do not. Can we attribute any difference in student performance at the schools to the graduate degree requirement? If we compare the incidence of cancer in industrial versus nonindustrial communities and find there is a higher rate in industrial communities, can we conclude that the "treatment" (presence of industry) is responsible for the higher incidence of cancer?

The basic logic of the static-groups comparison is that differences between groups that differ on a particular variable *may* be due to the variable. The difficult problem, of course, is determining whether the "treatment" is responsible for any obtained difference in performance. Since it is not possible to assign subjects to groups before introducing the "treatment" it is difficult to rule out other factors as being responsible for any obtained differences between groups. You can probably see by now that the static-groups design has several weaknesses; it is comparable to a subject variable comparison. We are not able to equate intact groups on all variables except one, and we are not able to equate two groups on all subject variables except one.

Factors Influencing Design Adequacy

In this section we will consider factors that can influence design adequacy. A design is adequate if the procedures allow you to determine whether the treatment had an effect on performance. If it can be argued that factors other than the treatment are responsible for any obtained difference in performance, then the design is not completely satisfactory. Nonexperimental designs are unsatisfactory because it is usually possible to list a *number* of factors, in addition to the treatment, that may be responsible for any obtained performance differences. All the factors to be considered are alternative explanations for performance differences attributed to a treatment manipulation.

History and Maturation. History and maturation both refer to events that occur between testings in a pretest-posttest situation or before testing in a single group observed once design. Maturation refers to events that take place within the individual. These events are relatively independent of the subject's situation or activity, they are general events. History effects, on the other hand, are specific; they depend on the subject's situation. For example, a student in college has different experiences than one who is not, but their maturational changes are probably similar.

The history factor can probably be best understood within the context of the single group, pretest-posttest design. A subject's history includes events besides the treatment that take place between the pretest and the posttest and may account for the pretest-posttest difference in performance. Only those events that are specific to the situation being investigated are part of the history.

Let us reconsider our single group, pretest-posttest design example in which twenty-five anxious students underwent therapy for their anxiety. If there is a significant decrease in the anxiety scores from the pretest to the posttest can we attribute the difference to the therapy? It is not reasonable to conclude that the therapy was responsible because there are several other factors that may be responsible for a decrease in the anxiety score. For example, if the investigator administered the first anxiety test to students during their first week at college, it is likely that the scores would be high. New students tend to be anxious; as they develop new friendships, pass examinations, and become acquainted with their professors, their anxiety usually decreases. These events, not the treatment, may be responsible for any reduction in anxiety. Or it may be that the therapy per se had no effect on anxiety, but the events associated with therapy did; for example, maybe the pretest-posttest difference can be attributed to the attention paid to the student independent of the therapy given. The same reduction might occur by taking each of the twenty-five students for coffee, coke, or beer once a week instead of administering therapy. In short, several events that may occur between the pretest and posttest could change the test scores. A control group that is identical to the no treatment condition except for the treatment manipulation is needed.

The history factor poses an interpretational problem for the single group observed once design also. In both cases there is no way to know whether the treatment or other events occurring before testing are responsible for the level of performance.

Maturation refers to time-related processes within the subject that may influence performance. The processes could be neurological development, aging, fatigue, sexual arousal, and so on (Campbell & Stanley, 1963). A pretest-posttest difference may be due to maturational changes and not the treatment.

Let us reconsider our single group, pretest-posttest example in which fifty third-grade students are given an eight-week remedial reading program. It may be incorrect to attribute a significant increase in reading scores from pretest to posttest to the reading program because the change may be due to maturation. Perhaps neurological development during the eight weeks is responsible for the increase in reading scores. Maturation effects can be very powerful. Interpretational problems encountered when using a pretest-posttest, single group should increase as the length of time between the two tests increases.

Selection. Some designs do not allow the investigator to form equivalent groups before introducing the independent variable. If we are not able to form equivalent groups before treatment it is difficult to reach conclusions about the treatment effect since other factors may be responsible for the differences obtained. This problem has already been discussed in some detail in our discussion of subject variables. We said there that we can only *select* subject variables. We cannot, for example, *manipulate* the age of our subjects; we can only *select* subjects according to age.

The necessity for selection makes the interpretation of results from the static-groups design very difficult. Because the static-groups design involves a comparison of intact groups there is no good way to determine whether the groups differ on a number of variables in addition to the treatment variable. Let us reconsider our example of comparing the annual salaries of people between the ages of forty and fifty. We are likely to find that the annual salary of college graduates is considerably higher than for nongraduates but it does not necessarily follow that graduating from college is the important consideration. It is reasonable to expect the college group to differ from the noncollege group in other respects. College graduates may be more intelligent or motivated than nongraduates; perhaps they would be making more money than nongraduates even if they had not graduated. In short, the static-groups design is not a very good way to assess the effects of a treatment because so many other variables may be responsible for any group differences.

Sensitization, Measurement, and Demand Characteristics. Sensitization, measurement, and demand characteristics all refer to interpretational problems arising from the procedures used to assess a treatment effect. Sensitization and measurement refer to the fact that the assessment process may change the subject's behavior. If a single group, pretest-postttest design is used, any difference between the two scores may be a function of the procedure and not treatment; the pretest may *sensitize* the subject to the treatment effect.

It is possible to demonstrate sensitization by performing a 2 by 2 factorial, random groups design, as shown in Table 6-1. One variable is the treatment (yes versus no), and the other variable is the presence of a pretest (yes versus no). We can determine whether there is a treatment effect for the subjects who get the pretest, *and* we can determine whether there is a treatment effect for the subjects who do not get the pretest. We use the performance on the dependent measure, of course, to assess the treatment effect. If a treatment effect is obtained for subjects who took the pretest, and *no* treatment effect is obtained for those who did not, we have evidence of sensitization. A treatment effect is obtained only if a pretest is given.

The *measurement* factor can refer to the facts that a test may change the subjects, and different results may be obtained with reactive and nonreactive

TABLE 6-1

An Example to Demonstrate That the Effect of a Treatment May Depend on the Use of a Pretest

		Treatment	
		Yes	No
Pretest	Yes	$\bar{X} = 40$	$\bar{X} = 20$
	No	$\bar{X} = 20$	$\bar{X} = 20$

measures. You will remember that reactive and nonreactive measures differ; nonreactive measures are obtained in such a way that the observees are not aware that their behavior is being recorded. If the effect of a treatment depends on the type of dependent measure (reactive versus nonreactive), there is a measurement factor.

Demand characteristics are cues available to a subject in an experiment that may enable him to determine the "purpose" of the experiment. A subject who knows what the experimenter wants may respond to please or displease the experimenter. Obviously, we can expect demand characteristics to pose a greater interpretational problem if the subject has several cues about the purpose of the experiment (e.g., pretest and reactive measures) than if he has none. Because demand characteristics pose interpretational problems for experimental as well as nonexperimental designs, we will discuss them in more detail in the next chapter.

You need not be concerned about fine distinctions among sensitization, measurement, and demand characteristics because the distinction among these factors is, at best, blurred. Sensitization and measurement can probably be classified as examples of the demand characteristic factor since both of these factors can be viewed as cue effects. That is, sensitization may occur because subjects use the pretest to determine what the experimenter hopes to accomplish with the treatment. And a difference between reactive and nonreactive measures may be obtained because the subject is able to determine what the experimenter wants when a reactive measure is used and respond accordingly. We can call all three factors demand characteristics or we can use all three labels. It is probably better to remember all three labels because all three are used in research articles in the social sciences.

TABLE 6-2

Scores for a Group of Subjects on Two Equivalent Tests Having Perfect Reliability

Subject	Test 1 score	Test 2 score
1	130	130
2	63	63
3	89	89
4	46	46
5	113	113
6	79	79
7	103	103
8	99	99
9	116	116
10	61	61
11	80	80
12	89	89
13	125	125
14	55	55
15	92	92

Regression. When a single group, pretest-posttest design is used, differences between the two scores for each subject may be due to regression and not to the effect of the treatment manipulation. To discuss what is meant by regression and why regression is an important methodological consideration, it is first necessary to reconsider the concept of reliability.

We said that reliability can mean either consistency of measurement or accuracy of measurement. When considering reliability in terms of accuracy or precision we view each individual's score as having two components, a true score and an error score; that is, we *theorize* that there is a true score and an error score component. The true score component taps stable characteristics of the individual. It does not change over time unless there has been a basic change in the individual. The error component, on the other hand, does change over time. This component represents all the chance factors that are likely to influence performance at one time. Chance can increase the true score, decrease the true score, or leave it unchanged. Reliability is determined by the relative magnitudes of the true score and error score. If the error score is much smaller than the true score then chance fluctuations over time are small and, as a result the total score on each testing occasion will be determined primarily by the true score. In this case successive measurements will be accurate (they will be close to the true score) and consistent (they will yield about the same score) because the scores will be determined largely by the subject's stable characteristics. If, on the other hand, there is a large error score component, scores for repeated testings of the same individual are likely to vary widely.

The scores will probably be inaccurate (not close to the true score) and inconsistent since performance is determined largely by chance.

Let us consider what results might be obtained if each subject is given two tests and the tests are highly reliable or unreliable. If the tests have perfect reliability, then each test is tapping the same stable characteristics; the scores should not change from the first test to the second. This result is given in Table 6-2. Notice that all subjects have the same score for each test because we have assumed that there is no error component for each score. If we select subjects on the basis of their score on the first test we should not expect their scores on the second test to change unless we introduce a treatment that has a real effect between the first and second test.

Now let us use the same scores to demonstrate what might happen if the two tests are unreliable. If the scores reflect chance fluctuations only, then we should not expect each subject to achieve the same score for both tests. Each subject's score is assumed to reflect chance fluctuations only. We can *simulate* what might happen if only chance determines the score by using the same scores presented in Table 6-2. In this case, however, we will randomly assign the scores to subjects by placing each score on a piece of paper and blindly drawing them out of a hat. The first number is assigned to the first subject, the second to the second subject, and so on. We do this twice, once for each test. The results of such a random selection of numbers is presented in Table 6-3.

To understand the methodological implications of unreliability we need to

TABLE 6-3

Scores for a Group of Subjects on Two Tests Having Low Reliability

Subject	Test 1 score	Test 2 score
1	99	92
2	55	113
3	113	125
4	80	80
5	61	55
6	63	89
7	46	130
8	125	103
9	89	63
10	89	116
11	79	79
12	116	89
13	103	46
14	92	61
15	130	99

imagine that a single group, pretest-posttest is used and there is no treatment effect. Should we expect the mean pretest and posttest scores to differ? The answer to this question depends on two considerations—the reliability of the test and the selection of subjects. If the two tests correlate perfectly then the situation is comparable to the one depicted in Table 6-2. We should not expect the mean pretest score to differ from the mean posttest score, regardless of which subjects are selected for the experiment, because the tests are tapping the subjects' stable characteristics only. However, we can expect a marked change in the pretest and posttest scores if the subjects who have high pretest scores are selected *and* the pretest-posttest reliability is low.

We can simulate the second situation by selecting the five subjects who have the highest pretest scores from Table 6-3. The five highest scores are 113, 125, 116, 103, and 130 (subjects 3, 8, 12, 13, and 15); the mean of these five scores is 117.40. Now if we consider the five posttest scores for the *same* subjects we find that their scores are 125, 103, 89, 46, and 99; the mean is 92.40. We find that there is a marked change from pretest to posttest for subjects who have high scores on the pretest when chance factors determine each score because we *selected* those subjects who had high scores on the pretest. If their high scores were obtained by chance (i.e., they were lucky), there is no guarantee that they will also obtain high scores on the posttest (they may not be lucky again). In general, then, we can expect scores to decrease from pretest to posttest if subjects who have high scores on the pretest are selected and there is less than perfect pretest-posttest reliability.

The methodological implication of the above discussion should be clear. Rarely, if ever, do tests have perfect reliability, so we can expect chance fluctuations to have at least some influence on each subject's score. If we select subjects with high pretest scores, we should expect their posttest scores to be lower, even if there is no treatment effect. Therefore, if we get a change from pretest to posttest we do not know whether to attribute the change to the treatment or to the unreliability of our measuring instruments. The same situation holds if we select subjects who have low pretest scores, except that the posttest scores should increase. That is, if the pretest scores are used to select subjects who, by chance, had low scores, there is no guarantee that they will obtain low scores on the second test as well.

A change should be expected from pretest to posttest, even if there is no treatment effect, as long as the subjects selected have extreme pretest scores and the two tests lack perfect reliability. This change is called *regression*. The change from the pretest to the posttest is a tendency for the extreme scores to change in the direction of the mean score. To regress, in this case, means to approach or revert to the mean performance. The amount of regression will be related to the reliability of the two tests; it should increase as the correlation (reliability) of the two tests decreases.

The implication for the single group, pretest-posttest design is straightforward. We rarely, if ever, have a perfect correlation between two tests, even if the same test is given twice. Thus if we select subjects who have extreme pretest scores we must expect to get regression effects. One solution is to select only those subjects who have average scores on the pretest. In this case, we believe that we should not get regression effects if we start with average scores. Although this is true, we may not be able to select those people who have average scores on the pretest since, for the purpose of determining regression effects, it is best to define average in terms of the *population* mean. If our sample mean turns out to be an accurate estimate of the population mean, the procedure should eliminate any regression *toward* the mean. A better solution is to use a control group that is given both the pre- and posttest but not the independent variable. The use of a control group allows us to study only those subjects who have extreme scores on the pretest (e.g., high anxiety or low reading scores). In many cases we want to study subjects with extreme scores. It is necessary, of course, to make sure that the experimental and control groups are equivalent before introducing the treatment to the experimental group.

Evaluation of Nonexperimental Designs

Nonexperimental designs are inadequate because it is difficult to determine whether performance is influenced by the treatment or other confounding factors. The single group observed once design is confounded by history, maturation, selection, and possibly by demand characteristics. The single group, pretest-posttest design is confounded by history, maturation, measurement, regression, and possibly by sensitization. The static-groups design is confounded by the need for selection (see Campbell & Stanley, 1963). In short, these designs are simply not very good. Fortunately, we can usually avoid them because experimental designs are widely applicable. Sometimes, however, experimental designs are not suitable. If experimental designs are not appropriate, the student is encouraged to consider using a quasi-experimental approach before opting for a nonexperimental procedure. Nonexperimental designs should be used only as a last resort because their scientific usefulness is, at best, limited.

QUASI-EXPERIMENTAL DESIGNS

The Logic of Quasi-experimental Designs

As you will remember, the goal of science is to understand natural phenomena. We test our understanding of a phenomenon by making predictions about observable events. Frequently this means that we predict what effect a particular treatment will have on behavior. If our prediction does not square with the facts (i.e., the experimental outcome), we reject or modify our explanation of the phenomenon. The experimental method is very helpful because it allows us to assess accurately the effect of different treatments. The relationship between quasi-experimental designs and experimental designs depends on the use of a between-subject or within-subject comparison and on the amount of control the investigator has over nonmanipulated events. It is frequently possible to evaluate treatment effects with quasi-experimental techniques.

The basic logic behind the use of quasi-experimental designs is very simple. Because we cannot always form equivalent groups before introducing the treatment we need procedures that allow us to eliminate or minimize the influence of confounding factors. If we can rule out confounding variables, then we can conclude, with reasonable assurance, that the treatment is responsible for a significant difference in performance. We are usually not able to reach conclusions about treatment effects with nonexperimental designs because there are usually a number of confounding factors. Quasi-experiments are an improvement over nonexperiments because we can rule out most, if not all, confounding effects.

Examples of Quasi-experimental Designs

In this section we will consider two quasi-experimental approaches — the time-series design and the nonequivalent control group design. The time-series design is a within-subject design. The nonequivalent control group design is a between-subject design. We will see that the relationship between quasi-experimental and experimental designs can depend on whether we are interested in a between- or within-subject comparison. (See Campbell & Stanley (1963) for a detailed presentation of quasi-experimental designs.)

The Time-series Design. The time-series design is similar to the single group, pretest-posttest nonexperimental design in that performance is assessed before and after the treatment is introduced. The difference between the two designs is that performance is assessed *several* times before and after treatment with the time-series design. Since we have already considered the weaknesses of the single group, pretest-posttest nonexperimental design we know that a single assessment of performance before and after treatment is inadequate. We now need to ask what is gained by making periodic measurements of performance before and after treatment.

Let us assume that a federal law is passed forbidding the ownership and possession of handguns by private citizens after January 1, 1978. The problem is to assess what effect, if any, this law has on the incidence of violent crime. The experimental method is not appropriate, of course, because we cannot control who gets the treatment and who does not. The law applies to all citizens. However, we can assess the effect of the new law by noting the incidence of violent crime for the year before the law (1977) and the first year during which the law is in effect (1978). We have a single group, pretest-posttest, nonexperimental design because all citizens are given the treatment. Our result is presented in Figure 6-1.

You may conclude, at least initially, that the evidence supports the view that the law resulted in a reduction in the incidence of violent crimes. However, that may not be the case. The data presented in Figure 6-1 could result from a number of other situations. If we know the incidence of violent crime for several years before and after the effective date of the new law we should be better able to evaluate the plausibility of explanations for the decrease in violent crimes from 1977 to 1978. Four hypothetical patterns of results of a time-series analysis are presented in Figure 6-2.

Figure 6-2A suggests that the treatment (the new law) did not have any effect on the incidence of violent crimes. The decrease from 1977 to 1978 appears to be simply a continuation of a trend that started a few years earlier. There is little reason to attribute the change from 1977 to 1978 to the introduction of the treatment in early 1978 because the drop in the crime rate associated with the introduction of the treatment is not unusual. In this case it is more reasonable to conclude that something besides the availability of

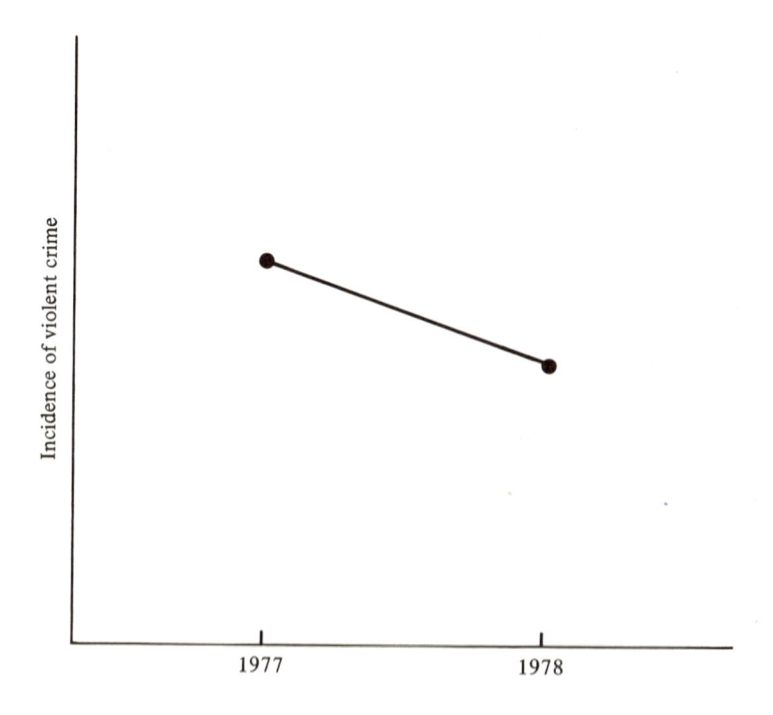

FIGURE 6-1

Incidence of violent crime for 1977 and 1978 (fictitious data)

FIGURE 6-2

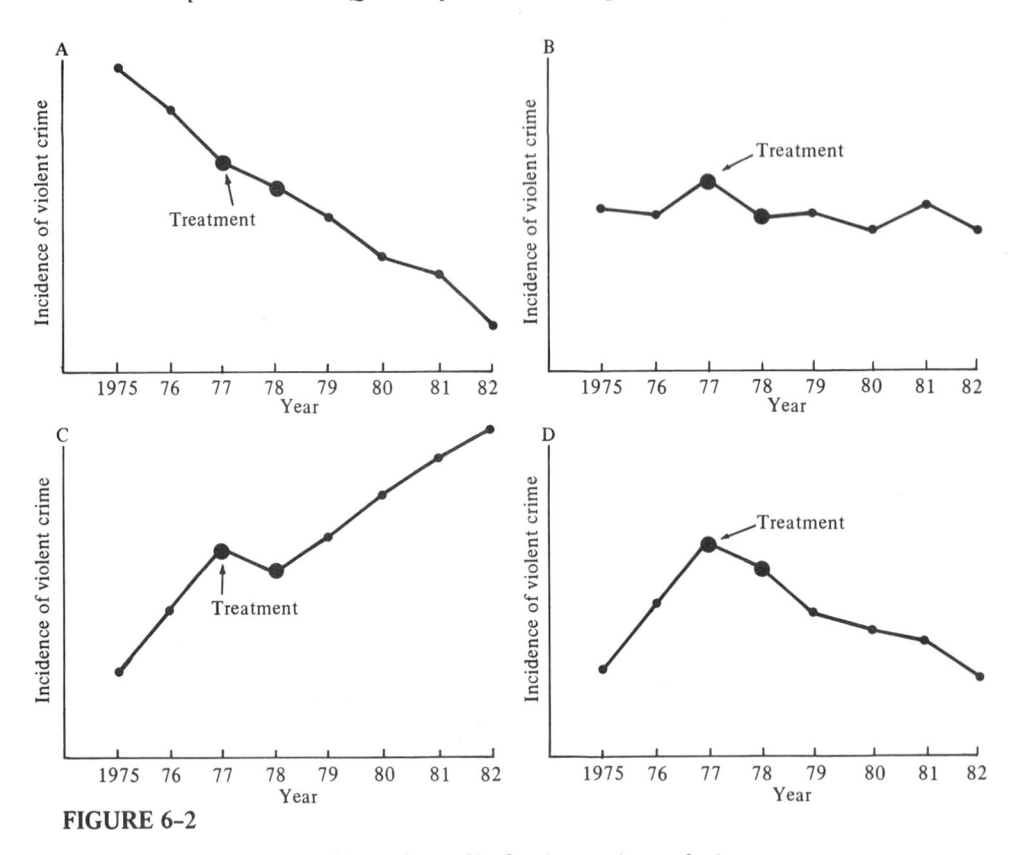

Four possible outcomes (hypothetical) of a time-series analysis

handguns is responsible for the decrease in violent crime. The results presented in Figure 6-2B also fail to support the importance of the handgun legislation. In this case 1977 seems to have been an unusual year for violent crime. Perhaps a number of "chance occurrences" (e.g., miserable weather conditions) during 1977 resulted in more violent crime. The reduction from 1977 to 1978 may be simply a *regression* effect. That is, if we have an unusual year we should expect a change in the direction of average performance (a regression effect) in the following year. It is difficult to evaluate social change because social changes are usually initiated in unusual years (Crano & Brewer, 1973). For example, a high incidence of violent crime may produce enough public protest to bring about handgun legislation. Or a period of low crime may result in legislation to abolish capital punishment. The social actions may parallel increases or decreases in the crime rate without having any effect on the crime rate.

The results presented in Figure 6-2C and D are consistent with the view that the handgun legislation has an effect on the incidence of violent crime. The results in Figure 6-2C suggest that the effect was only temporary. One might speculate that people deprived of handguns required time to develop other methods for committing violent crimes. The decline from 1977 to 1978 might reflect the fact that people were *temporarily* without weapons. The result depicted in Figure 6-2D is consonant with the view that the handgun legislation had a strong, long lasting effect on the incidence of violent crime. The continuous decline after the introduction of the treatment may simply reflect the fact that it takes time to reduce the supply of handguns. As the supply decreases, the incidence of violent crime decreases. There are other interpretations for the results presented in Figure 6-2C and D, of course. The important point is that these results are consistent with (i.e., they do not contradict) the view that handgun legislation has an effect. The results presented in Figure 6-2A and B do not support a treatment effect. Thus, the time-series design provides considerably better evidence than the single group, pretest-posttest design. If we consider only the evidence for 1977 and 1978 we cannot say very much about the effect of the legislation. The quasi-experimental design (time-series approach) is clearly better than the non-experimental procedure. However, the time-series design does have some limitations.

The major limitation of the time-series design is that an event other than treatment may be responsible for at least part of the performance change. The design does not control history effects because there is no equivalent control group that does not receive the treatment. Yet history is less of a problem with the time-series design than with the single group, pretest-posttest design because the use of multiple tests over time may allow us to identify the event that is responsible for the observed results. If the pattern of results is like that in Figure 6-2A we may reasonably conclude that the event responsible for the trend may have occurred many years before the treatment. There is no way to know when the responsible event occurred if we consider only the results for 1977 and 1978. If we consider all the years and obtain a result like the pattern presented in Figure 6-2D, then we can restrict rival hypotheses to events that took place around the time the treatment was introduced. If there is a plausible alternative hypothesis we will have to be cautious about concluding that the treatment was effective. For example, if the major television networks decided to cancel all programs depicting violence beginning January 1, 1978, there are two reasonable explanations for any reduction in the incidence of violent crime: handgun legislation and the elimination of television violence. If there are no reasonable rival hypotheses we can conclude, albeit tentatively, that the treatment was effective.

The handgun legislation example is a little misleading; one may infer that the investigator does not control the time at which the treatment is introduced; this may or may not be true. There are fewer problems of interpretation if the investigator controls the introduction of the treatment than if he does not. The reason for this is simple enough: if the investigator cannot decide when to introduce the treatment, the treatment may be introduced at an "unusual" time. That is, a number of changes may be implemented at the same time to alleviate an undesirable situation. For example, handgun legislation may be passed at about the same time that the major networks decide to cancel programs in which violence is depicted. If, on the other hand, the investigator decides when to introduce the treatment he can reduce the probability that another important event will occur (be introduced) at the same time. Thus there should be fewer rival hypotheses to consider if the investigator determines when the treatment is introduced.

The time-series design is useful for many situations. As the previous example indicates, it can be used to assess treatment effects in real situations. In this case it may be possible to generate rival hypotheses (i.e., other than the treatment) to account for the obtained result. Yet it is also possible to use the time-series design in situations where other events are not allowed to occur — for example, in laboratory experiments. In the laboratory the time-series design is very similar to some of the within-subject experimental designs considered in Chapter 5. For example, investigators who study operant conditioning frequently determine the response rate of subjects for a long period of time, introduce the treatment, and then determine the response rate for another long interval. If the response changes after the treatment they are likely to conclude that the treatment was responsible. This conclusion is usually reasonable because investigators try to minimize the possibility that any other event was introduced along with the treatment. The same logic applies for experiments conducted in more real-life situations except that there is a greater likelihood that some other event besides the treatment was responsible for the results.

The Nonequivalent, Control Group Design. The nonequivalent, control group design involves a comparison of groups that are *not* equivalent before the treatment is introduced. Nonequivalent groups usually occur when the treatment has to be presented to intact (static) groups. The design involves more than a comparison of intact groups on one dependent measure (i.e., more than a static-groups, nonexperimental design) because each group is given a pretest and a posttest, so it is possible to evaluate whether the pretest-posttest change is different for the treatment group than for the control group.

Let us assume that a foreign language instructor is interested in evaluating the effect of a new program for teaching the second-year German course. She teaches the same course twice, once at 9:00 A.M. and once at 2:00 P.M. The classes are not likely to be equivalent because students can select their classes. Therefore the student who enroll in the 9:00 class may already know more German or may be brighter than students who enroll in the 2:00 class. Although she cannot randomly assign the students to the two classes she can control the teaching approach that she uses for each class. She decides to use the new technique for the 2:00 class and the old technique for the 9:00 class. She administers the same German test to both classes on the first day of class and another test to both classes on the last day of class. She can then compare the amount of change from pretest to posttest for each group to evaluate the new instructional method relative to the old method. She has used a nonequivalent, control group design.

The methodological issue is whether this design is adequate. If the 2:00 class has a significantly greater increase from pretest to posttest than the 9:00 class can we conclude that the new instructional technique is better than the old technique? The answer depends on several considerations. It is necessary to assume that the experiment was conducted properly. That is, the instructor should be equally enthusiastic for the two classes, assign the same amount of homework, proceed at the same pace, and so on. If the experiment was performed properly, the next task is to consider rival hypotheses. Are there other explanations besides the treatment manipulation for the obtained results?

The evaluation of a design is a relative matter. We need to compare the strengths and weaknesses of this approach with those of other approaches. The design is clearly better than the single group, pretest-posttest design because we can compare the amount of change for the treatment group with the amount for the control group. Events other than the treatment that occur between the pretest and posttest should influence the two groups equally, and we do not have to be particularly concerned with ability differences between the two groups because we are interested in how the two groups change over a period of time. We should be able to evaluate the relative changes even though the groups are of unequal ability. Although history and maturation are confounding variables for the single group, pretest-posttest design, and the need for selection can confound the static-groups design, these factors do not *usually* pose interpretational problems for the nonequivalent, control-group design. Yet, that design is not without weaknesses.

The nonequivalent, control group design does not have general weaknesses, but interpretational problems may arise under some circumstances. For example, if there are large differences between the treatment and control groups before the treatment is introduced there may be *differential regression* in the two conditions. To understand this point it is necessary to remember that the amount of regression is related to the selection of subjects. If subjects in the treatment group have extreme scores (e.g., very low scores) on the pretest and the subjects in the control group do not, there may be more regression for the treatment group than for the control group. Similarly, if an experiment is conducted with young children and there are large differences between the treatment group and control group on the pretest, differences in the amount of change from pretest to posttest could be the result of maturational instead of treatment effects. Exceptionally bright children may develop faster than average children, so both groups should have similar pretest performance levels.

We have said that the pretest may sensitize the subjects in the treatment condition to the treatment; a treatment effect may be obtained only if a pretest is given. Sensitization or demand characteristics pose greater interpretational problems in some areas than others. There is usually not much of a problem in research on teaching methods, for example, because the tests used can be identical or very similar to the tests normally given. Investigators interested in opinion or attitude change, however, need to be more concerned about this interpretational problem, because a pretest about opinions or attitudes may make the subject very sensitive to the treatment manipulation.

COMPARISON OF THE DESIGNS

Experimental, quasi-experimental, and nonexperimental designs have various strengths and weaknesses in relation to each other. Before considering the strengths and weaknesses of the three classes of designs we need to discuss whether the classifications themselves are reliable.

Classification of Designs

The ease of classifying designs depends, at least in part, on whether between-subject or within-subject comparisons are made. When we make between-subject comparisons we can distinguish experimental designs from others on the basis of how groups are formed. If subjects are randomly assigned to conditions before the treatment is introduced and the groups are treated identically except for the treatment, we have an experimental design. Matched-groups designs in which subjects are randomly assigned to conditions after matching are one type of experimental design. Between-subject comparisons that do not involve random assignment of subjects to groups at some point are either quasi-experimental, nonexperimental, or "subject variable" designs. The distinction between quasi-experimental and nonexperimental designs can be made on the basis of the number of confounding factors that are present. If there are several possible confounding factors (e.g., history, maturation, selection), the design is nonexperimental. In general it is usually fairly easy to classify between-subject comparisons according to the type of design used. Within-subject comparisons are more difficult.

It is frequently difficult to classify designs involving within-subject comparisons because there is no clear procedural difference between the classes of designs; we do not use random assignment procedures to assign subjects to the conditions when we make within-subject comparisons. One solution is to distinguish experimental, quasi-experimental, and nonexperimental designs on the basis of the number of confounding factors present. If it is unlikely that there are any confounding factors, the experimental label is appropriate. If there are several confounding factors, the nonexperimental label is appropriate. If there is a possibility that there is one or more confounding factors, the quasi-experimental label is appropriate. In short, the classification of a design can be determined by the amount of control the investigator has over nonmanipulated variables. Thus, within-subject comparisons made in well-controlled laboratory situations can usually be classified as experimental, whereas within-subject comparisons made in real-life situations are more likely to be classified as quasi-experimental or nonexperimental. Although there is no simple rule for putting within-subject designs into categories it does not matter greatly how a design is classified as long as you know what, if any, confounding factors are present.

Internal and External Validity

In Chapter 1 we said that validity can refer to experiments as well as to measurement. Internal validity refers to whether the effect was due to the treatment administered in a specific experiment. External validity refers to whether a treatment effect can be generalized. A treatment effect that cannot be generalized beyond the specific experimental conditions lacks external validity. A treatment effect that can be obtained in the real world (i.e., in different settings, with different populations of subjects, and so forth) has external validity (see Campbell, 1957). Internal validity is a precondition for external validity. A treatment that has external validity also has internal validity. It does not necessarily follow, however, that a treatment that has an effect in the laboratory (i.e., has internal validity) will also have an effect in real-world situations. We can usually establish internal validity by use of appropriate designs and by controlling for potential confounding variables, but establishing external validity is a matter of degree. External validity refers to the generality of a finding; it will not be established merely because a treatment is administered in a realistic setting. We cannot establish external validity completely because there are so many different situations in which a treatment can be evaluated.

The strengths and weaknesses of the different types of designs can be discussed in terms of internal and external validity. Nonexperimental designs lack internal validity, so they usually have little or no usefulness. Nonexperimental designs rarely enable one to determine the effectiveness of a treatment, so there is no sound basis for discussing the generality of the treatment effect. In short, nonexperimental designs are not very useful for establishing internal or external validity.

Experimental designs provide the best way of establishing internal validity but they are usually not as useful as quasi-experimental designs for establishing external validity because investigators usually cannot use random assignment in real-life situations. Besides, there is usually a trade-off between internal and external validity. If an experimenter has control over all or most of the nonmanipulated variables, the probability of detecting a real effect of the treatment should be high. In general, one is more likely to detect a real effect of a treatment in the laboratory than in real life. If the generality of the research finding is not a matter of concern, the experimental method provides the best way to establish internal validity. As we mentioned in Chapter 1, the extent to which generalization of research findings is possible depends, in part, on the research area considered.

Investigators interested in physiology, perception, attention, and basic learning and memory usually do not have to be greatly concerned about the problem of generality. It is reasonable for these investigators to study the relationships among variables under fixed conditions (i.e., use experimental designs) and then generalize their findings. Often they can *assume* external validity because there is little reason to believe that the phenomena they study depend on individual differences. For example, the memory system is believed to be pretty much the same for people who differ in intelligence, beauty, socioeconomic status, personality, age, weight, and so on.

Generality is more important for investigators interested in personality, social behavior, or instruction. In these areas the effect of treatment manipulations (e.g., type of instructional technique) frequently depends on the type of person participating in the experiment. External validity cannot be assumed; it must be established. Quasi-experimental designs can be very useful in these areas because they frequently allow investigators to establish internal and external validity.

Quasi-experimental designs can often be used to assess treatment effects when it is not possible or feasible to use experimental designs. They may be useful when research is performed in real-life situations such as classrooms, medical clinics, and so forth. One should not conclude, however, that it is always impossible to use experimental designs in real-life situations. This is clearly not the case. If either a quasi-experimental or experimental approach can be used, the investigator should, all else being equal, adopt the experimental approach. Quasi-experimental approaches are valuable when it is not possible to use an experimental approach, but they should not be selected without first considering whether an experimental design can be used.

The use of experimental designs in real-life situations should increase as more people discover that these designs can be very useful for investigating applied problems. For example, an experimental design is currently being used to compare the effects of tonsillectomies for children with the effects of medical treatment such as antibiotic therapy. The investigators are trying to discover whether physicians have been too quick to recommend tonsillectomies — at an average cost of around $550 per operation. Perhaps children would be better off with their tonsils. A research team (see *Newsweek,* February 23, 1976, p. 79) obtained the consent of parents to *randomly assign* the children to have surgery or to be treated medically. The two groups will be studied for several years to assess the relative effectiveness of tonsillectomies and medical treatment. If the groups differ significantly, it will be possible to attribute differences to the effect of the treatment.

SUMMARY

Three nonexperimental designs were considered to give the reader an understanding of what factors influence design adequacy. The factors that have an influence are history, maturation, selection, measurement, demand characteristics, sensitization, and regression. History and maturation refer to events (other than the treatment) that may account for differences in performance. The history factor includes only those events that are specific to the situation being investigated. Maturation refers to time-related processes within the individual that may influence performance. Selection refers to the fact that some designs do not allow the investigator to form equivalent groups before introducing the independent variable. Measurement and sensitization refer to the fact that the assessment process may change the subject's behavior. Demand characteristics are those cues available to a subject that may enable him to determine the purpose of the experiment. Regression is a change from pretest to posttest that results if the pretest-posttest measures are not perfectly reliable and subjects with extreme pretest scores are selected. Nonexperimental designs are inadequate because it is difficult to determine whether performance is influenced by the treatment or to one or more of the above confounding factors.

The basic logic behind the use of quasi-experimental designs is very simple. Because it is not always possible to form equivalent groups before introducing the treatment we need procedures that allow us to eliminate or minimize the influence of confounding factors; quasi-experimental designs provide such procedures. The influence of confounding factors can be minimized by assessing performance several times before and after the experimental treatment (time-series design) or by using a nonequivalent, control-group design. The nonequivalent, control-group design involves a comparison of groups that are *not* equivalent before introducing the treatment. Each group is given a pretest and a posttest, so it is possible to evaluate whether the pretest-posttest change is different for the treatment group than for the control group.

An experiment has internal validity if a treatment has an effect. It has external validity if a treatment effect can be generalized. Internal and external validity are related since internal validity is a precondition for external validity. Nonexperimental designs are not useful for establishing internal or external validity. Experimental designs provide the best way of establishing internal validity, but they are frequently not as useful as quasi-experimental designs for establishing external validity because investigators are *usually* not free to use random assignment procedures in real-life situations. Quasi-experimental designs are useful because they can frequently be used to assess treatment effects when it is not possible or feasible to use experimental designs.

QUESTIONS

1. Give examples, other than the ones mentioned in the text, of the following nonexperimental designs. To what extent, if any, are these designs "used" in your everyday decision making? What are the weaknesses of each?
    a. Single group observed once
    b. Single group, pretest-posttest
    c. Static-groups
2. Distinguish between the history and maturation factor.
3. In what way, if any, does a static-groups design differ from a subject variable experiment in which subjects are assigned to conditions on the basis of a personal characteristic (e.g., shyness)?
4. How could you determine whether there is a sensitization effect?
5. Why is it necessary to understand regression effects? What influences the magnitude of regression?
6. What is the logic behind quasi-experimental designs?
7. Give examples, other than the ones mentioned in the text, of a time-series design and a nonequivalent, control-group design. Why are these designs useful?
8. Distinguish between internal and external validity.
9. What determines the relative importance of internal and external validity for individual investigators?
10. Can experimental designs be used to establish external validity? Why?

performing the experiment 7

In this chapter we will consider difficulties that the experimenter may encounter while executing the experiment. The student who has accepted the invitation to be an active participant has already made many decisions. He has selected a problem area of interest and generated a testable idea. If the experimental method is appropriate the task becomes an exercise in hypothesis testing. The experimenter is interested in whether the planned manipulation affects performance. A testable idea must predict that an independent variable will have an effect on a performance variable. The research hypothesis is that the independent variable will have an effect; the null hypothesis is that it will not.

The factors to consider in selecting a design have been discussed. After selecting the appropriate design, the experimenter needs to consider the problems involved in collecting the data. He has to obtain the necessary facilities and equipment, select and obtain subjects, and decide what testing procedures are most appropriate. He has to be aware of the ways that inadequate testing procedures can confound an experiment, so that these hazards can be avoided. The procedures and problems in conducting an experiment are discussed in this chapter.

FACILITIES, SPECIAL SKILLS, AND EQUIPMENT

The facilities, special skills, and equipment that researchers use vary greatly depending on the problem to be investigated. For example, physiological psychologists usually have surgical skills, knowledge of instrumentation, and elaborate facilities and equipment. Investigators who use computers for the collection and analysis of data frequently have considerable understanding of computer technology. Although technical skills and elaborate equipment are not necessary or even useful in some areas of psychological research, it is clear that many problems could not be investigated without the use of complicated equipment. For example, multivariate analyses (more than one dependent measure) would be very difficult to do without computers. And physiological psychologists have been able to study the innermost portions of the brain only *after* the development of stereotaxic, stimulating, and recording instruments.

The Role of Computers

The importance of computers in psychological research has increased markedly during the last decade. They are now commonplace tools for analyzing the results of experiments. They make possible the analysis of data that would otherwise be virtually impossible to analyze. Moreover, computers have become useful for much more than data analysis — they are used extensively as a means of data collection. It would be impossible to perform some experiments if computers were not available. In many cases the computer has replaced the experimenter for data collection because it can do the job more efficiently. It can also allow an investigator to avoid procedural difficulties. For example, if the data are collected by having the subject interact solely with a computer, there is no chance that it will, inadvertently, give the subject clues regarding the purpose of the experiment.

Computers are also used in developing ideas for experiments; sometimes a researcher will develop ideas about behavior by noting and testing similarities between computers and humans. For example, a scientist interested in understanding how humans make sense of auditory input might try to build a machine that interprets what it hears. Is it possible to develop a machine that can type out whatever you say? Or, is it possible to develop a machine that will sort mail by analyzing the handwritten addresses on letters? The theorist who considers the problems involved in building a machine (programming a computer) to perform human functions is forced to consider a number of difficult problems. By wrestling with these problems he may develop ideas about human functioning. In short, computers are useful in all three of the major stages of investigation: formulating ideas, collecting relevant data, and analyzing the data. There is little doubt that they will continue to play an important role in psychological research.

Selecting a Laboratory

There are very few limits on where and how data can be collected. Experiments need not be conducted in the laboratory. Data can be collected in a classroom, at a football game, in a bar, in a laboratory, and elsewhere. The only limits on where and how the data should be collected are ethical, practical, and methodological. A laboratory is a good place to work because distractions can be kept to a minimum. With more control over the situation there is less chance that the dependent measure will be influenced by other variables.

To illustrate, let us assume that you want to conduct a three-group, random-groups experiment. It is necessary to test the subjects individually, but the materials are such that the subject can perform the task in many different settings, such as a laboratory, home, bar, or classroom. The problem is to decide whether or not all subjects should be required to come to the laboratory.

The other option is to take the materials and look for subjects in blocks of three. If you find three people in a dormitory who are willing to participate, you can *randomly assign* each of them to one of the three conditions and then test the subjects in the dormitory. Next, you find three classmates who are willing to stay after class to serve in the experiment. You *randomly assign* them to the three conditions. You repeat this procedure with successive blocks of three subjects in various locations until you have collected the data. (This design is frequently called a randomized block design, a special kind of random-groups design. In this case subjects are grouped, or blocked, according to location.) You want to know in what way, if any, the data that are gathered in the various locations will differ from the data that would have been obtained from the same subjects in a single location (e.g., a laboratory).

Number of Laboratories and Confounding. Your first reaction may be that the experiment that was conducted in various locations is confounded, whereas one conducted in the laboratory would not have been confounded. This is an erroneous belief. To argue convincingly that an experiment is confounded it is necessary to demonstrate that the level of the confounding variable was different for the various treatment conditions. For example, if all subjects in one condition were tested in a bar, all subjects in another condition were tested in a classroom, and all subjects in the third condition were tested in a dormitory, the experiment would be confounded. You would not know whether to attribute the results to the independent variable or the location variable. If the level of the confounding variable (i.e., the locations) differs for the treatment conditions, then it is reasonable to argue that the location variable may have been responsible for any obtained differences between conditions.

However, in the case considered above, one subject in each condition was tested in each of the locations. Since the levels of the location variables were the same for all conditions, it is unreasonable to argue that the different locations produced differences between the treatment conditions. The locations were *controlled* in that each location was used once for each condition. When you are convinced that the use of various locations did not confound the experiment you can consider the effect of using different locations.

Number of Laboratories and Within-group Variance. Let us assume that some locations are more conducive to high performance than others. If the type of location influences performance and every subject in each condition is tested in a different location, then the within-group variance should be greater for the experiment conducted in several locations than for the experiment conducted in the laboratory. Any variable that increases the within-group estimates of population variance will decrease the likelihood of rejecting the null hypothesis when the independent variable actually has an effect. Thus the use of several locations will result in a more stringent test of the treatment manipulation and will decrease the chance of detecting a "real" effect of an independent variable when the effect is small. If a significant difference is obtained under these stringent conditions one can be confident that the independent variable has an effect.

Deciding Where to Conduct the Experiment. There is no set of rules that can be applied to determine whether it is better to test subjects in the laboratory or in real-life situations. In making this decision one should consider the ethical, practical, and methodological problems raised by the particular experiment. After doing so one may decide that the decision as to whether a single laboratory or various locations should be used for testing is arbitrary. There are many such decisions to be made in conducting research. If one's interest is in obtaining significant differences between treatment means, the "arbitrary" decisions should be made in such a way that the likelihood of obtaining significant differences is maximized; in this case the investigator would decide to test all subjects in the laboratory. However, an investigator who is only interested in manipulations that have a large effect and generality is likely to opt for the use of various locations; he may not consider the manipulation very interesting or important unless the effect can be obtained in "real-life" situations.

Procedures Specific to Research Areas

If the problem area of interest has been studied by other researchers, it is likely that certain procedures have been used so often that they can be considered standard. If an idea can be tested by using a standard procedure, the results of one experiment can be compared with those of other investigations in which the same procedure was used. If different experiments share a common procedure the facts can be organized on this basis. More important, new findings can be evaluated primarily in terms of the independent variable manipulations that the experimenter made and not in terms of arbitrary experimental procedures.

Although there are good reasons for adopting standard procedures, there is a danger in doing so. The difficulty is that a standard procedure may be taken for granted, causing investigators to become less creative in generating and testing ideas. If an idea can be tested by using a standard procedure there is little reason to adopt a new one. However, if the idea cannot be tested by standard procedures, then the procedures, not the idea, should be discarded. A standard set of procedures can be considered a tool. If the tool is useful, use it; if it is not useful, set it aside. Investigators should be willing to evaluate the standard procedures of their research area to determine whether these procedures are helping or hindering the development of the field.

SUBJECTS

Selection of Subjects

Psychologists have used many kinds of subjects for psychological research, but rats, pigeons, rhesus monkeys, and humans are used most frequently. The concentration on only a few kinds of lower animals has not gone without criticism. For example, Beach (1950) and Lockard (1968) have bemoaned the fact that psychologists have used the albino rat so extensively. One reason for the emphasis on rats, pigeons, rhesus monkeys, and humans is availability. A researcher interested in using lower animals can purchase rats, pigeons, or monkeys from private sources.

The decision about whether to use humans or lower animals will probably be dictated by the nature of the research problem. Many manipulations can be made with animals that would be impossible or unethical with humans. For example, genetic studies and physiological studies either must be done, or are better done, with lower animals as subjects.

Use of Human Subjects. The use of human subjects in psychological experiments poses special problems. As is the case when lower animals are the subjects, availability will be an important determinant of which subjects are selected. The problem of obtaining people who are willing to serve in psychological experiments is generally aggravated by a lack of money to pay people for their time. Thus, the experimenter is forced to abandon the research or to seek other means of obtaining subjects.

The most common way to obtain subjects for experiments is to ask students in introductory psychology classes to participate. The ethical problems involved in recruiting subjects from classes are considerable. Psychology departments and instructors typically use a variety of procedures to ensure that the rights of participants are not violated. From the experimenter's point of view the crucial considerations are obtaining the participant's informed consent whenever possible and treating the participant with respect and dignity. Experimenters should resolve any ethical issues before testing any subjects. (The ethical principles for conducting research are presented in Chapter 1.)

Use of More than One Type of Subject. Some researchers may be fortunate enough to have several subject populations available and may decide, therefore, to compare them. If the only point of interest is to compare two subject populations on some dependent variable, then it will only be possible to conclude that one population does better on the task than the other. It is not reasonable to attribute the difference to any specific variable because there is no way of knowing all the variables on which the two populations differ. Of course there are many occasions when it is important to know which population will do better on a particular task. The investigator may want to compare the populations for practical reasons or to determine whether there is a phenomenon to investigate further. If he obtains differences between populations, then he can design additional studies in an attempt to discover the reasons for the differences.

Number of Subjects per Condition

The number of subjects tested in each condition should depend on the effect of the independent variable, the type of design, and whether the investigator is interested in detecting small effects. If the independent variable manipulation is so powerful that all the subjects in the experimental group are better than the best subject in the control group, then there is no need to test more than the usual number of subjects. The usual number of subjects can be determined by referring to research journals. Investigators in a single field tend to test approximately the same number of subjects per condition. If the groups are shown to be equivalent before the independent variable is introduced then there is some justification for using fewer than the normal number of subjects.

The issue of how many subjects to test boils down to a question of belief. The task is to convince the scientific community that the results of the experiment are attributable to the independent variable and not solely to chance, or worse, to a nonmanipulated but confounding variable. The purpose of conducting and analyzing experiments is to convince others and yourself of the effectiveness or ineffectiveness of a particular manipulation. Thus, the astute approach is to determine what would convince other investigators and then meet or better their criteria. For any experiment there are usually computational advantages to having an equal number of subjects in each condition.

For some problems a large amount of data can be obtained from a single subject. For example, in some perceptual studies in which within-subject designs are used, the same subject can be tested for long periods. The combination of a large number of observations on each subject and a within-subject design generally results in a need for fewer subjects. If you are interested in detecting *any effect* due to the independent variable, no matter how small, and you are forced to use a between-subject design, then you should test a large number of subjects in each group. The probability of detecting a real difference increases, all things being equal, as the number of subjects per condition increases. Yet if one has to test a great many subjects in each condition to obtain a significant difference statistically, it is questionable whether the effect has any psychological importance.

Individual or Group Testing

All Conditions Represented. The nature of the experiment may allow testing of subjects individually or in groups. The obvious reason for testing in groups is to collect the data more rapidly. Testing subjects in each of the conditions at the same time may make it possible to gather all the data with just one session. Besides the obvious practical advantage here there may be a methodological advantage. There may be less within-group variance when subjects are all tested at the same time than when they are tested individually. The reason for the expected difference in within-group variance is that situational testing variables are likely to influence the group-tested and individually tested subjects differentially. Let us look at an example.

Assume that a two-group, random-groups design is used and that subjects can be tested individually or in groups. The experimenter decides to test individually the sixteen subjects in each group. Let us further assume that it takes one hour to test a subject and that the experimenter has two free hours in the morning and two hours in the afternoon. One subject from each condition is tested in the morning and one from each condition in the afternoon. Thus, half the subjects in each group will be tested in the morning and half in the afternoon. If subjects perform differently at different times of the day, then the time-of-day effect should increase within-group variance but should affect all groups equally. A similar argument can be made for many other time-related variables. There is likely to be less within-group variance when subjects are tested at the same time if time-related variables have an effect on the dependent measure.

Even though all the situational variables should be the same for subjects tested at the same time, the size of the groups may have some effect on performance. For example, some subjects may cooperate more fully when they are tested individually. The failure of some subjects to follow instructions could have an effect on the difference between group means, since uncooperative subjects may not be assigned equally to all conditions. Such failure to follow instructions should cause within-group variance to increase. Thus, the advantages and disadvantages of group and individual testing depend on the problem.

One Condition Represented. If subjects cannot be tested in all conditions at the same time, then it is questionable whether anything other than individual testing should be used. For example, it may be possible to test many subjects at the same time but only subjects from one condition in any one session. If there were three treatments, one could test all the subjects in the first condition, then all the subjects in the second, and then all the subjects in the third. This is a poor procedure because there are several confounding variables (e.g., order of testing, experience of the experimenter) that may be responsible for any obtained mean differences. Testing subjects individually instead would permit an order of testing that would balance the effects of the confounding variables over the three conditions so that differences between treatments could be attributed to the effect of the independent variable.

Let us assume that you acknowledge that individual testing is methodologically sound and testing all the subjects in one treatment condition at the same time is unacceptable. If you can test subjects from only one condition in any one session, is it permissible to test more than one at a time? Assume that you decide to test three subjects from the same condition at the same time. If you test a total of fifteen subjects in each condition then you will have five different testing sessions for each condition. In order to balance the effects of time-related variables (e.g., time of day, experience of the experimenter), you determine the order of testing randomly with the restriction that the number of subjects tested in one condition does not exceed the number tested in the other conditions by more than three. The issue is whether testing the subjects in blocks of three is acceptable. It should be clear that this procedure is much better than testing *all* the subjects from one condition at the same time. Yet the likelihood of balancing out time-related variables is greater if subjects are tested individually than if they are tested in groups of three.

It is not possible to conclude that testing in blocks of two or more is right or wrong. Some investigators will object to this procedure. They will argue that the data from each block of subjects should be treated as though it were obtained from one subject. That is, that for statistical purposes the mean score for each block of subjects should be treated as the score for one subject. If each block of subjects is treated as one subject, then there is little advantage to testing subjects in blocks. However, other investigators will accept this procedure as methodologically sound and analyze the data in the same way that they would if each subject were tested individually.

The decision as to whether testing subjects from the same condition in blocks is permissible is a question of judgment. Those who believe that this procedure balances out the effects of time-related variables are likely to use it and accept its use by others. Those who are skeptical will probably not use it and will be reluctant to accept the findings of experimenters who do. It is unlikely, however, that very many investigators will accept or reject the results of an experiment solely on the basis of whether or not subjects from the same condition were tested in blocks of two or more. They are more likely to evaluate the experimental procedure along with such factors as the magnitude of the effect, and the consistency of the results with earlier findings.

CONFOUNDING

Number of Experimenters

The nature of an experiment may be such that the data can be collected much more rapidly or efficiently if there are two or more experimenters. In such a case, each experimenter must, of course, test the same number of subjects in each condition so that significant group differences can be attributed to the effect of the independent variable and not to the use of different experimenters. If one experimenter tests all the subjects in one treatment condition and another tests all the subjects in the other condition, the experiment would be confounded (assuming the experimenter was not the intended independent variable).

The methodological considerations in using two or more experimenters are similar to those in using two or more laboratories to collect the data. If the characteristics of the experimenters influence the performance of the subjects and both experimenters test subjects in all conditions, then the within-group variance will increase and the chances of obtaining significant mean differences will decrease.

Demand Characteristics

Nature of Demand Characteristics. Assume that you are engaged in doing research on a problem in which you have great personal interest. In addition, you may have a considerable amount of bias. It would probably be gratifying to you to have any prediction you might make supported by experimental results. Yet you should want the results to reflect the true state of affairs and not your bias, so it is important to minimize the likelihood that your biases will affect the results. The work of Orne (1959, 1962) and Rosenthal (1963, 1966) has demonstrated that the experimenter's expectations or biases can influence the results of psychological experiments. Orne points out that a human subject will, generally, attempt to determine the purpose of the experiment and then do what is necessary to make it succeed.

As we saw in the last chapter, each experiment has *demand characteristics* from the point of view of the subject. Subjects are sometimes able to determine what the experimenter wants and respond accordingly. Moreover, the effect of finding out what the experimenter wants may be influenced markedly by the treatment condition the subject is in, because experimenters rarely want the same performance from subjects in different treatment conditions. If the subject detects that he is in the "special" group, his interest and performance level may increase. And, if he detects that he is in the "control" group, his interest and performance may decrease. Such an experiment is confounded because there is no way to know whether the results are due to the independent variable or to the effect of demand characteristics.

It is also possible, of course, that the subjects will determine what the experimenter wants and then respond in just the opposite way. Yet most subjects tend to be cooperative. You can assess whether a subject is cooperative by asking him to hold a large chunk of ice. If you return forty minutes later and the subject is sitting in a puddle of water clutching a small chunk of ice, you have a cooperative subject (Hanley, 1969).

Pervasiveness of Demand Characteristics. Although there is no question that experimenter bias and demand characteristics can influence the results of psychological studies, there is disagreement over the pervasiveness of the effect. Neisser (1967) attributed the findings of some dream, imagery, perceptual defense, perceptual fragmentation, sensory deprivation, shadowing, subliminal perception, visual search, visual word recognition, and word association experiments to the effects of demand characteristics. In many cases the subject will probably be able to pick up cues from the experimenter or from other characteristics of the experiment to determine what is expected. Then he has the option of "cooperating" with the experimenter. Yet Barber and Silver (1968) argue that the effect of experimenter bias is difficult to demonstrate and less pervasive than Rosenthal claims.

In any case, you should do whatever is necessary to eliminate or at least minimize the effect of demand characteristics. When you provide cues that enable the subjects to discern what results you want you have a confounded experiment. Any significant mean differences could be attributed to the effect of the independent variable or to the demand characteristics. Perhaps the subjects were only trying to please you by doing what you wanted them to do.

The extent to which demand characteristics confound an experiment will depend on the nature of the problem. For example, in studying the experimental control of dreaming one should take precautions to eliminate or minimize the effects of demand characteristics. Direct instruction or hypnosis can be used to attempt to influence dream content, but it is difficult to determine the success of such an attempt. Perhaps the subjects will react to the demand characteristics of the experiment and report the type of dream they think the investigator wants them to report, regardless of their actual dreams. Patients in psychoanalysis tend to report having the type of dreams that their analysts expect. Patients of Adlerians have Adlerian dreams, patients of Freudians have Freudian dreams, and so on. Is this because the analysts are controlling the dream content? Or is the effect due to demand characteristics?

At the opposite extreme, in a study in which all conditions are tested at the same time and the experimenter does not have any knowledge of what condition each subject is being tested in and the subjects are not able to detect whether they are in an experimental or control condition, there is little reason to be concerned with the confounding effects of demand characteristics.

Experimenter Attitude and Demand Characteristics. You should evaluate your attitude and your experiment to assess whether demand characteristics are likely to be responsible for differences between the groups. If you are interested in obtaining the facts, you will want to eliminate any possible confounding effect due to demand characteristics. But if you are intent on obtaining support for your theoretical notions regardless of the facts, you should change your attitude or not do research. The task of determining the facts is difficult enough without adding personal biases.

It is necessary to distinguish between biases that affect the selection of a problem area and the generating of ideas, and those that affect the *testing* of ideas. Because experimenters should select problems and hypotheses in which they have a personal interest, a certain amount of bias is probably inevitable in planning an experiment. However, personal biases should not be allowed to influence the testing process.

To illustrate, suppose you have a great deal of personal interest in a football team, the Mudville Mites. You are extremely biased in their favor. You watch them practice, lead the fans in cheering, and extol their virtues while imbibing in the local gin mill. Moreover, you believe that winning is everything. Yet when it comes time for the test, you want it to be unbiased. You would not think of bribing the opponents or an official. You want the Mudville Mites to win on their merit alone. Similarly, you should want your ideas to be tested on their merit alone, or you should get out of the business of testing ideas. If you carry your biases into the testing arena, then you risk not giving your ideas a fair test.

Controlling Demand Characteristics. If you select a problem in which demand characteristics could be a problem you should design your experiment in such a way that the effects of these characteristics can be assessed. For example, if one group of subjects is more likely to detect the real purpose of the experiment than the other group, you may try to manipulate the cooperativeness of the subjects (by providing incentives or by adopting a gentle, considerate manner for only one group) as an additional independent variable. If you are able to manipulate cooperativeness and if the other independent variable produces the predicted effect for both cooperative and uncooperative subjects, you may reasonably conclude that the results are not due to demand characteristics.

Even if there is little reason to think that subjects can discern the purpose of the experiment or detect how you "want" them to perform, you should take precautions against demand characteristics; subjects may be very perceptive. Sometimes it is possible to test them without knowing the particular condition to which each is assigned. When subjects are tested individually, however, it is usually impossible for the experimenter not to know the condition of each. In such a case it may help to have them tested by another experimenter who is unaware of the purpose of the experiment. Care should be taken to ensure that he is unbiased. In some cases, it is feasible to "bias" experimenters in opposite directions and analyze for the effect of biasing.

In short, you should be aware that subjects may determine what you are trying to do and may perform accordingly. The danger of confounding the experiment in this way is present in both between-subject and within-subject designs, but is usually a greater threat in within-subject designs. In fact, a consideration of demand characteristics may lead you to choose a between-subject design if testing each subject in all conditions would disclose the purpose of the experiment. Also, it may lead you to automate the experiment as much as possible. For example, the instructions could be tape recorded to minimize the possibility that the experimenter, while reading the instructions, would provide differential cues to subjects in the various conditions.

Confounding with a Between-subject Design

Failure to Obtain Equivalent Groups. A confounding that is specific to between-subject designs is the failure to obtain equivalent groups, or the destruction of such groups. As you recall, each subject receives only one level of each independent variable for a between-subject design. It is important that there be a high probability of obtaining equivalent groups before the independent variable is introduced. Therefore, except for the limits of the design and procedure, it is necessary to assign subjects to conditions on a random basis. If a matched-groups design is used, subjects should be assigned randomly with the restriction that the groups be equated on the matching variable. As long as the independent variable is something other than a subject variable manipulation, there should be little difficulty in obtaining equivalent groups *most of the time* through the use of random assignment.

Random assignment will not always produce equivalent groups, so you have to expect to be wrong a small portion of the time when you reject the null hypothesis. Investigators have to be able to live with a small probability of error; the task is to keep it small. If you want to manipulate a subject variable, there is virtually no procedure that allows you to be reasonably confident that the groups are equivalent except for the subject variable of interest. For example, if you want to manipulate political party, Republican versus Democratic, how are you going to obtain two groups that are equivalent except for their political beliefs? You cannot use random assignment because political belief determines the subject's condition. Even if you were to randomly select from the entire population of Republicans and Democrats to obtain your sample, you could not be certain that any obtained differences in your dependent measure were attributable to political belief. Obviously, Republicans and Democrats differ on variables other than political belief (e.g., wealth and occupation).

Destruction of Equivalent Groups. Even when equivalent groups have been obtained by the use of random assignment, the nature of the independent variable may destroy their equivalence. For example, assume that you are interested in how performance on a task is influenced by the difficulty of the preceding task. The question of interest is whether a subject is more likely to perform at a higher level if the earlier laboratory experience were easy or if it were difficult. The subjects are randomly assigned to the two conditions. The experiment requires that each subject participate in two separate sessions on successive days. All subjects are given the same task on Day 2. On Day 1, one group of subjects is given a fairly easy task and the other group a more difficult task. After the subjects complete their tasks, you thank them and ask them to return the next day for another session. Unfortunately, all the subjects do not return the second day. Of the twenty subjects who had easy tasks, eighteen return for the second day. Of the twenty who had difficult tasks only twelve return.

You are a little disturbed by the fact that some of the subjects did not return for the second session, but you analyze the data for those who did. You find that the subjects who performed difficult tasks on Day 1 have a higher mean performance on Day 2 than those who performed easy tasks even though all subjects were given the same task for Day 2. You conclude that, at least for this task, subjects tend to perform better if their previous laboratory experience was difficult than if it was easy. Is this conclusion justified?

It should be clear that the nature of the independent variable may have resulted in the destruction of equivalent groups. One could argue that the group differences are a result of nonequivalent groups. It is plausible that the eight subjects with difficult tasks who did not return for Day 2 were unlike the twelve who did return. More specifically, they may have been duller than the twelve others. Thus one could argue that those twelve subjects were, on the average, brighter than the eighteen subjects who performed the easy task. If more subjects are lost in one condition than in the other, the equivalence of the groups may be destroyed.

The destruction of equivalent groups is likely to be a serious methodological problem in making a survey. Assume that the nature of the survey is the manipulation and that each form is mailed to a randomly selected sample of 100 subjects. Unless there is a high return of the surveys it is difficult to know whether the subjects who respond are typical of the sample of 100 that received each form.

Failure to Control Nonmanipulated Variables. At the risk of laboring the obvious, let us point out again that investigators must control for the effects of nonmanipulated variables. The experimenter should make every effort to see that the groups differ only with respect to the intended manipulation. For example, if an investigator is studying a new drug's effect on humans it is important to treat the subjects in all groups alike except for the drug. This means that control subjects should be given seemingly identical injections or pills. The person giving the treatments should not know who gets the real drug and who gets the placebo. If subjects were told what treatment they were to receive, there would be no way to determine whether the effects were due to the drug or to the fact that subjects knew they were receiving a special treatment.

There are a number of ways that an experiment can be confounded by failure to control nonmanipulated variables. For example, if the independent variable is the type of strategy subjects are asked to employ, the experimenter should take care not to sound more encouraging in one condition than another. And he should make sure that all subjects are given the same amount of time to perform the task that is used to assess the independent variable. In short, the investigator should examine the procedures carefully to make sure that only the intended manipulation is made. It is necessary to control for nonmanipulated variables regardless of whether a between-subject or within-subject design is used.

Confounding with a Within-subject Design

The principal problem of confounding with a within-subject design is failure to counterbalance for practice and time-related effects. As you remember, each subject receives every level of the independent variable in a within-subject design. Since it is not possible to present all the levels of the independent variable at the same time, it is necessary to control for the effects of practice and time by making sure that each treatment is presented at each stage of practice an equal number of times. In addition, in some cases it is a good idea to have each treatment precede and follow every other treatment an equal number of times. This is particularly important if there is reason to believe that the effect of a treatment will be influenced by the immediately preceding treatment.

TESTING THE SUBJECTS

The difficulties involved in obtaining the data will vary with the particular problem investigated. Sometimes you may have to do an extensive amount of work to get ready to conduct the experiment. Such tasks as recruiting subjects, finding a place to conduct the experiment, writing instructions for the subjects, preparing materials, and obtaining equipment can involve a lot of time and energy. Yet this stage of the research is extremely important. It is a good idea to double-check all preparations to make sure that you do not manipulate more than the independent variable, thereby confounding the experiment.

If you make a mistake while conducting the experiment (e.g., give a subject the wrong instructions or the wrong amount of time), then you should replace the subject with another. Replacing subjects is no particular problem as long as it is not differential for conditions. If it is differential (i.e., if many subjects are lost in one condition and few subjects in the other conditions), the groups may not be equivalent. And you should not, of course, intentionally make mistakes in an effort to eliminate the subjects who are not performing as you would like. Moreover, it is important that you have the same attitude toward all subjects. You should not be friendly toward some and unfriendly toward others, even if you do prefer to test members of the opposite sex.

You should test a few subjects to make sure that the procedures, materials, and equipment are satisfactory before obtaining data that you will analyze. That is, you may want to conduct a short pilot study first. The results obtained by testing a few subjects in each condition should enable you to evaluate the arbitrary decisions (e.g., the amount of time, the nature of the materials), allow you to assess the clarity of the instructions, and give you an opportunity to eliminate errors in your behavior as experimenter. After you are confident that you can perform the experiment properly, you can begin collecting the data.

SUMMARY

The facilities, special skills, and equipment that researchers use vary greatly depending on the problem investigated. Computers are used extensively in psychological research to collect and analyze data, and as models of information processing. The major disadvantage to the use of complicated equipment is that it sometimes becomes an end in itself rather than a means for evaluating ideas.

Experiments need not be conducted in laboratories or in a single setting. The only limits on where and how data can be collected are ethical, practical, and methodological. The use of different settings does not necessarily confound the results of an experiment but it is likely to increase the within-group variance if the locations have any influence on performance. There are no rules to determine whether experiments should be conducted in laboratories or real-life situations. Statistical results are usually better for tests conducted in laboratories, but generalization is easier from real-life situations.

The use of standard procedures for collecting data enables investigators to compare the findings of many different experiments and to evaluate new experiments according to their results, not their procedures. One disadvantage is that investigators may be less creative in generating and testing ideas if they restrict themselves to standard procedures. The other danger is that the study of procedures may become an end instead of a means.

Psychologists use many kinds of subjects, both human and nonhuman. The major factor influencing subject selection is availability. The number of subjects that should be tested in each condition depends on the nature of the independent variable, the type of design, and the researcher's interest in detecting small effects. If it is possible to test subjects in each of the conditions at the same time, there is usually a statistical advantage to testing in groups rather than individually. If it is not possible to test subjects in more than one condition at the same time then it is questionable whether anything other than individual testing should be used.

Each experiment has demand characteristics from the point of view of the subject. The effect of finding out what the experimenter "wants" may be influenced greatly by the subject's treatment condition because experimenters rarely expect the same performance from subjects in different treatment conditions. The results of the experiment may be determined more by the subject's detection of the experimenter's expectations than by the effect of the independent variable, i.e., demand characteristics may threaten to confound many experiments. Although there is disagreement regarding the pervasiveness of the effect, there is little reason not to take steps to minimize, control, or assess the effects of demand characteristics.

The principal confounding problem with between-subject designs is the failure to obtain equivalent groups and the destruction of equivalent groups. In within-subject designs, the principal confounding problem is the failure to counterbalance for practice and time-related effects.

QUESTIONS

1. What are the advantages and disadvantages of collecting the data in one setting rather than in several settings?
2. What are the advantages and disadvantages of using standard procedures when testing subjects?
3. What factors determine how many subjects should be tested in each condition?
4. What are the advantages and disadvantages of testing subjects individually or in groups? Why is the number of conditions represented during group testing an important consideration?
5. What are demand characteristics and why are they an important methodological consideration?
6. What are some general ways in which confounding may occur in a between-subject design? In a within-subject design?
7. An investigator was interested in the effect of experiences at a university on the stands students take on controversial issues. She obtained a random sample of 100 freshmen, 100 sophomores, 100 juniors, and 100 seniors at a large state university. All 400 students agreed to take a test. The investigator found a direct relationship between the number of years at the institution and the score on the test. Freshmen tended to be conservative, and seniors tended to be liberal. Assume that the test was reliable and valid. The investigator concluded that the experiences at the university caused the students to become more liberal. Do you agree with her conclusions? Why?
8. An investigator was interested in the effect of violence in movies on the amount of violence reported in dreams. He randomly assigned a group of 100 subjects to two groups so that there were an equal number of subjects in each group. Each subject agreed to attend the movie of the investigator's choice

if the investigator provided the ticket. One group viewed a very violent movie and the other group viewed a nonviolent movie. The subjects also agreed to record any dreams that they remembered having during the night immediately following the movie. The investigator analyzed the dreams for violent content and found there was a significantly higher incidence of violence for the subjects who saw the violent movie. He concluded that viewing a violent movie has a tendency to cause one to have violent dreams. Do you agree with this conclusion? Why?

9. An investigator was concerned with the effect of fear arousal on learning. She was keenly aware of the ethical problems involved in performing an experiment of this type. The subjects were told that there was a possibility that they would receive some "pretty stiff" shocks if their performance on a learning task was low. Each subject was promised five dollars for participating. After hearing about the general nature of the experiment, forty subjects agreed to participate. These subjects were randomly assigned to the two conditions in such a way that there were twenty subjects in each. The investigator then told the subjects whether they were in the shock or no shock condition. Six subjects in the shock condition then decided not to participate, so the experimenter recruited six more as replacements. The shock and no shock subjects were tested on a learning task. None of them received any shock, of course. The independent variable was whether they *expected* to receive shock for low performance. The results revealed that the subjects who expected a shock performed better than the subjects who expected no shock. The investigator concluded that the expectation of a shock resulted in higher performance on the learning task. Do you agree with her conclusion? Why?

DESCRIBING, ANALYZING, AND REPORTING RESULTS

methods and procedures for describing results

8

In this chapter we will discuss the description of results obtained with observational techniques and the experimental method. Because investigators frequently manipulate independent variables to determine whether the manipulation has an effect on dependent variables, the description of results is often synonymous with the description of the scores subjects obtain on the dependent measure(s). It is not necessary to use the experimental method to obtain such scores, but the label *dependent measure* is generally restricted to cases in which this method is used.

The words *performance measure* or *behavioral measure* are usually used as labels for results obtained with a method other than the experimental. Yet in describing results it makes little difference whether the scores are called performance measures or dependent measures. An investigator who observes the performance of an organism without manipulating an independent variable still must describe the behavior observed. Or, if two measures are obtained on each subject, the investigator can describe the degree of the relationship between them by computing a correlation. Thus, investigators must describe their results whether they use observational techniques, the correlational approach, or the quasi-experimental or experimental method. The procedures and methods that can be used to describe results depend on the level of measurement obtained. Therefore, our first task is to consider the levels of measurement.

LEVEL OF MEASUREMENT AND PERFORMANCE VARIABLES

In Chapter 1 we defined measurement as the use of rules to assign numbers to objects or events. The rules used determine the level of measurement that

161

is obtained and, consequently, the operations that can be performed on the numbers. We will see later, for example, that it is necessary to classify the dependent variable according to the level of measurement obtained in order to select an appropriate statistical test. The four levels of measurement are nominal, ordinal, interval, and ratio.

Nominal or Categorical Measurement

A nominal classification system is one in which the different classes (categories) are qualitatively related. Brands of soap or beer are examples of such a system. There is no single, quantitative variable that can be used to distinguish different brands. The differences between categories of a nominal system are of kind, not of degree. They are qualitative, not quantitative.

It is fairly easy to construct nominal classification systems because the primary task is to select categories that are qualitatively related. Social scientists and laymen have not been reluctant to create such systems. You probably have at least a tendency to place people in categories. For example, you may classify them as right-handed or left-handed, male or female, workers or politicians, introverted or extraverted, warm or cold, assertive or timid. If the categories are qualitatively different, they belong to a nominal system. For many research problems it is important to be able to determine the number of individuals in each category so that the factors influencing the assignment to categories and the relationship between classification systems can be determined.

Ordinal Measurement

For nominal data it is assumed that differences between categories are of kind, not degree. However, a single continuum will frequently underlie a particular classification system. For example, the categories of normal, neurotic, and psychotic all describe degrees of maladjustment. If there is good reason to believe that a single dimension underlies a classification system it may be useful to rank the categories and treat the results as ordinal rather than nominal data. People in the normal, neurotic, and psychotic categories can be given the scores of 0, 1, and 2, respectively. The numbers indicate the *relative* amount of maladjustment. The difference in maladjustment between individuals in the 0 and 1 categories is not necessarily the same as the difference between those in the 1 and 2 categories. Of course, assignment to these categories must be reliable if the system is to be useful.

Since it is usually possible to argue that subjects in different categories differ on one or more quantitative variables, you may conclude that it is good strategy to "convert" nominal measurement to ordinal by "detecting" an underlying quantitative dimension. This is not necessarily a good idea, however, because often there is no sound basis for selecting a quantitative dimension.

Consider, for example, the classification of people according to political party. It can be argued that several factors, such as income, status, values, and occupation, underlie this classification. We would not want to substitute one of the underlying factors (e.g., wealth) for political party, however, because wealth and political party are not always related. For instance, Republicans tend to be wealthier than Democrats, but there are also very wealthy Democrats and very poor Republicans. The use of the income (a quantitative measure) is not a good substitute for political party. There appears to be no single quantitative variable that can be used to classify people accurately according to their political preferences. Therefore it is better to remain at the nominal level of measurement. If subjects in different categories differ in a number of ways it is more reasonable to maintain a nominal classification than to attempt to rank the categories (i.e., Republican, Democrat, Independent) on the basis of a single quantitative variable.

The point is that an ordinal scale represents a quantitative difference, whereas a nominal classification system does not. Ordinal data can be obtained whenever it is possible to rank subjects or events along a single dimension. For example, if you rank individuals according to physical strength or performance on a midterm you are using an ordinal scale. An ordinal scale is one in which the scale values are quantitatively related, but the differences between successive values are not necessarily equal.

When numbers are used to indicate the amount of a particular characteristic but the differences between successive units of measurement are not necessarily equal, ordinal data are obtained. For example, if the members of a class are ranked according to leadership ability, the difference in ability between members 4 and 8 is not necessarily the same as the difference between members 16 and 20. But if a dependent measure does have equal intervals between successive units on the scale, then *interval* data are obtained.

Interval and Ratio Measurement

For interval data the scale values are related by a single, underlying quantitative dimension, and there are equal intervals between successive values. Fahrenheit temperature is a good example of an interval scale. The units reflect a quantitative difference and the intervals between successive units are equal. For example, the difference between 80 and 100 degrees Fahrenheit is the same as the difference between 40 and 60 degrees. These are *equal volumetric changes* in the thermometer. Yet the Fahrenheit scale is not a ratio scale because the ratio obtained by dividing one temperature by another is not meaningful. It is meaningless to say that 50 degrees is twice as warm as 25 degrees.

164   Methods and Procedures for Describing Results

A ratio scale has equal intervals between successive units *and* an absolute zero. If a scale has these two features it is meaningful to consider the ratio of two numbers on the scale. Weight is a good example of a ratio scale; it has an absolute zero and equal intervals between successive units. It is meaningful to say that a 200-pound person weighs twice as much as a 100-pound person.

Determining the Level of Measurement

It is usually easy to ascertain whether the level of measurement is nominal because one can readily determine whether values on a scale are quantitatively or qualitatively related. And for our purposes it makes no difference whether measurement is at the interval or ratio level. The major task is to decide whether the performance measure is interval or ordinal.

Unfortunately that task is not always simple. For example, scores on questionnaires, intelligence tests, and achievement tests are frequently viewed as interval data, but this view can be disputed. If the items are not homogeneous one can argue that the differences between successive units are not equal. Often it is unclear whether they are equal; then the investigator has to decide whether to regard the measurement as ordinal or interval. There are advantages to having interval data, so when in doubt most investigators treat their data as interval. Those who prefer a more conservative approach, however, will treat their data as ordinal.

DESCRIPTIVE MEASURES

The level of measurement determines the descriptive measures that can be computed. Description is straightforward with nominal data; it is only necessary to indicate the number of cases in each category. Each subject provides the same amount of data, namely, one case in a particular category. However, if ordinal or interval data are obtained, the subjects will almost certainly attain different scores. Therefore it is more difficult to describe performance on the dependent measure. It is necessary to obtain average scores, and the way they are obtained will usually differ for ordinal and interval data because interval scores are additive and ordinal scores are not. It makes sense to add scores to obtain averages only if the differences between successive units on the scale are equal (i.e., they mean the same thing).

Our major goal in this section is to consider how interval data can be described. Because some of the measures to be discussed do not involve the addition or subtraction of individual scores, they are applicable to ordinal data as well. The steps in obtaining the various descriptive measures can be studied in the context of an example.

Let us assume that the performance measure is the number of strokes needed to complete a round of golf. The first step is to decide the level of the performance measure. It is clearly not nominal because the scores have a quantitative rather than a qualitative relationship. A slight case could be made for regarding the scores as ordinal data; one could argue that the difference between successive units is not necessarily equal. For example, the difference between a 2 and a 5, on a par 4 hole, may appear to you, if you are a golfer, to be much greater than the difference between a 7 and a 10 on the same hole. However, since most investigators and golfers would probably conclude that a stroke counts as a stroke regardless of quality, the scores can be viewed as interval measures. (That is, we will treat data as interval if there is some doubt about whether the scores are instances of ordinal or interval measurement). Now that we have determined that the level of measurement of the performance variable is interval, the next task is to describe the scores. There are two basic sets of descriptive measures for interval data: measures of central tendency and measures of variability.

Measures of Central Tendency

We fluctuate. Our performance varies with time of day, amount of sleep, level of interest, and so on. If the task is to decide who is better at a particular activity, such as golf, one should be reluctant to base the decision on limited information. To illustrate, assume that you decide to determine whether you are a better golfer than Dana, one of your friends. You both agree to play eighteen holes of golf per day for ten consecutive days.

After playing the tenth round you adjourn to a local pub to analyze the data. The question boils down, you both believe, to assessing who has the better *average* performance. Measures of central tendency must be computed in order to describe your average performance. Since you both want to appear fair, you agree to compute three different measures of central tendency: the mode, median, and mean. The scores for the ten rounds of golf for each player are presented in Table 8-1.

The Mode. The mode is the most frequently occurring score. An examination of Table 8-1 reveals that neither player had any total more than once. Therefore it is not possible to determine a modal score for each player. To compute a modal score at least one score has to be obtained more than once. For example, if a golfer has rounds of 73, 73, 74, 75, 76, 79, 82, 88, 88, and 88, her modal score would be 88 — not a good measure of her average performance. The mode can be very misleading because only the most frequent score is used; the mode does not provide any information about the other scores. The median and the mean make greater use of the evidence available.

The Median. The median is the value that divides the distribution in half after the scores are placed in ascending or descending order. The first step, then, is to place the scores in Table 8-1 in ascending order. The order for Dana is 82, 84, 85, 86, 88, 89, 90, 91, 92, and 93. The ascending order for your rounds is 79, 80, 82, 84, 85, 86, 87, 92, 99, and 116. Because there

TABLE 8-1

The Scores for Each of Ten Rounds of Golf for Dana and You (fictitious data)

Day	You	Dana
1	80	90
2	85	84
3	87	82
4	99	85
5	116	91
6	86	89
7	82	93
8	84	92
9	92	86
10	79	88

are ten scores, the middle score is half-way between the fifth and sixth. You have a median of 85.5 and Dana has a median of 88.5. You are pleased with the median scores as they indicate that, on the average, you are three strokes better than Dana. She argues that the median is not a satisfactory measure because it does not utilize all the available information. For example, even if your four lowest scores were reduced by 20, the median would be unaffected. The median is simply not sensitive to changes in extreme scores. In this case, Dana argues, the mean is a better measure. Note that the median score is useful with ordinal as well as interval data because it is not necessary to add or subtract scores to compute this measure.

The Mean. The mean is computed by adding all the scores and dividing by the number of scores. To compute the mean total score for the ten rounds of golf, the individual round totals are added, and then divided by the number of scores used to obtain the total (i.e., 10). Your total number of strokes for the ten rounds was 890. You divide this by 10 to obtain a mean score of 89. The symbol $\overline{X}$ (called x-bar) is used as a label for the mean. Dana has a mean of 88 (880 divided by 10). She can argue that, on the average, you are one stroke poorer. You reply that you are three strokes better if median performance is considered.

Dana insists that the mean is much better than the median because all the scores are used in making the computation. You answer that this is not necessarily a favorable characteristic. You believe that extreme scores should be discounted instead of being emphasized. The days you scored 79, 99, and 116 were very unusual days for you emotionally. You scored 99 on the day you heard your mother was coming for a visit, 116 on the day of her arrival, and 79 on the day she left. Obviously, you argue, such extreme scores should not be used to compute typical performance. The mean is influenced unduly by extremes.

A less debatable example can be used to demonstrate the influence of extreme scores on the mean. Let us assume a woman is seeking employment with a small company and the president of the company informs her that the average annual salary for executive personnel is $60,000. She is impressed but skeptical. On further inquiry she finds that the figure represents the mean salary. The president makes $200,000 a year, and the other four executives each make $25,000 a year. The mean for the five executives is $60,000. In this case, however, the median salary of $25,000 is, from the prospective employee's point of view, a much more useful measure of central tendency, and the choice of the median measure over the mean is clear-cut.

The effort to determine the better golfer, however, is at an impasse. The two major measures of central tendency yield conflicting results, and there is no ultimate authority that you can appeal to for truth. The argument that extreme scores should not be used to determine performance can be countered by asserting that good golfers are consistent. Their scores rarely deviate much from their typical performance. A good golfer should not have a bad day just because her mother is coming to visit.

By now you should be ready to concede that the question is not soluble. The measures used to assess central tendency may not be in agreement regarding which set of scores is higher if there are extreme scores and if the scores are of about the same magnitude. The important issue, of course, is what the measures of central tendency reveal about the obtained scores, not which of the three is best. The suitability of the measures depends on the distribution of the scores. Although we enjoy making value judgments there is little to be gained by doing so for measures of central tendency. It is more important to understand the strengths and weaknesses of each.

The mode is simply the most frequently occurring score, so it usually has limited usefulness. The mean utilizes more of the available information than the median but it is not appropriate for describing ordinal data. If there are extreme scores you may prefer the median because the mean is greatly influenced by extremes.

Measures of Variability

The Range. If you want to measure the extent to which scores vary you will find that the range is the simplest measure but that it is usually inadequate. The range is the difference score obtained by subtracting the smallest score from the largest. Although the computation is very easy, the measure is usually inadequate because it is based entirely on two scores. For the golf match example, you have a range of 37 (116 minus 79) and Dana has a range of 11 (93 minus 82). If there are only a few extreme scores, the range may give an unsatisfactory description of the variability of the scores. The variance is far more precise because all the scores are used in its computation.

Variance. The concept of variance is extremely important. You will remember that we can analyze variance (i.e., compare between- and within-group estimates of population variance) to assess treatment effects. In later chapters we will see that by analyzing variance we can also explain individual differences in behavior. Before we can analyze variance, we need to have a firm understanding of how variance is computed. Let us review and expand our discussion of the computation of variance as we presented it in Chapter 4.

In measuring the extent to which scores vary it is convenient to have a reference point, the mean. It is then possible to find the difference between each score and the mean and to add up the difference scores. That is, one can determine how much, if any, each score *deviates* from the mean by subtracting the score from the mean or the mean from the score. If this is done for each score and these deviations from the mean are added, the sum will be equal to zero.

The sum of the deviations from the mean is not a suitable measure of variability because it will always be zero; the sum of the positive deviations is always equal to the sum of the negative deviations. The problem could be solved by ignoring the minus sign and adding all the deviations regardless of sign. Although this procedure would yield a measure of variability, there are statistical and practical reasons for using, instead, a measure obtained by squaring each deviation from the mean.

The variance of a population is the sum of the squared deviations from the mean divided by the number of scores. In computing the variance for a sample of less than thirty scores from a population, the sum of the squared deviations is divided by the number of scores minus one. The reason for subtracting one is to obtain a more accurate estimate of population variance. Over the long haul, the sum of the squared deviations divided by the number of scores minus one provides a better estimate than the sum of the squared deviations divided by the total number of scores. If there are more than thirty scores, however, the variance is not influenced very much by which divisor is used.

Some investigators divide by the number of scores if their sole concern is *describing* the scores, and they divide by the number of scores minus one if their concern is *estimating* population variance. Since variance is usually computed for small samples (i.e., less than thirty scores per group or sample) and not for the entire population, many investigators always divide by the number of scores minus one. They do not bother to distinguish between a variance for description and one for estimation; the variance for estimation fulfills both functions. In this text variance will always be computed by dividing by the number of scores minus one, regardless of the size of the sample. The symbol s^2 is usually used for sample variance.

The scores from the golf match example are used to demonstrate the computation of variance. The scores for your ten rounds of golf and the variance computation are presented in Table 8-2. If you are unclear about how to use the deviation method you should study this table further. Then, take Dana's golf scores (82, 84, 85, 86, 88, 89, 90, 91, 92, and 93) and compute the variance using the deviation method. If your computation is correct you will obtain a variance of 13.33. Notice that your scores are considerably more variable than Dana's.

Using the deviation method should give you a good understanding of variance. It should be clear from the computation that the variance is nothing more than a measure of the extent to which scores differ from the mean score. However, this method of computation becomes cumbersome as the number of scores increases, particularly if the mean is not a whole number.

An example is presented in Table 8-3 to demonstrate both the deviation method and a computational method for computing the variance. The X refers to any score. The symbol $\bar{X}$ is used for the mean. The sigma (Σ) sign indicates the summing operation; the numbers denoted by the symbol following the sigma are *added*. Thus, the first term in the numerator for the computational formula is obtained by squaring each score and then summing

TABLE 8-2

The Total Scores for Each of Ten Rounds of Golf and the Computation of the Variance of These Scores. (The deviation scores are obtained by subtracting the mean from each score.)

Golf score (X)	Deviation score $(X - \bar{X})$	Squared deviation score $(X - \bar{X})^2$
79	− 10	100
80	− 9	81
82	− 7	49
84	− 5	25
85	− 4	16
86	− 3	9
87	− 2	4
92	+ 3	9
99	+ 10	100
116	+ 27	729
Sum = 890	Sum = 0	Sum = 1122

$\bar{X} = 89$ Variance = $\dfrac{\text{Sum of the squared deviation scores}}{\text{Number of scores minus 1}}$

Variance = $\dfrac{1122}{9}$ = 124.67

TABLE 8-3

An Example of the Calculation of the Variance by the Deviational and Computational Formulas

	Deviational method		Computational method
Scores	$(X - \bar{X})$	$(X - \bar{X})^2$	Scores
38	−5.25	27.56	38
55	11.75	138.06	55
62	18.75	351.56	62
25	−18.25	333.06	25
31	−12.25	150.06	31
46	2.75	7.56	46
45	1.75	3.06	45
50	6.75	45.56	50
42	−1.25	1.56	42
39	−4.25	18.06	39
41	−2.25	5.06	41
45	1.75	3.06	45
	Sum = 0	Sum = 1084.22	T = 519

$\bar{X} = 43.25$

$$\text{Variance} = \frac{\Sigma(X - \bar{X})^2}{n - 1}$$

$$= \frac{1084.22}{11}$$

$$= 98.57$$

$\Sigma X^2 = 23{,}531$

$$\text{Variance} = \frac{\Sigma X^2 - \frac{(T)^2}{n}}{n - 1}$$

$$= \frac{23{,}531 - \frac{269{,}361}{12}}{11}$$

$$= \frac{1084.25}{11}$$

$$= 98.57$$

the squared scores. It is important to note that the scores are squared *before* they are added. The T in the formula refers to the total of all the scores, and the n refers to the number of scores. The second term in the numerator for the computational formula is obtained by squaring the total and dividing by the number of scores. The denominator is simply the number of scores minus one. A comparison of the two formulas reveals that the denominators are the same and the numerators are mathematically equal. The numerator of the computational formula is simply another way to calculate the sum of the squared deviation scores. It should be clear that the calculation of variance is easier with the computational formula, particularly if a calculator is available.

Standard Deviation. The computation of the standard deviation is easy if the variance has already been computed because the standard deviation is equal to the square root of the variance. It is a more useful descriptive measure than the variance because it is in the same units as the mean, whereas the variance is in different units than the mean. The fact that the variance is essentially an average *squared* deviation from the mean makes it somewhat unsatisfactory as a descriptive measure. In considering the difference between two means it is useful to have a variability measure that is in the same units as the means. This measure can be obtained by taking the square root of the variance. The resulting standard deviation is used extensively as a measure of variability and can also be used as a unit of measurement. The symbol s is used to denote the standard deviation of a sample.

STANDARD DEVIATION AS A UNIT OF MEASUREMENT

Z-scores

The standard deviation can be used as a unit of measurement. An individual can determine how many standard deviation units she is above or below the mean by determining the difference between the mean and the obtained score and then dividing the difference by the standard deviation for the total set of scores. For example, let us assume that you obtain a score of 84 on a history midterm. The mean for the class was 74 and the standard deviation was 10. If you subtract the mean score for the history exam from your score you obtain a difference of 10. You then divide this difference by the standard deviation of 10 and obtain a quotient of 1 — you were one standard deviation unit above the mean on the history exam. The formula for computing a z-score is:

$$z = \frac{X - \overline{X}}{s}$$

where X refers to any score, $\overline{X}$ is the mean for the sample, and s is the standard deviation for the sample.

Z-scores can be used to compare scores from different distributions to determine a person's relative standing in each distribution. For example, assume that you are enrolled in a large psychology class and a large history class. As indicated in the above example, you obtain a score of 84 on the history exam. The mean is 74 and the standard deviation is 10. Your score on the psychology midterm is 69. The mean score was 60 and the standard deviation was 3. The question is whether your performance, relative to the other members of each class, was higher on the psychology or history exam. As we indicated previously, you were one standard deviation unit above the mean on the history exam, $z = +1$. Your z-score for the psychology exam is equal to $+3$ $[(69 - 60)/3 = 3]$. Even though you were ten points above the mean on the history exam and only nine points above on the psychology, your performance relative to other members of each class was far better in psychology than in history.

Z-scores and Normal Distributions

The use of the standard deviation as a unit can be clarified by considering the normal frequency distribution in Figure 8-1. The normal distribution is extremely important because many variables are distributed normally. That is, scores tend to cluster around the mean, and the probability of obtaining a particular score decreases as the difference between the score and the mean increases, as is indicated in Figure 8-1. The standard deviation unit can be used to indicate the relative position of a score, particularly if the properties of the distribution of scores are known. Let us assume that the scores on the history and psychology midterms were normally distributed.

Figure 8-1 can be used to show why a score of three standard deviations above the mean is considerably better than a score of one standard deviation above. The height of the curve indicates the relative frequency of each score. The area under the curve can be used to determine the probability of obtaining a score greater or less than a particular score. It can be readily seen that the probability of obtaining a score of three standard deviations above the mean is considerably less than the probability of obtaining a score of one standard deviation above. The first probability is represented by the dark shaded area in Figure 8-1, the second by the entire shaded area, both dark and light. A score of 69 or more on the psychology exam was obtained by only a few students, whereas a score of 84 or more on the history exam was

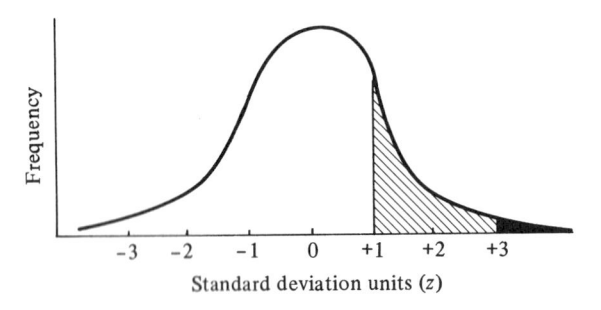

FIGURE 8-1

Areas under the curve of the standard normal distribution for a z-score of +1 or greater (entire shaded area) and a z-score of +3 (dark shaded area)

more common. In short, the scores from normal distributions can be transformed into a single distribution having a mean of zero and a standard deviation of one. This distribution is called the standard normal distribution. The transformation allows us to compare scores from normal distributions that have different means and variances.

If the distribution is normal, approximately 68% of the scores will be within one standard deviation above and below the mean, approximately 95% will be within two standard deviations, and approximately 99% will be within three standard deviations. A score that is three or more standard deviations above the mean is an unusually high score.

Z-scores and Nonnormal Distributions

You should not conclude that *all* scores (i.e., behaviors or measures of behavior) are normally distributed. Although many variables are normally distributed, other distributions are possible. Four types are presented in Figure 8-2. If the scores are distributed as in A, the distribution is said to be skewed positive. If they are distributed as in B, it is said to be skewed negative. Distributions are skewed if there are more scores on one end than the other. They are symmetrical if there are the same number of high and low scores. The direction of the skew of a nonsymmetrical distribution can be determined by examining the extreme scores or "tail" of the distribution. If the extreme scores are below the mean the distribution is said to be skewed negative; if they are above the mean it is skewed positive.

The interpretation of a score expressed in standard deviation units depends on the distribution. For example, the probability of obtaining a score that is at least two standard deviations above the mean is equal to the probability of obtaining a score that is at least two standard deviations below the mean if the distribution is symmetrical as in distributions C and D. This is not true if the distribution is skewed. There is a greater probability of obtaining a score that is at least two standard deviations above than a score that is at least two standard deviations below the mean if the scores are distributed as in A. The reverse is true if they are distributed as in B. One has to be careful when comparing scores from two distributions (e.g., the history and the psychology tests) if the distributions are not very similar.

Distributions may vary considerably in their flatness or peakedness. The flatness or peakedness of a distribution or curve is called kurtosis. A distribution or curve that is flat is platykurtic. One that is steep is leptokurtic. And one that falls between these two extremes is mesokurtic. The normal curve is mesokurtic. The curve in Figure 8-2C is platykurtic, and that in Figure 8-2D is leptokurtic.

Figure 8-2 demonstrates that the size of the standard deviation is related to the shape of the distribution. In Figure 8-2D the scores are clustered close

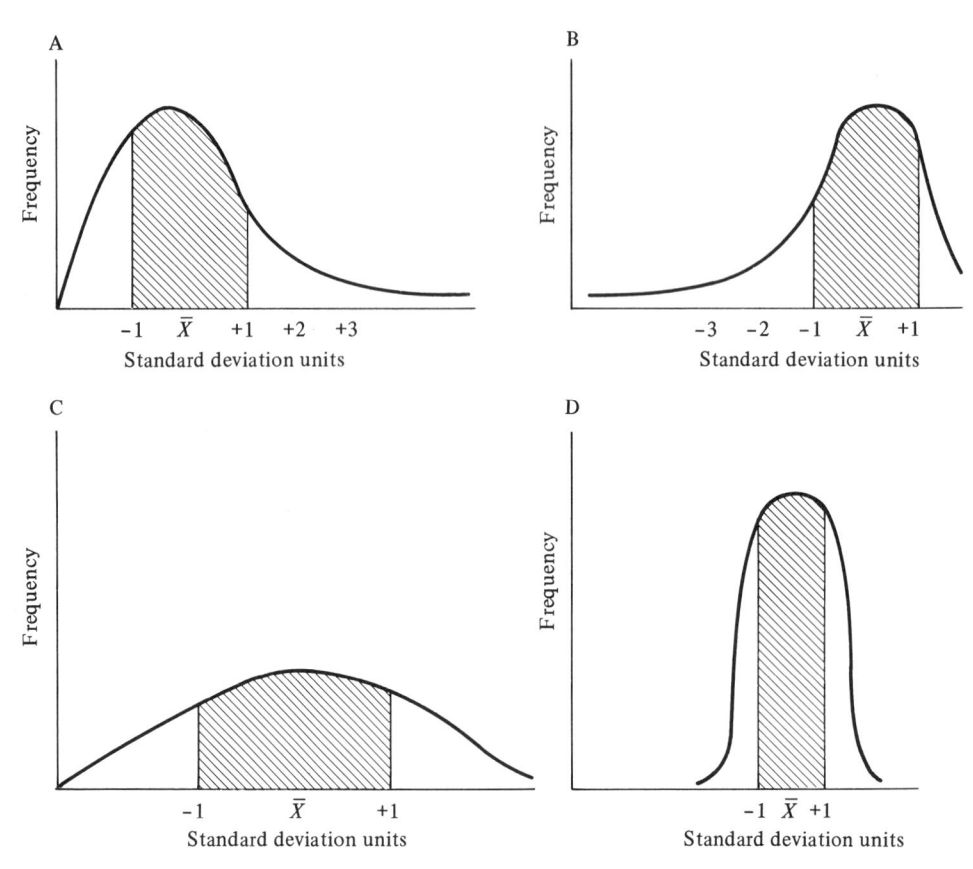

174 *Methods and Procedures for Describing Results*

FIGURE 8-2

The above four distributions differ markedly from the normal distribution in Figure 8-1. Distribution A is skewed positive, and Distribution B is skewed negative. Distribution C is platykurtic, and Distribution D is leptokurtic. The shaded area of each curve indicates the portion of the curve within one standard deviation above or below the mean.

to the mean so the size of the standard deviation is small. In Figure 8-2C the scores do not cluster tightly around the mean so the standard deviation is larger. This should not be any surprise, of course, because the standard deviation is a measure of the extent to which scores cluster around the mean. It is a particularly useful unit of measurement because it increases as the variability of the scores increases. As a result, when the score is expressed in standard deviation units one can get a firm motion of its relative position in a distribution and, therefore, of the probability of obtaining it if only chance is operating. For most distributions the probability of obtaining a score that is within one standard deviation of the mean is between .6 and .7. An examination of the distributions in Figure 8-2 reveals that the shaded portions of each figure include about 60% to 70% of the area below each curve. The probability of obtaining a score that is within one standard deviation of the mean (i.e., plus or minus one standard deviation) is about the same for these four distributions. (To review probability as the area under a curve, go back to Chapter 3.)

Z-scores and Other Derived Scores

Raw scores are the scores obtained on a test or performance measure. If you answer 83 out of 113 questions on a psychology final exam, your raw score is 83. The raw score, in isolation, does not convey very much information. We do not know whether this score is average or lower or higher than the other scores. Derived scores such as z-scores are useful because they provide a frame of reference. Much more information is conveyed by giving the z-score that corresponds to a raw score of 83 than by simply giving the raw score. If, for example, the z-score is +2, we know that the person's relative standing is high. Although z-scores are very useful for conveying relative standing, there are some minor inconveniences in using these derived scores. In many cases they are not useful for communication and they frequently require the use of negative numbers and decimals. Decimals are necessary because too much information would be lost if z-scores were rounded to the nearest whole number. There is considerable difference between a z-score of 2 and one of 2.49. Z-scores cannot always be used for communicating information about a person's standing because many people do not know what they are.

Some derived scores are based on z-scores. The logic behind many derived scores is that scores are *equivalent* if they are the same number of standard deviations above or below the mean in their respective distributions. (Note that we are interested in the equivalence of *scores*. Equivalence has a different meaning when used in reference to groups.) For example, scores that are 2.3 standard deviations above the mean in both distributions are equivalent. Given this definition of equivalence we can convert scores to any new distribution. We can *arbitrarily* decide what we want the mean and standard deviation for the new distribution to be.

Let us assume that we want to convert a raw score of 72 obtained from a distribution having a mean of 80 and a standard deviation of 4 to an equivalent score in a distribution that has a mean of 500 and a standard deviation of 100. Our task is to make sure that the score is the same number of standard deviations above or below the mean in both distributions. The first task is to determine the z-score for the old distribution. We use the z-score formula and insert the values for X, $\overline{X}$, and s. The result of our calculation gives us a z-score of -2.

$$z = \frac{X - \overline{X}}{s}$$

$$z = \frac{72 - 80}{4}$$

$$z = -2$$

Our score is two standard deviations below the mean. The next task is to determine what score is equivalent to this score in a new distribution having a mean of 500 and a standard deviation of 100. The answer, of course, is 300 because 300 is also two standard deviations below the mean. In short, the fact that equivalence can be defined in terms of standard deviations makes it possible to convert a distribution (set) of scores to a new distribution having a specified mean and standard deviation. Transformations of this sort are useful because they allow us to avoid the minor inconveniences associated with z-scores (i.e., communication, negative numbers, and decimals). The scores of most standardized tests (e.g., Graduate Record Examination, Army General Classification Test, Wechsler Adult Intelligence Scale) are transformed so that the scores are easy to interpret. It is, for example, easier to interpret a score (communicate relative standing) if the mean is 100 and the standard deviation is 10 than if the mean is 89 and the standard deviation is 7.

DESCRIBING THE RESULTS OF EXPERIMENTS

Now that you have been introduced to measures of central tendency and variability you have the basic tools necessary to describe the results of most experiments. Even though you have the tools it is likely that you are not quite sure how to use them; you may not know when to compute a particular measure or how to present it once it has been computed. One particularly suitable way to present the results of experiments is to use tables and figures. Once again, we will use examples to demonstrate how results can be described for different kinds of experiments, including those in which nominal, ordinal, and interval data are collected.

Nominal Data

Political party can be used as an example of a nominal classification system because party preference is a qualitative distinction. Assume that an investigator wanted to assess the effect of a campaign to persuade voters to become Democrats. She took a random sample of 200 registered voters in a small town and learned the political party preference of each. Then she initiated a campaign to persuade voters to register as Democrats. After the campaign was concluded she took another sample of 200 registered voters from the same town. The sample was random with the restriction that anyone selected in the first sample was not used in the second. Once again, the political preference of everyone selected was determined. How should the investigator describe the results?

There is no need to compute measures of central tendency or variability because each person selected contributes the same score. That is, each must indicate a preference for only one category — Democrat, Republican, or Independent. Therefore, it is easy to describe the results. All that is needed is the number of voters who selected each category. Of course, the results are calculated separately for the two samples so that the effect of the political campaign can be assessed. These results are presented in Table 8-4. Notice that the table's title gives a fairly complete explanation of the table's contents. The title should be as complete as possible so the reader does not have to "discover" what information is in the table by reading the text.

It is not necessary to present the results in the form of a table. It would have been sufficient simply to state the number of voters who selected the Democratic, Republican, and Independent parties before the political campaign (70, 70, and 60, respectively) and the number who selected each party after the campaign (90, 60, and 50). When there are only a few numbers there is no compelling reason to present them in a table. However, as the amount of data to report increases it frequently becomes necessary to use a table or figure to present the results. You will be prepared to analyze the results presented in Table 8-4 after reading Chapter 10.

Ordinal Data

Let us assume that the problem is to assess the effects of a plan to build courage. The independent variable is whether or not the subject has participated in the plan. The dependent measure is the ranking of the experimental and control subjects according to successfulness. The proponents of the plan claim that people who complete the self-esteem course have a greater

TABLE 8-4

The Number of Voters in Each Sample of 200 Who Selected Each Political Party Before and After the Political Campaign to Encourage Voters to Become Democrats (fictitious data)

Nature of the sample	Political party preference		
	Democrat	Republican	Independent
Selected before the campaign	70	70	60
Selected after the campaign	90	60	50

178 *Methods and Procedures for Describing Results*

probability of being successful than those who do not. The random-groups design is used. Thirty subjects are randomly assigned to the experimental and control conditions such that there are fifteen subjects in each. The experimental subjects receive a "Learn How to Be Courageous" course and control subjects do not. Five years after completion of the course an evaluation team that is unaware of the purpose of the experiment obtains enough information to rank the thirty subjects according to degree of success. The most successful person is given the rank of 30 and the least successful the rank of 1. How should the experimenter describe the results of this experiment?

Each subject's rank and treatment condition are given in Table 8-5. All the facts are presented in this way so that the reader can consider how best to describe the results. It is not correct to conclude that the results should be described as they are in Table 8-5. In most cases it is not necessary to present the rank for each subject. Usually, the principal concern is with whether the independent variable has an effect.

The effect of the independent variable is assessed by comparing the rankings of the experimental and control subjects. Since the level of measurement is ordinal it is not permissible to add the ranks of the subjects in each group to obtain average scores. Adding the ranks for descriptive purposes is not defensible unless there is reason to believe that the differences between successive ranks are equal. In this case there is no reason to believe that the

TABLE 8-5

The Rank of Each Subject in the Experimental (E) and Control (C) Conditions for the "Learn to Be Courageous" Experiment. (The rank of 1 indicates the least successful subject; the rank of 30 indicates the most successful subject—fictitious data.)

Subject	Condition	Rank	Subject	Condition	Rank
F. T.	C	1	K. S.	C	16
D. J.	C	2	D. A.	E	17
W. L.	C	3	W. H.	E	18
T. J.	C	4	A. M.	C	19
D. B.	C	5	R. M.	E	20
R. T.	C	6	R. W.	C	21
T. A.	C	7	G. V.	E	22
D. A.	E	8	M. K.	C	23
C. N.	C	9	L. W.	E	24
S. S.	E	10	J. S.	E	25
C. W.	C	11	T. S.	E	26
S. J.	C	12	C. G.	E	27
R. C.	E	13	T. B.	E	28
F. H.	C	14	H. B.	E	29
M. F.	E	15	B. C.	E	30

data are any more than ordinal. You should not conclude, however, that ranks are never added; some statistical tests with ordinal data require adding rank scores.

Probably the best way to describe the data in Table 8-5 is to indicate the number of subjects in each condition who are above the median rank. If the results are attributable to chance the number of experimental and control subjects above the median rank of 15.5 should be approximately equal. The fact that eleven of the fifteen subjects above the median are experimental subjects suggests that the independent variable had an effect. A statement of the number of experimental and control subjects above the median rank in combination with the results of an appropriate statistical test should demonstrate the effect of the independent variable. You will be able to analyze the results in Table 8-5 after reading Chapter 10.

Interval and Ratio Data

The task of describing the results of experiments in which interval or ratio data are obtained is more involved than with a lower level of measurement because of the need to compute measures of central tendency and variability. However, such computations are not difficult. Often the problem is deciding what measures to compute and how to present them. Once more, we will use examples to indicate some of the difficulties investigators may encounter.

Driver Education Example. An investigator uses a two-group, random-groups design to assess the effect of a driver education program on subsequent driving performance. The facilities at the school are limited, so only half of the students who want to take the driver education course can be accepted. To be fair, the students are randomly selected. This set of circumstances, though unfortunate from the point of view of those not selected for the program, provides an excellent opportunity to evaluate its effectiveness.

The independent variable is whether or not the student has received the driver education program. There are fifty students in each condition. Those not selected for the program learn to drive by other methods such as self-instruction, or instruction by a parent or sibling. The dependent measure is the number of arrests for driving violations in the ten-year period after learning to drive. Assume that the investigator has no difficulty learning the number of arrests for each subject. How should the results be described?

The score for each subject is, of course, the number of arrests in the ten-year period. The effect of the independent variable is assessed by comparing the average performance of the two groups. In most experiments in which interval data are obtained, the mean will be selected as the best measure of central tendency. However, if the distribution is markedly skewed, the median is likely to be a better indicator because the mean is influenced greatly by extreme scores. In this case, let us assume that the distribution of scores in each group is fairly symmetrical. Thus, the first task is to obtain the mean number of arrests for the two groups. Assume that the mean was 2.13 arrests for the driver education group and 3.07 for the control group. Is this all the information needed to describe the results of the experiment?

It is necessary to know the mean performance of the two groups, but this information is not sufficient to assess whether the independent variable had an effect. It is not clear whether the obtained result is a common or rare outcome if only chance is operating. Therefore, an appropriate statistical test must be performed to determine whether the null hypothesis can be rejected. The important point is that the results of many experiments in which interval data are obtained can be adequately described by presenting the mean for each treatment condition and the results of an appropriate statistical test.

It is also a good idea to present a measure of variability, usually the standard deviation, for each condition. By comparing the standard deviations one can determine whether the treatments influenced the fluctuations within conditions, make predictions about the effect of treatments on variability as well as on mean performance, and estimate chance fluctuation. Statistical tests can be used to assess whether the conditions differ significantly, but many investigators prefer to present a measure of the variability within each condition as well. There is no set rule about presenting measures of variability. Some readers prefer to see a measure of variability for each condition. Others are satisfied with a measure of central tendency (usually a mean) and the results of statistical tests. It is a good idea to present measures of variability whenever convenient, since some readers will appreciate having this information.

Factorial Design Example. Assume that a 2 by 2 factorial design is used to assess the effects of two independent variables. There are two levels of each independent variable, so there are four different treatment conditions. One independent variable is a subject variable (male versus female). The second independent variable is a nonsubject variable, the type of task (verbal versus nonverbal). The dependent measure is the score of each subject on a thirty-item test. Once again, the mean performance of each group is the most useful measure of central tendency. The task is to decide the best way to report the results.

In this case the results could be presented in the text, in a table, or in a figure because there are only a few measures to report. When there are many measures to present we may have to use either a figure or a table, depending on the experiment. If we are in doubt we should prepare the results both ways and then ask a few colleagues which presentation is clearer. The results of our example are presented in Table 8-6. Notice that the use of a table allows us to present the standard deviations for each condition as well as for the mean performance. Tables are generally to be preferred over figures if the standard deviations are of particular interest (i.e., if they differ markedly as a function of the condition).

The nature of the independent variable will usually determine the type of figure used. If it is qualitative we should use a bar graph; if quantitative, a line

TABLE 8-6

The Mean Number of Correct Responses and the Standard Deviations for the Four Conditions of a Hypothetical Experiment

Sex	Statistic	Type of Task	
		Verbal	Nonverbal
Male	$\bar{X}$	17.00	21.00
	s	2.33	2.05
Female	$\bar{X}$	21.00	17.00
	s	1.95	2.40

graph. In this example the levels of each independent variable differ qualitatively, so a bar graph is appropriate (Figure 8-3). As usual, the magnitude of the dependent measure is indicated on the ordinate or vertical axis. The independent variable is presented on the abscissa (horizontal axis) or in the

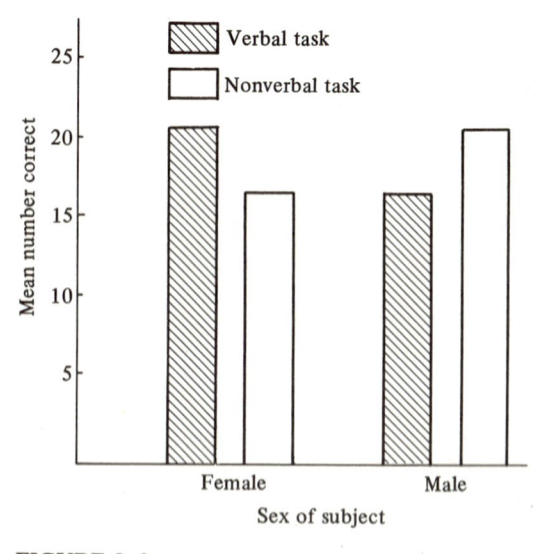

FIGURE 8-3

The mean number of correct responses on a thirty-item verbal task and a thirty-item nonverbal task as a function of sex (fictitious data)

182 Methods and Procedures for Describing Results

body of the figure by using different kinds of lines, by labeling the lines differently, or, as here, by shading the bars differently. Figure 8-3 indicates that there is probably a significant interaction between the type of task variable and the sex variable. Males do better on the nonverbal task, females on the verbal. A statistical test is needed to determine whether the interaction is significant. You will be able to perform this test after studying the material in Chapter 11.

When the independent variable is a quantitative manipulation a line graph should be used. Assume that the two independent variables are motivational level and task difficulty. In this case, the results of the hypothetical experiment could be presented as in Figure 8-4.

Instructional Method Example. Assume that an investigator was interested in the effect of instructional method (A, B, or C) on course performance. She divided the course into six segments and gave a forty-item test at the conclusion of each segment; the six tests were equally difficult. She used the random-groups design, with ten subjects in each condition. The number of items each subject answered correctly on each of the six tests is presented in Table 8-7. Our task is to consider how these results can best be presented. We are concerned with whether the method manipulation had an effect, whether performance changed over course segments, and whether performance over course segments is related to the type of instructional method. Can we assess these effects simply by examining the raw scores?

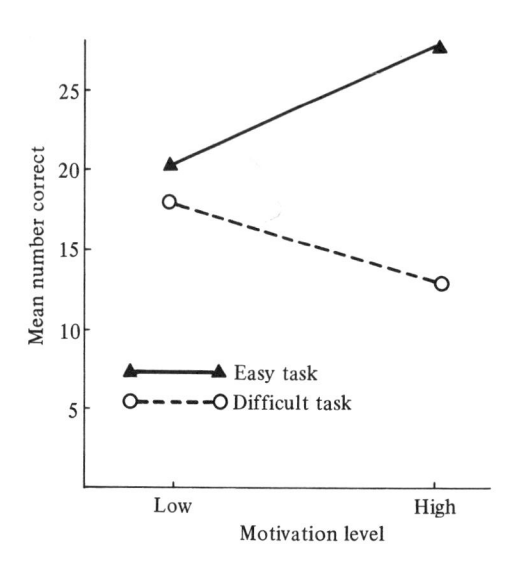

FIGURE 8-4

The mean number of correct responses on a thirty-item easy task and a thirty-item difficult task as a function of the motivational level of the subject (fictitious data)

TABLE 8-7

The Raw Scores, Totals, Means, and Standard Deviations for the Six Segments of of the Course for Each of the Three Instruction Conditions (fictitious data)

Method	Statistics and subject number	1	2	3	4	5	6
A	1	25	21	24	26	24	26
	2	26	24	22	29	23	20
	3	23	25	24	25	23	24
	4	28	24	26	28	20	21
	5	26	27	29	24	25	26
	6	17	14	21	20	22	20
	7	16	23	21	22	20	19
	8	14	22	18	21	23	25
	9	30	26	27	24	20	22
	10	30	29	24	29	20	22
	Total	235	235	236	248	220	225
	$\bar{X}$	23.5	23.5	23.6	24.8	22.0	22.5
	s	5.85	4.09	3.24	3.22	1.89	2.59
B	11	26	20	19	14	13	15
	12	29	26	22	20	17	15
	13	33	25	21	22	19	20
	14	21	22	16	14	13	14
	15	32	26	19	16	17	14
	16	17	19	14	15	14	13
	17	26	20	16	17	22	19
	18	24	22	22	17	14	15
	19	23	21	18	18	16	17
	20	27	17	23	19	13	9
	Total	258	218	190	172	158	151
	$\bar{X}$	25.8	21.8	19.0	17.2	15.8	15.1
	s	4.87	3.08	3.02	2.62	3.01	3.11
C	21	18	19	16	16	19	28
	22	14	16	17	17	22	26
	23	13	11	13	15	24	26
	24	16	18	14	13	23	27
	25	12	10	12	14	19	28
	26	12	14	16	18	16	22
	27	19	17	14	16	18	21
	28	12	13	14	15	17	17
	29	9	11	10	14	22	28
	30	12	9	16	19	25	29
	Total	137	138	142	157	205	252
	$\bar{X}$	13.7	13.8	14.2	15.7	20.5	25.2
	s	3.09	3.55	2.15	1.89	3.11	3.91

184 *Methods and Procedures for Describing Results*

An examination of Table 8-7 should reveal that it is extremely difficult, if not impossible, to understand what happened in the experiment by considering only the raw scores. We cannot process this much material at one time; there are simply too many raw scores. Therefore we want to select some of this data to describe the results of the experiment. What data should we present and how should we present it?

There should be little doubt that we need to compute measures of central tendency — in this case means — and variability. The measures that we compute are dictated by the questions we want to answer. Since we are interested in both the method manipulation and performance changes over the six segments we need to compute the mean and standard deviation separately for each method in each segment. The results of these computations are presented in Table 8-7. An examination of the means reveals that there were some interesting changes in performance over the six segments in the different conditions. That is, subjects taught by Method A performed at about the same level for all six segments; subjects receiving Method B got worse as the course progressed; and subjects receiving Method C got better as the course progressed. When a task involves a number of stages or trials and we are interested in performance at the various stages, we can show the changes best by a figure. Our results are presented in Figure 8-5. Notice that the six segments of the course are plotted on the abscissa. If, as in this case, each subject obtains more than one score on the dependent variable, the variable on which the repeated measures are obtained is plotted on the abscissa. It is necessary to present the results for each of the six segments because the interesting changes in performance over the six segments would not have been described if the investigator had decided to present an overall measure of average performance for each of the three conditions. There is, of course, no need to present the raw scores given in Table 8-7. The investigator used these raw scores to compute the means that are presented in Figure 8-5.

Autistic Boy Example. For the last example, assume that you are an undetected observer in a school for the mentally retarded. The experiment that takes place will be "natural" in the sense that only the alert, undetected observer will realize that an experiment is being conducted. The data are collected by observing the behavior of a young autistic boy and of the ward attendant from 2:00 to 3:00 P.M., Monday through Friday, for nine weeks. The independent variable is the attention the ward attendant gives the boy whenever the boy engages in self-destructive acts. The dependent measure is the number of self-destructive acts committed by the boy in each one-hour observation period. The question of interest is whether the behavior of the ward attendant is at least partially responsible for the child's self-destructive acts.

During the reinforcement sessions in the first three-week observation period (see Figure 8-6) the ward attendant responds only after the boy commits

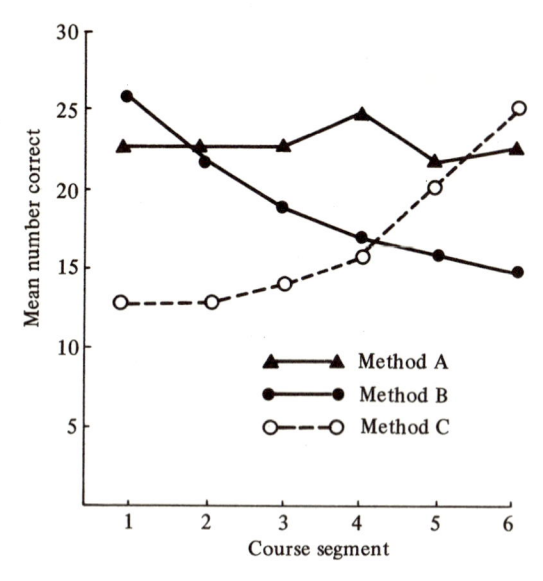

FIGURE 8-5

The mean performance on the test items for the six segments of the course for each of the three methods of instruction (fictitious data)

some self-destructive act. The reason for this selective attention is easily understood. The ward is overcrowded and understaffed, so the attendant has to move from one crisis to another. Because there are many children seeking her attention, only those who are most in need receive it. In short, the situation is such that one effective way for the boy to receive attention is to do something unusual. In this case the unusual behavior is a self-destructive act.

For the second three-week period (Extinction Sessions) the ward attendant changes strategy. She has noticed that the level of self-destructive acts is high on the ward and believes her own responses may be partially to blame. Therefore she decides to attend only to those children who are *not* engaging in self-destructive acts. The others are to be ignored.

This procedure is followed for three weeks until an administrator happens to pass the ward when a few children are engaging in self-destructive acts. The administrator is amazed that the ward attendant is ignoring these children and, instead, is playing with the other seemingly contented children. She makes it clear that the attendant had better change her behavior, so during the last three weeks, again reinforcement sessions, the attendant responds to unusual behavior on the part of the children. How should the results of this "natural experiment" be described?

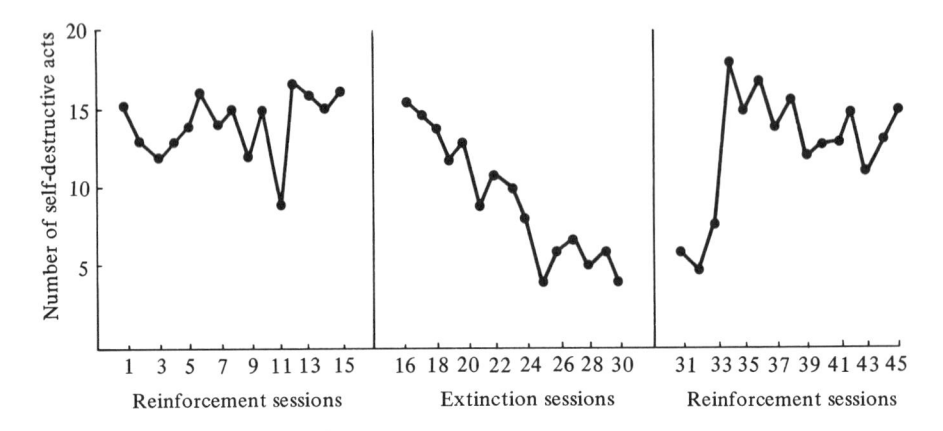

186 Methods and Procedures for Describing Results

FIGURE 8-6

The number of self-destructive acts as a function of the reaction to these acts by the ward attendant (fictitious data)

In this case there is no need to compute measures of central tendency or variability or to perform statistical tests. The only task is to report the number of self-destructive acts over the nine-week period. It is crucial to have session by session reporting as this is the only way that the effect of the manipulation can be assessed. The "natural experiment" is an instance of a within-subject design in which only one subject is tested. To evaluate the effectiveness of the independent variable one must compare the level of responding for the different treatment conditions.

If the level of responding is fairly stable from session to session within a treatment period and changes when a new treatment is introduced, then there is reason to believe that the treatment is responsible for the behavioral change. An examination of the results for the forty-five sessions should enable us to determine whether the treatment manipulation had any effect. These results are presented in Figure 8-6. Notice that the sessions are plotted on the abscissa, the number of destructive acts per session on the ordinate. The results suggest that the manipulation had an effect.

EVALUATING RESULTS

Evaluation cannot be clearly separated from description. One can argue that the evaluation of a particular result is one step in the description process. That is, determining whether a particular outcome is a rare or common event if chance only is operating can be considered a descriptive task. However, some readers will prefer to distinguish between the procedures involved in obtaining descriptive measures, which are discussed in this chapter, and the statistical tests involved in deciding to reject or not reject the null hypothesis. Bear in mind, however, that it may not be necessary to use statistical tests to evaluate a particular outcome. The distinction between describing and evaluating results is not always clear.

SUMMARY

There are four levels of measurement: nominal, ordinal, interval, and ratio. A nominal classification system is one in which the categories are qualitatively related. An ordinal scale is one in which the scale values are quantitatively related, but the differences between successive values are not necessarily equal. An interval scale has the properties of an ordinal scale *and* equal differences between successive scale values. A ratio scale has all the properties of an interval scale plus an absolute zero. The level of measurement determines how data can be described and evaluated.

There are two major sets of descriptive measures: measures of central tendency and measures of variability. The mode, median, and mean are measures of central tendency. The mode is the most frequently occurring score. The median is the value that divides the distribution in half after the scores are placed in ascending or descending rank order. The mean is the arithmetic average. For most investigators the mean is the most useful and the mode the least useful measure of central tendency. The range, variance, and standard deviation are measures of variability. The range is the difference between the smallest and largest score. The variance is the average squared deviation from the mean. The standard deviation is the square root of the variance. Standard deviations are useful as units of measurement.

The type of descriptive measure that is computed and the way the data are reported depend on the level of measurement. If nominal data are obtained, the results can be described by indicating the number of subjects assigned to each category. If ordinal data are obtained, the results can frequently be described by indicating the number of experimental subjects above the median rank plus the results of an appropriate statistical test. If interval data are obtained, it is usually necessary to compute mean scores for each treatment. The mean scores can be reported in the text, in tables, or in figures. The use of tables and figures is warranted if there are a large number of means to report or if a table or figure would provide a clearer picture of the results. If a figure is used, the nature of the independent variable is an important consideration. Bar graphs are used for qualitative manipulations and line graphs for quantitative manipulations. Tables are particularly useful when there are many means *and* measures of variability (e.g., standard deviations) to report. Investigators who prefer to present measures of variability usually use tables instead of figures because tables allow them to present measures of variability more easily.

188   Methods and Procedures for Describing Results

QUESTIONS

1. What level of measurement is obtained in each of these examples? Why?
   a. Three hundred subjects are asked to give their political party preference: Republican, Democratic, or Independent.
   b. The thirty members of a class are ranked according to height. The shortest person is assigned the number 1; the second shortest, the number 2, and so on.
   c. A thirty-item questionnaire designed to measure altruism is administered to 100 people. A score from 1 to 30 is obtained for each person.
   d. The independent variable is whether subjects use the new "hair grower" scalp treatment. The dependent variable is the number of hairs in a square-inch patch on the top of each subject's head.
   e. A free association test is administered. The amount of time each person takes to respond to each word is the performance measure. An average responding time is computed for each subject.
   f. Three judges rate twenty subjects on cooperation. Each judge rates each subject on a nine point scale from 1 (very uncooperative) to 9 (very cooperative). The median of the three judgments is used as the score for each subject.
2. Each of ten subjects was given a twenty-item current events test. The number of correct responses for each subject is given below. What are the mode, median, and mean scores? The scores are: 8, 13, 16, 14, 12, 13, 19, 6, 10, and 9.
3. What are the mode, median, and mean if the following scores are obtained: 14, 16, 16, 14, 16, 14, 14, 16, 14, 16?
4. What are the mode, median, and mean if the following scores are obtained: 18, 19, 3, 4, 8, 15, 2, 3, 3, 5? Is one measure of central tendency preferred over the others?
5. In Figure 8-2A would you expect the mean to be less than, equal to, or greater than the median? What would be the relationship between the mean and median for Figure 8-2B? Figure 8-2C?
6. Assume that you have the money and the inclination to sponsor a young golfer on the professional tour. Golfer A has a mean score of 72 and a standard deviation of four for 100 rounds. Golfer B has a mean score of 71.5 and a standard deviation of two for the same 100 rounds. Which golfer would you sponsor and why? (There is no right or wrong answer to this question.)
7. Compute the range, variance, and standard deviation for each set of scores given in Questions 2, 3, and 4.
8. What is the advantage of using the standard deviation as a unit of measurement?
9. Jane has taken two tests of self-esteem. On the first test she had a score of 25. The mean for the first test was 20 and the standard deviation was four. On the second test she scored 78. The mean for the second test was 70 and the standard deviation was nine. Which test indicates that Jane has higher self-esteem? Assume that the scores on both tests are normally distributed.

10. The results tabulated below were obtained in a learning experiment. Each subject was presented a list of fifteen common nouns and was asked to recall as many as possible. Five subjects were given a mnemonic system and five were left to their own devices. Describe the results. Compute the mean performance of each group for each trial and plot the results in a figure.

	Mnemonic group				Control group		
Subject number	Trial 1	Trial 2	Trial 3	Subject number	Trial 1	Trial 2	Trial 3
1	10	12	15	1	6	8	10
2	12	15	15	2	9	10	13
3	9	9	13	3	4	9	13
4	15	15	15	4	7	10	15
5	13	14	15	5	8	10	12

correlation 9

In Chapter 2 we learned that the correlational approach makes it possible to specify the degree of relationship between variables, to predict performance, and to test rival hypotheses about the relationships among variables. Now it is time to consider correlation in greater detail. We will look primarily at the steps in computing three correlation coefficients: the phi coefficient, and the rank-order and product-moment correlations. Scattergrams are used in the second section where we discuss possible relationships between variables and the role of correlational techniques in studying these relationships. The final section is devoted primarily to a variance view of correlation in which the product-moment correlation is emphasized.

COMPUTING CORRELATION COEFFICIENTS

The procedures that can be used to assess the degree of relationship between variables depend on the level of measurement for each variable. The phi coefficient can be computed if both variables are nominal. The rank-order correlation is appropriate if both variables are ordinal. The Pearson product-moment is appropriate if interval or ratio data are obtained.

Nominal Data and the Phi Coefficient

The phi (ϕ) coefficient is useful for assessing the degree of relationship between two variables when each variable is at the nominal level of measurement and dichotomous (i.e., there are only two levels of each variable). For example, we can evaluate the relationship between personality and sex by classifying individuals into two personality categories (introvert or extravert) and two categories of sex (male or female). Let us assume that we administered a personality test to 300 introductory psychology students and found 50 students who could be classified as introverted and 70 students who could be classified as extraverted. After determining the sex of each student we placed each student in *one* of the four possible categories obtained by considering both sex and personality (see Table 9-1). The next step is to compute the phi coefficient for the results presented in Table 9-1.

The formula for the phi coefficient is

$$\phi = \frac{(bc - ad)}{\sqrt{(j)(k)(l)(m)}}$$

where a, b, c, and d refer to the frequencies in the four cells of the 2 by 2 contingency table. In this case, $a = 20$, $b = 45$, $c = 30$, and $d = 25$. The letters j and k refer to the two row totals, and the letters l and m refer to the two column totals. In this case, $j = 65$, $k = 55$, $l = 50$, and $m = 70$. If we insert these values in the formula for the phi coefficient we obtain the following result:

$$\phi = \frac{(45)(30) - (20)(25)}{\sqrt{(65)(55)(50)(70)}}$$

$$\phi = \frac{1350 - 500}{\sqrt{12,512,500}}$$

$$\phi = \frac{850}{3537}$$

$$\phi = .24.$$

There is a low positive relationship between sex and personality. Females are more likely to be extraverted than introverted, and males are more likely to be introverted than extraverted. (Remember that these data are fictitious.) Yet the relationship is not strong because the correlation is only .24. The phi coefficient value and the other correlation coefficients to be considered shortly can assume any value from −1.00 to +1.00. Now let us assume that we have performed another experiment and obtained the results shown in Table 9-2. A comparison of the results presented in the two tables reveals that the degree of relationship between the two variables is considerably higher in Table 9-2. If all the females are extraverted and all the males are introverted, the relationship between this personality measure and sex is as high as it can be. We can predict personality accurately if we know the sex of the individual; if we know the personality of the individual we can accurately predict the sex. The accuracy of prediction is related to the degree of relationship. We are not able to accurately predict personality from sex if the correlation is .24, as is the case for the results presented in Table 9-1. Given the results in Table 9-1

192   *Correlation*

TABLE 9-1

The Number of Students in Each of the Four Classifications Determined by Personality and Sex (fictitious data)

Sex	Personality		Row total
	Introverted	Extraverted	
Female	a 20	b 45	j = 65
Male	c 30	d 25	k = 55
Column total	l = 50	m = 70	

we are more likely to be correct if we predict that a male is introverted than if we predict that he is extraverted, but we are likely to be wrong some of the time.

The value of the phi coefficient for the results presented in Table 9-2 is 1.00. The value for the phi coefficient would be −1.00 if either the rows (which present the data for males in the *a* and *b* categories) or the columns (which give the data for extraverts in categories *a* and *c*) were interchanged. The sign of the phi coefficient (plus or minus) does not have any meaning when nominal categories are used; it depends on how we arrange the 2 by 2 contingency table.

TABLE 9-2

The Number of Students in Each of the Four Classifications Determined by Personality and Sex (fictitious data)

Sex	Personality		Row total
	Introverted	Extraverted	
Female	a 0	b 65	j = 65
Male	c 55	d 0	k = 55
Column total	l = 55	m = 65	

Ordinal Data and the Rank-order Correlation

Computation of the Rank-order Correlation. Assume that you and another judge, named Harry, rate twelve male adult seals on aggressiveness. The rank of 1 is assigned to the most aggressive seal and 12 to the least aggressive. Then a correlation is computed between the two sets of rankings to determine the extent of agreement. Since rank data are obtained, a rank-order correlation can be computed. The two sets of rankings are presented in Table 9-3. There are no tied scores in this table. If two subjects had been ranked the same the two ranks in question would have been summed (e.g.,

TABLE 9-3

The Two Sets of Rankings for the Twelve Adult Male Seals and the Computation of the Rank-order Correlation. (The symbol d is used to indicate the difference between the rankings for each seal.)

Seals	Your ranking	Harry's ranking	d	d²
Killer	1	2	−1	1
Clyde	2	3	−1	1
Harry	3	1	2	4
Pete	4	4	0	0
Popeye	5	5	0	0
Fred	6	7	−1	1
George	7	6	1	1
Jack	8	9	−1	1
Adam	9	8	1	1
Sleepy	10	10	0	0
Milktoast	11	11	0	0
Fearful	12	12	0	0

Sum of $d^2 = 10$

$N = 12$

$$r_s = 1 - \frac{6(\Sigma d^2)}{N(N^2 - 1)}$$

$$r_s = 1 - \frac{6(10)}{12(144 - 1)}$$

$$r_s = 1 - \frac{60}{1716}$$

$$r_s = 1 - .035$$

$$r_s = .965$$

3 + 4 = 7) and both subjects given the mean of the tied ranks (e.g., 3.5). (If there were a large number of tied scores on a particular measure, the formula given below would not be appropriate.) The formula for computing the rank-order correlation is:

$$r_s = 1 - \frac{6(\Sigma d^2)}{N(N^2 - 1)}.$$

In this formula r_s is used to designate the rank-order correlation. The sigma (Σ) is a symbol for the summing operation. The symbol d refers to the difference between the ranks for each subject. In this case d^2 follows the summation sign so the squared difference scores are added. The N refers to the number of pairs of scores, in this case 12. The 1 and 6 are always used in this formula so they are called constants. Investigators use the symbol r_s for the rank-order correlation when it is computed for a sample and the Greek letter rho (ρ) when it is computed for the population.

Magnitude of the Rank-order Correlation. The magnitude of the rank-order correlation indicates the degree of relationship between two variables. It is free to fluctuate between -1.00 and $+1.00$. Notice that if the two sets of rankings were identical all the difference scores would be zero and, of course, the sum of the squared differences would also be zero. Since six multiplied by zero is zero, the numerator would be zero. And since zero divided by any number is zero, the second term of the equation would be zero. Thus the value of r_s when the two sets of ranks are identical is equal to $+1.00$.

Assume that your rankings are as presented in Table 9-3, but that Harry gives Killer a rank of 12, Clyde a rank of 11, and so on down the list. In this case the sum of the squared difference scores is as large as it can possibly be. If you do not believe this, arrange the rankings in any way you choose to produce a larger squared difference score. When you have a set of rankings as in the present example, only the sum of the squared difference scores is free to vary. You should experiment with different sets of rankings, computing the sum of the squared difference scores until you are convinced that r_s tends to be close to $+1.00$ when subjects with a high rank on one measure have a high rank on the other, middle ranks go with middle ranks, and low ranks with low, and that r_s tends to be close to -1.00 when subjects with a high rank on one measure have a low rank on the other, and middle ranks go with middle. The rank-order correlation tends to be about zero when individuals with a high rank on one measure may have a high, middle, or low rank on the other measure. In short, r_s varies from -1.00 to $+1.00$ depending on the degree and type of relationship between the two variables.

Interval Data and the Product-moment Correlation

In general, the comments made about the rank-order correlation are appropriate for the product-moment correlation except that the rank-order is used for ordinal data and the product-moment for interval data. To demonstrate the steps involved in computing the product-moment correlation we will use as our example the correlation between the intelligence of children adopted within the first three months of life and the intelligence of their genetic parents. The IQs of the adopted children were determined after they had attained adulthood. The IQ scores and the computation of the Pearson product-moment correlation are presented in Table 9-4. Computation of the correlation is easy if a calculator is used.

Computation of the Product-moment Correlation. The formula and computations in Table 9-4 require some explanation. The X refers to the mean intelligence score of each pair of genetic parents, the Y to the IQ score of each adopted child, and the large N to the number of families considered (pairs of scores). The sigma indicates that the summing operation is per-

TABLE 9-4

Average IQs of the Two Genetic Parents and the Adopted Child's IQ and the Product-moment Correlation for These Measures (fictitious data)

Family	Parents (X)	Child (Y)	XY
A	102	105	10,710
B	112	109	12,208
C	89	110	9,790
D	102	120	12,240
E	75	80	6,000
F	130	132	17,160
G	83	100	8,300
H	112	120	13,440
I	87	86	7,482
J	99	135	13,365
K	102	110	11,220
L	120	94	11,280
M	74	91	6,734
N	115	116	13,340

$\Sigma X = 1402 \quad \Sigma Y = 1508 \quad \Sigma XY = 153{,}269$
$\Sigma X^2 = 144{,}106 \quad \Sigma Y^2 = 165{,}924$

$$r = \frac{N\Sigma XY - (\Sigma X)(\Sigma Y)}{\sqrt{[N\Sigma X^2 - (\Sigma X)^2][N\Sigma Y^2 - (\Sigma Y)^2]}}$$

$$r = \frac{14(153{,}269) - (1402)(1508)}{\sqrt{[14(144{,}106) - (1402)^2][14(165{,}924) - (1508)^2]}}$$

$r = .63$

formed. Thus, for ΣX you would sum the X scores. For ΣX^2 you would sum the squared X scores. It is important to distinguish between the ΣX^2 and the (ΣX^2). The ΣX^2 means that each score is squared and then the *squared scores* are summed. The $(\Sigma X)^2$ means that the scores are summed and then the *total score* is squared. The same is true for ΣY^2 and $(\Sigma Y)^2$. For ΣXY you would multiply each XY pair and sum the products. This is all done for you in Table 9-4. After completing these computations it is a simple matter to insert the values into the formula and compute the correlation.

Magnitude of the Product-moment Correlation. Once again, the magnitude of the correlation depends on the pairings of scores. That is, some index is needed of the extent to which high X scores go with high Y scores. The product-moment correlation is an excellent index of this relationship. The magnitude of the correlation indicates whether the IQs of genetic parents and children are related when the children do not live with their genetic parents.

The magnitude of the correlation is unrelated to the absolute magnitudes of the intelligence scores; the correlation would be unaffected if 25 IQ points were added to the score of each child. The important factor is whether the high scores for one measure (parents with high scores) are paired with the high scores of the other measure (children with high scores). If you keep the same set of scores for the parents and the same set for the children and manipulate the pairings you will, of course, produce marked changes in the obtained product-moment correlation. These changes will, however, influence only one term in the product-moment correlation formula, namely, $N\Sigma XY$. The values for the other terms will remain the same. Thus, to demonstrate that the product-moment correlation assesses the extent to which high scores go with high scores, just manipulate the pairings and note the result. The sum of the X times Y cross-products is the largest when high scores of X are paired with high scores of Y.

SCATTERGRAMS AND CORRELATION

Nature of Scattergrams

The computation of the correlation coefficient provides a single measure of the degree of relationship between two variables, but this measure, by itself, may not provide a complete picture of the relationship between the variables. For cases in which interval data are obtained we can usually get a better understanding of the relationship between two variables if we make a scattergram *and* compute the correlation. A scattergram (sometimes called a scatterplot) is a plot of the scores made by the same individuals on two different variables presented in the form of a figure. Four scattergrams are presented in Figure 9-1. The values for one variable are presented on the abscissa, the values for the second on the ordinate. Since each subject has a score for each measure, each subject's performance can be represented as a dot. The loca-

Scattergrams and Correlation

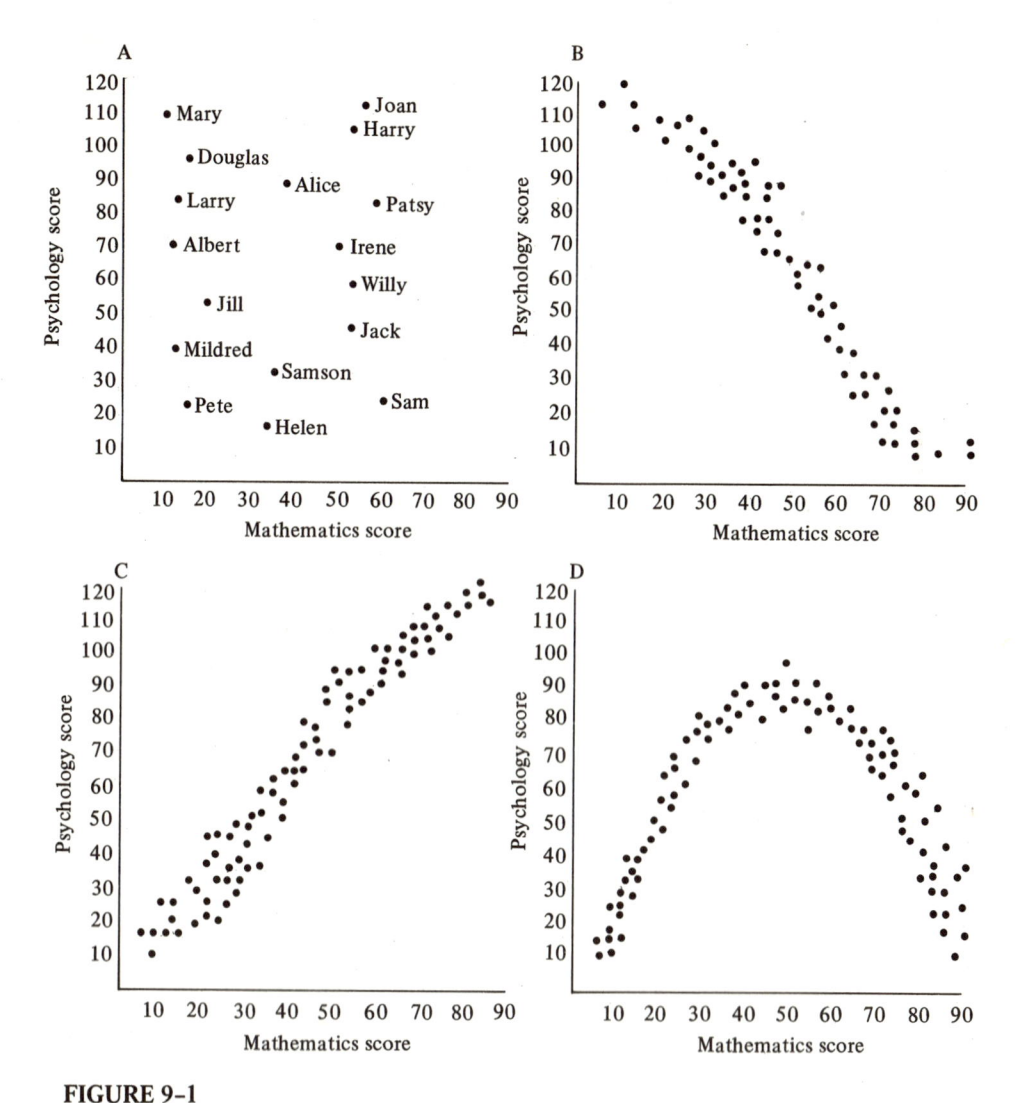

FIGURE 9-1

The scattergram for four different relationships between psychology and mathematics performance (fictitious data)

tion of the dot for each person is determined by his or her score on the two measures being considered. Figure 9-1A shows the name of the person represented by each dot. For example, Alice has a score of 40 on the mathematics test and 90 on the psychology test. Pete has a score of 18 on the mathematics test and 23 on the psychology test.

The first three scattergrams in Figure 9-1 represent a zero, a negative, and a positive correlation, respectively, between the two variables. The fourth plot represents a more complex relationship, to be discussed shortly. You may wish to examine the plot that corresponds to each of these three relationships. Remember that a high positive correlation is obtained when high scores go with high scores, low with low, and middle with middle. When high scores go with low scores and middle scores with middle, a high negative correlation is obtained. In a zero correlation, individuals with high scores on one measure may have high, medium, or low scores on the second measure.

The Relationship between Variables

The scattergrams in Figure 9-1 show linear and nonlinear relationships between the two variables. When two variables are linearly related an increase in one is accompanied by a constant increase (or a decrease if the variables have a negative relationship) in the other for the entire range of both variables. The effect of an increase in one variable on the other does not depend on the value considered. For example, if $Y = 2X$, the variables Y and X are linearly related. If X increases one unit, Y always increases two units.

When two variables have a *perfect* linear relationship all the dots of the scattergram can be connected by a single straight line. The scattergrams in Figure 9-1B and C do not depict a perfect linear relationship but they do describe a linear relationship because a single straight line could be drawn that would describe the relationship between the two variables reasonably well. Such a line could be drawn in Figure 9-1B, for example, because an increase in X (mathematics score) is, in general, accompanied by a constant decrease in Y (psychology score) for the entire range of both variables. The scattergram in Figure 9-1D, on the other hand, is not linear. A single straight line would not describe the relationship between the two variables.

Let us consider another figure in order to discuss linearity and monotonicity. Four relationships between variables X and Y are plotted in Figure 9-2. Figure 9-2A depicts a linear relationship. Linear relationships are also monotonic, but monotonic relationships are not necessarily linear. When two variables have a positive monotonic relationship an increase in one is accompanied by an increase in the other, but the increase is not necessarily the same for the entire range of both variables. For example, if $Y = X^3$, the two variables X and Y are monotonically but not linearly related. An increase in X is accompanied by an increase in Y, but each increase in X will not increase Y by the same amount. This relationship is depicted in Figure 9-2B. A relationship is nonmonotonic if an increase in one variable is sometimes accompanied by an increase and sometimes by a decrease in the other variable. For example, in Figure 9-2C and D an increase in X is sometimes accompanied by a decrease in Y and sometimes by an increase in Y.

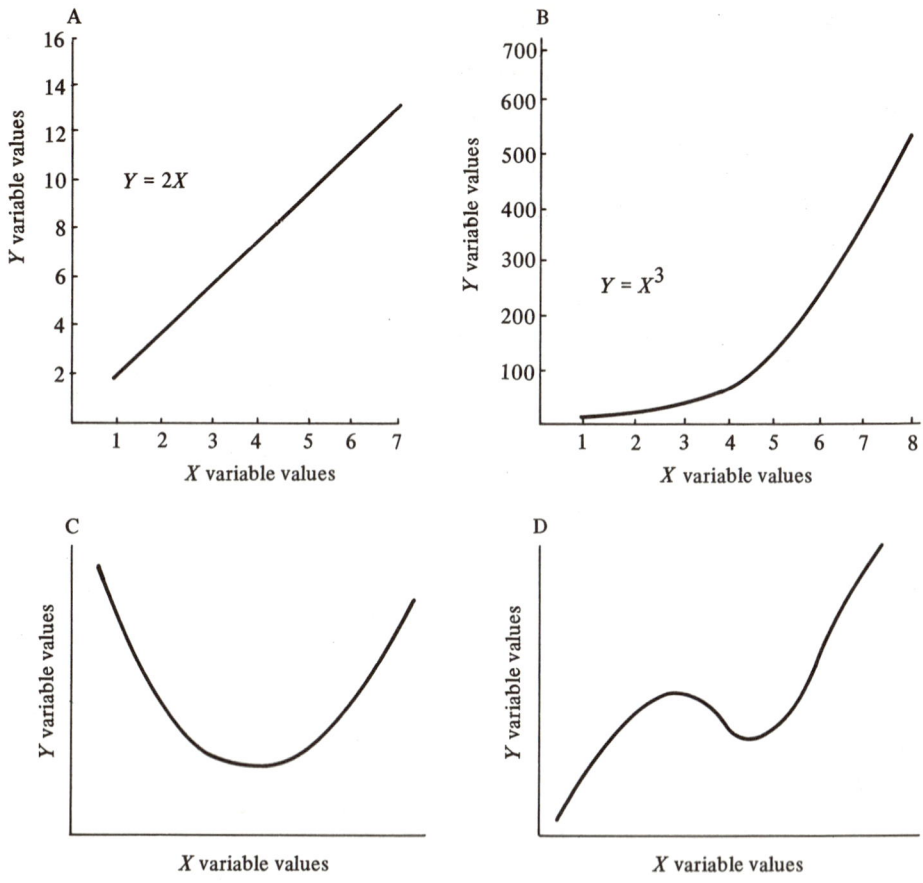

FIGURE 9-2

The relationship between variables X and Y is linear in A and nonlinear in B, C, and D. (The curves in A and B both represent monotonic relationships between variables X and Y. The curves in C and D are nonmonotonic.)

Correlation and the Relationship between Variables

The Pearson product-moment correlation is useful for assessing the degree to which two variables are linearly related. The magnitude of the correlation, when all else is equal, is related to the extent to which the dots of the scattergram cluster around a straight line. The correlation for the results depicted in Figure 9-1C is higher than for the results depicted in Figure 9-1D because we can draw a single straight line that will be close to the data points in the former case but not in the latter. Since the product-moment correlation is designed for assessing the extent to which two variables are linearly related it is usually not useful for assessing nonmonotonic or nonlinear relationships.

The Spearman rank-order correlation allows us to assess the monotonicity of two variables because we ignore the amount of increase in Y accompanying an increase in X when we rank order. For example, if we rank fifteen people on the basis of height, we do not measure the difference in height for people assigned successive ranks. The difference in height between subjects 3 and 4 may be much greater than the difference between subjects 14 and 15. Because we ignore the absolute difference (or we do not assess it in the first place) between successive ranks we cannot say whether an increase in one variable is accompanied by a *constant* increase in the other. All we assess is the extent to which an increase in one variable means an increase in the other. Thus, a high rank-order correlation can be obtained if the two variables are monotonically related, even though they are not linearly related. It follows that investigators should not claim that two variables are *linearly* related just because a high rank-order correlation is obtained. They *may* be linearly related, but some monotonic relationships are nonlinear. A scattergram is a useful way to assess whether the relationship is linear, monotonic, or nonmonotonic. None of the correlational techniques discussed allows us to assess nonmonotonic relations. A consideration of these is beyond the scope of this text; we can, however, plot the results in a scattergram to gain a pictorial representation of the relationship.

Regression

The regression line is the straight line drawn so that the sum of the squared deviations from each point to the line is a minimum. That is, we select the line that gives us the smallest sum when we add all the squared deviations from each point to the line. If the correlation is not perfect we can draw two regression lines: one to minimize the sum of the squared deviations when considering horizontal distance and one to minimize the sum of the squared deviations when considering vertical distance. We can consider whether individuals with the same score on X differ in their performance on the Y variable, or we can consider whether individuals with the same score on Y differ in their performance on the X variable. Fortunately we only need to discuss one of the regression lines because the principles to be considered are the same for both. We will consider the extent to which people with the same score on X differ in their performance on the Y variable. That is, we will consider how accurately we can predict a person's score on the Y variable if we know the person's score on X. We can always define the known score as X and the score we want to predict as Y.

The magnitude of the correlation, all else being equal, is determined by the extent to which the data points hug the regression line. If all the points fall on the regression line, the correlation is either $+1.00$ or -1.00, as in Figures 9-3A and B. When this correlation is obtained we can predict Y ac-

FIGURE 9-3

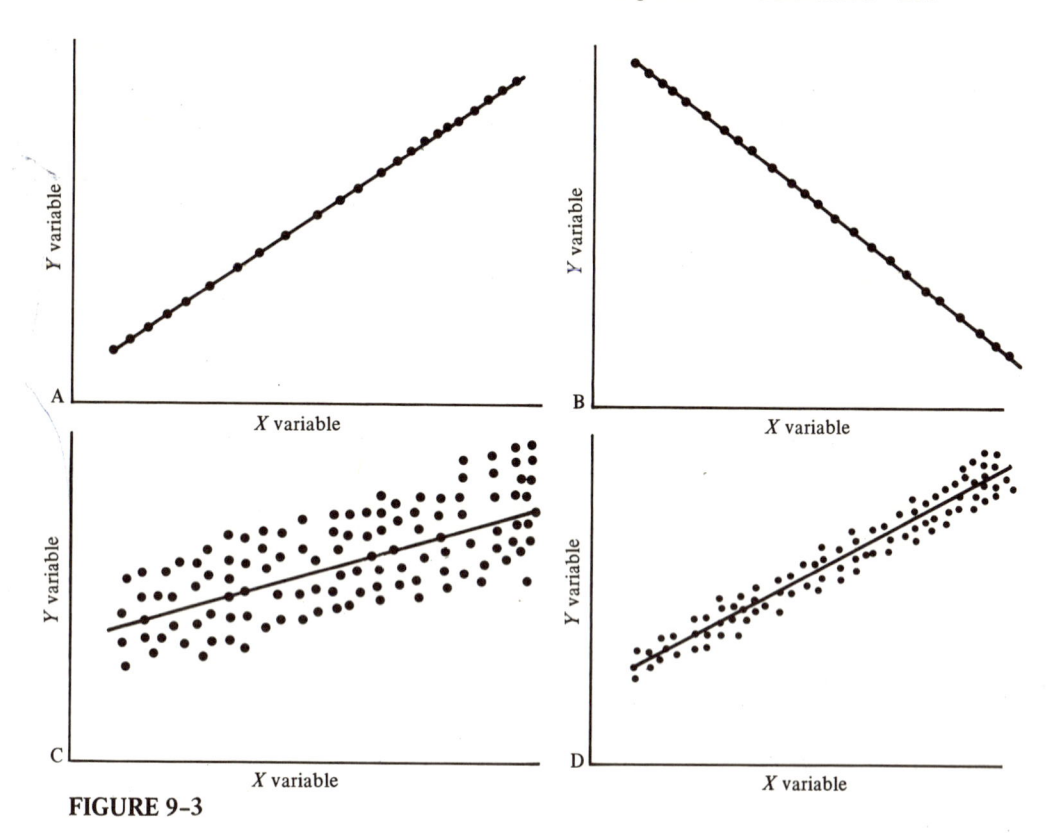

The scattergrams and regression lines for four different relationships between variables X and Y

curately if we know X. If the points do not cluster around the regression line, the correlation will be low, as in Figure 9-3C. Then, knowing X will not tell us very much about Y. We can still predict a Y score given X, but we cannot expect our prediction to be accurate. It is better to use the regression line to make the prediction than to simply predict the mean score for the Y variable (i.e., predict the mean score for Y regardless of the value of X) because X and Y are still related. That is, subjects who have high scores on X will still have higher Y scores than those who have low scores on X. A moderately high correlation is depicted in Figure 9-3D. Our predictions about Y when we know X should be more accurate for Figure 9-3D than for Figure 9-3C because the data points are closer to the regression line.

The scattergrams presented in Figure 9-3 should enable you to see that the accuracy of prediction is related to the extent to which the data points fall on the regression line. However, you should *not* conclude that scattergrams are used for making these predictions or that regression lines are determined by simply drawing the straight line that appears to minimize the sum of the squared deviations from each point to the regression line. A procedure called the method of least squares is used to determine the *equation* for the regression line, and the accuracy of prediction is quantified by calculating the standard error of estimate. We will not consider these statistical methods because the methods, though of interest to investigators who use correlation for prediction, are not essential for computing and understanding correlation. Students interested in these methods should consult standard statistics texts.

In summary, we can make scattergrams to represent pictorially the relationship between two variables. The scattergram provides information about the linearity and monotonicity of the relationship and about its magnitude. The magnitude of the correlation, when all else is equal, is directly related to the extent to which the data points hug the regression line. When all the data points are on the line the correlation is perfect (i.e., +1.00 or −1.00). Correlation can be used for prediction because we can predict performance if we know a subject's score on one variable (X-score) and the regression line for the two variables (obtained from the data of other subjects of course). The accuracy of our prediction is directly related to the magnitude of the correlation between the two variables.

UNDERSTANDING CORRELATION

Estimation

The correlation obtained with a sample (a statistic) can be used to estimate the correlation between two variables (a parameter) when the sample is randomly selected from the larger population. The accuracy of the estimate should increase, all things being equal, as the size of the sample increases. If the sample is not randomly selected, then using the sample correlation to estimate the correlation in the population is not warranted. Even when the sample is random a correlation of considerable magnitude may be due to chance; that is, it may be obtained even though the two variables are unrelated in the population.

When the two variables are unrelated, subjects with a high score on one variable may have a high, medium, or low score on the other. If, by chance, the investigator selects more individuals who have similar scores on the two variables than dissimilar scores, she may conclude, erroneously, that the two variables are related. A table to assess the statistical significance of rank-order correlations is presented in Appendix C-6, and a table to assess the statistical significance of product-moment correlations in Appendix C-7. These tables allow us to determine whether an obtained correlation can reasonably be attributed to chance. If the correlation exceeds the table value we can reject the null hypothesis that the population correlation is zero.

Variance and Correlation

In our earlier statement — the magnitude of the correlation, all else being equal, is directly related to the extent to which the data points hug a straight line — the qualifier *all else being equal* is necessary because the magnitude of the correlation is not determined solely by the closeness of scores to the regression line. It is determined by their closeness relative to the total fluctuation in Y-scores, computed by calculating the variance. When we have scores on two variables (i.e., an X-score and a Y-score) for each subject, we can split the Y variance into two components: the variance that does not depend on changes in X (variance around the regression line) and the variance that does depend on changes in X (variance of the Y' or predicted scores).

To keep the computations as simple as possible, let us assume that we have an X-score and a Y-score for each of six persons as given in Table 9-5. A scattergram and regression line are presented in Figure 9-4. The first step is to compute the variance for the Y-scores.

The Variance for Y-scores. The variance of the Y-scores is computed by the deviation method in Table 9-5. We determine the mean for the Y-scores, subtract the mean from each score, square each difference score, sum the squared scores, and divide by the number of scores minus one. Since we have both X- and Y-scores we use the symbol $\bar{Y}$ to indicate the mean for the Y-scores and Y to indicate any Y-score. We can now partition the fluctuations in Y into our two components.

Variance of Y-scores Independent of X. If fluctuations in Y are unrelated or independent of changes in X, then the value of X is not responsible for the

TABLE 9-5

The X-scores and Y-scores for Each of Six Subjects and the Computation of the Variance for the Y-scores

Subject	X-scores	Y-scores	$(Y - \bar{Y})$	$(Y - \bar{Y})^2$
A	5	2	−4	16
B	5	6	0	0
C	10	4	−2	4
D	10	8	2	4
E	15	6	0	0
F	15	10	4	16
		Sum = 36		Sum = 40
		$\bar{Y} = 6$		

$$s^2 = \frac{\Sigma(Y - \bar{Y})^2}{n - 1} = \frac{40}{5} = 8$$

FIGURE 9-4

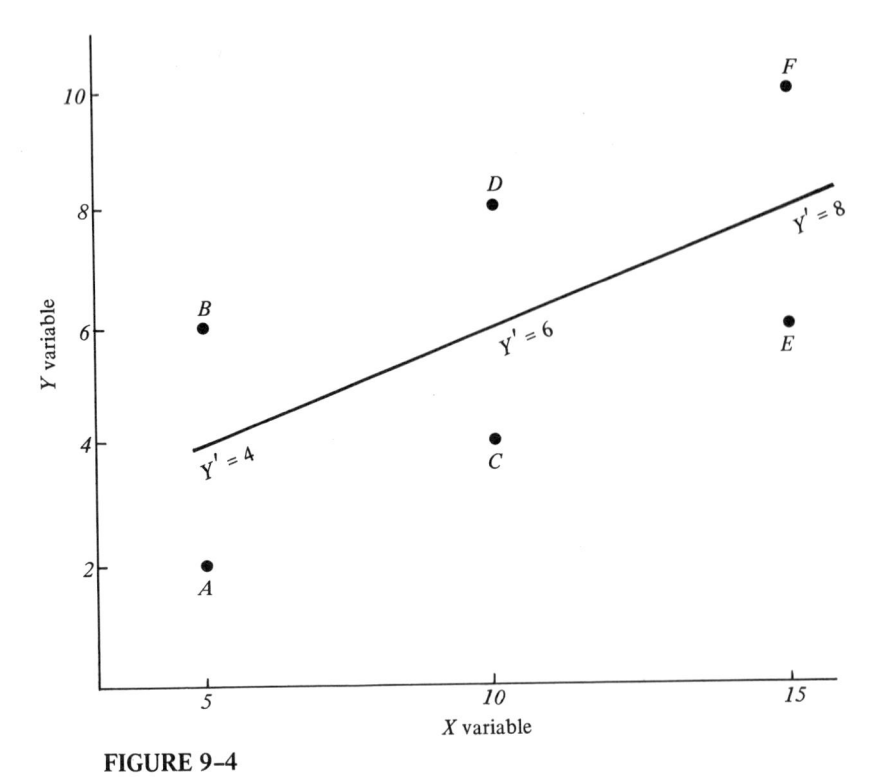

The scattergram for the hypothetical data presented in Table 9-5 and the regression line for predicting Y given X

fluctuations in Y. If two individuals have the same X-score but different Y-scores we cannot attribute the difference between the Y-scores to X because their X-scores are the same. Something besides the X-variable must be responsible for their different Y-scores. For example, subjects A and B have the same score on the X variable but different scores on the Y variable. The two tests (X and Y) are not measuring exactly the same capacities, abilities, or whatever. If they were, A and B would have the same score on Y. We can determine the amount of variance in Y that is independent of changes in X by determining the fluctuation of the Y-scores around the regression line.

The computation of the variance in Y that is independent of changes in X is presented in Table 9-6. It is basically the same as that used for the total variance in Y. The difference is that we use Y' (called Y prime) instead of the mean for Y (i.e., Y' instead of $\overline{Y}$). Y' is the Y-score you would predict when you know X. Thus, if we obtain X-scores for additional subjects and use these scores to predict Y, we should expect subjects with a score of 15 on X to have higher Y-scores than subjects with a score of 5 on X. The predicted

TABLE 9-6

The Computation of the Variance in Y-scores That Is Independent of Changes in the X-score for the Results Presented in Table 9-5

Subject	Y-score	Y'-score	(Y - Y')	(Y - Y')²
A	2	4	-2	4
B	6	4	2	4
C	4	6	-2	4
D	8	6	2	4
E	6	8	-2	4
F	10	8	2	4
				Sum = 24

$$s^2 = \frac{\Sigma(Y - Y')^2}{n - 1} = \frac{24}{5} = 4.80$$

score is the point on the regression line. Over the long haul it results in the most accurate prediction of Y-scores. To determine the fluctuation of Y-scores for subjects with the same X score, we determine the amount of fluctuation around the predicted score (regression line). The use of Y' in place of $\overline{Y}$ yields this variance. Notice that the variance in Y independent of changes in X is 4.80 (Table 9-6), less than the total variance in Y (8.00). The next step is to compute the variance in Y that is related to changes in X.

Variance of Y-scores Related to X. If we say that people get different Y-scores because they have different X-scores or that different Y-scores are related to different X-scores, we are saying that fluctuations in Y can be accounted for or "explained" in terms of X. The abilities necessary to do well on the Y test are the same as the abilities required to do well on the X test. Or the X variable might be directly responsible for the differences in the Y-scores. For example, if the X variable is the number of hours spent studying and the Y variable is performance on the final exam, we might expect that performance on the final exam would be related to the number of hours spent studying. The interesting question is how *much* of the fluctuation of Y-scores (e.g., performance on the final exam) can be accounted for by the X variable. If we want to account for individual differences in performance (e.g., fluctuations in performance on final examinations) we need to find the variables that account for the most fluctuation. An X variable that accounts for a large portion of the variance in Y-scores is, obviously, more important than an X variable that accounts for a small amount of the variance. The amount of variance accounted for is thus a "yardstick" by which we can evaluate the importance of X variables. The amount of time spent studying is more im-

206 Correlation

portant if it accounts for 50% of the variance of the final exam scores than if it only accounts for 4%.

The computation of the variance in Y-scores related to changes in X-scores for our hypothetical example is presented in Table 9-7. If the variance of Y-scores is related to changes in X we should predict different Y-scores when we know the X score. If we predict the same Y-score for all values of X it should be clear that the X variable does not account for differences in performance on the Y variable. The amount of variance in Y-scores that is related to the X variable is a function of the variance of Y' (i.e., the predicted scores). The computation of the variance of Y'-scores is a simple matter in this case. Each subject has a Y'-score because there is a Y'-score for each of the three scores for the X variable. That is, a Y'-score can be assigned to each subject on the basis of their score on the X variable. The symbol $\overline{Y'}$ is used for the mean of the Y' scores. The variance in Y-scores related to changes in X is equal to 3.20. Notice that the variance in Y-scores related to changes in X-scores is less than the total variance of the Y-scores. The variance in Y-scores related to changes in X-scores (i.e., 3.20) plus the variance in Y-scores independent of changes in X-scores (i.e., 4.80) is equal to the variance of the Y-scores (8.00). This is *always* the case. The ratio of the variance in Y-scores related to changes in X divided by the total variance of Y-scores gives us the portion of the Y-score variance that is accounted for (the explained variance). We can assess the relative importance of X variables if we know this ratio. Fortunately it is easily obtained when we know the correlation between the X and Y variables. The amount of Y-score variance that is related

TABLE 9-7

The Computation of the Variance in Y-scores That Is Related to Changes in the X-score for the Results Presented in Table 9-5

Subject	Y' score	$(Y' - \overline{Y'})$	$(Y' - \overline{Y'})^2$
A	4	−2	4
B	4	−2	4
C	6	0	0
D	6	0	0
E	8	2	4
F	8	2	4
	Sum = 36		Sum = 16
		$\overline{Y'} = 6$	

$$s^2 = \frac{\Sigma(Y' - \overline{Y'})^2}{n - 1} = \frac{16}{5} = 3.20$$

to the X-score is 3.20, and the total variance of the Y-scores is 8.00. Thus the amount of Y-score variance accounted for is 3.20/8.00 or .40. Forty percent of the Y-score fluctuations is related to changes in X-scores.

The Coefficient of Determination

The ratio of the Y-score variance related to X divided by the total Y-score variance is equal to r^2. As you will remember, the symbol r is used for the product-moment correlation. The square of r (i.e., r^2) is called the coefficient of determination. You can think of r^2 as the coefficient that allows us to determine how much of the variance of Y-scores is related to changes in X-scores. If we know the correlation it is very simple to compute the coefficient of determination; all we have to do is square r. For example, if $r = .30$, then $r^2 = .09$. In this case 9% of the variance of the Y-scores can be accounted for in terms of changes in X-scores.

You are encouraged to compute the product-moment correlation for the results presented in Table 9-5 using the formula presented in Table 9-4. If you perform this calculation you will find that the product-moment correlation for the results in Table 9-5 is equal to .63. (It is only a coincidence that the correlation for the results in Table 9-4 is also .63.) We can determine the coefficient of determination by squaring r. Thus, r^2 is equal to .40, as we discovered by computing the correlation.

The coefficient of determination allows us to compare the importance of X-variables. We can say that a variable that accounts for 40% of the Y-score variance is more important than a variable that accounts for only 10%. Many investigators find the coefficient of determination a more useful measure than the correlation because the interpretation is clear. Although the two measures are closely related the correlation has to be quite large before very much variance is accounted for. This can be seen by examining Table 9-8, but it can be seen most dramatically by comparing correlations of .00 and .10 with correlations of .90 and 1.00. A correlation of .10 accounts for 1% more variance than a correlation of zero. A correlation of 1.00 accounts for 19% more variance than a correlation of .90.

Range Restriction and Correlation

Our final task is to discuss factors that influence the magnitude of the correlation. There are three variances to consider: the total variance of the Y-scores, the Y-score variance related to changes in X-scores, and the Y-score variance unrelated to changes in X-scores. Because the total variance of the Y-scores is equal to the sum of the other two it follows that once we know two we can determine the third. That is, we can compute the correlation if we know two of these variances. We cannot compute the correlation if we know only one. It is not completely correct to say that the magnitude of the

TABLE 9-8

The Relationship between the Magnitude of the Product-moment Correlation and the Amount of Variance Accounted for (coefficient of determination)

Correlation	Variance accounted for
.00	0%
.10	1%
.20	4%
.30	9%
.40	16%
.50	25%
.60	36%
.70	49%
.80	64%
.90	81%
1.00	100%

correlation is a function of the extent to which the data points hug the regression line; that is true only if we assume that the total variance of the Y-scores does not change. Only when the total variance of the Y-scores (i.e., the variance to be accounted for) does not change can we say that the magnitude of the correlation is a function of the extent to which the data points hug the regression line.

It is also true, however, that the magnitude of the correlation is a function of the total Y-score variance if the variance of the data points around the regression line remains constant. Let us consider two situations, A and B. Assume that the variance of the Y-scores is 500 for Situation A and 300 for Situation B. Yet in both cases the Y-score variance that is independent of X-scores is the same (say, 150). That is, the variance of the data points around the regression line is the same for both situations. The correlations are not the same, however, because there is more Y-score variance related to changes in X-scores in Situation A ($500 - 150 = 350$) than in Situation B ($300 - 150 = 150$). Thus, the coefficient of determination is equal to .70 in Situation A ($350/500 = .70$) and equal to .50 in Situation B ($150/300 = .50$). The respective correlations are 0.84 for Situation A and 0.71 for Situation B.

The point is that factors that reduce the total variance of Y-scores can reduce the correlation even though the variance of the data points around the regression line is unaffected. The total variance of the Y-scores can be reduced by the selection procedures used to obtain subjects. For example, we might expect less total variance in Y-scores if subjects from a select population are chosen (e.g., college students at the University of Massachusetts) than if subjects are selected from the general population. The selection of subjects from a homogeneous population is likely to result in a lower correlation if there is a significant (i.e., nonzero) correlation between the two variables in the population.

In general, it is not a good idea to select subjects from a homogeneous group if you want to study the degree of relationship between two variables. The extreme case of range restriction is obtained when all subjects have the same score on the Y variable. When this result is obtained it does not make any sense to compute a correlation. We must remember that the purpose of correlation is to account for the variance of Y-scores. When there is no variance to account for there is no reason to compute the correlation.

SUMMARY

Correlations are extremely useful measures because they allow a precise indication of the degree of relationship between two variables. The procedures that can be used depend on the level of measurement. The phi coefficient, rank-order correlation, and product-moment correlation are appropriate for nominal, ordinal, and interval data, respectively. Correlation coefficients are free to fluctuate between -1.00 and $+1.00$. The rank-order correlation indicates the degree to which two variables are monotonically related, the product-moment correlation the degree to which they are linearly related.

Scattergrams are a useful way to describe pictorially the relationship between two variables. We can view correlation in terms of the accuracy with which a regression line describes the relationship between two variables. The regression line is defined as the straight line for which the sum of the squared deviations from each point to the line is a minimum. The magnitude of the correlation, all else being equal, is related to the extent to which the data points hug the regression line.

When we have two scores (an X-score and a Y-score) for each subject we can split the variance of Y-scores into two components. One component is the amount of variance in Y independent of changes in X (variance around the regression line). The second component is variance in Y-scores related to changes in X (the variance of the predicted scores). We are primarily interested in the ratio between the Y-score variance related to X-scores and the total Y-score variance. This ratio is equal to r^2, the coefficient of determination. This is the coefficient that allows us to determine how much of the variance of Y-scores is related to changes in X-scores. It thus allows us to compare the importance of X-variables. Restrictions in the range of one or both variables can reduce the correlation.

QUESTIONS

1. An investigator sampled 150 registered voters to determine their positions on handgun legislation. Of the 75 males, 50 opposed and 25 favored the legislation. Of the 75 females, 15 opposed and 60 favored the legislation. Compute a phi coefficient to determine the relationship between sex and attitude toward handgun legislation.
2. Ten members randomly selected from a bridge club having 300 members were rated on aggressiveness and on skill in playing bridge. Do a rank-order and a product-moment correlation. What do you have to do to the scores before computing a rank-order correlation? What size correlation would you expect if all 300 club members were used as subjects?

Subject number	Bridge	Aggressiveness
1	15	12
2	19	18
3	14	16
4	10	13
5	6	14
6	25	22
7	21	18
8	4	10
9	19	23
10	11	16

3. What size product-moment correlation would you obtain with the following results? Is it necessary to compute this correlation?

Subject number	Bridge	Aggressiveness
1	1	10
2	2	20
3	3	30
4	4	40
5	5	50
6	6	60
7	7	70
8	8	80
9	9	90
10	10	100

4. What size product-moment correlation would you obtain with the following results? Is it necessary to compute this correlation?

Subject number	Bridge	Aggressiveness
1	74	23
2	70	25
3	68	29
4	66	31
5	64	34
6	60	37
7	54	42
8	53	46
9	52	53
10	31	59

5. Assume that you test each of fifteen subjects randomly selected from a larger population on two tests and then compute the correlation between the tests. Will the correlation you obtain be the same as if you had tested the whole population instead of a sample of fifteen? What would be your best guess of the relationship between the two variables if you tested only fifteen subjects? What should happen to the accuracy of the estimate of the population correlation as the sample size increases?
6. Assume that two variables you are interested in (e.g., beauty and intelligence) are unrelated. That is, the real correlation is zero; the null hypothesis of no relationship between the variables is true. If you were to randomly select a sample of forty subjects, administer the tests, and compute the correlation, would you expect to obtain a correlation of zero? If you were to repeat this procedure 100,000 times with a new sample each time, what would you call the distribution of results you obtain? How would the distribution of results be influenced by the size of the sample?
7. What factors are likely to influence the magnitude of a correlation?
8. What is the difference between linearity and monotonicity?
9. What is a regression line? What is it used for?
10. What is the coefficient of determination? Why is it an important measure?
11. Why is it useful to partition the Y-score variance into two components? What are the two components? How large is each component when the correlation is zero, $+1.00$, and -1.00?
12. Explain why a range restriction usually results in a lower correlation.

statistical analysis of between-subject designs: nominal and ordinal data

10

In Chapters 10 through 12 we will consider certain statistical tests for analyzing the results of experiments. Statistical tests allow investigators to determine whether a particular experimental outcome is a common or rare event if only chance is operating. The result of the statistical analysis can then be used to determine whether the null hypothesis should be rejected. Although some investigators may obtain only experimental results that are obviously common or obviously rare, thus rendering statistical tests unnecessary, most investigators in the social sciences have frequent use for statistical tests. When an investigator needs to perform a statistical test on a particular experimental result the first task is to select an appropriate test.

SELECTING A STATISTICAL TEST

Selecting an appropriate test is crucial because only then will the results of the statistical analysis be meaningful. Notice that the task is to select *an* appropriate test and not *the* appropriate test. It is often possible to use more than one test. Our goal, however, is not to discuss the relative merits of different statistical tests but to provide a scheme for selecting an appropriate one. Then we will consider the steps involved in performing each of the selected tests.

The type of test that is appropriate depends on the type of design used and the level of measurement obtained. Two main designs and three levels of measurement are of interest to social scientists; there are six possible combinations of measurement level and design type. We can select an appropriate statistical test for each using the information in Table 10-1. To use the table we must determine what kind of design was used and what level of measurement was obtained. For example, if a within-subject design was used and ordinal data were obtained, the Wilcoxon test would be suitable.

The structure of Table 10-1 should help you recall what you know about the two major types of experimental design. A between-subject analysis is used with random-groups designs and with subject variable manipulations. In both of these cases it is necessary to compare the performance of different subjects to assess the effect of a manipulation; the comparison is between subjects. A matched-groups design can be analyzed as either a between-subject or within-subject design. If the matching is accomplished by equating the means and standard deviations of each group on the matching variable, then a between-subject analysis is used. If the matching is accomplished on a subject by subject basis, a within-subject analysis is usually used.

THE CHI SQUARE TEST

Obtained and Expected Frequencies

The chi square test allows the investigator to assess whether the obtained frequencies in a set of categories differ significantly from the expected frequencies. The test is appropriate when each subject is placed in one and only one category. The obtained frequencies are the number of subjects placed in each category. The expected frequency in each category is generally determined by assuming that the variable of interest has no effect. That is, the expected frequencies are usually computed by accepting the null

TABLE 10-1

Statistical Tests for the Two Major Types of Experimental Design and Three Levels of Measurement Combinations

Type of design	Level of measurement		
	Nominal	*Ordinal*	*Interval or ratio*

Between-subject
  a. Random-groups
  b. Subject variables
  c. Matched-groups
	Chi square test	Median test or Wilcoxon-Mann-Whitney test	Analysis of variance or *t*-test

Within-subject
  a. Within-subject
  b. Matched-groups
	Cochran *Q* test	Wilcoxon test	Analysis of variance or *t*-test

hypothesis. When the obtained frequencies are sufficiently different from the expected frequencies it is reasonable to conclude that the manipulation is in some way responsible for the difference.

Computation of Chi Square

The formula for computing the chi square is:

$$\chi^2 = \Sigma \frac{(O - E)^2}{E}$$

where O is the obtained frequency of a given category and E is the expected frequency. The actual computation is simple. The expected frequency is subtracted from the obtained frequency for each category; the difference is squared and divided by the expected frequency. This is done for each category. The chi square value is the sum of the values obtained with each category.

Evaluation of Chi Square

The next step is to determine whether the chi square value is large enough to permit rejection of the view that the observed results are attributable to chance. Note that as the discrepancy between the obtained and expected values increases, the value of χ^2 will increase. If the chi square value is significant, the null hypothesis can be rejected. To assess the significance of the chi square, one must refer to a table of chi square values. However, since it is necessary to understand *degrees of freedom* to use the table of chi square values properly, we will first consider this question.

Degrees of Freedom. The degrees of freedom are calculated by determining the number of obtained category frequencies that are "free to vary" when the total number of subjects is determined. For example, if the subjects are assigned to two categories there is one degree of freedom. Once the obtained frequency is determined for one category it is determined for the other. Only one category is free to vary and there is one degree of freedom. For current purposes, degrees of freedom can be defined as the number of categories in which the obtained frequencies are free to vary if the size of the total sample is determined: if 100 people are assigned to three different categories there would be two degrees of freedom. Once the number of people in the first two categories is determined the number in the third is determined. Only the frequencies in two of the categories are free to vary if the total number of subjects is 100.

Chi Square Table. A table of chi square values is presented in Appendix C-2. The table values are based on chi square sampling distributions that would occur if chance only were operating. Given the chi square distribution, we can determine the probability of obtaining a chi square of a particular magnitude. If chance only is operating, the probability of obtaining a large value for the chi square test is less likely than obtaining a small value. For example, if there is one degree of freedom there is only one chance in 100 that a chi square value of 6.635 or greater will be obtained if chance only is operating. Since this result is unlikely, purely on the basis of chance, it is reasonable to conclude that the manipulation plus chance effects, and not just chance, are responsible for the obtained effect.

In general, the table value that is appropriate for evaluating a statistical test is determined by the significance level, degrees of freedom, and whether a one-tailed or two-tailed test is desired. You will probably remember from the discussion in Chapter 3 that in most cases two-tailed tests should be preferred over one-tailed tests. When a two-tailed test is used the results can be evaluated regardless of their direction. For example, the investigator does not have to predict whether the experimental subjects will be better or worse than the control subjects, just that the independent variable will influence behavior. Table values are a little higher for two-tailed than one-tailed tests for any significance level and degrees of freedom value.

All the values in the chi square table in Appendix C-2, however, are for two-tailed tests because it is not meaningful to use a one-tailed test for a chi square value if there is more than one degree of freedom. The use of the table is very simple. One selects a significance level (usually .05) and determines the appropriate degrees of freedom. Let us assume that there is one degree of freedom and the .05 significance level has been adopted. By referring to the table one can see that a value of 3.841 is needed to reject the null hypothesis at the .05 level of significance. If the obtained chi square value is greater than the table value, the null hypothesis is rejected; if it is less than the table value, the null hypothesis cannot be rejected. The use of examples should help to clarify the steps involved in using the chi square test.

CHI SQUARE AND SUBJECT VARIABLES

The chi square test can be used to evaluate subject variables and nonsubject variables. The use of chi square to evaluate subject variables is very similar to the use of correlational techniques in that cause-effect conclusions are not warranted in either case.

Personality and Sex Example

Let us assume that we randomly select a sample of 200 college students and administer a test for assertiveness. The test allows us to classify each individual as either assertive or nonassertive. We are interested in knowing whether females are more or less assertive than males. The results of our hypothetical experiment are presented in Table 10-2. It is important to note

216 *Analysis of Between-subject Designs: Nominal and Ordinal Data*

TABLE 10-2

The Number of Students in Each of the Four Classifications Determined by Personality and Sex (fictitious data)

Sex	Personality		Row total
	Assertive	Nonassertive	
Female	O = 40 E = 55	O = 70 E = 55	110
Male	O = 60 E = 45	O = 30 E = 45	90
Column total	100	100	200

Computation of the chi square value

$$\chi^2 = \Sigma \frac{(O-E)^2}{E}$$

$$\chi^2 = \frac{(40-55)^2}{55} + \frac{(70-55)^2}{55} + \frac{(60-45)^2}{45} + \frac{(30-45)^2}{45}$$

$$\chi^2 = 4.09 + 4.09 + 5.00 + 5.00$$

$$\chi^2 = 18.18$$

that each student is placed in one and only one of the four possible categories. The chi square test can be used to determine whether the two variables are related.

Calculating Expected Frequencies. By examining Table 10-2 we see that there are two frequencies in each of the four cells of the table. The observed (O) frequencies are determined by the results of the data collection. In this case there were 40 assertive and 70 nonassertive females, and 60 assertive and 30 nonassertive males. The letter O is used for observed or obtained frequencies; the letter E is used for expected frequencies. The next task is to determine the expected frequencies.

To determine the expected frequency for each category in the body of the table we need to calculate the probability that an individual will be classified in each row *and* in each column when the row and column totals are determined. If the two variables of interest are unrelated, chance only should determine the obtained frequencies in each of the four categories. There are two ways to compute the expected frequencies, a hard way and an easy way.

The hard way to compute each expected frequency is to use the fact that the probability of an event is the number of favorable events divided by the total number of possible events if only chance is operating. In this case the probability of an event in the first row is .55 (110/200) and the probability for the second row is .45 (90/200). The probability for each of the two columns is .50 (100/200). When we are given the probability for each row and column we can obtain the probability for each category (cell) in the body of the table by multiplying the row probability by the column probability. That is, if we assume that personality and sex are unrelated we will find that the probability that an individual will be placed in a particular category is equal to the probability of his being in the row of the particular category multiplied by the probability of his being in the column of the category. Appendix A-1 contains additional information about computing the joint probability of independent events. To get the expected frequency for each category, the probability for each is multiplied by the total frequency, in this case 200.

The easy way to compute each expected frequency is to multiply the column total by the row total and divide by the total number of subjects. For example, to compute the expected frequency for the assertive and female cell the row total of 110 is multiplied by the column total of 100 and the product is divided by 200, the total number of subjects. This way is far easier than the procedure discussed above and the result is exactly the same. It skips the needless step of multiplying and dividing by the total number of subjects. The more complicated procedure was presented to demonstrate that the expected frequencies are obtained by determining what is probable if only chance is operating.

Computation of Chi Square. The computation of the chi square is presented in Table 10-2. The expected frequency is subtracted from the obtained frequency for each category; the difference is squared and divided by the expected frequency. The same procedure is used for each category, and then the values obtained for each are summed. In this case the obtained chi square value is equal to 18.18. The next step is to evaluate this value.

Evaluation of Chi Square. The question is whether the chi square value of 18.18 is large enough so that the hypothesis that the observed results are attributed to chance can be rejected. If the chi square value is significant the results suggest that assertiveness and sex are related. If the chi square value is not significant there is no reason to believe that they are related. The chi square value is assessed by referring to the table in Appendix C-2.

The problem of determining degrees of freedom for chi square causes little difficulty if you observe that the totals for the rows and columns are "fixed" (not free to vary). They do not provide information about the independence or dependence of the variables; they are only the starting points for assessing independence or dependence — they are fixed. Therefore it is easy to compute the number of degrees of freedom simply by counting the number of obtained category frequencies that are free to vary. In the present example, only one cell frequency is free to vary; the others are determined (There is only one degree of freedom). The reader who does not see that there is only one degree of freedom should prepare a few 2 by 2 contingency tables similar to Table 10-2. Fill in the totals for each row and column and then fill in the "obtained" category frequencies. If you do this you should soon prove to yourself that you have one degree of freedom; that is, once you have filled in the obtained value for one of the cells, the values in the rest are determined. If you compute the degrees of freedom for tables that have different numbers of categories you should soon realize that the number of degrees of freedom for a chi square with two variables is always equal to the number of rows minus one times the number of columns minus one.

An examination of the table of chi square values in Appendix C-2 reveals that a value of 3.841 is needed to reject the null hypothesis at the .05 level of significance with one degree of freedom. The use of the .05 level is somewhat arbitrary. Some investigators may prefer a more stringent (e.g., .01) or in rare cases a more lenient (e.g., .10) significance level. The factor to consider in adopting a significance level is whether you prefer to minimize the probability of making a Type 1 or a Type 2 error. If you decrease the probability of making one kind of error you increase the probability of making the other. Therefore, most investigators adopt the .05 significance level. Since the obtained chi square value of 18.18 is greater than the table value of 3.841, the null hypothesis is rejected. The results support the view that there is a relationship between assertiveness and sex. For the fictitious data presented here, males are more assertive than females. Although investigators tend to select the .05 significance level they usually report the highest significance level obtained simply because more information is conveyed when the highest level is reported. For example, if an investigator reports that a chi square is significant at the .01 level it is, of course, also significant at the .05 level. The reverse is not true.

Chi Square and the Phi Coefficient. It is possible to compute a phi coefficient (see Chapter 9) when both variables are at the nominal level of measurement and dichotomous, as in the present example. The phi coefficient for this example is equal to .3015. The question of interest is the relationship between chi square and the phi coefficient.

The two measures are related. We can obtain one when we have the other because $\chi^2 = n\phi^2$. In this case $n = 200$, so $\chi^2 = 200\,(.3015)^2 = 18.18$. The phi coefficient reveals the degree of relationship between two variables. The chi square reveals whether we can reject the null hypothesis of no relationship between the two variables. If the results are a rare event when only chance is operating we can conclude that more than chance is operating. We can conclude that the variables are related. The chi square test is usually more useful than the phi coefficient measure because it is not limited to dichotomous variables.

Marital Adjustment Example

The chi square test can be used to evaluate the relationship between variables that have more than two levels. Let us consider such an example. Assume that you believe a satisfactory childhood has considerable influence on marital adjustment and you decide to test your hypothesis. You develop one detailed questionnaire to assess the extent to which childhood experiences were pleasant and another to evaluate marital adjustment.

You do not have any elaborate theory about why the experiences of childhood should be related to marital happiness. Mostly it is gut level feeling you have about people. You believe that the child who has experienced such delights as playing jacks, playing hopscotch, building a treehouse, collecting trading cards, flying a kite, chasing frogs, or tipping over a canoe is much better equipped for the problems of marriage than one who has spent a duller childhood. A person who has had an enjoyable childhood has reason to be optimistic about the future. Perhaps you think back to the first time you "stole" cookies from the cookie jar, to your first trip to the circus, or to your first love. Surely, you reason, these experiences can be a continued source of pleasure in the adult years. Or perhaps you believe that a person learns how to enjoy life early. You may believe that one has to learn how to laugh at oneself, how to relax, and how to turn an unpleasant event into a pleasant one by using wit — that a sense of humor is important and that its elements are acquired early. You test your view by randomly selecting 450 people from a population of married people and classify them into nine categories based on their early life experiences and marital adjustment.

The results of the experiment are presented in Table 10-3. The 450 people are placed in the nine mutually exclusive categories. Keep in mind that you are not concerned with the number of people who have poor, medium, or good marriages, nor with the number who have pleasant, average, or unpleasant childhoods. The number of people in each of these large categories is used as the starting point for assessing whether the two variables are related. You are interested in the obtained, relative to the expected, frequencies in the nine categories in the body of the table, not in the frequencies in the margins (total for each row and column).

Calculating Expected Frequencies. To determine the expected frequencies for each category in the body of the table we determine the probability that an individual will be classified in each row *and* in each column if the row and column totals are determined. In determining the expected frequencies we assume that only chance determines the frequency for each category. The

TABLE 10-3

Obtained and Expected Frequencies for Each of the Nine Categories of Childhood Experiences and Marital Success. The Computation of the Chi Square Value Is Included (fictitious data).

Childhood experiences	Marital success			Row total
	Poor	Medium	Good	
Unpleasant	O = 60 E = 33.33	O = 50 E = 50.00	O = 40 E = 66.67	150
Average	O = 30 E = 33.33	O = 60 E = 50.00	O = 60 E = 66.67	150
Pleasant	O = 10 E = 33.33	O = 40 E = 50.00	O = 100 E = 66.67	150
Column total	100	150	200	450

Computation of the chi square value

$$\chi^2 = \Sigma \frac{(O - E)^2}{E}$$

$$\chi^2 = \frac{(60 - 33.33)^2}{33.33} + \frac{(50 - 50.00)^2}{50} + \frac{(40 - 66.67)^2}{66.67} + \frac{(30 - 33.33)^2}{33.33} + \frac{(60 - 50.00)^2}{50}$$

$$+ \frac{(60 - 66.67)^2}{66.67} + \frac{(10 - 33.33)^2}{33.33} + \frac{(40 - 50.00)^2}{50} + \frac{(100 - 66.67)^2}{66.67}$$

$$\chi^2 = 21.34 + 0 + 10.67 + .33 + 2.00 + .67 + 16.33 + 2.00 + 16.66$$

$$\chi^2 = 70.00$$

---

simple way to compute the expected frequencies is to multiply the column total by the row total and divide by the total number of subjects. For example, to compute the expected frequency for the unpleasant childhood experiences and poor marital success cell, the row total of 150 is multiplied by the column total of 100, and the product is divided by 450, the total number of subjects.

Computing and Evaluating the Chi Square. The procedure for computing the chi square value is identical to that used for the earlier example. The computation is presented in Table 10-3. Following the computation of the chi square, the degrees of freedom should be determined, and then the table in Appendix C-2 should be used to obtain the appropriate table value. If the obtained chi square value is greater than the table value the null hypothesis should be rejected.

The problem of determining degrees of freedom for chi square causes little difficulty if you observe that the totals for the rows and columns are fixed. Here only four cell frequencies are free to vary; the others are determined (There are four degrees of freedom).

After computing the degrees of freedom and the chi square it is a simple matter to refer to the chi square table in Appendix C-2 to find that the obtained value of 70.00 is significant at the .01 level since it exceeds the table value of 13.28. Thus, the null hypothesis of independence is rejected. It appears that childhood experiences and marital success are related. Once again because subject variables were selected it is incorrect to conclude that the relationship is causal. When the variables of interest are subject variables correlational techniques can also be used. For example, one could compute a correlation between marital success and childhood happiness using the scores on the questionnaires or by performing the chi square test that has just been presented.

Because the two examples demonstrating the use of chi square have involved classifying individuals on the basis of subject variables, let us consider examples that involve nonsubject variable manipulations. Chi square is extremely useful for many purposes; its use is not limited to subject variable manipulations.

CHI SQUARE AND NONSUBJECT VARIABLES

Political Views Example

The use of the chi square test is essentially the same regardless of whether a subject or nonsubject variable is manipulated. Assume that an investigator with considerable wealth and resources wants to assess whether it is possible to persuade people to become socialists, moderates, or conservatives. He believes there are at least two important aspects to influencing political opinions and voting behavior: indoctrinating subjects in the arguments for a particular position and reinforcing them for holding it. He tests this view by investigating the effects on subsequent political behaviors of a two-year indoctrination program. Three programs are used, each designed to produce either socialists, moderates, or conservatives. You can decide what might be the best curriculum and reward structure for such programs and can wrestle with the ethical issues of whether such indoctrination should be undertaken.

Design and Procedures. A group of 300 adults is obtained, from all walks of life, between the ages of eighteen and forty. The subjects are randomly assigned to three groups with the restrictions that there be 100 subjects in each group and that married couples be assigned to the same group. That is, the random-groups design is used. The subjects are paid well for serving in the experiment. During the two-year experimental manipulation the investigator has virtually complete control over everything the subjects read, whom they are allowed to converse with, what they are praised for, and so on.

After the indoctrination period the subjects do not receive any further monetary reward. Ten years after the termination of the program, judges unaware of the purpose of the experiment classify each subject as a socialist, moderate, or conservative. The principal concern is whether the political views that the subjects hold after ten years were influenced by the indoctrination program they received.

Calculating and Evaluating the Chi Square. The results of the experiment are presented in Table 10-4. The evaluation procedure is essentially identical to that used for the last example. It is necessary to compute an expected frequency for each category and then determine whether the obtained frequencies are significantly different. This is done, of course, by computing a chi square. The calculations for the chi square are also included in Table 10-4. To evaluate whether the chi square is statistically significant, the table in Appendix C-2 is used to determine whether the obtained value exceeds the table value for four degrees of freedom and the significance level (say, .05) that is adopted. In this case the chi square value of 2.72 is less than the table value of 9.488, so it is not possible to reject the null hypothesis. There is no support for the view that one can change political views over a ten-year period with the indoctrination programs employed. If the chi square had been significant the differences in political opinion could have been attributed to the independent variable.

The Median Test: Vitamin C Example

The median test can be used to evaluate between-subject designs when ordinal data are obtained. It requires, however, that the ordinal data be treated like nominal data since the median test is a special application of the chi square test. A single example should be sufficient to familiarize you with this test. Assume that an investigator is interested in the effect of Vitamin C on general health.

Experimental Method. The investigator is particularly concerned with whether or not Vitamin C helps to prevent colds, so cold symptoms are given a high weighting by the judges who assess the general health of each subject. Thirty army recruits in basic training who volunteered for the experiment are randomly assigned to two groups with the restriction that there be fifteen subjects in each group. Each subject in the experimental group takes massive doses of Vitamin C each day for three months. Each subject in the control group takes massive doses of a placebo.

The dependent measure is the general health of the subjects for the three months during which experimental subjects take Vitamin C. The judges, who

TABLE 10-4

The Number of Obtained and Expected Frequencies in Each Political Category for the Subjects Who Received Each Political Indoctrination Program. The Computation of the Chi Square Value Is Included (fictitious data).

Type of indoctrina-tion program	Ten years after indoctrination			Row total
	Socialist	Moderate	Conservative	
Socialist	O = 25 E = 30	O = 42 E = 40	O = 33 E = 30	100
Moderate	O = 35 E = 30	O = 36 E = 40	O = 29 E = 30	100
Conservative	O = 30 E = 30	O = 42 E = 40	O = 28 E = 30	100
Column total	90	120	90	300

Computation of the chi square value

$$\chi^2 = \Sigma \frac{(O-E)^2}{E}$$

$$\chi^2 = \frac{(25-30)^2}{30} + \frac{(42-40)^2}{40} + \frac{(33-30)^2}{30} + \frac{(35-30)^2}{30} + \frac{(36-40)^2}{40}$$

$$+ \frac{(29-30)^2}{30} + \frac{(30-30)^2}{30} + \frac{(42-40)^2}{40} + \frac{(28-30)^2}{30}$$

$$\chi^2 = .83 + .10 + .30 + .83 + .40 + .03 + 0 + .10 + .13$$

$$\chi^2 = 2.72$$

are unaware of the condition each subject is in, rank the subjects on the basis of general health for the entire three-month period. The rank of 1 is assigned to the subject with the best health, the rank of 30 to the subject with the worst health. Initially the experimenter hoped it would be possible to rank the thirty subjects without allowing ties, but the judges, after several attempts to make fine discriminations, decide that ties are permissible.

Results. The ranking of the thirty subjects is presented in Table 10-5. Although each subject's score is a rank in this particular experiment, it is not necessary to rank subjects directly on the dependent measure in order to use the median test. One could obtain a score for each subject and then rank the scores. In any case, it is necessary to arrive at one overall ranking of the thirty subjects. Given the results in Table 10-5, we must decide whether the results should be attributed to chance or to the effect of the manipulation.

Computing and Evaluating the Chi Square. One way to assess the significance of the results is to use the chi square test. The results can be analyzed in essentially the same way as if nominal data had been obtained. The only difference is that it is necessary to categorize subjects on the basis of their group (experimental or control) and on whether they are above or below the median rank. Then there will be four categories for the thirty subjects. Each subject can be counted in only one of the four.

The obtained and expected frequencies in each category are presented in Table 10-6. The chi square value is computed in exactly the same way that it is for nominal data. After computing the chi square value and determining the degrees of freedom, the table in Appendix C-2 is used to assess whether the obtained value (with one degree of freedom) is large enough to reject the null hypothesis. In this case the chi square value of 6.53 is greater than the table value (3.841) with one degree of freedom and the .05 level of significance, so the null hypothesis is rejected. It appears that Vitamin C tends to improve health. (You should remember that the results are fictitious.)

You should now understand how to compute a chi square and evaluate it for statistical significance. If you do much research in the social sciences you are very likely to use the chi square sooner or later. It is probably used as much as any other single statistical tool. It is one of the few good tools for analyzing nominal data. Another reason for its popularity is that it is easy to

TABLE 10-5

The Rank for Each Subject in the Experimental (E) and Control (C) Conditions for the Vitamin C Experiment (fictitious data)

Subject	Condition	Rank	Subject	Condition	Rank
A. B.	E	1	R. M.	E	16
T. B.	E	2	C. B.	C	17
C. S.	C	3	P. D.	E	18
K. P.	E	4.5	C. W.	C	19
L. W.	E	4.5	G. C.	E	20
S. B.	C	6	D. H.	C	21
W. C.	E	7	R. F.	E	22
C. C.	E	8	K. Z.	C	23
J. K.	E	9	J. F.	C	24
F. S.	C	10.5	J. P.	C	25
E. T.	E	10.5	L. W.	C	26
J. D.	C	12	L. S.	C	27
B. B.	E	13	J. M.	C	28
A. D.	E	14	A. M.	C	29
G. D.	E	15	R. R.	C	30

TABLE 10-6

The Obtained and Expected Frequencies for the Four Categories in the Experiment on the Effect of Vitamin C on General Health. The computation of the Chi Square Value Is Included (fictitious data).

Condition	General health		Row total
	Above median	Below median	
Vitamin C (Experimental)	O = 11 E = 7.5	O = 4 E = 7.5	15
Control	O = 4 E = 7.5	O = 11 E = 7.5	15
Column total	15	15	30

Computation of the chi square value

$$\chi^2 = \Sigma \frac{(O - E)^2}{E}$$

$$\chi^2 = \frac{(11 - 7.5)^2}{7.5} + \frac{(4 - 7.5)^2}{7.5} + \frac{(4 - 7.5)^2}{7.5} + \frac{(11 - 7.5)^2}{7.5}$$

$$\chi^2 = 1.633 + 1.633 + 1.633 + 1.633$$

$$\chi^2 = 6.532$$

compute and evaluate. Even though the use of the chi square is generally straightforward, there are some pitfalls to be avoided in using this tool.

RESTRICTIONS ON THE USE OF CHI SQUARE

There are three restrictions to be aware of in using the chi square test. First, the test is appropriate only if the frequency measures are independent. In simplest terms this means that only one measure is obtained for each subject. Each subject can be placed in one and only one category. Second, the data must be in frequency form. There is little problem with this restriction as long as the chi square test is understood to be appropriate when individuals are assigned to categories. The data of interest are the number of individuals assigned to each.

Third, the test should not be used if the expected frequencies are too small. What is considered too small will vary somewhat with the number of variables and the total number of subjects. In any case, the test can be used with confidence as long as none of the expected frequencies is equal to or less than five. When there are expected frequencies of less than five the number of subjects should be increased so that the expected frequencies increase. Or it may be possible to combine categories so that those which have expected frequencies of less than five are eliminated. If neither of these options is suitable another test of significance (e.g., Fisher-Yates Exact Probability Test) should be used.

WILCOXON-MANN-WHITNEY TEST

A disadvantage to the use of the chi square test (median test) when ordinal data are obtained is that all the available information is not used since the rather crude classification of above versus below the median is employed. Any two ranks above the median count the same, and any two ranks below the median count the same. That is, ordinal data are treated like nominal data. The Wilcoxon-Mann-Whitney test takes into account the differences between ranks on the same side of the median.

Computational Steps

Let us return to the example of the effect of Vitamin C on general health and use the Wilcoxon-Mann-Whitney test. The first step is to obtain a ranking of the subjects similar to that in Table 10-5. The principal concern is the sum of the ranks for the experimental subjects and for the control subjects. The sum of each of these ranks is presented in Table 10-7. You should compute the sum of the ranks for each group and then select the smaller sum. In this case the sum of the ranks for the experimental group is selected because it is less than the sum of the control group.

The two groups have the same number of subjects, so it is reasonable to expect that the sums should be about the same if only chance is operating. As one sum decreases the other must increase because together they must equal the sum for all the subjects regardless of group. Because the two sums are directly related, the results of a two-group experiment can be evaluated by considering the sum of ranks for just one group. That is, the effect of the manipulation can be assessed by considering the magnitude of the sum of ranks for one group. The issue is whether the smaller sum is small enough that the obtained results would be a rare event if only chance were operating.

A complication arises if there is an unequal number of subjects in the two groups because we cannot simply add the ranks for each group and take the smaller sum. We must compute the sum for the smaller group (called T) and then compute another value, T' (called T prime), by using the following formula:

$$T' = N_1(N_1 + N_2 + 1) - T$$

TABLE 10-7

The Sum of the Ranks for the Experimental and Control Subjects for the Results Presented in Table 10-5

Experimental	Control
1	3
2	6
4.5	10.5
4.5	12
7	17
8	19
9	21
10.5	23
13	24
14	25
15	26
16	27
18	28
20	29
22	30
Sum = 164.5	Sum = 300.5

where N_1 is the number of subjects in the smaller group, and N_2 is the number of subjects in the larger group. We then select T or T', whichever is *smaller*. The formula is necessary because the sum of the ranks is related to the number of subjects in each group. For example, all else being equal, the sum for a group of 20 subjects will be higher than the sum for a group of 10 subjects. The formula allows us to remove the bias inherent in having a different number of subjects in the two conditions so that our totals (T and T') yield performance measures uninfluenced by differences in group size. The symbols T and T' are shorthand for total. They should not be confused with the t-test, a significance test used for interval data that is considered in the next chapter.

Evaluating the Test

The smaller sum is evaluated by referring to Appendix C-3. To determine the appropriate table value you must decide on a level of significance (say, .05) and determine the number of subjects in each group (in this case fifteen). If the two groups are of unequal size, then you must refer to the appropriate column for the smaller group and the appropriate row for the larger group. If the groups are the same size, of course, it doesn't make any difference. For the present example the correct table value is 184 for the .05 level of significance and fifteen subjects per group.

If the smaller of the two group sums is *equal to or less than* the table value, the null hypothesis is rejected. In this case the null hypothesis is rejected because the obtained sum of 164.5 is less than 184. The Wilcoxon-Mann-Whitney test is consistent with the median test in revealing that the probability of obtaining these results by chance is less than .05. On the basis of chance a value smaller than the table value should be obtained about five times in one hundred attempts. Since this is an unlikely event it is reasonable to conclude that the results are not attributable to chance. The investigator can conclude that the manipulation was responsible for the obtained difference between groups.

Characteristics of the Test

The Wilcoxon-Mann-Whitney test is easy to compute and evaluate for significance. The table that is used to evaluate the obtained sum of ranks for the smaller of the two samples is appropriate only if each group has twenty or fewer subjects. This should not be a problem, however, because it is unlikely that you will have more than twenty subjects in one group. If you do you can refer to Kruskal and Wallis (1952) to learn how to evaluate the sum of ranks for larger groups. Also, note that the obtained value must be smaller than the appropriate table value in order to be significant. This is unusual; in most significance tests the obtained value has to be larger than the table value to be significant.

If there are many tied scores the value of the sum of ranks may be affected. Obviously, tied scores will not have any effect when the subjects with the tied scores are in the same group, since the ranks are summed for each group. However, when the ties are between groups, the smaller sum of ranks tends to decrease and, therefore, the likelihood of rejecting the null hypothesis increases. When there are many tied ranks between groups you may want to adopt a more stringent significance level (say, the .01 instead of the .05) or resolve the ties in the way that affords a more conservative test of the research hypothesis. For example, if you have predicted that the experimental subjects will have lower ranks than the control subjects, in the case of a between-group tie you should give the control subject the lower of the two ranks and the experimental subject the higher, instead of giving both subjects the average.

If there are more than two treatments to be compared and each subject obtains a score on some ordinal measure, it is possible to use the Wilcoxon-Mann-Whitney test. However, only two conditions can be compared at the same time. If there are a number of treatments to compare (e.g., five separate comparisons) it is usually a good idea to adopt a stringent significance level so that the significance level per experiment is not too lenient. For example, if five comparisons are made and the .05 is used for each, then the significance level for the entire experiment is five times .05 or .25, whereas if the .01 level is used for each comparison, then the significance level for the entire experiment is still only .05. Many investigators prefer to use the more stringent significance level when making multiple comparisons.

SUMMARY

The type of statistical test that is appropriate depends on the type of design and the level of measurement obtained. Appropriate tests for the six major combinations of measurement level and design type are presented in Table 10.1.

The chi square test is used to analyze between-subject designs in which nominal data are obtained. The basic task is to determine whether the obtained frequencies in a set of categories differ significantly from the expected frequencies. Expected frequencies are calculated by assuming the null hypothesis is true.

Chi square value is computed by subtracting the expected frequency from the obtained frequency for a category, squaring the difference, and dividing by the expected frequency. This is done for each category. The chi square value is the sum of the values obtained for each category. The obtained chi square is evaluated by comparing it with the appropriate value in the chi square table. If the obtained value exceeds the table value, the chi square is significant.

The median test is a special application of the chi square test. All subjects are ranked and then split into two categories — above the median and below the median. A chi square test is used to determine whether the number of experimental subjects above the median is greater or less than what can be expected on the basis of chance.

There are three restrictions on the use of the chi square test. The test is appropriate only in frequency measures are independent. The data must be in frequency form. And the test should not be used if the expected frequencies are too small.

The Wilcoxon-Mann-Whitney test is appropriate for between-subject designs in which ordinal data are obtained. Like the median test this test is only appropriate for evaluating two conditions at a time. All subjects are rank ordered and the sum of ranks for both groups is obtained. The smaller sum is then evaluated by comparing it with the appropriate table value. If the obtained sum is smaller than the table sum the results are significant.

QUESTIONS

1. Determine the expected frequency for each category (cell) in the following table. In determining the expected frequencies you should assume, of course,

that the two variables are unrelated. There are 400 subjects in this experiment.

Variable 1

	Poor	Good	
A	25	75	100
B	37.5	112.5	150
C	37.5	112.5	150
	100	300	

Variable 2 (row label)

2. A sample of fifty Democrats, fifty Republicans, and fifty Independents is obtained to check the view that wealth and political preference are related. An annual income of $18,000 is used as the criterion of wealth. It is possible to classify each individual according to political party and income. Each can be placed in one category only. Do a chi square test to determine if the two variables are related.

Political party

		Republicans	Democrats	Independents	
Wealth	Below $18,000	O = 15, E = 23.3	O = 30, 23.3	O = 25, 23.3	70
	Above $18,000	O = 35, E = 26.7	O = 20, 26.7	O = 25, 26.7	80
		50	50	50	150

$2.95 + 1.93 + .124 + 2.58 + 1.68 + .108 = 9.372$

3. Is there any similarity between deciding whether two subject variables are related by using a chi square test and computing a correlation between the two subject variables?

4. Let us assume you are interested in the relationship between parental smoking (i.e., one or both parents smoke or neither parent smokes) and whether their children smoke when they become adults. In order to test your view you randomly select 200 adults between the ages of twenty-one and thirty and assess whether they smoke and whether their parents smoked when they were children. One variable is whether the parents smoked; the second is whether the subject smokes. The hypothetical results for this experiment are presented below. Do a chi square test to determine whether the variables are related.

Subject

	Smokes	Does not smoke
One or both parents smoke	70	40
Neither parent smokes	37	53

Parents

5. Assume that you analyze the fictitious results presented in Question 4 further by considering the results for male and female subjects separately. The results of this breakdown of the data are presented below. Do a chi square test for the female subjects only. Are the variables related? Do a chi square test for the male subjects only. Are the variables related?

Male subjects

	Smokes	Does not smoke
Smoke	50	10
Do not smoke	10	25

Parents

Female subjects

	Smokes	Does not smoke
Smoke	20	30
Do not smoke	27	28

Parents

6. What are the limitations of the chi square test?
7. Assume that you want to evaluate a new program of instruction. You randomly assign twelve subjects to the treatment (experimental) condition and twelve to the control condition. After the treatment, judges who are not aware of the treatment manipulation rank the subjects according to their performance on a criterion test. You obtain the results given below. Did the treatment have an effect? Use the median test to evaluate your results.

232 Analysis of Between-subject Designs: Nominal and Ordinal Data

Subject	Condition	Rank
a	E	1
b	E	2
c	E	3
d	C	4
e	E	5
f	C	6
g	E	7
h	E	8
i	C	9
j	C	10
k	E	11
l	E	12
m	E	13
n	E	14
o	E	15
p	C	16
q	E	17
r	C	18
s	C	19
t	C	20
u	C	21
v	C	22
w	C	23
x	C	24

8. Repeat the above analysis, but this time use the Wilcoxon-Mann-Whitney Test.

statistical analysis of between-subject designs: interval data (11)

Although the *t*-test is not useful for analyzing complex designs, there are some good reasons to be familiar with it. Students who examine psychological literature are almost certain to encounter it and will benefit from knowing how it is computed. A second reason for considering the *t*-test is that many students have little interest or need to analyze complicated experimental designs. They want to learn the basic principles of doing research in the social sciences but are not interested in preparing for a research career. It is certainly possible to consider many important aspects of psychological research without performing the analysis of variance. Some instructors prefer to emphasize research methodology and minimize statistical analysis by performing experiments that can be analyzed by the *t*-test. This is an especially appealing approach when the students have been introduced to the *t*-test in a previous statistics course (often, the statistics course that serves as a prerequisite for the methodology course). Some instructors consider the *t*-test less difficult to learn than the analysis of variance and some consider it more difficult. The student who learns how to use both tests will be able to judge their relative difficulties according to his own view.

THE *t*-TEST

Assume that an experiment was conducted comparing the verbal ability of left- and right-handed people to support a theory of cerebral dominance. The dependent measure is the verbal portion of a standardized intelligence test. The independent variable is handedness (right versus left), a subject variable. We select subjects according to this variable. Because there are many more right-handed than left-handed people in the population, the number of subjects selected for each condition does not reflect the proportion in the general population. Assume that we randomly select eight left-handed subjects from a pool of left-handed people and ten right-handed people from a pool of right-handed people. The results of this hypothetical experiment are presented in Table 11-1. We can compute a *t*-test for this between-subject comparison to determine whether the group differences should be attributed to chance fluctuation only or to chance fluctuation plus the treatment. If we obtain a significant *t*-value we can say that handedness is related to verbal ability.

Computation of the *t*-Test

The formula and computational steps involved in computing the *t-test* for between-subject comparisons are presented in Table 11-1. The subscripts 1 and 2 (e.g., n_1 and n_2) are used to denote the two groups. The symbols X, $\overline{X}$, and n, refer to any score, the mean, and the number of subjects in each group; this is the same terminology we used earlier. The letters SS are shorthand for the sum of squares, which is a short form of the term *sum of squared deviations from the mean*. You will remember that we computed the sum of the squared deviations from the mean when we computed the variance in Chapters 4 and 8.

Although the computation of the *t*-test for this example may look complicated, it is not difficult if you first get the ΣX, $\overline{X}$, ΣX^2, and n for each group. Then you should compute the sum of squares for each group and insert values in the formula. Remember that the ΣX^2 is obtained by squaring each score and summing the squared scores and the $(\Sigma X)^2$ is obtained by adding the scores to obtain a total score and then squaring the total score. You should not have any difficulty following the computational steps given in Table 11-1 as long as you take one step at a time. It is necessary to have a calculator, preferably one that allows you to determine the square root in one operation.

The obtained *t*-value is negative in this case because we subtracted the mean for the left-handed subjects from the mean for the right-handed subjects. This was arbitrary. We could have subtracted the mean for the right-handed subjects from the mean for the left-handed subjects. If there are theoretical reasons for expecting one group to be better than the other, the means can be subtracted to give a positive *t* value if the prediction is supported and a negative *t* value if the prediction is not supported. The sign (positive or negative) can be used to indicate whether the results are in the direction predicted but it does not affect the significance of the obtained value unless a one-tailed test

TABLE 11-1

The Verbal Ability Scores for Eight Left-handed and Ten Right-handed Subjects (fictitious data)

	Right-handed	Left-handed
	109	110
	97	125
	114	107
	93	117
	98	96
	99	103
	105	99
	107	105
	104	
	100	
ΣX	1,026	862
$\bar{X}$	102.60	107.75
ΣX^2	105,630	93,514
n	10	8

Computation of t

$$t = \frac{\bar{X}_1 - \bar{X}_2}{\sqrt{\left(\frac{SS_1 + SS_2}{(n_1 - 1) + (n_2 - 1)}\right)\left(\frac{1}{n_1} + \frac{1}{n_2}\right)}}$$

$$t = \frac{102.60 - 107.75}{\sqrt{\left(\frac{362.40 + 633.50}{(10 - 1) + (8 - 1)}\right)\left(\frac{1}{10} + \frac{1}{8}\right)}}$$

$$t = \frac{-5.15}{\sqrt{\left(\frac{995.90}{16}\right)(0.10 + 0.125)}}$$

$$t = \frac{-5.15}{\sqrt{(62.244)(0.225)}}$$

$$t = \frac{-5.15}{\sqrt{14.005}}$$

$$t = \frac{-5.15}{3.742}$$

$$t = -1.376$$

Computation of sums of squares

$$SS_1 = \Sigma X_1^2 - \frac{(\Sigma X)^2}{n_1}$$

$$SS_1 = 105,630 - \frac{(1026)^2}{10}$$

$$SS_1 = 105,630 - 105,267.60$$

$$SS_1 = 362.40$$

$$SS_2 = \Sigma X_2^2 - \frac{(\Sigma X)^2}{n_2}$$

$$SS_2 = 93,514 - \frac{(862)^2}{8}$$

$$SS_2 = 93,514 - 92,880.50$$

$$SS_2 = 633.50$$

is used to evaluate t. As was pointed out in Chapter 3, the use of a one-tailed test is rarely justified.

Evaluating the Obtained t Value

The obtained t value is evaluated for statistical significance by comparing it with a table value. The table in Appendix C-5 shows the likelihood of the obtained t value occurring if chance only is operating. To find the appropriate table value for comparison we must know the degrees of freedom and select a significance level. Assume that the .05 significance level is selected. The number of degrees of freedom is determined by counting the number of scores that are free to vary when each group total is determined. If the group total is fixed all the scores in each group except one are free to vary. (Refer to Table 11-1 where the group total is fixed and count the number of scores in each group that are free to vary.) It should be clear that the degrees of freedom for each group is one less than the number of subjects in each group. In this case there are sixteen degrees of freedom because there are ten subjects in one group (nine scores free to vary) and eight subjects in the other group (seven scores free to vary). The t value needed to reject the null hypothesis at the .05 level (two-tailed) is 2.120. Because the obtained t value is less than that (i.e., 1.376) we cannot reject the null hypothesis. The hypothetical results do not support the view that handedness is related to verbal ability.

You should now be able to use the formula presented in Table 11-1 to analyze two-group experiments in which between-subject designs are used. When there are more than two groups in the experiment the t-test can be repeated until all groups are compared. For example, if there are three groups, A, B, and C, a t-test could be performed between groups A and B, between groups A and C, and between groups B and C. However, it is usually a good idea to adopt a more stringent significance level (e.g., .01 instead of .05) if several comparisons are to be made. Adopting a more stringent significance level keeps the significance level per experiment from becoming too high. What is too high will, of course, depend on the goals of the investigator. If she is interested in keeping the probability of making a Type 1 error low for the entire experiment she should adopt a stringent significance level for each comparison. For example, if five comparisons are made (i.e., five t-tests are computed) and the .01 level is adopted, the significance level for the experiment will be approximately .05.

On the other hand, when there are several comparisons it is more likely that one or more treatments will be effective than when there is only one comparison. Therefore, a stringent significance level will increase the probability of making a Type 2 error. The question is which type of error the investigator would rather avoid. Many investigators adopt a more stringent significance level when making multiple comparisons; some do not. We will consider this issue again later in this chapter.

LOGIC OF THE ANALYSIS OF VARIANCE

The logic of the analysis of variance was discussed in considerable detail in Chapter 4 to give us a framework for viewing experimental design. Between-group and within-group estimates of population variance were computed with the deviation method. Performance of these computations with the deviation method is an excellent vehicle for understanding the logic behind the analysis of variance. The reader who has forgotten the earlier discussion is encouraged to re-examine the first portion of Chapter 4 before continuing. We will *briefly* consider the logic here as a quick overview.

Obtaining Two Estimates of Population Variance

The crux of the analysis of variance with the random-groups design is to obtain two independent estimates of population variance. The variance of each group is an estimate of population variance, so there are as many estimates as there are groups. However, it is necessary to obtain a single estimate based on the variance within each sample. Therefore, an average of the sample variances is the best within-group estimate of population variance. The within-group variance measure increases as the fluctuations between subjects in the same group increase.

The other estimate of population variance is based on group means. When the null hypothesis is true the group means can be considered a distribution of sample means from the same population. This distribution of sample means can be used to obtain another estimate of population variance. Since the second estimate is based on group means it is a between-group estimate. The first estimate of population variance is influenced by fluctuations *within* each group and the second, which is based on means, by fluctuations *between* groups (between means). A proof that two independent estimates of population variance can be obtained, one based on within-group and the other on between-group variance, is presented in Appendix A-2. The reader will need to read this chapter to understand the proof.

Comparing the Two Variance Estimates

The two estimates of population variance can be compared to assess the effect of the independent variable. If chance only is operating (i.e., if the null hypothesis is true), the two estimates should be about the same. However, when the independent variable has an effect there should be greater differences between the group means than if there were no effect. The reason is simple enough. If the independent variable does not have an effect the group means are all estimates of the same population mean. However, if it does have an effect the group means will not all be estimates of the same mean because the manipulation will result in an increase or decrease in the experimental group mean. The between-group fluctuations will increase when the independent variable has an effect, but there is no reason to expect within-group fluctuations to increase.

The crux of the analysis of variance test is to compare the between-group and within-group estimates of population variance. If the two are about the same, there is no reason to reject the null hypothesis. If the between-group estimate is considerably larger than the within-group estimate the null hypothesis can be rejected.

ANALYSIS OF VARIANCE WITH ONE INDEPENDENT VARIABLE

Assume that an investigator is interested in how a person's willingness to buy is influenced by the aggressiveness of the salesperson. The investigator plays the role of a salesperson and measures the effect of her assertiveness on sales. The independent variable is whether she plays her role with low, medium, or high aggressiveness when making the sales pitch (with "information content" of the sales pitch equated for the three roles). Thirty prospective customers are randomly assigned to the three conditions with the restriction that there be ten subjects in each group. The effectiveness of each treatment is measured by the total dollar value of the sales to each customer. Thus, a random-groups design was used and interval data were obtained.

The results of the experiment are presented in Table 11-2. Our task is to

TABLE 11-2

The Total Dollar Value of Each Sale for the Ten Subjects in the Three Experimental Conditions (fictitious data)

	Low aggressiveness	Medium aggressiveness	High aggressiveness
	9	21	36
	11	23	32
	5	24	30
	17	15	25
	13	22	32
	10	26	37
	12	19	27
	11	20	33
	15	18	29
	12	21	31
ΣX	115	209	312
ΣX^2	1419	4457	9858

determine whether the different sales pitches influenced sales. The analysis of variance is an appropriate statistical test. We will consider some basic terminology before doing the actual computation.

Sum of Squares

The basic task in performing an analysis of variance for this type of experiment is to compute the sum of squares total (SS_{tot}), the sum of squares between groups (SS_{bg}), and the sum of squares within groups (SS_{wg}). The task is simplified somewhat in that the SS_{tot} is equal to the SS_{bg} plus the SS_{wg}. Thus, given two values, we can obtain the third by subtraction. There are two ways to obtain the values we are interested in. One way is to use the deviation formulas. For example, to obtain the SS_{tot} by the deviation method the overall mean is subtracted from each score, each difference is squared, and all of the squared difference scores are added. Another way is to use computational formulas to obtain the three values.

The use of the deviation method is a good way to understand what the computation of the analysis of variance is all about because the deviations are obtained directly. This was the procedure that was used to obtain the sum of the squared deviations from the mean in Chapter 4, and it works well for examples like those presented in Appendix A-4 and Chapter 4 because the means are whole numbers, not fractions. The deviation method is cumbersome in most cases, however, because means are rarely whole numbers. The computation of squared deviations from the mean is usually laborious. We will use the computational formulas, which are much easier to handle, particularly if a calculator is available. If you want to convince yourself that the deviation and computational formulas are comparable, refer to Appendix A-5. Or if you want to examine the proof for the assertion that the SS_{tot} equals SS_{bg} plus SS_{wg}, refer to Appendix A-3.

Let us now perform an analysis of variance on the data in Table 11-2. Again, the basic task is to compute the SS_{tot}, the SS_{bg} and the SS_{wg}. Because we will be working with group totals and the sum of the squared scores, you may prefer to obtain these values before considering the three formulas. If you refer to Table 11-2, you will see that the total for each group and the sum of the squared scores for each group have been calculated. The overall total can be obtained by adding the group totals.

Computation of the Sum of Squares Total. The first step is to compute the SS_{tot}. The formula for the computation of SS_{tot} is:

$$SS_{tot} = \Sigma\Sigma X^2 - \frac{(T)^2}{N}$$

The summation signs (sigmas) mean that you add; the numbers denoted by the symbol following the sigmas are added. The X in the formula refers to any score. In this case each score is squared and then all the squared scores are added. It is important to note that the scores are squared *before* they are added. There are two summation signs because the squared scores in each group are added and then the group totals are added (i.e., this can be regarded as two separate adding operations). If all the scores are squared and added, the obtained value is 15,734. The T in the formula (the total for all the scores) is squared and then divided by N (the total number of scores, in this case 30). The computation of the SS_{tot} is presented in Table 11-3. The next step is to compute the SS_{bg}.

Computation of the Sum of Squares between Groups. The formula for the SS_{bg} is:

$$SS_{bg} = \Sigma \frac{(\text{group total})^2}{n} - \frac{(T)^2}{N}$$

The n is the symbol for the number of scores in each group. Each group total is squared and divided by the number of scores in that group. If there are the same number of subjects in each group, each group total can be squared and all the totals can be summed before dividing by the number of subjects in each group. If there is an unequal number of subjects in each group, each group total is squared and divided by the number of subjects in that group before summing the values across groups. Having an unequal number of subjects in each group does not cause problems if only one independent variable is studied and the number in each group is *about* the same. The last term in the formula is identical to the last term in the formula for the SS_{tot}. Since this value has already been computed, it is not necessary to do it again. The computation of SS_{bg} for our example is presented in Table 11-3.

Computation of the Sum of Squares within Groups. The computation of the SS_{wg} is very easy; since the value can be obtained by subtracting the SS_{bg} from the SS_{tot}. This follows because $SS_{tot} = SS_{bg} + SS_{wg}$. Obviously, if a mistake is made in computing the SS_{tot} or the SS_{bg} it is not possible to obtain the correct SS_{wg} by subtraction, so it is a good idea to compute the SS_{wg} directly as well. If the results are the same with both methods you can proceed with confidence. To compute the SS_{wg} directly each group is taken individually and SS is computed for that group only. After this is done for all the groups, the values that were obtained are summed. The total is equal to the SS_{wg}. If the work is done correctly the SS_{tot} will be equal to the SS_{bg} plus the SS_{wg}. The computation of the SS_{wg} by the subtraction method and the direct method is presented in Table 11-3.

The sum of squares can be zero (e.g., all groups have identical means), but never negative. A negative *sum of squares* indicates a mistake.

However, positive and negative *scores* should not be of any concern; the presence of both positive and negative numbers will have no effect on the analysis. Yet, if the negative numbers bother you they can be eliminated by adding a constant greater than the largest negative number to every score.

TABLE 11-3

Computation of the Analysis of Variance for the Data Presented in Table 11-2

$$SS_{tot} = \Sigma\Sigma X^2 - \frac{(T)^2}{N}$$

$$SS_{tot} = 15,734 - \frac{(636)^2}{30}$$

$$SS_{tot} = 2250.80$$

$$SS_{bg} = \Sigma \frac{(\text{group total})^2}{n} - \frac{(T)^2}{N}$$

$$SS_{bg} = \frac{(115)^2 + (209)^2 + (312)^2}{10} - \frac{(636)^2}{30}$$

$$SS_{bg} = \frac{154,250}{10} - \frac{(636)^2}{30}$$

$$SS_{bg} = 1941.80$$

$$SS_{wg} = SS_{tot} - SS_{bg}$$

$$SS_{wg} = 2250.80 - 1941.80$$

$$SS_{wg} = 309.00$$

or

$$SS_{wg} = \left[1419 - \frac{(115)^2}{10}\right] + \left[4457 - \frac{(209)^2}{10}\right] + \left[9858 - \frac{(312)^2}{10}\right]$$

$$SS_{wg} = 96.5 + 88.9 + 123.6$$

$$SS_{wg} = 309.00$$

Adding a constant to each score has no effect on the analysis of variance significance test.

Analysis of Variance Table

Source of Variance. The next step is to prepare the analysis of variance table. This table provides a convenient way to arrive at the estimates of population variance and compare the estimates. An analysis of variance table for our example is Table 11-4. The first column is labeled *source*. This is shorthand for *source of variance*. Recall that there are two independent estimates of population variance, one based on within-group variance, the other on between-group variance; these are the two sources.

Degrees of Freedom. The second column is labeled *degrees of freedom (df)*. The degrees of freedom for analysis of variance can be understood in about the same way as degrees of freedom for the chi square. The task is to determine the number of scores that are free to vary when the total is determined. To determine the degrees of freedom between groups, each group total and the overall total are considered. When the overall total is fixed, all the group totals except one are free to vary. Thus, the degrees of freedom between groups is one less than the number of groups. Since the symbol k is used to denote the number of groups, the degrees of freedom between groups is $k - 1$.

To compute the degrees of freedom within groups it is necessary to consider the number of scores in each group and the group total. When the group total is fixed all the scores in each group except one are free to vary. If you refer to Table 11-2 and count the number of scores in each group that are free to vary when the group total is fixed it should be clear that the degrees of freedom for each group is one less than the number of subjects in each group. When n is used to denote the number of subjects in each group the degrees of freedom for each group is equal to $n - 1$. Since there are k different groups, the number of degrees of freedom within groups is equal to $k(n - 1)$ if there are the same number of subjects in each group. The degrees of freedom for SS_{tot} is equal to the total number of scores minus one. The degrees of freedom between groups and within groups together should equal the degrees of freedom for SS_{tot}.

The SS, MS, and F Columns. The third column is for the sum of squares. Because these values have already been determined it is only necessary to record them in the table.

The fourth column is labeled *mean square (MS)*. The mean square is

TABLE 11-4

Analysis of Variance Table for the Experiment in Which the Effect of Aggressiveness on Selling Was Assessed

Source	df	SS	MS	F
Between groups	2	1941.80	970.90	84.87
Within groups	27	309.00	11.44	
Total	29	2250.80		

obtained by taking the *SS* for each source, in this case that between groups and within groups, and dividing by the degrees of freedom for that source. When chance only is operating, each mean square is an independent estimate of population variance. If the independent variable manipulation had an effect the between-group mean square should be larger than the within-group mean square.

The two are compared by dividing the between-group mean square by the within-group mean square. The value obtained is called an *F* value. It is recorded in the fifth column of the analysis of variance table. (The value is labeled *F* after Sir Ronald Fisher who is largely responsible for developing the analysis of variance significance test.) In this case the *F* value is recorded in the between-group row because the size of the *F* is used to assess whether the differences between groups are greater than should be expected if only chance is operating. After completing the analysis of variance table, there is only one more step. It is necessary to determine whether the obtained *F* value is statistically significant.

Evaluating the Obtained F Value

By now you have probably guessed that the obtained *F* value is evaluated for statistical significance by comparing it with a table value. If the between-group estimate is so much larger than the within-group estimate that the obtained *F* value is a rare event if only chance is operating, the results can be attributed to the independent variable. The table in Appendix C-4 is used to assess the likelihood of the obtained *F* value occurring if only chance is operating.

In order to find the appropriate table value for comparison we must know the number of degrees of freedom for each variance estimate and select a significance level. Assume that the .05 level of significance is selected. The number of degrees of freedom for the between-group estimate indicates the appropriate column to refer to in the table, and the number of degrees of freedom for the within-group estimate indicates the appropriate row. In this case there are two degrees of freedom for the between-group and twenty-seven degrees of freedom for the within-group estimate. The table in Appendix C-4 does not have a value for two and twenty-seven degrees of freedom so it is necessary to use the next *smaller* degree of freedom for the within-group estimate. An examination of Column 2 and Row 26 reveals a table value of 3.37 corresponding to the .05 significance level. Thus, in order to reject the null hypothesis at the .05 level of significance, the obtained *F* value has to be equal to or greater than 3.37. Because the obtained *F* value of 84.87 is greater than 3.37, the null hypothesis is rejected. The results of this experiment are very unlikely if only chance is operating. Therefore, it appears that the level of aggressiveness influenced the dollar value of the sales, if, of course, the experiment was properly designed and executed.

Follow-up Tests

The previous analysis reveals that the level of aggressiveness influenced the dollar value of the sales, but it does not indicate whether medium aggressiveness differs significantly from high aggressiveness or from low aggressiveness. It tells us only that there is a significant difference between low and high aggressiveness. If an independent variable with more than two levels produces a significant effect it is possible to conclude that the groups that do the best and the worst differ significantly, but it is not possible to make statements about comparisons between the other groups.

The relative effectiveness of different levels of the independent variable is usually not a major concern if a quantitative manipulation is made and a monotonic relationship is observed. In the present example, the major interest is in whether aggressiveness has an effect, not in the relative effectiveness of different levels of aggressiveness. However, when a qualitative manipulation is made (e.g., three different instructional techniques are used), one should compare the levels of the independent variable. It is important to know whether the groups differ significantly and *which* groups differ significantly. To obtain that information one must perform follow-up tests.

As was mentioned earlier some investigators adopt a more stringent significance level when making follow-up tests (e.g., they make all possible comparisons of four groups taking two at a time). If five or less comparisons that are not theoretically justified are to be made, you can adopt a more stringent significance level. The significance level for the experiment is roughly equal to the number of comparisons times the significance level: if the .01 significance level is adopted for each of five comparisons, the significance level for the experiment would be approximately .05. If there are theoretical reasons for making each comparison (i.e., the comparisons are preplanned), many investigators do not adopt a more stringent significance level for each comparison.

It is not uncommon for investigators to use the analysis of variance to analyze the effect of an independent variable having more than two levels and then, if necessary, use the *t*-test to complete the analysis by comparing the performance of two groups at a time. There is nothing wrong with this procedure. It just seems unnecessary to use the *t*-test because the follow-up tests can be made with the analysis of variance. The *t*-test, analysis of variance, or a number of other tests can be used as follow-up tests.

An appropriate follow-up test is to repeat the analysis of variance for the comparisons of interest. For example, if three instructional techniques (A, B, and C) were tested it may be interesting to know if A and B differ, if B and C differ, and if A and C differ. If the overall analysis is significant at least one, and maybe all, of these comparisons will be significant. To make each comparison it is necessary to consider two groups at a time, not three. For example, to compare A and B the investigator should ignore Group C entirely.

It is a good idea to use the mean square and degrees of freedom from the overall analysis when making a follow-up comparison because the within-group estimate of population variance is not likely to be affected by the treatment manipulation. Therefore, the best within-group estimate is obtained when all groups are considered. For instance, in the previous example of aggressiveness and dollar value of sales it is possible to do an analysis of variance for the low and medium conditions only. High aggressiveness is ignored completely. The between-group estimate of population variance is based only on the low and medium groups. However, the overall within-group estimate of population variance (i.e., 11.44 with twenty-seven degrees of freedom) can be used to evaluate the low versus medium comparison. The degrees of freedom for the obtained F value would be one and twenty-seven.

Relationship between the t- and F-Tests

The relationship between the t- and F-tests can be demonstrated by performing an analysis of variance on the results reported in Table 11-1. The computation of this analysis of variance is presented in Table 11-5. The procedure for computing the sum of squares total and the sum of squares within groups is identical to the example presented in Table 11-3. There is a *slight* difference in the computation of the sum of squares between groups because there is an unequal number of subjects in the two groups. As should be clear from the computation of the SS_{bg} presented in Table 11-5 it is necessary to square each group total and divide by the number of subjects in that group before summing the values across groups. When there are the same number of subjects in each group we square each group total, sum the squared scores, and divide by the number of subjects in each group. The only other difference is in the computation of the degrees of freedom within groups. We cannot simply multiply the number of groups (k) by $n - 1$ because n is not the same for each group. We have to determine the number of scores that are free to vary for each group separately and then sum the degrees of freedom across groups to obtain the total degrees of freedom within groups.

The evaluation of the obtained F value is identical to the procedure used earlier. We refer to Appendix C-4 to find the tabled value that corresponds to one and sixteen degrees of freedom and the .05 significance level. This value is 4.49. Since the obtained F value of 1.88 is less than the tabled value we cannot reject the null hypothesis. The analysis of variance and the t-test yield comparable results; we cannot reject the null hypothesis in either case.

It is easy to specify the relationship between the t- and F-tests because F equals t^2. You can take the square root of an F value to obtain a t value or you can square a t value to obtain F. This makes sense only when you have a two-condition comparison, of course, because the t-test is limited to two-condition comparisons. You can square the t value obtained in Table 11-1 (−1.376) to demonstrate that the squared value (1.89) is equal to the

TABLE 11-5

Computation of the Analysis of Variance for the Data Presented in Table 11-1

$$SS_{tot} = \Sigma\Sigma X^2 - \frac{(T)^2}{N}$$

$$SS_{tot} = 199,144 - \frac{(1,888)^2}{18}$$

$$SS_{tot} = 199,144 - 198,030.22$$

$$SS_{tot} = 1113.78$$

$$SS_{bg} = \Sigma \frac{(\text{group total})^2}{n} - \frac{(T)^2}{N}$$

$$SS_{bg} = \frac{(1026)^2}{10} + \frac{(862)^2}{8} - \frac{(1888)^2}{18}$$

$$SS_{bg} = 105,267.60 + 92,880 - 198,030.22$$

$$SS_{bg} = 117.38$$

$$SS_{wg} = SS_{tot} - SS_{bg}$$

$$SS_{wg} = 1113.78 - 117.38$$

$$SS_{wg} = 996.40$$

Source	df	SS	MS	F
Between groups	1	117.38	117.38	1.88
Within groups	16	996.40	62.28	
Total	17	1113.78		

F value obtained in Table 11-5. Except for a slight rounding error of .01 the two values are equal. That is, $t^2 = 1.89$, and $F = 1.88$.

The tabled values for t and F are related in the same way (i.e., $F = t^2$). You can demonstrate this relationship by selecting a significance level (say .05) and comparing the table values for each degree of freedom value. For the F distribution we use one degree of freedom for the numerator because there is only one degree of freedom when two groups are compared. If we compare the .05 significance level for any of the within-group degrees of freedom we will find that the tabled values of t, when squared, will equal the tabled values for *F*. This point is demonstrated in Table 11-6. Corresponding table values of *t* and *F* were selected. As can readily be seen, *F* equals t^2. In short, the student who learns how to use the analysis of variance test does not need to bother with the *t*-test. This holds true for the analysis of between-subject designs (considered in this chapter) and within-subject designs (considered in the next chapter).

The discussion of the statistical analysis of between-subject design experiments in which one independent variable is studied is now concluded. We have considered the *t*-test, the analysis of variance, and the relationship between them. The next step is to consider the analysis of experiments in which two independent variables are studied. Before going on to the next example it is very important that we have a firm understanding of the steps used in performing an analysis of variance.

To master the steps you should do the actual computations for several examples. If a calculator is available compute the analysis of variance for the results in Table 11-2 by referring to the text material and Table 11-2 only. If you can do it without referring to Table 11-3, you should be ready to continue on. This is also a good time to turn to the problems at the end of the chapter and work those that require an analysis of variance to be performed with just one independent variable. Such practice will facilitate your understanding of the next section.

ANALYSIS OF VARIANCE WITH TWO INDEPENDENT VARIABLES

Assume that an investigator is interested in the quality of instruction and the quality of the student body at a particular institution. He has witnessed both outstanding and abysmal examples of instruction and has had contact with students who take their course work very seriously and with students who consider higher education a farce. He wonders what can be done to improve the quality of instruction.

TABLE 11-6

The Tabled Values for t *and* F *for the .05 Significance Level for Several Degrees of Freedom within Groups*

Degrees of freedom	Tabled t values	Tabled F values
1	12.706	161.00
4	2.776	7.71
10	2.228	4.96
16	2.120	4.49
40	2.021	4.08

Combination of Subject and Nonsubject Variable Manipulations

The investigator is convinced that learning is a very complicated phenomenon. He has rejected the view that there is a single best way to present material because he has witnessed various styles that appear to be effective. Moreover, the emphasis on the quality of instruction, although important, is only one side of the problem. After all, regardless of the quality of instruction the student still has complete veto power over all learning. If he decides not to learn there is no way that an instructional program of whatever quality will succeed; it is also necessary to consider the quality or state of the learner. A particular instructional program may be effective for one kind of learner but not for another. The investigator decides to test this view by conducting an experiment.

Nonsubject Variable Manipulation. There are many models of instruction, and each approach has its advocates and critics. The investigator decides to study the effect of the instructor's style. He selects a content-oriented formal approach for one style and a motivation-oriented informal approach for the other. For the formal approach he uses few examples and makes little or no attempt to entertain the students or relate the material to "real-life" situations. He does not take any responsibility for motivating the student. If the student is not self-motivated that is his own problem. The instructor's role is to present the material in a well-organized manner without garnishment; the student's role is to learn it. The instructor does not encourage the students to relate to him on a personal basis.

For the informal approach the instructor uses many examples. He tries to use examples that are amusing or help the student relate the material to real-life situations. He also tries to motivate the students to learn and encourages them to be very informal with him both inside and outside of the classroom. In short, he attempts to relate to them personally.

Subject Variable Manipulation. The investigator believes that the effectiveness of each instructional approach may depend on the characteristics of the students. Some students may want to relate to their instructors on a personal basis and have the instructor attempt to motivate them. Others, however, may have little or no interest in a personal relationship with the instructor. They do not want the instructor to attempt to motivate them because they believe they are able to cope with their motivational problems. In short, the investigator believes that students can be placed in two large categories, which he calls "low academic motivation" and "high academic motivation." A questionnaire is designed to determine motivation level. Assume that the questionnaire is reliable and valid.

Method. The two independent variables are the instructional approach and the type of student. The dependent variable is course performance as assessed by the total number of points each student accumulates. The final grade is based on the number of points. The behavioral objectives are the same for both instructional techniques and the students are informed of these objectives. The evaluation process is consistent with the stated objectives. Every level of each independent variable is combined with every level of every other independent variable and the number of observations are the same for each combination of treatments. In this case there are two levels of instruction and two kinds of students, so there are four conditions. This is called a 2 by 2 factorial design because there are two levels of each of two independent variables.

A questionnaire designed to assess academic motivation is presented to a group of 200 students. Then the top thirty-two students (high motivation) and the bottom thirty-two (low motivation) are selected. The top thirty-two are randomly assigned to the two instructional conditions with the restriction that there be sixteen subjects in each group. The same procedure is used for the bottom thirty-two. It is important that there be the same number of subjects in each of the four conditions. The two groups of high motivation students differ with respect to the instructional manipulation, as do the two groups of low motivation students. Assume that all methodological or procedural problems are handled properly and that the data are collected with a minimum of difficulty.

Results. The total number of points each student accumulated in the four experimental conditions is presented in Table 11-7. The task is to determine whether the independent variables had an effect on course performance. The analysis of variance is an appropriate statistical test. The level of measurement is interval, and a between-subject design was used.

Computing Analysis of Variance

The procedure for analyzing this experiment is very similar to that used for the previous example. In fact, the initial steps are identical to the steps used when only one independent variable is manipulated. The basic task is to compute the SS_{tot}, SS_{bg}, and SS_{wg}, in that order. It is necessary to compute the sum of the scores for each group and the sum of the squared scores for each group in order to compute the three sums of squares.

Computing the SS_{tot}, SS_{bg}, *and* SS_{wg}. The formula for the computation of the SS_{tot} is:

$$SS_{tot} = \Sigma\Sigma X^2 - \frac{(T)^2}{N}.$$

As we know, the first term is obtained by squaring the score for each subject and then adding all the squared scores. To obtain the value for the second term the total for all the scores is squared and then divided by the total number of scores (in this case 64). The formula for the SS_{bg} is:

$$SS_{bg} = \Sigma \frac{(\text{group total})^2}{n} - \frac{(T)^2}{N}.$$

TABLE 11-7

The Total Number of Points for Each Student in the Four Experimental Conditions (fictitious data)

Academic motivation	Instructional approach	
	Content-oriented, formal	Motivation-oriented, informal
Low	102 112 95 100 117 76 128 $\Sigma X_2 = 1{,}660$ 81 $\Sigma X^2 = 176{,}660$ 109 88 $\bar{X} = 103.75$ 111 93 124 84 135 105	164 165 175 181 140 138 160 $\Sigma X_2 = 2{,}480$ 156 $\Sigma X^2 = 389{,}468$ 133 154 $\bar{X} = 155.00$ 159 152 113 185 146 159
High	189 168 137 175 165 173 162 $\Sigma X_2 = 2{,}608$ 198 $\Sigma X^2 = 430{,}050$ 150 158 $\bar{X} = 163.00$ 147 173 156 177 129 151	132 94 118 153 109 100 127 $\Sigma X_2 = 1{,}869$ 104 $\Sigma X^2 = 221{,}891$ 120 135 $\bar{X} = 116.81$ 107 110 103 108 121 128

Thus, to obtain the first term each group total is squared and the squared group totals are added and then divided by the number of subjects in each group (in this case 16). The second term was already computed when the SS_{tot} was computed. Since the SS_{tot} is equal to the SS_{bg} plus the SS_{wg}, the SS_{wg} can be obtained by substraction (or by computing a SS for each group separately and then adding these values). The next step is to assess each independent variable separately. To do this we must look at the experiment in a slightly different manner. One independent variable has to be ignored while the other is evaluated. The computations are presented in Table 11-8.

Computing a Sum of Squares for Each Independent Variable. This step in the analysis requires a little flexibility or imagination on the part of the student. The formula for the SS_{bg} is used extensively but the definition of a group changes as the effect of each independent variable is assessed. The first term in the SS_{bg} formula is obtained by squaring each group total, adding the squared scores, and dividing by the number of scores in each group. The same procedure is used to evaluate the effect of each independent variable separately, but the way the groups are defined changes. Therefore the student has to look at the experiment from several points of view. The way the groups are defined will also determine the label given to the SS_{bg}. The SS_{bg} is very useful because it can be used to evaluate the effect of each independent variable separately. These points should shortly become clear.

The effect of the instructional manipulation can be evaluated by viewing the experiment as a two-group experiment. There are low and high motivation students in each of the instructional groups. The type of student variable is collapsed in order to evaluate the effect of instruction. If the type of student variable is ignored, there are thirty-two students in one instructional group and thirty-two in the other; imagine that academic motivation was not manipulated and that thirty-two students were tested with each instructional approach. The SS_{bg} can be obtained for each of the two instruction groups to assess the effect of the instructional manipulation. If these two groups differ markedly the difference can be attributed to the instructional manipulation. It is not reasonable to attribute these group differences to the type of student manipulation because there are low and high motivation students in each group.

Although the SS_{bg} formula is used to assess the instructional effect it is more appropriate to label the sum of squares obtained the $SS_{instruction}$ to minimize confusion. A between-group sum of squares is obtained but is it of a particular kind. It is the sum of squares obtained by comparing the subjects who had one instructional technique with the subjects who had the other, so it makes good sense to label it the $SS_{instruction}$. The computation of the $SS_{instruction}$ is presented in Table 11-8.

A similar procedure is used to obtain a sum of squares for the type of student effect. In this case, one group consists of thirty-two low motivation students and the other of thirty-two high motivation students. Once again the SS_{bg} formula is used. A total is obtained for each of the two groups. These totals are squared, then added, and then divided by the number of subjects in each group (thirty-two). The resultant value is labeled the $SS_{type\ of\ student}$. Now consider the differences among all four groups.

Computing the Sum of Squares for the Interaction. Let us consider the factors, besides chance, that might cause the four group totals to differ. If

TABLE 11-8

Computation of the Analysis of Variance for the Data Presented in Table 11-7

$$SS_{tot} = \Sigma\Sigma X^2 - \frac{(T)^2}{N}$$

$$SS_{tot} = 1,218,069 - \frac{(8617)^2}{64}$$

$$SS_{tot} = 57,870.73$$

$$SS_{bg} = \Sigma \frac{(\text{group total})^2}{n} - \frac{(T)^2}{N}$$

$$SS_{bg} = \frac{(2608)^2 + (1660)^2 + (1869)^2 + (2480)^2}{16} - \frac{(8617)^2}{64}$$

$$SS_{bg} = \frac{19,200,825}{16} - \frac{(8617)^2}{64}$$

$$SS_{bg} = 39,853.29$$

$$SS_{wg} = SS_{tot} - SS_{bg}$$

$$SS_{wg} = 57,870.73 - 39,853.29$$

$$SS_{wg} = 18,017.44$$

$$SS_{instruction} = \Sigma \frac{(\text{group total})^2}{n} - \frac{(T)^2}{N}$$

$$SS_{instruction} = \frac{(4268)^2 + (4349)^2}{32} - \frac{(8617)^2}{64}$$

$$SS_{instructuon} = 102.51$$

$$SS_{type\ of\ student} = \Sigma \frac{(\text{group total})^2}{n} - \frac{(T)^2}{N}$$

$$SS_{type\ of\ student} = \frac{(4477)^2 + (4140)^2}{32} - \frac{(8617)^2}{64}$$

$$SS_{type\ of\ student} = 1,774.51$$

$$SS_{I \times S} = SS_{bg} - SS_{instruction} - SS_{type\ of\ student}$$

$$SS_{I \times S} = 39,853.29 - 102.51 - 1774.51$$

$$SS_{I \times S} = 37,976.27$$

the instruction and type of student manipulations influence course performance, these manipulations will cause the four group totals to vary. Yet the $SS_{instruction}$ and the $SS_{type\ of\ student}$ may not account for all the differences among the groups. Determining the "overall" effect of instruction or type of student does not afford an assessment of the extent to which the effect of one of the manipulations (say, instruction) depends on the level of the other independent variable (type of student). If the effect of one depends on the level of the other, the two variables are said to *interact*.

The interaction effect is assessed by determining the extent to which the $SS_{instruction}$ and $SS_{type\ of\ student}$ effects account for all the differences among the four groups. That is, the sum of squares for instruction by type of student is computed by subtracting the $SS_{instruction}$ and $SS_{type\ of\ student}$ effects from the SS_{bg}. The interaction effect is the difference among the four groups that is not accounted for by the instruction effect and the type of student effect. This computation is also presented in Table 11-8. Interaction effects are considered in greater detail following the completion of the computations for this example. Now that all the sums of squares have been computed, the analysis of variance table can be considered.

The Analysis of Variance Table

Source of Variance. The analysis of variance table for this example is Table 11-9. The principal difference between this table and the one for the earlier example is that the between-group source of variance is replaced with an instruction, a type of student, and instruction by the type of student. It is necessary to consider the between-group differences in terms of these three *independent* effects rather than in terms of an overall between-group effect. The effects are independent in that the statistical significance of any one of them does not depend on the significance, or lack of it, of any other. The within-group variance is used in the same way that it was when only one independent variable was considered.

TABLE 11-9

Analysis of Variance Table for the Experiment Investigating the Effect of Type of Instruction and Type of Student on Course Performance

Source of variance	df	SS	MS	F
Instruction (*I*)	1	102.51	102.51	.34
Type of student (*S*)	1	1,774.51	1,774.51	5.91
I × *S*	1	37,976.27	37,976.27	126.47
Within-group	60	18,017.44	300.29	
Total	63	57,870.73		

Degrees of Freedom. The degrees of freedom are determined in essentially the same way as when there is only one independent variable. The degrees of freedom for the instruction effect is equal to one because there are only two instruction groups. When calculating the instruction effect, the type of student variable was collapsed. This left two groups of thirty-two subjects each. Because the overall total is fixed, only one group total is free to vary. By the same reasoning, the degrees of freedom for the type of student effect is also equal to one.

A simple way to remember how to compute the degrees of freedom for any interaction is to keep in mind that a multiplication sign is used to label an interaction (e.g., *instruction × type of student*). The degrees of freedom for any interaction effect can be obtained by multiplying the degrees of freedom for the variables involved. In this case there is one degree of freedom for the interaction because the product of the degrees of freedom for the two variables is equal to one.

Note that the sum of the degrees of freedom for the three effects is equal to that which would have been obtained if the overall between-group effect had been assessed. Since there were four independent groups there would be three degrees of freedom for the between-group effect. There are sixty degrees of freedom for the SS_{wg} because there are four groups and sixteen subjects per group ($k(n-1) = 4(15) = 60$).

The SS, MS, *and* F *Columns.* The column for *SS* should not cause any difficulty because the sum of squares for each effect has been computed. The task is simply to record the values in the table. The values for the *MS* column are obtained by dividing the *SS* values for each effect by the degrees of freedom for that effect. The *F* value for each effect is obtained by dividing the mean square for the effect by the within-group mean square. In this case there are three separate effects. Each effect is evaluated by comparing the obtained *F* value with the appropriate table value. You will recall that in this case there are one and sixty degrees of freedom for each effect. If the .05 significance level is adopted, an obtained *F* value of 4.00 or greater (see Appendix C-4) is needed in order to have a statistically significant effect. We find that the type of student effect and instruction by type of student interaction are significant, but the instruction effect is not significant.

INTERACTIONS

Let us look at the results of this experiment in greater detail. The interpretation of the effect of a single variable (main effect) is usually straightforward. The particular manipulation either produces a statistically significant effect or it does not. In this case, the type of student manipulation produced a statistically significant effect and the instruction manipulation did not. Because the type of student manipulation is a subject variable, one cannot be confident that the obtained difference between the groups was due solely to motivational differences. Perhaps some other subject variable that correlates with academic motivation was actually responsible. For example, the two motivational groups may have differed in intelligence.

At this point you may be ready to conclude that the results of the experiment are not very interesting. The instruction manipulation did not result in a statistically significant effect and the one significant main effect is difficult to interpret because it involved a subject variable manipulation. Perhaps the experimenter wasted a lot of time. It would have been much simpler to correlate the academic motivation measure with course performance than to conduct an elaborate experiment. Of course, one could argue that there was no way of knowing that the instruction manipulation would not have an effect. Obviously, investigators should be prepared to accept the fact that their notions may be incorrect. In this case, however, there is little reason for gloom. The interaction is statistically significant, and it has practical and theoretical importance.

Definition of an Interaction

Many people have a difficult time understanding interactions, so a brief review may be useful. An interaction between two independent variables means that the effect of one depends on the level of the other. In our example the effect of instruction proved to depend on the type of student. In simple terms, the content-oriented formal approach produced better results with the highly motivated students ($\overline{X}$ of 163.00 versus $\overline{X}$ of 116.81), and the motivation-oriented informal approach produced better results with the less motivated students ($\overline{X}$ of 155.00 versus $\overline{X}$ of 103.75). These results are presented in Table 11-7. (Remember that these results are fictitious; they may not represent the true state of affairs.) The instruction effect would have been different if only high motivation or only low motivation students had been used. Even though the *overall* instructional manipulation did not have an effect, the finding indicates that the effectiveness of a particular instructional approach depends on the type of student.

Importance of Interactions

It is extremely unlikely that one can attain a satisfactory understanding of behavior without considering how variables interact. It is, of course, important to determine the main effects of particular independent variables on performance, but it is also important to determine the conditions under which the independent variable manipulation is effective or ineffective. If you can see that interactions are important you should also be able to see the importance of understanding the procedures for assessing interactions. Interactions are important when nonsubject variables are studied (e.g., the effects of different drugs in isolation or in combination) and when nonsubject variables are studied in combination with subject variables. Let us consider this latter situation further.

The investigation of interactions is one way to circumvent some of the interpretational difficulties in studying subject variables. The fact that the effectiveness of a particular variable depends on the type of subject is important even if there is no way to be confident that the right label is used for the subject variable. If it is possible to separate subjects into categories and then find a nonsubject variable manipulation that is differentially effective depending on the category of subjects considered, the finding is easy to interpret. It is essentially irrelevant what label is used for the categories. The important point is that the sorting is *useful* if the effectiveness of a nonsubject variable manipulation depends on the type of subject.

A common misconception about interactions is that one or more of the variables must be significant to obtain a significant interaction. This is simply not true, particularly when only two independent variables are manipulated. Main effects are independent of each other and they are independent of interactions. One can assess whether variables are independent of each other by determining whether they interact, but they can interact without producing main effects and vice versa. Let us consider a few pictorial examples in order to clarify the relationship between main effects and interactions.

Relationship between Interactions and Main Effects

Let us assume an experiment is conducted in which instructional method (Method 1 and Method 2) and type of student (social science major and natural science major) are varied. Course performance is the dependent variable. Four possible outcomes of the experiment are presented in Figure 11-1. The type of student variable is plotted on the abscissa (natural science on the left, social science on the right) and the instructional method variable is indicated by the shading of the bars (shaded bars for Method 1, blank bars for Method 2). Performance on the dependent measure (course performance) is plotted on the ordinate (vertical axis). The height of each bar indicates the course performance for that particular condition. For example, in Figure 11-1A the natural science students who receive Method 1 (shaded bar on the left) had the same level of performance as the social science students who received Method 2 (blank bar on the right). Let us consider Figure 11-1A to evaluate whether there are main effects or interactions. Assume that the within-group mean square is quite small so that the differences that appear to be significant *are* significant.

We evaluate main effects by considering one independent variable at a time. If we ignore method and compare the two kinds of students in Figure 11-1A we see that the average performance (average height of the bars) for

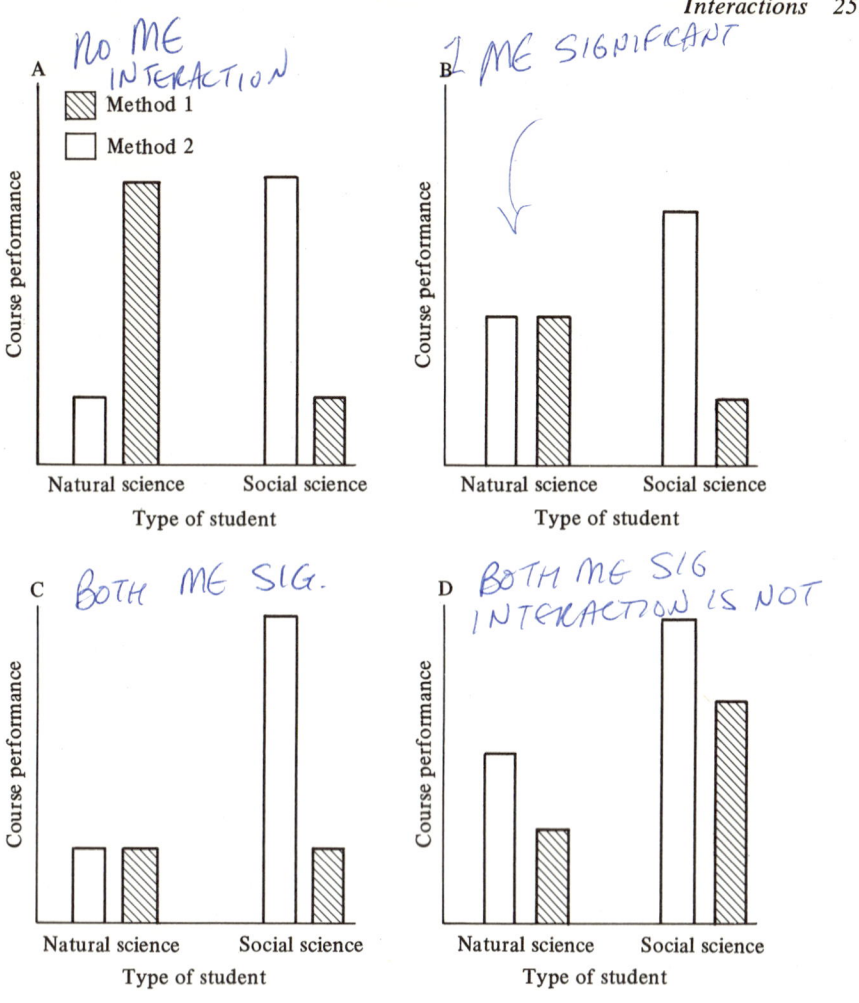

FIGURE 11-1

Course performance as a function of the type of student and instruction method (fictitious data)

social science students is about the same as for natural science students. Similarly, if we compare the two methods (i.e., if we ignore the type of student variable), we find that the two blank bars are about the same average height as the two shaded bars. There are no main effects; however, there is an interaction. The effect of method is much different for natural science students (1 is better than 2) than for social science students (2 is better than 1). The interaction is important because it qualified the interpretation of the main effects. If we only considered the main effects we would conclude that neither independent variable had an effect. This would be misleading, however, because

258 *Analysis of Between-subject Designs: Interval Data*

the variables do have an effect under certain conditions. For example, there is an effect of method if only natural science students are considered or if only social science students are considered. Similarly, natural science students are better than social science students if only Method 1 is considered, and social science students are better than natural science students if only Method 2 is considered.

In short, the interpretation of a main effect for an independent variable is straightforward as long as the independent variable does not interact with another independent variable. If the independent variable does interact with another independent variable the interaction is likely to be more important than the main effect. The interaction allows us to specify the *conditions* under which the independent variable has an effect.

A consideration of the remaining three figures (B, C, and D) is left as an exercise. If you consider B and C you should find that the effectiveness of the method depends on the type of student. In Figure 11-1B one main effect is significant and in Figure 11-1C both main effects are significant. In Figure 11-1D both main effects are significant but the interaction is not.

Each part of Figure 11-1 is drawn as a bar graph because it is unlikely that there is a single quantitative dimension underlying the independent variable of type of student. The type of student variable is more accurately classified as a qualitative rather than a quantitative variable. If we have a quantitative variable we can use line graphs instead of bar graphs. The same results presented in Figure 11-1 are presented in Figure 11-2 as line graphs. The type of student variable has been changed to quantitative ability. In this case quantitative ability (low versus high) is plotted on the abscissa and the method is indicated by the type of line (solid for Method 1 and dashed for Method 2). Once again course performance is plotted on the ordinate. There are four groups so there are four means plotted in each of the four figures. The four means are represented by the four dots in Figure 11-2A. We connect the two dots that represent the mean performance for the Method 1 conditions with a solid line. We connect the two dots that represent the mean performance for the Method 2 conditions with a dashed line. The two dots on the left indicate the mean performance for the two low quantitative ability conditions. The two dots on the right indicate the mean performance for the two high quantitative ability conditions. We have used lines instead of bars because it is reasonable to suggest that method and quantitative ability are related for more than just the two levels of quantitative ability considered. For example, in Figure 11-2A the results suggest that performance with Method 1 decreases as quantitative ability increases, whereas performance with Method 2 increases as quantitative ability increases.

If you examine the four figures carefully you should conclude — assuming that the within-groups mean square is quite small — that for A, B, and C the interaction is probably significant and the main effects may or may not be significant. In the fourth case (Figure 11-2D) both main effects are probably sig-

FIGURE 11-2

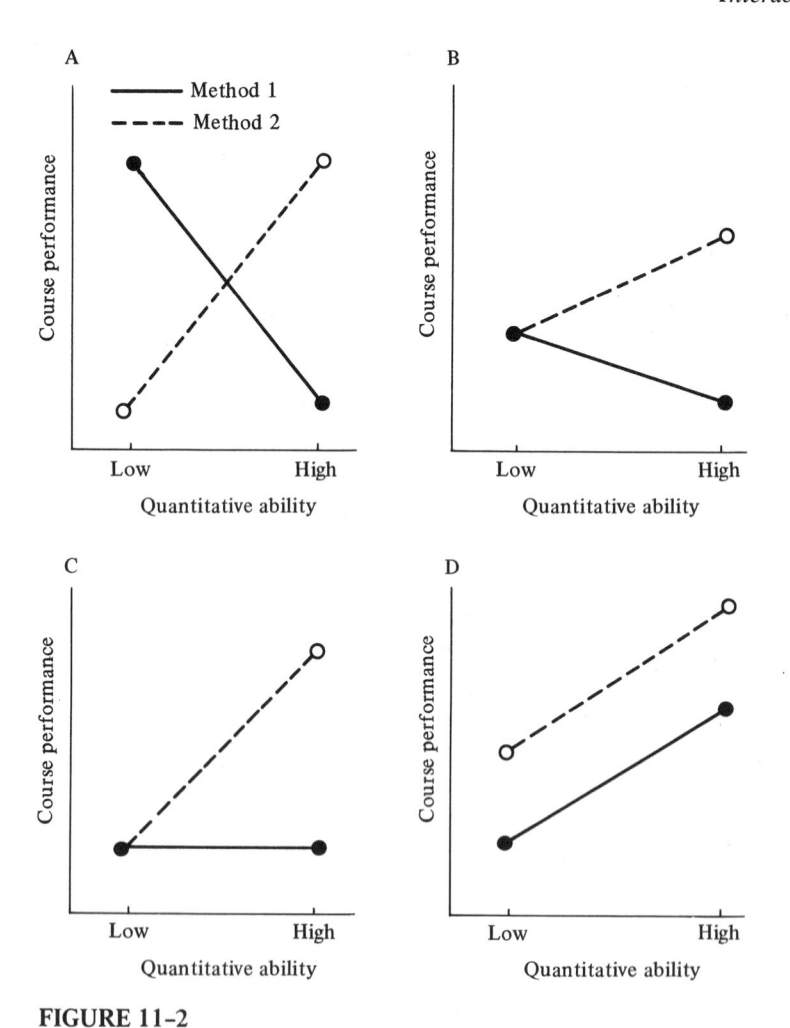

Course performance as a function of the instructional method and the quantitative ability of the students (fictitious data)

nificant but the interaction is not. It is necessary, of course, to perform statistical tests (in this case analysis of variance) to determine whether a particular effect is significant. We need to determine whether a particular outcome is rare or common if only chance is operating. We cannot do this simply by looking at a table or figure because the table or figure may not contain any information about the size of the chance fluctuations (e.g., the within-group mean square). An examination of a table or figure is a useful way to assess which effects are *likely* to be significant and which are not. There are other potential outcomes that would have the same significant effects (i.e., there are patterns of performance other than that given in C which might result in significant main effects and a significant interaction). The figures merely help us to visualize various possible outcomes.

ASSUMPTIONS OF THE ANALYSIS OF VARIANCE

The assumptions underlying the analysis of variance depend on the model used. Only the fixed effects model is considered in this text. Conclusions are drawn only about the levels of the independent variable actually manipulated. For the fixed effects model, one makes two assumptions: that the variances of the samples are homogenous and that the distributions within each sample are normal.

Homogeneity of Variance

The independent variable is expected to influence the extent to which the groups differ but not the fluctuations within a particular group. The within-group fluctuations are expected to be about the same regardless of the treatment. If, however, the manipulation influences the within-group variance (i.e., there is significantly greater fluctuation within one group than within another), the assumption of homogeneity of variance has been violated. Our task is to assess whether the within-group fluctuations (variance) are greater than should be expected on the basis of chance. This task can be accomplished by dividing the variance of the group having the greatest variance by that of the group having the smallest variance. The resultant quotient is called the F_{max} value.

The F_{max} value can be evaluated by referring to Appendix C-6. To find the correct table value the number of groups and the size of each group must be considered. The number of groups is used to determine the correct column and the degrees of freedom for each group (i.e., the number of subjects minus one) is used to determine the correct row. The values are given for both the .05 and .01 level of significance. For example, if there are six groups and sixteen subjects in each group, the F_{max} value has to be equal to or greater than 4.68 in order to conclude that the variances are heterogeneous. If the table does not include the value for your degrees of freedom, you should use the next lower value (e.g., 10 instead of 12) if you are interested in obtaining a significant F_{max} value, and the next highest (e.g., 12 instead of 10) if you are interested in obtaining a nonsignificant F_{max} value. Since investigators are usually interested in obtaining an F_{max} value that is not significant, the next highest degree of freedom is usually used whenever the table does not include the value for your degrees of freedom. If the variances are heterogeneous, i.e., if a significant F_{max} value is obtained, then the assumption of homogeneity of variance has not been met.

Assume that an investigator performs the F_{max} test and obtains a significant value. There is good reason to believe that the sample variances are not homogeneous. The question then is what investigators should do when heterogeneous variances are obtained. Although there is some disagreement on this point, most statisticians think that violating the assumption of homogeneity of variance is not too serious a problem. If this assumption is violated the experimenter is likely to reject the null hypothesis more often than is justified. The likelihood of error is a function of the size of the sample and the extent of the heterogeneity of the variances. Yet there is usually little cause for concern in that the violation of this assumption tends to have very little effect on the accuracy of the analysis of variance test. If the assumption has been violated a more stringent significance level (say, .01 instead of .05) should probably be used.

On the other hand, the significant F_{max} value may be a very interesting finding. If the independent variable influenced the within-group variance for some groups and not others, this suggests that subjects in the group(s) with the high variance were influenced differentially by the treatment. If the performance of some subjects and not of others is influenced, then the task for the experimenter is to determine why. In short, the fact that a treatment influences variance can be viewed as a finding *to be explained,* not merely as a failure to meet the assumption of the analysis of variance test.

Normality of Each Sample Distribution

The fact that the analysis of variance is so robust (i.e., insensitive) with respect to violations of homogeneity of variance has led many investigators to ignore the assumption and not to test for homogeneity of variance. Because the analysis of variance test is also robust with respect to the assumption of the normality of the distribution within each sample, many investigators ignore this assumption as well. Violations of the normality assumption do not have much effect on the validity of the test. However, some readers may want to know how to determine whether this assumption has been met.

The assumption can be evaluated by plotting the deviation of each score from its *group* mean. If the frequency distribution of these deviation scores for all groups combined is fairly normal (symmetrical and mesokurtic), the assumption is satisfied. If the assumption is not satisfied (i.e., if the distribution is markedly skewed) the investigator may elect to use a statistical test that does not require this assumption (see Siegel, 1956).

SUMMARY

The *t*-test or the analysis of variance can be used to evaluate the statistical significance of results of between-subject designs in which interval data are obtained. The *t*-test is appropriate for comparing two conditions at a time; the analysis of variance can be used for two or more groups at a time. The two significance tests are directly related in that the F value is always equal to t^2 when the two tests are performed on the same results.

The steps involved in obtaining a t value or F value are straightforward. The formula for the t-test and an example to demonstrate the computational steps are presented in Table 11-1. The computation of the analysis of variance for an experiment with one independent variable consists primarily of obtaining two estimates of population variance. The between-group estimate of population variance (mean square) is obtained by dividing the sum of squares between groups by its degrees of freedom. The within-group estimate of population variance (mean square) is obtained by dividing the sum of squares within groups by its degrees of freedom. The mean square between groups is divided by the mean square within groups to obtain an F value for the effect of the independent variable. The F value is evaluated by comparing it to the appropriate table value. If the obtained value exceeds the table value, the null hypothesis is rejected.

The analysis of variance for experiments in which more than one independent variable is manipulated is similar to that used for one independent variable. The major difference is that the sum of squares between groups is broken up to assess the effect of each independent variable and the interaction of the independent variables separately. It is not necessary to obtain a significant main effect to obtain a significant interaction.

The two major assumptions of the analysis of variance are homogeneity of variance and normality of each sample distribution. Slight violations of these assumptions do not have much effect on the accuracy of the analysis of variance test.

QUESTIONS

1. Why is it important to obtain two independent estimates of population variance?
2. Do an analysis of variance to determine whether the effect of the independent variable influenced performance. Present the analysis of variance table. The random-groups design was used and interval data were obtained. Or, perform a t-test on the first two groups only.

Group I	Group II	Group III
16	26	21
2	19	6
18	31	12
3	6	18
14	22	2
25	3	24
9	16	5
20	22	19

3. Do a *t*-test to determine whether the effect of the independent variable influenced performance. Once again, the random-groups design was used and interval data were obtained.

Group I	Group II
19	25
22	26
16	27
25	24
19	24
23	28

4. The investigator was interested in whether the attitude of the experimenter toward a child would affect the child's ability to perform a manual dexterity task. While meeting the child and introducing him to the task, the experimenter was either very friendly to the child or very businesslike. The child's task was to drop as many marbles as possible into a jar. The dependent measure was the number of marbles in the jar after one minute. The random-groups design was used. Analyze the results of the experiment and state the conclusions.

Friendly experimenter	Businesslike experimenter
20	34
30	35
36	29
26	31
22	27
23	33
32	26
28	30
24	
25	

5. Do an analysis of variance to determine whether the level of the independent variable influenced performance. Present the analysis of variance table. A random-groups design was used and interval data were obtained.

Group I	Group II	Group III
42	47	40
39	49	41
36	45	35
44	51	39
40	53	36
41	44	40
38	52	38
42	49	37
35	47	35
41	53	37
40	51	39

6. Do the follow up tests for the data in Question 5 to determine which groups differ significantly.
7. An investigator was interested in the amount of money different types of people would give to help free George Grimley from prison after an unfair trial. The two types of subjects used were humanitarians and lawyers. (Those who qualified for both categories were not used in the study.) The investigator also used two approaches: an emotional approach based on the plight of poor George Grimley and his family of fifteen children, and a judicial approach based on the legal precedents that could be set by the case. The dependent measure was the amount of money given. Random assignment was used to assign people to the type of approach. Present the analysis of variance table.

Type of participant

		Humanitarian	Lawyer
Type of appeal	Emotional	26 24 23 27 25 25 24 26	20 19 16 19 18 17 16 15
	Judicial	19 17 18 14 16 17 15 16	28 26 24 27 26 22 24 25

8. Do an analysis of variance to determine whether the effect of two independent variables — type of task and anxiety level — influence performance. Do the two variables interact? The random-groups design was used for the type of task manipulation. Anxiety level is a subject variable. Interval data were obtained.

		Type of task	
		Easy	*Difficult*
Anxiety	Low	9 10 8 7 9 10 11 9	6 5 7 8 6 5 6 7
	High	10 11 9 10 12 13 14 12	2 3 4 3 4 3 5 4

9. Draw a figure for the results obtained in Question 8.
10. What are the assumptions of analysis of variance?

analysis of within-subject and matched-groups designs 12

A few words need to be said about matched-groups designs and between-subject analyses before we consider statistical tests for within-subject and matched-groups designs. A matched-groups design can be considered a halfway step between a within-subject and a between-subject design. The way the matching is carried out determines which type of analysis is appropriate. When groups are matched by equating the group means and variances on the matching variables, the between-subject analyses discussed in Chapters 10 and 11 should be used. If they are matched on a subject by subject basis, then the analyses discussed in this chapter are appropriate.

The major purpose of this chapter is to acquaint you with statistical tools for analyzing experiments in which related samples are obtained. The samples may be related in that each subject is tested under each treatment condition (within-subject design), or the subjects in each treatment condition may be matched with subjects in the other treatment conditions on a subject by subject basis. As in the previous two chapters, the type of statistical tool will depend on the level of measurement of the dependent variable. The levels of measurement are examined in the same order as before, namely, nominal, ordinal, and interval. The steps in computing each test are considered in the context of an example.

NOMINAL DATA

Nominal Data Example

Imagine that an experimenter is interested in how to persuade people to stop smoking. An experiment is conducted to test the effectiveness of two different treatments relative to no treatment. For one treatment condition an aversive stimulus is paired with smoking in an attempt to make smoking unpleasant. The stimulus is an electric shock of sufficient intensity to be annoying but weak enough that no physical damage is done. The second treatment condition combines emotional and intellectual appeals intended to convince subjects that it would be in their own best interest to stop smoking. This approach involves presenting the evidence that smoking causes lung cancer, familiarizing subjects with the consequences of lung cancer, and so on. The third is a no treatment condition. The three conditions are labeled "shock," "verbal," and "control," respectively.

The two treatment conditions are administered for a two-hour period, four times a week for one month. The control subjects are also seen for the same amount of time, but their sessions are spent discussing issues unrelated to smoking, such as community problems. At the conclusion of the treatment period the experimenter checks periodically with the subjects and with their associates to determine whether they have, in fact, quit smoking. Success is defined as smoking a mean of five or fewer cigarettes a day for two months. The dependent measure requires classifying each person into the success or failure category. Assume that the experimenter has little difficulty classifying the subjects. For our purposes the success and failure categories are qualitatively different. That is, the dependent measure is to be treated as nominal data even though it could be viewed as an instance of a higher level of measurement.

The experimenter believes that the length of time a person has been smoking prior to treatment and the amount of smoking per day prior to treatment are likely to be related to the difficulty of breaking the cigarette habit. Therefore he decides to match the three groups on the basis of prior smoking habits. From the sample of smokers he identifies groups of three persons who have essentially the same smoking history. He then *randomly assigns* them to the three conditions in such a way that one subject is in each condition. This process is repeated until three groups of twenty subjects each are obtained.

Results. The results of the experiment are presented in Table 12-1. Notice that there are twenty subjects in each condition and that the three subjects in the same row are matched with respect to prior smoking history. Each subject has a score of 0 (failure) or 1 (success). The issue is whether the three groups differ significantly in the number of successes. A significance test is used to assess whether the obtained differences are greater than can reasonably be expected on the basis of chance. In this case a test is needed that can be performed with a matched-groups (or within-subject) design which yields nominal data. The Cochran Q test (Cochran, 1950) is suitable.

TABLE 12-1

The Results of an Experiment Investigating the Effect of Two Treatments, Relative to a Control, in Reducing the Incidence of Smoking (fictitious data)

Row	Control	Verbal approach	Shock approach	Total
a	0	1	1	2
b	1	1	0	2
c	0	0	1	1
d	0	1	1	2
e	0	0	0	0
f	1	1	1	3
g	0	0	0	0
h	1	1	1	3
i	0	1	1	2
j	0	0	1	1
k	1	0	1	2
l	0	1	0	1
m	1	1	0	2
n	0	0	0	0
o	0	1	1	2
p	0	0	0	0
q	1	1	1	3
r	0	0	0	0
s	0	1	1	2
t	1	1	1	3
group total	7	12	12	$T = 31$
(group total)^2	49	144	144	$\Sigma(\text{row total})^2 = 71$

$$Q = \frac{(k-1)\,[k\,\Sigma(\text{group total})^2 - (T)^2]}{k\,(\Sigma \text{ row totals}) - \Sigma(\text{row totals})^2}$$

$$Q = \frac{2\,[3\,(49 + 144 + 144) - (31)^2]}{3\,(31) - 71}$$

$$Q = 4.55$$

Cochran Q Test

Computing the Q Value. The data in Table 12-1 are in the correct form for the use of the Cochran Q test in that each subject is placed in either a success or failure category. To make possible the use of the Cochran Q test, the dependent measure must be dichotomous (e.g., success or failure, yes or no, pass or fail, consent or refuse). A zero is always assigned to individuals in one category and a one to individuals in the other. Also, the data in

Table 12-1 are in correct form in that the treatment conditions are represented in the columns, and the number of observations in each condition is equal to the number of rows.

The value of Q can then be computed by the formula:

$$Q = \frac{(k-1)\,[k\,\Sigma(\text{group total})^2 - (T)^2]}{k\,(\Sigma\,\text{row totals}) - \Sigma(\text{row totals})^2}$$

As in earlier examples, k is equal to the number of conditions (groups) and T is equal to the total of all the scores. The group totals refer, of course, to the totals for each condition. The computation of the Q value is presented in Table 12-1. Following the computation of Q, the next step is to evaluate Q to determine whether the obtained value is statistically significant.

Evaluating the Q *Value.* The obtained Q value is evaluated for significance in essentially the same way as the chi square. That is, since the two are essentially equal, the chi square distribution can be used to evaluate Q. The number of degrees of freedom for the Cochran Q test is equal to $k-1$. The value in the chi square table with $k-1$ degrees of freedom is the appropriate table value with which to evaluate the obtained Q value. If the .05 significance level is adopted a Q value of 5.991 or higher (see Appendix C-2) is needed to reject the null hypothesis. In this case the obtained value of 4.55 is less than the value needed so it is not possible to reject the null hypothesis. The probability of this particular outcome is greater than 5% if chance only is operating.

Uses of the Cochran Q *Test.* To use the Cochran Q test the number of observations per condition should not be too small (not less than, say, ten). Note also that the Cochran Q test can be used with a within-subject as well as a matched-groups design. For example, a perception experiment could be performed in which each subject receives three different conditions of illumination. The condition of illumination is the independent variable. The task is to determine whether the subject is a success or failure under each of the three conditions. In this case there would be three observations from each subject so the observations in each row would be one subject's data. The Cochran Q test could be used to analyze this experiment in the same way that it was used to analyze the matched-groups experiment. However, if it is possible to do more than classify subjects into one of two categories, information is wasted by classifying them into two categories and using the Cochran Q test.

ORDINAL DATA

Ordinal Data Example

Assume that an experimenter is interested in the effect of a training program to reduce or eliminate shyness. The investigator has a test for shyness that we will assume to be reliable and valid. The test scores are treated as ordinal measurement because it is not clear that the intervals between successive units are equal. It is clear, however, that the test scores are at least at the ordinal level of measurement and that differences between test scores are ordinal. We can rank the differences between test scores obtained by testing each individual twice. All subjects are given a pretest, the treatment, and then a posttest. You may wish to consider the methodological weaknesses of this nonexperimental design (see Chapter 6) and perhaps suggest how the design might be changed to remove the weaknesses. Our task will be to consider a significance test for evaluating the pretest-posttest difference.

The results of this hypothetical experiment are presented in Table 12-2. Twelve subjects are randomly selected for the treatment from a population of introductory psychology students who indicated that they were shy. The question of interest is whether the pretest-posttest differences, if any, can be attributed solely to chance fluctuations or whether something besides chance (e.g., the treatment, regression, history) is operating. The Wilcoxon test can be used to evaluate the statistical significance of the results.

The Wilcoxon Test

Computations for the Wilcoxon Test. The computation of the Wilcoxon test for the results of the experiment on shyness is presented in Table 12-2. As shown in the table, each subject has two scores, in this case a pretest and posttest score. We want to examine the two sets of scores to assess whether

TABLE 12-2

The Pretest and Posttest Shyness Scores for the Twelve Subjects Who Received the Treatment and the Computations for the Wilcoxon Test (fictitious data)

Subject	Pretest	Posttest	Sign	Difference	Rank difference	Signed rank difference
A	45	38	+	7	8.0	+8.0
B	34	23	+	11	10.0	+10.0
C	31	35	−	4	4.0	−4.0
D	50	48	+	2	1.5	+1.5
E	22	19	+	3	3.0	+3.0
F	39	45	−	6	6.5	−6.5
G	42	30	+	12	11.0	+11.0
H	25	20	+	5	5.0	+5.0
I	50	30	+	20	12.0	+12.0
J	42	44	−	2	1.5	−1.5
K	36	30	+	6	6.5	+6.5
L	23	14	+	9	9.0	+9.0

Sum of positive ranks = 66

Sum of negative ranks = 12

the obtained differences between the two sets is a rare or common event if chance only is operating. The first step is to subtract one score from the other for each subject to obtain a difference score. It does not matter which score is subtracted (i.e., pretest score minus posttest score or vice versa) as long as we are consistent. However, we cannot use any subject who has the same score on the two tests. That is, a difference score of zero is not permitted. Subjects with a difference score of zero are dropped from the analysis completely. We keep the sign of the difference and the amount of the difference separate because we want to rank the difference scores independent of sign. The ranked difference scores are presented in the sixth column of Table 12-2. When there are tied scores we assign the average of the tied ranks. The last column is obtained by taking the sign (Column 4) and placing it next to the rank difference (Column 6) to obtain the signed rank difference (Column 7). Then we add the positive ranks and the negative ranks. We compare the smaller sum with a tabled value to determine whether the results are statistically significant.

Evaluation of the Wilcoxon Test. The smaller sum, in this case the sum of the negative ranks, is called the W value (for Wilcoxon). In this case W is 12. We need to determine whether this value is a rare or common occurrence if chance only is operating. In order to do this we compare the obtained value with a distribution of W values obtained by referring to Appendix C-6. To find the appropriate tabled value we need to adopt a significance level and know the number of subjects (i.e., the number of pairs of scores). Let us adopt the .05 significance level (two-tailed). Because there are twelve subjects, the tabled value is 13. Our W value of 12 is lower than the tabled value of 13 so we can reject the null hypothesis. For the Wilcoxon test the obtained value must be less than the tabled value in order to be significant.

In this case we can reject the null hypothesis but it does not follow necessarily that we can attribute the results to chance fluctuation *plus* the treatment effect. There may be variables other than the treatment that are responsible for the statistically significant reduction in the shyness scores from pretest to posttest. The significance test allows us to conclude that more than chance is operating but it does not allow us to specify exactly what "more than chance" means. We can attribute statistically significant results to the effect of the treatment only when we have used experimental procedures that make alternative interpretations unlikely. There are several other plausible interpretations for a statistically significant result obtained with a pretest-posttest, nonexperimental design.

INTERVAL DATA

Interval Data Example

Assume that an investigator is interested in evaluating a theory of aggression in which aggressive behavior is viewed in terms of survival. The view is simply that aggressive behaviors are necessary for the survival of those species that kill other animals for food. Perhaps hunger in lower animals results in increased aggressiveness. That is, the internal stimuli associated with hunger may also be associated with aggressiveness. Our investigator decided to assess whether aggressiveness is related to hunger in children.

Assume that the investigator has access to young children at a summer camp. The investigator has control over the time each child eats because it is necessary to stagger the eating times at the dining hall. The children eat their evening meal at 5:00, 6:00, or 7:00 P.M. Children who eat early (i.e., 5:00 P.M.) are free to play afterward; children who eat late (i.e., 7:00 P.M.) are free to play before eating. Thus it is possible to observe the play behavior of children at 6:00 P.M. to determine the relationship between aggressive behaviors and time since the last meal. Each child is observed for one hour, starting at 6:00 P.M., on two days. On one day the child eats at 5:00 P.M., on the other day at 7:00 P.M. The order of the conditions (i.e., 5:00 P.M. versus 7:00 P.M.) is counterbalanced across conditions so that the nature of the treatment is not confounded with the order of the treatments. A within-subject design is used and interval data (number of aggressive acts) are obtained.

One can ponder the methodological, ethical, and interpretational problems inherent in an experiment of this nature. One can consider the problems of defining hunger and aggressiveness, demand characteristics, possible differential transfer, and so on. Or one may want to consider other approaches that could be used to investigate the relationship between hunger and aggression. Our concern will be with the analysis of results obtained with a within-subject design in which interval data are obtained. In this case the level of measurement is ratio because there is an absolute zero and one can argue that there are equal intervals between successive units of measurement. We are not interested in differences between interval and ratio measures because this distinction is not important for the statistical procedures considered. Here, interval data can mean interval or ratio.

The *t*-Test

The results of our hypothetical, within-subject design experiment are presented in Table 12-3. We will perform two statistical tests, the *t*-test and analysis of variance, and then consider the relationship between the two tests. The computations for a *t*-test with related samples is also presented in Table 12-3. Notice that this is not the same *t*-test that was used in Chapter 11. The *t*-test for a between-subject design differs from the *t*-test for a within-subject design. The formula for the *t*-test for a within-subject design (often called a correlated or direct difference *t*-test) is not very complicated.

It is important to realize that there are two scores for each subject. The first step is to subtract the second score from the first and then square the difference score. When this has been done for each subject the difference

TABLE 12-3

The Results of a Hypothetical Experiment Investigating the Effect of Hunger on the Number of Aggressive Acts and the Computation of the t-test

Subject	Hungry	Not hungry	D	D^2
A	8	4	4	16
B	22	18	4	16
C	9	1	8	64
D	4	7	-3	9
E	6	6	0	0
F	14	12	2	4
G	17	3	14	196
H	12	13	-1	1
I	9	2	7	49
J	11	8	3	9
K	19	14	5	25
L	2	1	1	1

$\bar{X}_1 = 11.08 \qquad \bar{X}_2 = 7.42 \qquad \Sigma D = 44 \qquad \Sigma D^2 = 390 \qquad n = 12$

$$t = \frac{\bar{X}_1 - \bar{X}_2}{\sqrt{\dfrac{\Sigma D^2 - \dfrac{(\Sigma D)^2}{n}}{n(n-1)}}}$$

$$t = \frac{11.08 - 7.42}{\sqrt{\dfrac{390 - \dfrac{(44)^2}{12}}{12(12-1)}}}$$

$$t = \frac{11.08 - 7.42}{\sqrt{\dfrac{390 - 161.333}{132}}}$$

$$t = \frac{3.66}{\sqrt{1.7323}}$$

$$t = \frac{3.66}{1.316}$$

$$t = 2.781$$

scores are summed and the squared difference scores are summed. The sign is important when summing the difference scores; the plus scores are added and the minus scores are subtracted. The next step is to compute the mean for each set of scores (i.e., the mean for the hungry condition and the mean for the not hungry condition) and determine the total number of subjects (i.e., the value for n). Note that n indicates the number of *subjects,* not the number of scores. After these values are obtained, it is a simple task to insert these values in the formula for t and compute the t value, if a calculator is available. The obtained t value is equal to 2.781. The next step is to find the statistical significance of this t value.

The t value is evaluated for significance by comparing it with the appropriate tabled value in Appendix C-5. Let us assume that we select the .05 significance level (two-tailed). The next task is to determine the number of degrees of freedom. In this case the number of degrees of freedom is equal to the number of subjects minus one. The logic for this equation can be appreciated by examining Table 12-3. If you examine the computations for the t value you should appreciate the fact that the difference score (i.e., the sum of squares of the difference scores) is used to determine the t value, not the fluctuations of the scores within each of the two conditions. There is only one D-score per subject, so, if the total for D is "fixed," there are $n - 1$ scores (D-scores in this case) that are free to vary. There are eleven degrees of freedom in this case (twelve subjects) so the tabled value is 2.179. Because the obtained value of 2.781 is higher than the tabled value we can reject the null hypothesis.

Analysis of Variance

Let us consider the results of the experiment on hunger and aggressiveness behavior again, but this time we will perform an analysis of variance instead of the t-test. The results and analysis of the experiment are presented in Table 12-4. Note that the analysis differs somewhat from that performed for a between-subject design. The first step is to obtain the SS_{tot}. This value is obtained in exactly the same way as for a between-subject design. Next the $SS_{conditions}$ is obtained. *Conditions* is a label for the independent variable. For example, if the independent variable is type of social setting, *social setting* could be substituted for *conditions.* This value is obtained in the same way that the main effects for the independent variables were obtained for the between-subject design. The $SS_{subjects}$ is obtained after the $SS_{conditions}$ and it is obtained in the same way except that the totals for each subject (row totals) are used instead of the column totals. After the subject totals are squared and then added the sum is divided by two because there are two scores for each subject. The next step is to obtain the sum of squares for the interaction of conditions by subjects by subtracting the $SS_{conditions}$ and $SS_{subjects}$ from the SS_{tot}.

The analysis of variance table for the present example is also presented in Table 12-4. The degrees of freedom and the mean square values are obtained in the same manner as for a between-subject analysis. Note that the F value

TABLE 12-4

The Results and Analysis of a Hypothetical Experiment Investigating the Effect of Hunger on Aggressiveness

Subject	Hungry	Not hungry	Total
A	8	4	12
B	22	18	40
C	9	1	10
D	4	7	11
E	6	6	12
F	14	12	26
G	17	3	20
H	12	13	25
I	9	2	11
J	11	8	19
K	19	14	33
L	2	1	3
X	133	89	222
X^2	1877	1013	5390

$$SS_{tot} = \Sigma\Sigma X^2 - \frac{(T)^2}{N}$$

$$SS_{tot} = 2890 - \frac{(222)^2}{24}$$

$$SS_{tot} = 2890 - 2053.50$$

$$SS_{tot} = 836.50$$

$$SS_{conditions} = \Sigma \frac{(\text{group total})^2}{n} - \frac{(T)^2}{N}$$

$$SS_{conditions} = \frac{(133)^2 + (89)^2}{12} - \frac{(222)^2}{24}$$

$$SS_{conditions} = 2134.17 - 2053.50$$

$$SS_{conditions} = 80.67$$

(Continued on next page)

TABLE 12-4 continued

$$SS_{subjects} = \Sigma \frac{(\text{subject total})^2}{\# \text{ of conditions}} - \frac{(T)^2}{N}$$

$$SS_{subjects} = \frac{5390}{2} - \frac{(222)^2}{24}$$

$$SS_{subjects} = 641.50$$

$$SS_{subjects \times conditions} = SS_{tot} - SS_{conditions} - SS_{subjects}$$

$$SS_{s \times c} = 836.50 - 80.67 - 641.50$$

$$SS_{s \times c} = 114.33$$

Source	df	SS	MS	F
Conditions (C)	1	80.67	80.67	7.76
Subjects (S)	11	641.50	58.32	
C × S	11	114.33	10.39	
Total	23	836.50		

for conditions is obtained by dividing the mean square for conditions by the mean square for the conditions by subjects interaction. An F value for subjects is not computed. The main concern is whether the conditions produced a significant effect, not whether the subject effect is significant. A significant F for subjects would tell us only that subjects differ in performance on the dependent measure. Since it is well known that subjects differ in performance, this F value would be of little interest.

The evaluation of the obtained F value is accomplished by comparing the obtained value of 7.76 with the appropriate tabled value. In this case there are one and eleven degrees of freedom, so the tabled value (see Appendix C-4) corresponding to the .05 significance level is equal to 4.84. Because the obtained value is greater than the tabled value we can reject the null hypothesis. The results for the t-test and analysis of variance are consistent; we reject the null hypothesis in both cases.

In performing the above analysis with the t- or F-test we have to assume that the mean square of conditions by subjects provides a suitable estimate of chance fluctuation only. The extent to which this assumption is justified frequently depends on the research area considered. Investigators who do not have to be particularly concerned about interactions between subject and nonsubject variables (see the discussion of parsimony in Chapter 1) can usually use the above analysis. If there is reason to believe that the effect of the treatment depends on the type of subject the above analysis may not be appropriate.

An investigator who is concerned about the differential effect of treatments on subjects can, of course, combine subject variable with nonsubject variable manipulations to determine whether the two kinds of variables interact.

Relationships between the *t*- and *F*-Tests

A comparison of the results for the analysis of variance test and *t*-test reveals, once again, that $F = t^2$. That is, except for a slight rounding error the *t* value of 2.781 when squared equals the value for F (7.76). Because we can reach the same conclusion about the statistical significance of the results with either test we can use either.

The advantage of the *t*-test is that it may be a little easier to compute. You can compare the computations in Tables 12-3 and 12-4 and decide which set of computations is easier. Your decision may depend on the equipment you have available. For example, you may find the *t*-test easier if your calculator enables you to compute the square root in one step but does not allow you to square X and sum the squared scores in one operation. The student who considers the *t*-test easier to compute and who does not expect to compare more than two conditions at a time may opt for the *t*-test over the *F*-test.

The disadvantage of the *t*-test is that it is only good for comparing the performance of two groups (between-subject design) or two conditions (within-subject design). So, if you are interested in comparing more than two conditions or performing statistical tests on experiments with more than one independent variable to test for interactions you need to know how to perform the analysis of variance. This test enables you to analyze experiments in which there are more than two levels for the independent variable, more than one independent variable, and more than one type of design. Analysis of variance can be used to evaluate mixed design experiments, in which one independent variable is a within-subject manipulation and the other is a between-subject manipulation.

SUMMARY

The statistical tests discussed in this chapter are appropriate for within-subject designs and for matched-groups designs if the matching is done on a subject by subject basis. The Cochran Q test is appropriate for nominal data, the Wilcoxon test for ordinal data, and the analysis of variance and *t*-test for interval data. The steps involved in using the Cochran Q and Wilcoxon tests are fairly straightforward.

Using the analysis of variance to analyze experiments with matched-groups or within-subject designs is quite similar to using it with between-subject designs. The major difference is that fluctuations within subjects or within matched sets of subjects are used to evaluate the effect of the independent variable. This estimate of chance fluctuation is the interaction of conditions by subjects if a within-subject design is used. The *t*-test is fairly easy to compute but it is only useful for two-condition comparisons.

QUESTIONS

1. An experiment was conducted to assess the effects of two treatments. A within-subject design was used and nominal data were obtained. Perform the appropriate statistical test to determine whether the treatments differed in effectiveness. A score of 1 indicates success and a score of 0 indicates failure. The presentation order of the conditions was counterbalanced so that half the subjects were given Treatment A first and the other half were given Treatment B first.

Subject	Treatment A	Treatment B
a	0	0
b	0	1
c	0	1
d	1	1
e	0	1
f	0	1
g	1	1
h	0	1
i	1	0
j	0	1
k	0	1
l	0	1
m	0	1
n	1	1
o	0	1
p	1	0

2. An experiment was conducted in which a within-subject design was used. Subjects were tested under Condition A and Condition B. The dependent measure was whether subjects were successful or unsuccessful under each testing condition. They were given a score of 0 if they were unsuccessful and a score of 1 if successful. Do the appropriate analysis to determine if the condition manipulation had any effect. In this case, you should treat the success versus failure categorization as an instance of a nominal classification.

Subject	Condition A	Condition B
1	0	0
2	1	0
3	1	0
4	1	0
5	1	0
6	1	0
7	1	1
8	0	1
9	1	0

3. Assume that the same experiment was conducted as in Question 2 but that ordinal data were obtained. Do the appropriate analysis. Then assume that the data are at the interval level of measurement and perform an appropriate statistical analysis.

Subject	Condition A	Condition B
1	24	19
2	23	18
3	31	23
4	18	14
5	29	22
6	20	16
7	26	31
8	17	19
9	12	10

4. An experiment was conducted to assess the effect of three treatments. A within-subject design was used and interval data obtained. Each subject obtained a score for each of three treatment conditions. A high score indicates good performance. Do an analysis to determine whether the three treatments differed in effectiveness. The order of the treatments was counterbalanced. Or, use a *t*-test to compare treatments A and B.

Subject	Treatment A	Treatment B	Treatment C
a	23	18	45
b	26	23	41
c	25	17	38
d	27	19	42
e	31	24	35
f	28	28	29
g	24	21	33
h	22	17	39
i	27	25	32
j	26	35	38
k	25	21	41
l	41	32	55
m	18	11	42
n	28	33	43

5. Analyze the results obtained in the above experiment as if a between-subject design had been used. That is, imagine that fourteen subjects were tested in each of the three conditions and the above scores obtained. Do you expect to obtain a higher *F* value for the treatment manipulation with the between-subject or the within-subject analysis? Why?

evaluating and reporting results 13

In this chapter we will examine some of the difficulties encountered in evaluating and reporting results. Our task is to consider whether the results are worth reporting and, if they are, where and how they should be reported. This is not easy. There is no accepted standard for evaluating research, no prescribed place to send the manuscript, and no single set of principles to follow in writing the report. The experimenter has to make decisions. Deciding whether his results are worth reporting means that he will have to consider their psychological significance.

THE PSYCHOLOGICAL SIGNIFICANCE OF RESULTS

Statistical versus Psychological Significance

Statistical significance refers to the likelihood that an event can be attributed to chance effects. Psychological significance refers to whether or not a particular finding is a contribution to knowledge. The fact that a result is statistically significant does not mean, necessarily, that it is of psychological significance. The psychological significance of a study is determined by the quality of the idea, the adequacy of the test, and the clarity of the results. All three are important.

To evaluate the results for psychological significance you should reconsider your research idea. It is true that the merit of the idea was evaluated at length before the experiment was conducted, but it is likely that a lot of time has passed since the earlier evaluation. You may have insights that you lacked previously.

Evaluating the Quality of Ideas

It is difficult to make general statements about the process of evaluating ideas. In some cases evaluation will be easy because the idea is clearly important or unimportant. For example, if you demonstrate a finding that has already been demonstrated numerous times, you have not made a contribution to knowledge. On the other hand, if you establish a new phenomenon or provide an explanation for a previously unexplained phenomenon your contribution is probably worthwhile. Several people usually participate in judging whether a particular finding makes a contribution to knowledge. The investigator assesses the value of his work at various stages in the investigation, particularly the planning stage. He usually asks colleagues to participate in this evaluation. When the results are submitted for publication, the work is usually evaluated by specialists in the same area. Most journal editors insist that research findings pass a contribution to knowledge test as one step in determining whether the findings should be published.

Adequacy of the Test

If the idea passes the quality evaluation the next step is to consider the adequacy of the test. Did the experimental manipulation provide a fair test of the prediction? Were there any confounding variables? Could the results have turned out in such a way that the idea would have been proved incorrect? An adequate test of an idea is obtained only if the results can refute as well as support the assertions to be tested.

Sometimes an experimental design fails to yield an adequate test of the idea owing to unforeseen problems. For example, an investigator may decide to test the effectiveness of different learning strategies by manipulating the strategy instructions to each group. If differences are obtained between the groups, there is no problem. However, if differences are not obtained, it will be very difficult to determine whether the strategies actually do not differ in effectiveness or the subjects simply failed to use the strategy they were told to use. If the test is inadequate there is little choice but to start over by devising a better test. If the test is adequate the next task is to consider the clarity of the results.

Definitiveness of the Results

Evaluating the results for clarity involves both statistical and nonstatistical considerations. If statistically significant, easily interpreted results are obtained the investigator is very fortunate. Interpretational problems arise when the results are not as clear as the experimenter would have liked. For example, when two predictions are made and one is clearly supported and the other is not, there will be interpretational problems. If both predictions follow from

282   Evaluating and Reporting Results

the theoretical view the investigator is likely to be ambivalent about the results. In evaluating the clarity of results one should consider whether it is possible to draw firm conclusions from the findings. If the predictions received firm support and the experiment was a fair test of the predictions and the research idea was equal to or better than ideas already reported in refereed scientific journals, then it is fair to conclude that the findings are psychologically significant.

We can distinguish between nonsignificant, which refers to the lack of statistical significance, and insignificant, which refers to the lack of psychological significance. Let us assume that the results lack psychological significance. At this point the investigator may be very discouraged. He has spent a lot of time and energy on an insignificant result. Clearly he has reason to be discouraged but it may be incorrect to conclude that he gained nothing but a few more gray hairs and a higher hostility level. He may now be in a good position to redesign the experiment and conduct it properly, having discovered some of the pitfalls in conducting research.

It is not uncommon for an investigator to make mistakes that invalidate the results of the experiment. His task is then to decide whether the test was inadequate or the idea was wrong. If the test was inadequate, the experimenter may have some firm notions about how a better test could be made. If the idea was wrong, perhaps an alternative theoretical notion is now worthy of test. The point is that experimenters should not be surprised if their first attempts at research do not come out as well as they had hoped. Many research projects do not yield the anticipated results. Let us assume, however, that the results are clear and important. The next task is to report the findings.

REPORTING THE FINDINGS

The Decision to Report Research Findings

Importance of the Findings. It would appear that the only factor in deciding whether to report research findings is their psychological significance. If you have something important to report you are likely to be eager to have it in print. If you have rather uninteresting results there is usually little reason to bother reporting them. However, there may be situations that make it necessary to report insignificant or nonsignificant results. For example, an instructor may insist that his students report the less-than-exciting results of a laboratory experiment in order to gain skill in making and evaluating reports.

Graphic Phobia. There is at least one additional factor that may influence the decision whether to report findings. For lack of a better term, let us call this factor *graphic phobia* (i.e., fear of writing). In some cases anxiety about writing may be related to the lack of psychologically significant findings. Yet many people experience anxiety about writing even when they are convinced that the finding should be reported or even when they have excellent "external justification" (e.g., being required to report a laboratory experiment). You can expect to be a little anxious about reporting the findings because writing can be both a reinforcing and a punishing experience. This point requires further elaboration.

We have said before that one should attempt to find a research problem of genuine personal interest. An experimenter is not likely to derive much satisfaction from research unless it is intrinsically rewarding. Let us assume that you did find a problem of personal interest. You generated an idea that you believe to be excellent, designed an experiment to test it, and obtained statistically significant results. You evaluate all that you have done and conclude that the findings are psychologically significant. You are extremely excited by this chain of events. Now it is time to report the findings so that others can evaluate the work.

If the experiment required a large commitment you will undoubtedly want the finished manuscript to reflect this. Perhaps friends and relatives know that you have been conducting a research project, and they are interested in learning the results. How, you may ask, can one possibly communicate all the excitement, frustration, confusion, depression, and insight that went into the research project? The answer is that one cannot, and should not, as this would detract from the major goal of reporting the findings. Perhaps the objective approach that investigators convey on the printed page has led some students to conclude that scientists are a cool, unemotional lot. However, the reader who has experienced some of the rewards and punishments of doing research should know better. In short, don't be overly concerned if you sweat a little while preparing the manuscript.

Factors to Consider Before Writing

Selecting the Audience. If the findings are worth reporting the next task is to consider what audience to reach and how to reach it. Scores of journals publish research findings about behavior and mental activity. Your task is to select the most appropriate journal or other medium. To determine the proper audience it is necessary to assess the extent to which the finding is of general interest.

If the finding has broad significance it may be reasonable to inform the major communications networks. If it is likely to be of interest to scientists in other disciplines a journal should be selected that is widely read among scientists (e.g., *Science* or *Scientific American*). If it is of interest mainly to psychologists, a psychological journal should be selected. If it is of interest to psychologists working on a particular problem only, a specialized psychological journal would be appropriate. If the finding is unimportant it may only be necessary to notify the one other person in the world who is interested. You accomplish this by calling your mother.

It is important to take care in selecting the place to submit the manuscript

284 Evaluating and Reporting Results

because if an inappropriate journal is chosen your time and that of the journal editor will be wasted. The manuscript will be returned and you will be advised to send it elsewhere. Since the format varies for different journals it will then be necessary to make changes in the manuscript so that it conforms to the style of a second journal. Investigators often decide where they want to submit their articles by the time they are ready to start writing. If you have not familiarized yourself with the journals that publish articles in your area of interest you should do so before starting to write.

Following the Correct Format. After you have selected a journal you should study recent issues to learn the style used in that journal. Often there will be instructions for investigators who plan to submit manuscripts to the journal. It is also a good idea to obtain a copy of the style manual published by the American Psychological Association (1200 Seventeenth Street, N.W., Washington, D.C., 20036). This manual provides useful information for preparing a manuscript. It is still necessary to examine recent issues of the journal you are interested in, however, because each journal usually has slight deviations from the general style.

Now let us turn to general problems encountered in manuscript preparation. We will examine the four major sections of a research article: introduction, method, results, and discussion.

The Introduction Section

The four major sections of the manuscript correspond roughly to the four major stages of experimentation. One can conceptualize experimentation as involving an idea stage in which the problem area is selected and testable ideas are generated, a testing stage in which data are collected, a results stage in which the effects are determined and evaluated for statistical significance, and an overall evaluation stage in which the possible value of the finding to the state of knowledge in the field is considered.

The introduction corresponds to the idea stage. The goal in the introduction should be to familiarize the reader with the problem, the insights for problem solution, and the procedure for testing the insights. One should say why the predictions, if supported, will be of psychological significance. The task of writing an introduction is usually more difficult than it first appears, often because of poor organization and a failure to assess accurately how much background information is needed.

Selecting the Relevant Prior Research. The amount of background information needed will depend on the nature of the problem, the audience, and the journal. Obviously, if the readers of the journal already know a great deal about the problem it is not necessary to present much background information in the introduction. To do so would be to waste journal space and the reader's time. Yet the investigator does have an obligation to consider the earlier work most directly related to his study. He should realize that it is extremely unlikely that the idea is completely new. The chances are that someone investigated a similar idea but not in quite the same way or in the same context or for the same purpose. At the very least the reader should be informed about the previous work that is most closely related to the study to be reported. Planning the organization of the introduction should be relatively easy after a decision has been made about how much background information to provide. (Many instructors will insist that their students present a more extensive literature review than would be found in the introduction of a journal article.)

Organizing the Introduction. At the risk of laboring the obvious, it should be pointed out that one should plan the introduction before writing it. In many cases, unfortunately, little or no thought goes into planning. One needs to consider how much background material to present, the order in which to present it if there is more than one relevant study, the specific problem, the solution, and how the solution is to be tested. If the reader does not learn from the introduction what is going to be done and why, the introduction has not been written properly.

Indicating the Importance of the Problem. The introduction is the place to persuade the reader of the importance of the experiment. If you are ashamed of your idea you should not bother to report the study. If you are not ashamed of it you should talk about its psychological significance in the introduction. The reader should be told the basic plan for testing the idea, the results to be expected and how the results will support or refute the predictions. The specific details of the testing procedure, however, should be left for the method section.

The Method Section

The major task in the method section is to explain how the predictions were tested. If elaborate equipment or complicated materials were used it may be helpful to discuss this in a special subsection. If the experiment was extremely simple, no subheadings may be needed. In general, however, subheadings for design and procedure are useful.

Design. The reader should be told in the design subsection what was manipulated, correlated, or observed and what was measured. If the experimental method was used it is necessary to specify the independent variable(s) and dependent variable(s). In general the method section should proceed from the more overall aspects of the experiment (e.g., independent and dependent variables) to the more specific procedures employed. After reading the discussion of design the reader should have a clear view of what was manipulated and the type of design used to test the predictions. The specific procedures used in making the tests are reported in the procedure subsection.

Procedure. The task in the discussion of procedure is to tell exactly how the experiment was conducted so that the reader could repeat the experiment in essentially the same way. After writing the procedure subsection you should ask yourself whether the experiment could be completed by referring only to the information presented in the method section. The reader has to be told how subjects were obtained, how they were assigned to conditions, what materials were used, how much time was needed for each phase of the experiment, what the subjects were told, how the dependent measure was obtained, and so on. One way to present this information is to describe the procedure used to test the subjects in each of the conditions. It is a good idea to study the method sections of published journal articles to see how this is done. After the procedure is presented the next step is to consider the results of the experiment.

The Results Section

It is important to plan the results section before starting to write it. When you have completed all the statistical analyses you should have a clear notion of what aspects of the results are interesting and what aspects are not. For example, if there are two or more independent variables and only one produced a statistically significant effect, this variable, all things being equal, is going to be more interesting than the others. It is also important to double-check calculations to be sure that the reported results are identical to the obtained results.

Organizing the Results. The major task is to lead the reader through the results, pointing out what is significant and what is not. Your role is like that of a guide taking visitors through a museum. Make sure that the reader is made aware of the important results. The results have to be organized in such a way that the reader is not confronted with a large mass of data. The task is to give a simple, clear, and reasonably complete account of the results. Although the specific organization will depend on the particular study considered, there are a few points that need to be emphasized.

Presenting Data. There is usually no reason to present the raw data to the reader. You should simplify the data by presenting descriptive measures (e.g., measures of central tendency such as the mean) for each group. You may have to decide whether it would be better to present the descriptive measures in the text, in a figure, or in a table. There is no rule that can be applied in all circumstances. However, if there are many numbers to present (say, ten or more), probably a table or figure should be used. Often a figure cannot be used because there are too many means to present. In such a case the tabular presentation should be preferred. The choice between a table and a figure will often depend on the nature of the data.

If you are unsure of which way to present the measures of central tendency, frequency, or whatever, prepare them in different forms. Then it may become clear which mode of presentation is best. If you are still unsure which method is the clearest for the reader, ask a few friends or colleagues to judge. Do not present the same measures in two different ways in the manuscript as this may confuse or insult the reader.

Leading the Reader Through the Results. A very common mistake experimenters make in reporting results is presenting a measure of central tendency in a figure or table and then leaving the readers to their own devices. This is analogous to an unguided trip through a museum. If the results are simply presented in a table and the reader is expected to decide which values are important and which are unimportant, the investigator is not assuming the responsibilities of the guide. After all, by the time you report the results you should have thought about them for a long time and should be in a good position to point out what is important.

Amount of Data Presented. You should avoid, if possible, presenting a large amount of data. If you have an exceptionally interesting study in which there are many important measures there is little choice but to present a great deal of information. However, if a large amount of data is to be reported the burden on the guide is increased.

You should accept the fact that you are in a better position than the reader is to judge the importance of your data and should organize the results section to emphasize what is important. It is reasonable to ignore completely or just give passing notice to unimportant results. As long as your view of what is important is reasonably consistent with what others think you should have little difficulty with instructors, journal editors, or readers.

After presenting the basic descriptive measures you need to indicate what comparisons the reader should consider and whether they are statistically significant. If a complex analysis of variance was conducted you may decide to present the analysis of variance table. However, it is generally better to present the F values of interest without bothering to present the entire table. Once again, the task is to decide which method of presentation is easier for the reader. The plan of the results section, then, is to present the basic descriptive measures, point out the important comparisons, and indicate whether the differences between conditions are statistically significant.

Discussing the Results. Another question is how much discussion of the results is desirable in the results section. Some investigators prefer to present the bare results and save all discussion of them for the discussion section. Others prefer to say more about them in the results section. The nature of the experiment and the preferences of the investigator may influence the choice. If it would be clearer to discuss each finding right after presenting it, then it would be better to combine the discussion section with the results section.

Let us assume, however, that you do not want to eliminate the separate discussion section because it is necessary to provide an overall evaluation of the present findings and relate them to previous research. Yet you would still like to say something about each finding immediately after presenting it. Is it permissible to do so? The answer is *yes* if the discussion does not take you too far afield. In general you should avoid comparing your results with the results of earlier work as this may confuse the reader. It is usually best to concentrate on making concise remarks about the interesting aspects of *your* results. A consideration of the relationship of the findings to other findings, their psychological significance, and the overall state of the problem is usually best left for the discussion section.

The Discussion Section

The discussion section is similar to the introduction in that it is a place to consider the broader problem area of interest. The introduction can be regarded as the *before* and the discussion section as the *after*. In the introduction the state of the art before the investigation was examined. In the discussion section you should consider the state of the art after the investigation (i.e., how the investigation influenced knowledge about the phenomenon in question). The introduction offered the idea or insight that was expected to further the understanding of a particular phenomenon or produce a particular result. The insight is testable since certain predictions follow from it. In the discussion section, presented after the reader has been informed about the accuracy of the prediction, all the cards are on the table so it is time to assess the degree of success or failure.

Reporting an Important Finding. The ease of writing the discussion section will be determined in large part by the psychological significance of the findings and the quality and thoroughness of the introduction. If the understanding of a particular phenomenon has changed drastically because of your contribution, then, of course, you will want to emphasize the impact of your finding. The discussion section should be very enjoyable to write. Perhaps the finding has implications for further research, or perhaps it makes possible the reinterpretation of earlier work within a different theoretical framework. If the finding has practical application this may be emphasized in the discussion. The specific nature of the discussion will depend, of course, on the particular contribution.

Reporting a Finding of Some Interest. Another possibility is that the results, although clear, are not entirely consistent with earlier findings. Your task, therefore, is to compare your findings with those of other investigators and try to resolve the differences. Because you have the most recent evidence bearing on a particular problem you should be in a good position to evaluate the current state of knowledge. The experiment may provide evidence which suggests that one view is to be preferred over the others. In order to write this kind of discussion you may need to spend a lot of time studying the results of other investigators in an attempt to integrate the results. Yet the attempt at integration may result in additional insights that can be tested experimentally. Even if the results do not provide a complete solution to the problem of interest, they may suggest avenues for additional research.

Reporting Findings of Little Interest. Another possibility is that the results did essentially nothing to clarify the problem, but you still have to report the findings in order to gain experience. This kind of discussion is painful to write.

It is not feasible to concentrate on the extent of your contribution because this would only depress you. You cannot concentrate on a comparison of your results with those of other investigators because yours were not sufficiently clear to warrant the comparison. Thus there is little choice but to admit that your predictions were not supported and consider the possible reasons for the failure. The state of knowledge is the same as it was before your "contribution" except that you may be convinced that one idea, yours, is not a particularly useful insight. You have the unpleasant task of considering a problem for which you were unable to offer a good solution. However, since you probably learned a great deal about the problem, or at least thought a great deal about it, you may have a number of new ideas to present in the discussion section. If you can generate sufficiently interesting ideas you may wish to put them to an experimental test.

General Comments About Writing

After you have completed a draft of the four major sections you may be tempted to decide on a title, write an abstract or summary as required, prepare the tables or figures, list the references, and then type the manuscript for publication. This would be a mistake. There is almost no chance that the first draft would measure up to the standards of a professional journal. It is necessary to polish the manuscript. You polish it by recasting unclear statements, eliminating redundancy, correcting faulty organization, and remedying any other defects you can find. After you believe the manuscript is in fine shape it is a good idea to ask someone to read it and make criticisms.

One has to be very careful in choosing a critic. It is important to find someone who will criticize constructively. You are likely to be ego-involved in your work and, therefore, somewhat reluctant to accept even constructive criticism. If you are offered nonconstructive criticism (e.g., "I can't believe you passed freshman English!"), the only thing you gain is animosity toward the critic. There is also the danger of finding a critic who is so picayune that you doubt the value of the criticism. On the other hand, there is the danger of finding someone who is unwilling to make any criticism for fear of offending. What is needed is someone with a knowledge of language to objectively tell you how your paper reads. It may be difficult to find such a person, but you should know at least one who qualifies.

Once you have found this rare person you need to treat him with extreme care. It is important to take his comments seriously. If he says a statement is unclear you have to be willing to clarify it. It is irrelevant that the statement is clear to you. The important thing is that it be clear to others. After all, your purpose is to communicate your findings.

You may be frustrated by the criticism. You would probably prefer the critic to say that the manuscript is in excellent shape so that you could prepare it for publication. Task completion is usually a rewarding state of affairs so anything that delays it may be frustrating. Yet it is necessary to fight the urge to get the job over with at any cost. Once a manuscript is published there is no way to change it.

Preparing the Manuscript for Publication

As we have said, you should check recent issues of the journal you have in mind and any instructions for authors — such as instructions on the inside covers of the journal or in the publication manual of the American Psychological Association — before preparing the manuscript for publication. Unless you have special drawing talents you should find a professional draftsman to prepare the figures. The manuscript should be typed according to the specifications of the journal and the appropriate number of copies made. Then it is important to proofread carefully. After any errors are eliminated the manuscript is sent to the journal editor along with a covering letter asking that it be considered for the journal. After a reasonable length of time (in some cases an unreasonable length of time) you will receive a reply from the editor. The manuscript will be accepted as is, accepted subject to certain revisions, or rejected.

Let us assume that your manuscript has been accepted. Except for checking the printer's proofs the task is completed. You have generated an idea, devised a test for it, executed the test, determined the results, evaluated them, and published the findings. If you have been able to complete the entire cycle you should be very proud of yourself. Obviously, a tremendous amount of thought and effort is needed to conduct a successful research project. If you enjoyed testing your idea you may want to give serious thought to a research career. There is a need for people who can generate and test important ideas.

SUMMARY

It is important to distinguish between statistical and psychological significance. Statistical significance refers to the likelihood that an event can be attributed to chance effects. Psychological significance refers to whether a finding is a contribution to knowledge. The psychological significance of a study is determined by the quality of the idea tested, the adequacy of the test, and the clarity of the results.

The decision to report research findings should be based solely on their importance, but other factors frequently enter in. Some people are reluctant to report their findings because writing makes them nervous. One should expect to experience some anxiety while preparing a manuscript because research usually involves a tremendous personal commitment.

The four major sections of the manuscript correspond roughly to the four major stages of experimentation. The introduction corresponds to the idea stage, the method section to the testing stage, the results section to the evaluation of the obtained findings, and the discussion section to the overall evaluation.

The problems in writing the introduction are selecting the relevant prior research, organizing the introduction, and explaining how the proposed idea should contribute to knowledge. The reader should be told in the method section about how the idea was tested. It should be possible to repeat the experiment by referring only to the information presented in the method section. The problems in writing the results section include organizing the results and deciding what to present and how to present it. The nature of the discussion section will be influenced by whether the finding is of little interest, some interest, or great interest.

APPENDIX

This appendix to Chapter 13 is included to give the student preparing a laboratory report or the beginning researcher preparing a research article an example of a manuscript as submitted for publication. For this example each page of the manuscript is outlined and, when applicable, numbered so it is clear what sections require a new page and what sections do not. The cover page, abstract, tables, and figures are each on a separate page. Reference notes, references, footnotes, and figure captions are *started* on a new page. The running head on the first page (title page) is a short title (maximum of 60 spaces including punctuation and spaces between words). If the title is already short, then the running head and the title will be identical.

```
              Weapons as Aggression-Eliciting Stimuli

              Leonard Berkowitz and Anthony LePage

                     University of Wisconsin




        Running head:  Weapons as Aggression-Eliciting Stimuli
```

Reprinted by permission of the senior author and publisher from the *Journal of Personality and Social Psychology*, vol. 7 (1967), pp. 202–207.

Aggression
1

Abstract

An experiment was conducted to test the hypothesis that stimuli commonly associated with aggression can elicit aggressive responses from people ready to act aggressively. One hundred male university students received either one or seven shocks, supposedly from a peer, and were then given an opportunity to shock this person. In some cases a rifle and revolver were on the table near the shock key. These weapons were said to belong, or not to belong, to the available target person. In other instances there was nothing on the table near the shock key, while for a control group two badminton racquets were on the table near the key. The greatest number of shocks was given by the strongly aroused $\underline{S}$s (who had received seven shocks) when they were in the presence of the weapons. The guns had evidently elicited strong aggressive responses from the aroused men.

Aggression

2

Weapons as Aggression-Eliciting Stimuli[1]

Human behavior is often goal directed, guided by strategies and influenced by ego defenses and strivings for cognitive consistency. There clearly are situations, however, in which these purposive considerations are relatively unimportant regulators of action. Habitual behavior patterns become dominant on these occasions, and the person responds relatively automatically to the stimuli impinging upon him. Any really complete psychological system must deal with these stimulus-elicited, impulsive reactions as well as with more complex behavior patterns. More than this, we should also be able to specify the conditions under which the various behavior determinants increase or decrease in importance.

The senior author has long contended that many aggressive actions are controlled by the stimulus properties of the available targets rather than by anticipations of ends that might be served (Berkowitz, 1962, 1964, 1965). Perhaps because strong emotion results in an increased utilization of only the central cues in the immediate situation (Easterbrook, 1959; Walters & Parke, 1964), anger arousal can lead to impulsive aggressive responses which, for a short time at least, may be relatively free of cognitively mediated inhibitions against aggression or, for that matter, purposes and strategic considerations. This impulsive action is not necessarily pushed out by the anger, however. Berkowitz has suggested that appropriate cues must be present in the situation if aggressive responses are actually to occur. While there is

  Aggression

                                                               3

still considerable uncertainty as to just what characteristics
define aggressive cue properties, the association of a stimulus
with aggression evidently can enhance the aggressive cue value of
this stimulus. A variety of observations can be cited in support
of this reasoning (cf. Berkowitz, 1965).

   Direct eivdence for the present formulation can be found in a
study conducted by Loew (1965). His subjects, in being required to
learn a concept, either aggressive or neutral words, spoke either
20 aggressive or 20 neutral words aloud. Following this "learning
task," each subject was to give a peer in an adjacent room an
electric shock whenever this person made a mistake in his learning
problem. Allowed to vary the intensity of the shocks they administered over a 10-point continuum, the subjects who had uttered
the aggressive words gave shocks of significantly greater intensity
than did the subjects who had spoken the neutral words. The
aggressive words had evidently evoked implicit aggressive responses
from the subjects, even though they had not been angered beforehand,
which then led to the stronger attacks upon the target person in the
next room when he supposedly made errors.

   Cultural learning shared by many members of a society can also
associate external objects with aggression and thus affect the
objects' aggressive cue value. Weapons are a prime example. For
many men (and probably women as well) in our society, these
objects are closely associated with aggression. Assuming that the
weapons do not produce inhibitions that are stronger than the evoked
aggressive reactions (as would be the case, e.g., if the weapons

Aggression

4

were labeled as morally "bad"), the presence of the aggressive objects should generally lead to more intense attacks upon an available target than would occur in the presence of a neutral object.

The present experiment was designed to test this latter hypothesis. At one level, of course, the findings contribute to the current debate as to the desirability of restricting sales of firearms. Many arguments have been raised for such a restriction. Thus, according to recent statistics, Texas communities having virtually no prohibitions against firearms have a much higher homicide rate than other American cities possessing stringent firearm regulations, and J. Edgar Hoover has maintained in <u>Time</u> magazine that the availability of firearms is an important factor in murders (Anonymous, 1966). The experiment reported here seeks to determine how this influence may come about. The availability of weapons makes it easier for a person who wants to commit murder to do so. But, in addition, we ask whether weapons can serve as aggression-eliciting stimuli, causing an angered individual to display stronger violence than he would have shown in the absence of such weapons. Social significance aside, and at a more general theoretical level, this research also attempts to demonstrate that situational stimuli can exert "automatic" control over socially relevant human actions.

<u>Method</u>

<u>Subjects</u>

The subjects were 100 male undergraduates enrolled in the introductory psychology course at the University of Wisconsin who volun-

Aggression

5

teered for the experiment (without knowing its nature) in order to earn points counting toward their final grade. Thirty-nine other subjects had also been run, but were discarded because they suspected the experimenter's confederate (21), reported receiving fewer electric shocks than were actually given them (7), had not attended to information given them about the procedure (9), or were run while there was equipment malfunctioning (2).

Procedure

General design. Seven experimental conditions were established, six organized in a 2 x 3 factorial design, with the seventh group serving essentially as a control. Of the men in the factorial design, half were made to be angry with the confederate, while the other subjects received a friendlier treatment from him. All of the subjects were then given an opportunity to administer electric shocks to the confederate, but for two-thirds of the men there were weapons lying on the table near the shock apparatus. Half of these people were informed the weapons belonged to the confederate in order to test the hypothesis that aggressive stimuli which also were associated with the anger instigator would evoke the strongest aggressive reaction from the subjects. The other people seeing the weapons were told the weapons had been left by a previous experimenter. There was nothing on the table except the shock key when the last third of the subjects in both the angered and nonangered conditions gave the shocks. Finally, the seventh group consisted of angered men who gave shocks with two badminton racquets and shuttlecocks lying near the shock key. This condition sought to determine whether the presence of *any*

Aggression

6

object near the shock apparatus would reduce inhibitions against aggression, even if the object were not connected with aggressive behavior.

Experimental manipulations. When each subject arrived in the laboratory, he was informed that two men were required for the experiment and that they would have to wait for the second subject to appear. After a five-minute wait, the experimenter, acting annoyed, indicated that they had to begin because of his other commitments. He said he would have to look around outside to see if he could find another person who might serve as a substitute for the missing subject. In a few minutes the experimenter returned with the confederate. Depending upon the condition, this person was introduced as either a psychology student who had been about to sign up for another experiment or as a student who had been running another study.

The subject and confederate were told the experiment was a study of physiological reactions to stress. The stress would be created by mild electric shocks, and the subjects could withdraw, the experimenter said, if they objected to these shocks. (No subjects left.) Each person would have to solve a problem knowing that his performance would be evaluated by his partner. The "evaluations" would be in the form of electric shocks, with one shock signifying a very good rating and 10 shocks meaning the performance was judged as very bad. The men were then told what their problems were. The subject's task was to list ideas a publicity agent might employ in order to better a popular singer's record sales and public image. The other person (the confederate) had to think of things a used-car dealer might do in order to increase sales. The two were given 5 minutes to write their answers, and the papers were then collected by the experimenter who supposedly would exchange them.

Following this, the two were placed in separate rooms, supposedly so that they would not influence each other's galvanic skin response (GSR) reactions. The shock electrodes were placed on the subject's right forearm, and GSR electrodes were attached to fingers on his left hand, with wires trailing from the electrodes to the next room. The subject was told he would be the first to receive electric shocks as the evaluation of his problem solution. The experimenter left the subject's room saying he was going to turn on the GSR apparatus, went to the room containing the shock machine and the waiting confederate, and only then looked at the schedule indicating whether the subject was to be angered or not. He informed the confederate how many shocks the subject was to receive, and 30 seconds later the subject was given seven shocks (angered condition) or one shock (nonangered group). The experimenter then went back to the subject, while the confederate quickly arranged the table holding the shock key in the manner appropriate for the subject's condition. Upon entering the subject's room, the experimenter asked him how many shocks he had received and provided the subject with a brief questionnaire on which he was to rate his mood. As soon as this was completed, the subject was taken to the room holding the shock machine. Here the experimenter told the subject it was his turn to evaluate his partner's work. For one group in both the angered and nonangered conditions the shock key was alone on the table (no-object groups). For two other groups in each of

Aggression
8

these angered and nonangered conditions, however, a 12-gauge shotgun and a .38-caliber revolver were lying on the table near the key (aggressive-weapon conditions). One group in both the angered and nonangered conditions was informed the weapons belonged to the subject's partner. The subjects given this treatment had been told earlier that their partner was a student who had been conducting an experiment. They now were reminded of this, and the experimenter said the weapons were being used in some way by this person in his research (associated-weapons condition); the guns were to be disregarded. The other men were told simply the weapons "belong to someone else" who "must have been doing an experiment in here" (unassociated-weapons group), and they too were asked to disregard the guns. For the last treatment, one group of angered men found two badminton racquets and shuttlecocks lying on the table near the shock key, and these people were also told the equipment belonged to someone else (badminton-racquets group).

Immediately after this information was provided, the experimenter showed the subject what was supposedly his partner's answer to his assigned problem. The subject was reminded that he was to give the partner shocks as his evaluation and was informed that this was the last time shocks would be administered in the study. A second copy of the mood questionnaire was then completed by the subject after he had delivered the shocks. Following this, the subject was asked a number of oral questions about the experiment, including what, if any, suspicions he had. (No doubts were voiced about the presence of the weapons.) At the conclusion of this interview the experiment was ex-

Results

Effectiveness of Arousal Treatment

Analyses of variance of the responses to each of the mood scales following the receipt of the partner's evaluation indicate the prior-shock treatment succeeded in creating differences in anger arousal. The subjects getting seven shocks rated themselves as being significantly angrier than the subjects receiving only one shock, $F(1,84) = 20.65$, $p < .01$). There were no reliable differences among the groups within any one arousal level.

Aggression Toward Partner

The mean number of shocks administered in each experimental condition are given in Table 1. The hypothesis guiding the present study receives good support. The strongly provoked men delivered more frequent electrical attacks upon their tormentor in the presence of a

----
Insert Table 1 about here
----

weapon than when nonaggressive objects (the badminton racquets and shuttlecocks) were present or when only the shock key was on the table. An analysis of variance of the shock data for the six groups in the 3 x 2 factorial design (i.e., exclude the badminton racquets condition) revealed two significant effects. The subjects who received seven shocks delivered more shocks to the confederate than the subjects who received one shock $F(1,84) = 104.62$, $p < .001$. And, the Number of Shocks by Weapons Association interaction was significant,

$F(2,84) = 5.02$, $p < .01$. The significant interaction means that the effect of the presence of the weapons on the dependent measure was influenced by whether subjects were given one or seven shocks.

Discussion

Common sense, as well as a good deal of personality theorizing, both influenced to some extent by an egocentric view of human behavior as being caused almost exclusively by motives within the individual, generally neglect the type of weapons effect demonstrated in the present study. If a person holding a gun fires it, we are told either that he wanted to do so (consciously or unconsciously) or that he pulled the trigger "accidentally." The findings summarized here suggest yet another possibility: The presence of the weapon might have elicited an intense aggressive reaction from the person with the gun, assuming his inhibitions against aggression were relatively weak at the moment. Indeed, it is altogether conceivable that many hostile acts which supposedly stem from unconscious motivation really arise because of the operation of aggressive cues. Not realizing how these situational stimuli might elicit aggressive behavior, and not detecting the presence of these cures, the observer tends to locate the source of the action in some conjectured underlying, perhaps repressed, motive. Similarly, if he is a Skinnerian rather than a dynamically oriented clinician, he might also neglect the operation of aggression-eliciting stimuli by invoking the concept of operant behavior, and thus sidestep the issue altogether. The sources of the hostile action, for him, too, rest within the individual, with the behavior only steered or permitted by discriminative stimuli.

Aggression

11

Alternative explanations must be ruled out, however, before the present thesis can be regarded as confirmed. One obvious possibility is that the subjects in the weapons condition reacted to the demand characteristics of the situation as they saw them and exhibited the kind of behavior they thought was required of them. ("These guns on the table mean I'm supposed to be aggressive, so I'll give many shocks.") Several considerations appear to negate this explanation. First, there are the subject's own verbal reports. None of the subjects voiced any suspicions of the weapons and, furthermore, when they were queried generally denied that the weapons had any effect on them. But even those subjects who did express any doubts about the experiment typically acted like the other subjects.

Setting this aside, moreover, it is not altogether certain from the notion of demand characteristics that only the angered subjects would be inclined to act in conformity with the experimenter's supposed demands. The nonangered men in the weapons group did not display a heightened number of attacks on their partner. Would this have been predicted beforehand by researchers interested in demand characteristics? The last finding raises one final observation. Recent unpublished research by Allen and Bragg indicates that awareness of the experimenter's purpose does not necessarily result in an increased display of the behavior the experimenter supposedly desires. Dealing with one kind of socially disapproved action (conformity), Allen and Bragg demonstrated that high levels of experimentally induced awareness of the experimenter's interests generally produced a decreased level of the relevant behavior. Thus, if the subjects in

Aggression

12

our study had known the experimenter was interested in observing their aggressive behavior, they might well have given less, rather than more, shocks, since giving shocks is also socially disapproved. This type of phenomenon was also not observed in the weapons conditions.

Nevertheless, any one experiment cannot possibly definitely exclude all of the alternative explanations. Scientific hypotheses are only probability statements, and further research is needed to heighten the likelihood that the present reasoning is correct.

Aggression

13

References

Anonymous. A gun-toting nation. Time, August 12, 1966.

Berkowitz, L. Aggression: A social psychological analysis. New York: McGraw-Hill, 1962.

Berkowitz, L. Aggressive cues in aggressive behavior and hostility catharsis. Psychological Review, 1964, 71, 104-122.

Berkowitz, L. The concept of aggressive drive: Some additional considerations. In L. Berkowitz (Ed.), Advances in experimental social psychology. Vol.2. New York: Academic Press, 1965, pp. 301-329.

Easterbrook, J. A. The effect of emotion on cue utilization and the organization of behavior. Psychological Review, 1959, 66, 183-201.

Loew, C. A. Acquisition of a hostile attitude and its relationship to aggressive behavior. Unpublished doctoral dissertation, State University of Iowa, 1965.

Walters, R. H., & Parke, R. D. Social motivation, dependency, and susceptibility to social influence. In L. Berkowitz (Ed.), Advances in experimental social psychology. Vol.1. New York: Academic Press, 1964, pp. 231-276.

Aggression

14

Footnotes

[1] The present experiment was conducted by Anthony LePage under Leonard Berkowitz's supervision as part of a research program sponsored by Grant G-23988 from the National Science Foundation to the senior author.

Aggression

15

Table 1

Mean Number of Shocks Given in Each Condition

Condition	Shocks received	
	1	7
Associated weapons	2.60	6.07
Unassociated weapons	2.20	5.67
No object	3.07	4.67
Badminton racquets	----	4.60

appendix: proofs and examples A

1. PROBABILITY

In Chapter 3 the probability of an event was defined as the ratio of favorable events divided by the total possible events. For example, the probability of drawing a heart from a standard deck of playing cards is .25 because there are thirteen favorable events and fifty-two total possible events. In this example it is easy to determine the number of favorable events and the total number of events. But as the number of possible events and favorable events increases, or the complexity of the events increases, the task of determining the probability of an outcome becomes more difficult. For example, determining the probability of a particular sequence of events is usually more difficult than assessing the probability of a single event. Fortunately, in some instances it is possible to use rules to calculate the probability of events if the complexity or number of events precludes determining the probability directly by dividing the number of favorable events by the total number of possible events.

Multiplication Rule

The multiplication rule is useful because in many instances the probability of two independent events is known (e.g., the probability of obtaining heads when tossing a coin and the probability of obtaining a 4 with one roll of a die). The probability of obtaining both events in succession is calculated by multiplying the probabilities of the separate events. For example, the probability of tossing a head and then obtaining a 4 by rolling a die is .083 since the probability of obtaining a head is .50 and the probability of obtaining a 4 is .167. Thus, the probability of a *complex* outcome can be determined if the probability of the *components* of the

305

event is known. It is only necessary to multiply the probabilities of the components. It is assumed that the components are discrete, independent events. For example, the toss of the coin should not influence the roll of the die. Or, stated differently, if the probability of the joint occurrence of two events is equal to the probability of the occurrence of one event times the probability of the occurrence of the other event, the events are independent.

Permutations

In many instances it is useful to know the number of ways that objects or events can be arranged. An ordered arrangement is called a *permutation*. The total number of permutations of N objects or events is $N!$ The symbol ! is called *factorial*. $N!$ is the product of all successive integers from N to 1. For example, if an investigator has six different conditions and desires to counterbalance them completely, the number of permutations of the six conditions is 6! or $6 \times 5 \times 4 \times 3 \times 2 \times 1$ or 720. After determining the number of permutations, it is likely that the investigator will decide against complete counterbalancing of the six conditions.

If you do not believe there are 720 different orders of six objects or events, you can generate all possible orders. In generating the first order, you will find that there are six possible conditions for the first position, five for the second position, four for the third position, three for the fourth position, two for the fifth position, and only one for the sixth position. The reader who notes this relationship will only have to generate one order to realize that the number of possible permutations is $N!$ It is assumed that each condition can be used once and only once in each sequence.

In some cases it is not feasible or desirable to arrange the entire set of N objects or events. Instead, it is necessary to determine the number of ways of selecting and arranging a *portion* of the N objects. If r is equal to the number of objects selected and r is equal to or less than N, then the number of permutations of r objects selected from among N distinct objects is equal to:

$$\frac{N!}{(N-r)!}.$$

For example, if an investigator could only test three of six possible conditions in each session, r would equal 3 and N would equal 6. The number of permutations of the three conditions selected from the six conditions would be

$$\frac{6!}{(6-3)!}$$

or $6 \times 5 \times 4$ or 120.

In short, the number of possible arrangements of events can be determined by using the permutation formulas. When the total number of permutations is known, it is a fairly simple task to assess whether an obtained sequence is a rare or common event. However, for many purposes it is not important to consider the order of events but only the number of ways that r events can be selected from N events. If the ordering is not important then a way is needed to compute the number of combinations of N events taken r at a time. For permutations the order of the events is important. For combinations the order of the events is irrelevant.

Combinations

The number of ways of selecting r distinct combinations of N objects can be calculated by the formula

$$\frac{N!}{r!\,(N-r)!}.$$

For example, assume that an investigator wants to select four subjects, at random without replacement, from a group of ten subjects. How many ways could four subjects be selected from among the ten subjects? In this case $r = 4$ and $N = 10$. The number of combinations of ten things taken four at a time is equal to

$$\frac{10!}{4!\,6!} = 210.$$

Thus, the probability of obtaining any particular set of four subjects is 1/210 or .0047.

The use of the combination formula makes it possible to determine the probability of complex events. For example, the combination formula can be used to calculate the probability of being dealt a flush (all five cards of the same suit) in a game of stud poker. There are thirteen cards in each suit so it is necessary to determine the number of ways of selecting five distinct combinations of thirteen objects. That is, it is necessary to determine the number of different ways one can get a flush in each suit. The number of combinations is

$$\frac{13!}{5!\,(13-5)!} = 1287.$$

Since there are four different suits there are 5,148 different ways that one can be dealt a flush in stud poker. Thus, there are 5,148 favorable events. The total number of possible events is calculated by determining the number of possible poker hands that one can be dealt. This is determined by computing the number of combinations of fifty-two cards taken five at a time. The number of combinations is

$$\frac{52!}{5!\,(47)!} = 2{,}598{,}960.$$

Thus, the probability of being dealt a flush in a game of stud poker is 5,148/2,598,960 or slightly less than .002.

2. PROOF THAT TWO INDEPENDENT ESTIMATES OF POPULATION VARIANCE CAN BE OBTAINED IF THE NULL HYPOTHESIS IS TRUE

The following set of symbols are used in the proofs in Appendix A. It is assumed that there are the same number of scores in each condition or group.

n = number of scores in each group
X = any score
$\overline{X}_j$ = mean of group j
$\overline{X}.$ = mean for all groups combined or the grand mean
σ^2 = population variance
s^2 = sample variance
s = standard deviation of the sample
$s_{\bar{x}}$ = standard error of the sample

Within-group Estimate of Population Variance

The first step is to prove that the SS_{wg} divided by its degrees of freedom is equal to the sample variance. Remember that sample variance is the best estimate of population variance. The task, therefore, is to obtain two independent ways to compute s^2. If there is only one sample or group, the best estimate of population variance is the sample variance or

$$\frac{\Sigma (X - \overline{X}_j)^2}{n - 1}.$$

If there is more than one sample, the best estimate is obtained by pooling the k different estimates of population variance by summing them and dividing by k. Thus the best estimate of population variance is:

$$\frac{\Sigma\Sigma (X - \overline{X}_j)^2}{k(n - 1)} = s^2.$$

The double summation sign means that the values obtained by performing the indicated operations on the scores in each group are summed over groups.

The symbol s^2 is used because the obtained value is an estimate of population variance and not the actual population variance. An examination of the left side of the equation reveals that the numerator is equal to the SS_{wg} (i.e., the sum of the squared deviations of each score from its group mean) and the denominator is equal to the degrees of freedom for within groups. The number of scores that are free to vary in each group is equal to $n - 1$. Because there are k groups, the degrees of freedom for within groups is equal to $k(n - 1)$. In short, the SS_{wg} divided by its degrees of freedom provides one estimate of population variance.

Between-groups Estimate of Population Variance

The next task is to demonstrate that the SS_{bg} divided by its degrees of freedom also provides an estimate of population variance if the null hypothesis is true. In order to do this it is necessary to know that the standard deviation of the null hypothesis sampling distribution is called the *standard error*. Any time there is more than one group, the different groups comprise a sampling distribution, i.e., a distribution of samples. If the independent variable does not have an effect, the distribution can be considered a null hypothesis sampling distribution.

The standard error is equal to the standard deviation divided by the square root of n (i.e., $s_{\bar{x}} = \dfrac{s}{\sqrt{n}}$). Since it is necessary to work with the variance instead of the standard deviation, each side of the equation is squared. This gives Equation 1.

$$s_{\bar{x}}^2 = \frac{s^2}{n} \qquad (1)$$

If each side of Equation 1 is multiplied by n, an estimate of population variance is obtained since s^2 is an estimate of population variance.

$$ns_{\bar{x}}^2 = s^2 \qquad (2)$$

Since

$$s_{\bar{x}}^2 = \frac{\Sigma(\bar{X}_j - \bar{X}.)^2}{k-1}$$

the right hand value in this equation can be inserted in Equation 2 to give Equation 3.

$$\frac{\Sigma\, n(\bar{X}_j - \bar{X}.)^2}{k-1} = s^2 \qquad (3)$$

Note that the numerator of the left term in Equation 3 is equal to the SS_{bg} and the denominator is equal to the degrees of freedom for the SS_{bg}. Therefore, the SS_{bg} divided by its degrees of freedom provides an estimate of population variance when the null hypothesis is true. Since the SS_{bg} divided by its degrees of freedom and the SS_{wg} divided by its degrees of freedom provide independent estimates of population variance when the null hypothesis is true, these estimates can be compared in order to assess whether the null hypothesis is true. This point has already been discussed under the heading "Logic of Analysis of Variance."

3. PROOF THAT THE $SS_{tot} = SS_{bg} + SS_{wg}$

Once again, it is assumed that there are the same number of scores for each condition or group. The symbol notation is the same as the notation used in Appendix A-2. The first step is to show that the grand mean subtracted from any score is equal to the difference between the score and the group mean plus the difference between the group mean and the grand mean. This equation is obtained by simply adding and subtracting the group mean from the right side of the equation.

$$(X - \bar{X}.) = (X - \bar{X}_j) + (\bar{X}_j - \bar{X}.) \qquad (1)$$

Equation 1 applies to any score. Since the SS_{tot} is obtained by considering all scores, it is necessary to obtain the sum of the values obtained by performing the operation on every score in each group and for all groups. The double summation sign indicates that the values obtained by considering all the scores in each group and all the groups are added. Each side of Equation 2 is also squared since it is

310   Appendix A

necessary to consider squared deviations from the mean. Equation 3 is obtained by expanding the right side of Equation 2. Equation 3 reduces to Equation 4,

$$\Sigma\Sigma(X - \bar{X}.)^2 = \Sigma\Sigma[(X - \bar{X}_j) + (\bar{X}_j - \bar{X}.)]^2 \qquad (2)$$

$$\Sigma\Sigma(X - \bar{X}.)^2 = \Sigma\Sigma(X - \bar{X}_j)^2 + \Sigma\Sigma(\bar{X}_j - \bar{X}.)^2 \qquad (3)$$
$$+ 2\Sigma\Sigma(X - \bar{X}_j)(\bar{X}_j - \bar{X}.)$$

$$\Sigma\Sigma(X - \bar{X}.)^2 = \Sigma\Sigma(X - \bar{X}_j)^2 + \Sigma\Sigma(\bar{X}_j - \bar{X}.)^2 \qquad (4)$$

$$SS_{tot} = SS_{wg} + SS_{bg} \qquad (5)$$

because the deviations that are not squared sum to zero. That is, the last term in Equation 3 is equal to zero. The first term in Equation 4 is equal to the SS_{tot}; the second term is equal to the SS_{wg}; and the third term is equal to the SS_{bg}.

4. COMPUTATION OF THE ANALYSIS OF VARIANCE WITH THE DEVIATION FORMULAS

The hypothetical experiment was designed to investigate the influence of alcohol on motor performance. The independent variable was the amount of alcohol: 0, 1, 2, or 3 shots. The dependent variable was the number of total errors for each of the twenty-four players for a four-game series.

Number of errors

	0 Condition	1 Condition	2 Condition	3 Condition
	1	2	4	5
	2	3	5	6
	3	4	6	7
	1	2	4	5
	2	3	5	6
	3	4	6	7
Total	12	18	30	36
$\bar{X}$	2	3	5	6

Grand Mean equal to 4

$SS_{tot} = \Sigma\Sigma(X - \bar{X}.)^2$
$SS_{tot} = (9 + 4 + 1 + 9 + 4 + 1) + (4 + 1 + 0 + 4 + 1 + 0) +$
$\qquad (0 + 1 + 4 + 0 + 1 + 4) + (1 + 4 + 9 + 1 + 4 + 9)$
$SS_{tot} = 28 + 10 + 10 + 28$
$SS_{tot} = 76$

$SS_{bg} = \Sigma n(\bar{X}_j - \bar{X}.)^2$
$SS_{bg} = 6[(2)^2 + (1)^2 + (1)^2 + (2)^2]$
$SS_{bg} = 6 \, [10]$
$SS_{bg} = 60$

$SS_{wg} = SS_{tot} - SS_{bg}$
$SS_{wg} = 76 - 60$
$SS_{wg} = 16$
or

$SS_{wg} = \Sigma\Sigma[X - \bar{X}_j]^2$
$SS_{wg} = [(1^2 + 0^2 + 1^2 + 1^2 + 0^2 + 1^2) + (1^2 + 0^2 + 1^2 + 1^2 + 0^2 + 1^2) +$
$\qquad (1^2 + 0^2 + 1^2 + 1^2 + 0^2 + 1^2) + (1^2 + 0^2 + 1^2 + 1^2 + 0^2 + 1^2)]$
$SS_{wg} = 4 + 4 + 4 + 4$
$SS_{wg} = 16$

Analysis of variance table

Source	df	SS	MS	F
bg	3	60	20	25.00
wg	20	16	.80	
tot	23	76		

5. PROOF THAT THE DEVIATION AND COMPUTATIONAL FORMULAS FOR THE ANALYSIS OF VARIANCE ARE MATHEMATICALLY EQUIVALENT

Once again, it is assumed that there are an equal number of subjects in each condition. The symbol notation is the same as the notation used in Appendix A-2. In order to demonstrate that the deviation formulas are equivalent to the computational formulas, the computational formulas are derived from the deviation formulas. That is, the plan is to start with the deviation formulas and by a series of algebraic steps end up with the computational formulas. The student who has a weak background in algebra may elect to skip this proof. Another "proof" can be obtained by computing the analysis of variance in Appendix A-4 by using the computational formulas.

The SS_{tot}

$SS_{tot} = \Sigma\Sigma(X - \bar{X}.)^2 = \Sigma\Sigma(X^2 - 2\bar{X}.X + \bar{X}.^2)$ (1)

$SS_{tot} = \Sigma\Sigma X^2 - 2\bar{X}.\Sigma\Sigma X + \bar{X}.^2 \Sigma n$

$SS_{tot} = \Sigma\Sigma X^2 - \dfrac{2\Sigma\Sigma X(\Sigma\Sigma X)}{\Sigma n} + \dfrac{(\Sigma\Sigma X)^2 \Sigma n}{(\Sigma n)^2}$

$SS_{tot} = \Sigma\Sigma X^2 - \dfrac{2(\Sigma\Sigma X)^2}{\Sigma n} + \dfrac{(\Sigma\Sigma X)^2}{\Sigma n}$

$SS_{tot} = \Sigma\Sigma X^2 - \dfrac{(\Sigma\Sigma X)^2}{N}$

$SS_{tot} = \Sigma\Sigma X^2 - \dfrac{(T)^2}{N}$ (2)

In Equation 2, T is equal to the sum of all the scores and N is equal to the number of different scores.

The SS_{bg}

$$SS_{bg} = \Sigma n(\overline{X}_j - \overline{X}.)^2 \qquad (3)$$

$$SS_{bg} = \Sigma n(\overline{X}_j^2 - 2\overline{X}_j\overline{X}. + \overline{X}.^2)$$

$$SS_{bg} = \Sigma n\overline{X}_j^2 - 2\overline{X}.\Sigma n\overline{X}_j + \overline{X}.^2 \Sigma n$$

$$SS_{bg} = \frac{\Sigma(\Sigma X)^2}{n} - \frac{2(\Sigma\Sigma X)}{\Sigma n} \times \frac{\Sigma n(\Sigma X)}{n} + \frac{(\Sigma\Sigma X)^2}{\Sigma n}$$

$$SS_{bg} = \frac{\Sigma(\Sigma X)^2}{n} - \frac{2(\Sigma\Sigma X)^2}{\Sigma n} + \frac{(\Sigma\Sigma X)^2}{\Sigma n}$$

$$SS_{bg} = \frac{\Sigma(\Sigma X)^2}{n} - \frac{(\Sigma\Sigma X)^2}{N}$$

$$SS_{bg} = \frac{\Sigma(\text{group total})^2}{n} - \frac{(T)^2}{N} \qquad (4)$$

The SS_{wg}

$$SS_{wg} = SS_{tot} - SS_{bg}$$

appendix: research topics B

The purpose of this appendix is to present a few research topics that can be used as starting points for further research. Suggestions for research are made for each of the topics, but the task of selecting, planning, and executing a project is left to you. Planning and executing your own research project is an excellent way to gain an understanding of the various stages of experimentation and the relationships among them. Moreover, any student who becomes actively involved in a research project which is of personal interest is likely to find that research can be fun. If you do not find a topic to your liking in this appendix you should examine the journals that report research findings in psychology and the other social sciences. The topics in this appendix are not representative of the research areas investigated by social scientists because it was necessary to exclude those topics which require special skills, equipment, or an extensive knowledge of the area. Instructors who elect to emphasize a particular content area can offer alternative research topics.

TOPIC 1. THE LOST LETTER TECHNIQUE

Milgram (1969) describes a technique that can be used to assess public opinion and that avoids some of the problems inherent in the survey technique. The survey technique typically entails selecting a representative sample from a larger population and then questioning each subject in the sample. Its success is demonstrated by the fact that political polls tend to predict accurately the outcome of elections. The survey technique is a reactive measure, of course, because the person being interviewed is aware that some sort of "evaluation" is occurring.

The lost letter technique yields a nonreactive measure. The subjects are not aware, presumably, that their performance is being assessed, because the investigator does not select or make direct contact with them. The only contact between the investigator and the subjects is through a "lost letter." The investigator plants a number of self-addressed, stamped letters at various locations. The dependent measure is the number of letters that are mailed by the people who find them. Thus, the lost letter technique differs from the survey technique in that it assesses the willingness of individuals to carry out a particular act — to mail or not mail a letter — instead of assessing opinion directly.

In one of Milgram's studies, 400 letters were addressed in exactly the same way (to the same address in New Haven, Connecticut) except that they were directed either to Mr. Walter Carnap, to the Friends of the Communist Party, to the Friends of the Nazi Party, or to the Medical Research Associates. The words "Attention: Mr. Walter Carnap" were typed at the lower left on each of the 300 envelopes addressed to one of the organizations. The contents of every letter were the same. Walter Carnap was told that the plans for the meeting had changed because the speakers could not arrive in time. The letter was straightforward but suggestive in light of the organization involved. That is, the reader would be likely to infer that the sender (Max Thuringer) and addressee (Walter Carnap) were actively involved in the affairs of the organization, particularly in the recruitment of new members. The envelopes were distributed in various locations (sidewalks, shops, telephone booths) in ten preselected districts of New Haven. In addition, each envelope had been sealed so that, if the letter was posted, the investigator would be able to determine whether it had been opened.

The results were striking. The percentage of the 100 letters posted was very high for the letters to the Medical Research Associates (72%) and for the personal letters (71%), but very low (25%) for letters to the other two organizations. There was a greater tendency to open the letters addressed to the organizations, particularly the Communist (40%) and Nazi (32%) ones, than the personal letters (10%).

The Milgram technique can be used in several ways. It can be used to assess public opinion on a controversial issue by varying the name of the organization that is placed on the lost letters. If the issue is one about which people tend to be highly emotional, it may be interesting to compare the results of the lost letter technique with the results obtained with a survey technique. Or, the technique could be used to study how subject variables or location variables influence whether individuals will carry out a particular act. For example, if you lost a textbook that was clearly marked with your name, address, and telephone number, do you believe the probability of having it returned would be influenced by whether it was left in a chapel, dormitory, or classroom?

Reference

Milgram, S. The lost-letter technique. *Psychology Today,* June, 1969. 30-33; 66-68.

TOPIC 2. CORRELATION OF ABILITIES

Many problems can be investigated only by correlational and observational techniques. For example, beginning in 1921, Terman and his associates studied over fifteen hundred children who had IQs of 140 or above. The progress of the children was followed through the middle years of their adult lives. The major finding was that the gifted children were above average in characteristics other than intelligence. That is, there is a positive correlation between intelligence and health, social adaptability, and leadership. In general, the gifted children continued to be superior to their own generation as they grew older.

You are encouraged to design a correlational study which would yield data of personal interest. For example, you may be interested in whether performance in a methodology course is related to performance in nonmethodology courses, whether quantitative abilities are related to verbal abilities, or whether the amount of study time is related to course performance. Or, you could select a test of ability such as the Remote Associates Test (Mednick and Mednick, 1967), a memory test, or a vocabulary test and correlate performance on the test with another variable of interest.

The Remote Associates Test can be described as a search task. Each item consists of three stimulus words. The subject's task is to find a word that is related to all three of the stimulus words. For example, *party* is an acceptable solution to the stimulus triad of *line, birthday,* and *surprise.* A remote associates test similar to the Mednick test is published in the paperback entitled *Involvement in Psychology Today.* There are a number of ways to construct a memory test. For example, you could select a list of twenty-five common nouns, read it aloud to subjects at the rate of one word every five seconds, and then have them recall as many words as they can from the list in any order. A vocabulary test can be constructed by selecting words which differ in degree of difficulty. It is important to select enough words of intermediate difficulty so that individual differences among the subjects will be detected.

After the test has been constructed, the next step is to establish the reliability of the measure. Reliability can be assessed by correlating the performance of subjects on even-numbered items with their performance on odd-numbered items, by correlating the scores obtained by testing each subject twice with a time lag between the two testing sessions, or by correlating the performance of subjects on two comparable tests. For example, for the memory test, you could select fifty common nouns and randomly assign each noun to List 1 or List 2 with the restriction that there be twenty-five nouns in each list. Then you could test each subject on both lists. Half the subjects would receive List 1 and then List 2 and the other half the reverse order. The performance for each subject on the two lists could then be correlated.

If you have attempted to establish the reliability of a test you are likely to appreciate the fact that it is not a simple matter to construct a reliable test. A number of attempts may be necessary. After a reliable test has been constructed, it is reasonable to question whether test performance is related to other measures. Keep in mind that there should be logical or theoretical grounds for correlating variables. For example, one might ask whether performance on a memory test can predict performance in a course which requires extensive memorization. Unfortunately, it is still not uncommon for psychologists to construct a test and then correlate it with everything in sight. On the positive side, it should be noted that psychologists have developed very sophisticated correlational techniques. These techniques, which are beyond the scope of this text, allow investigators to "explain" correlations. And, if it is possible to obtain correlations between measures at different points in a subject's life, such data can be used to assess whether variables are causally related.

References

Crano, W. D., Kenny, D. A., & Campbell, D. T. Does intelligence cause achievement? A cross-lagged panel analysis. *Journal of Educational Psychology,* 1972, 63, 258–275.
Involvement in Psychology Today. Del Mar, California: CRM Books, 1970.
Mednick, S. A., & Mednick, M. T. *Examiner's Manual: Remote Associates Test.* Boston: Houghton-Mifflin, 1967.
Oden, M. H. The fulfillment of promise: forty year follow up of the Terman gifted group. *Genetic Psychology Monographs,* 1968, 77, 3–93.
Terman, L. M., & Oden, M. H. *The Gifted Child Grows Up.* Stanford, California: Stanford University Press, 1947.

TOPIC 3. MNEMONIC SYSTEMS

There are slight variations among mnemonic systems, but the basic components are essentially the same. The first phase of most systems involves the memorization of a series of "pegs." Generally, words are used as pegs and each word is numbered, with associations between numbers and words. A frequently used peg list is: 1-bun, 2-shoe, 3-tree, 4-door, 5-hive, 6-stick, 7-heaven, 8-gate, 9-line, 10-hen. Following the memorization of the peg words, new words can be memorized by using bizarre imagery to connect the new words to peg words. For example, if *automobile* is the first to-be-recalled word, the task is to conjure up a bizarre image connecting the first peg, *bun,* and *automobile.* A possible image might be a five-foot bun driving an automobile. The same principle is used for the remaining to-be-recalled words. At recall, the peg words, which are accessible because they have been well memorized, are presumed to elicit the visual images formed during the study trial and thus make the to-be-recalled words accessible.

The effectiveness of providing subjects with a plan for improving memory can be demonstrated by performing an experiment. The experimental subjects are given the list of peg words to memorize. It is important that they have the list extremely well memorized. Then they are told to use the peg list items to recall new items by linking each peg word with a to-be-recalled word by conjuring up a bizarre image of the two words. The control subjects do not receive a peg list. They are told to study the words so that they can recall them during the subsequent recall trial. The list of to-be-recalled words is read to subjects at a rate of one word every five seconds. Concrete words such as *automobile, paper, tiger,* and *football* are used. The typical finding (e.g., Bugelski, Kidd, & Segman, 1968) is that the experimental subjects perform much better than controls.

There is reason to believe that the way information is represented in images is related to the size of the image. Kosslyn (1975) had subjects conjure up images at the correct relative size next to a fly or an elephant. For example, subjects might be asked to conjure up an image of a cat next to an elephant or a cat next to a fly. The image was to be projected flush up against a large surface (e.g., a tennis backboard) such that the projected images "covered" most of the surface while still maintaining the relative size relationship between the two animals imaged. For our example, we can expect the image of a cat to be larger when paired with a fly than when paired with an elephant. Kosslyn found that more information was represented in large images than small images.

A number of experiments can be performed to study mnemonic systems and the role of imagery in mnemonics. For example, one could assess the effect of image size. If large images yield better performance than small images can we attribute the results to the size of the image? Do large images take longer to construct than small images? Does the effectiveness of a mnemonic system depend on the material to be memorized? Can children use imagery more effectively than adults?

References

Bower, G. H. Analysis of a mnemonic device. *American Scientist*, 1970, 58, 496–510.

Bugelski, B. R., Kidd, E., & Segman, J. Image as a mediator in one-trial paired-associate learning. *Journal of Experimental Psychology*, 1968, 76, 69–73.

Kosslyn, S. M. Information representation in visual images. *Cognitive Psychology*, 1975, 7, 341–370.

Wood, G. Mnemonic systems in recall. *Journal of Educational Psychology*, 1967, 58 (6, Pt. 2), 1–27.

TOPIC 4. INFORMATION PROCESSING

If you have thought about the acquisition of skills, you have probably noted that voluntary control is required during the early stages of skill acquisition. For example, in the early stages of learning to type one has to think about the letters that are being typed. As greater proficiency is developed it is no longer necessary to think about each individual letter. In fact, thinking about individual letters tends to result in more mistakes and a slower rate of typing. One explanation for this phenomenon is that the skilled typist processes units larger than single letters (e.g., words or phrases). The processing may only appear to be controlled by involuntary mechanisms because the use of larger units does not require all the capacity of the voluntary processing system.

It is possible to study the size of the unit or the nature of the unit that the skilled typist processes. Suppose, for example, that you were interested in determining whether a typist processes the meaning of the material to be typed. That is, you are interested in determining whether meaning units or nonmeaning units are processed. One way to answer this question is, of course, simply to ask skilled typists whether they pay attention to the meaning of the passage they are typing. Or, you could select two passages of equal difficulty and change the ordering of the nouns so that the meaning is disrupted without affecting the syntax and grammar. The normal and distorted versions of each passage are used equally often. Each typist receives the distorted version of one passage and the normal version of the other. The distortion should have a negative effect on typing performance only if the typist is processing the meaning of the passage being typed. If this manipulation has such an effect, it is possible to conclude that meaning units are being processed.

The size of the units being processed can be studied by taking a passage and varying the presentation order of its parts. For one condition the passage could be presented without any changes. For a second condition the sentences could be presented in a random order. For a third condition the sentences and the phrases within each sentence could be presented in a random order. For a fourth condition all the words could be ordered randomly. For a fifth condition the letters of each word could be scrambled. The effect of the various disruptions can then be used to determine the size of the unit that the typist is processing. For example, if there are no differences between the first four conditions and the fifth condition is the poorest, it is possible to conclude that the typist is processing word units.

References

Annett, J. Acquisition of skill. *British Medical Bulletin*, 1971, 27, 266–271.

TOPIC 5. AGGRESSION

There are several studies of aggression in which nonhumans are used as subjects. Animals have a strong tendency to attack each other if they are shocked on the feet (Ulrich & Azrin, 1962) or if a positive reinforcer is withdrawn (Azrin, Hutchinson, & Hake, 1966). In the Azrin, et al., study pigeons were trained to peck a disk, in a schedule that included both reinforcement and extinction. For the reinforcement periods food was delivered as a reward for pecking. For the extinction periods no food was delivered when the pigeons pecked the disk. When the two periods of reinforcement and extinction were alternated, the investigators found that the pigeons would attack a nearby pigeon during the extinction periods. Some of the pigeons attacked even when the "bystander" pigeon was a stuffed model.

The length of the attack on the other pigeon decreased as the length of the time since the last reinforcement increased, and it increased as the number of prior reinforcements increased. It was necessary to alternate reinforcement with extinction in order to get attack, and attack was produced only if the food delivered during the reinforcement period was eaten. That is, satiated pigeons were less likely to attack. The extinction-produced attacks were not attributable to a past history of aggression because the same effect was obtained with socially deprived pigeons. The authors concluded that the change from food reinforcement to extinction produced aggression. The reader who has recently been denied an anticipated reward should empathize with the pigeons in the Azrin, et al., study. Yet, it is difficult to demonstrate that the findings obtained with lower animals are applicable to the understanding of human aggression.

Aggression in humans cannot readily be studied through procedures comparable to those used with lower animals because of practical and ethical considerations. Investigators have demonstrated that human subjects tend to be aggressive after witnessing an aggressive act (e.g., Bandura, Ross, & Ross, 1963), but it is difficult to determine whether these effects are long-lasting or applicable to more "real-life" situations. The student who is interested in studying human aggression in natural situations is limited primarily to observational and correlational techniques. There are at least two problems that may be of interest. One is determining the level of aggression. Another is determining the antecedents of aggressive behavior.

The investigator who wants to assess the level of aggression can use a number of approaches. One approach is to obtain the incidence of violent crimes per 100,000 population over a period of years. It should be easy to obtain this data because law enforcement agencies keep records of violent crimes. If these records can be accepted as accurate (e.g., if there is no reason to believe the relationship between *actual* and *reported* crimes varied from year to year) *and* there is a trend toward more or less violence, the incidence of crime can be used as a starting point for determining the antecedent conditions. For example, if there is an increase in actual violence as inferred from police records and an increase in the incidence of violence in magazines, newspapers, movies, and television, it is reasonable to ask whether the relationship between depicted and actual violence is causal. If it is possible to obtain measures on actual and depicted violence at various times, it is possible to use correlational techniques that allow a cause-effect interpretation. The reader who is interested in this approach can refer to Eron, Huesmann, Lefkowitz, and Walder's (1972) article on television violence and aggression.

The suggestions made above are not realistic for the student who is interested in studying aggression but does not have the time or resources for an elaborate project. Instead, she may elect to study aggression using an observational technique. For example, one could design a questionnaire or interview people to assess attitudes toward violence. Why do some people enjoy watching movies that depict beatings, rapes, killings, shootouts, and slaughters? Is watching violence a novel experience? Is it a safety valve that allows people to release violence rather than commit violent acts? Do people learn to like violence? Another procedure would be to assess individual differences in preference for violence. How do people who enjoy watching violence differ from those people who do not? Or, one could assess whether people are satiated quickly on violence. For example, one could determine whether the repeat rate (people who see a particular movie more than once) is greater for violent or nonviolent movies. Marler (1976) considers the role of strangeness and familiarity on animal aggression and suggests that this may be the single most important variable for controlling animal aggression. You may be able to think of ways to assess the importance of the strangeness-familiarity variable for human aggression.

References

Ardrey, R. *The Territorial Imperative.* New York: Atheneum, 1966.

Azrin, N. H., Hutchinson, R. R., & Hake, D. F. Extinction-induced aggression. *Journal of the Experimental Analysis of Behavior,* 1966, 9, 191–204.

Bandura, A., Ross, D., & Ross, S. A. Imitation of film mediated aggressive models. *Journal of Abnormal and Social Psychology,* 1963, 66, 3–11.

Berkowitz, L. Experimental investigations of hostility catharsis. *Journal of Consulting and Clinical Psychology,* 1970, 35, 1–7.

Eron, L. D., Huesmann, L. R., Lefkowitz, M. M., & Walder, L. O. Does television violence cause aggression? *American Psychologist,* 1972, 27, 253–263.

Lorenz, K. *On Aggression.* New York: Harcourt Brace Jovanovich, 1966.

Marler, P. On animal aggression: The roles of strangeness and familiarity *American Psychologist,* 1976, 31, 239–246.

Smith, D., King, M., & Hoebel, B. Lateral hypothalamic control of killing: Evidence for a cholinoceptive mechanism. *Science,* 1970, 167, 900–901.

Ulrich, R. E., & Azrin, N. H. Reflexive fighting in response to aversive stimulation. *Journal of the Experimental Analysis of Behavior,* 1962, 5, 511–520.

Zimbardo, P. G., The human choice: Individuation, reason, and order versus deindividuation, impulse, and chaos. *Nebraska Symposium on Motivation, 1969,* 1970, 18, 237–307.

TOPIC 6. THE COCKTAIL PARTY PHENOMENON

The cocktail party phenomenon (Cherry, 1957) is the label given to the observation that it is possible to select a message to listen to and ignore other messages. Thus, at a cocktail party you can eavesdrop on the conversation behind you or attend to a different conversation, but not both. It is possible to switch back and forth between the two conversations but very difficult to comprehend both if the level of discourse is complex. The phenomenon of selective attention can be investigated using earphones that make it possible to send one message to one ear and a different message to the other ear. The subject has to repeat (shadow) the message in one ear. The message to be shadowed must be difficult enough to require full attention. Usually the material to be shadowed is made more difficult by presenting it faster.

The shadowing procedure makes it possible to study some interesting aspects of selective attention. One can consider whether subjects process any of the unattended message by varying the relationship between the attended and unattended message (Treisman, 1964) and by presenting high priority information (e.g., the subject's name) in the unattended message (Moray, 1959). The results of these studies reveal that subjects do process some of the unattended message.

The study of selective attention is usually performed with special equipment that makes it possible to control the messages presented to each ear, but elaborate equipment is not essential for all studies of selective attention. The student can study selective attention by presenting two messages simultaneously to both ears and requiring subjects to attend to only one. This is similar to the situation faced by the student who wants to study while a roommate is playing the stereo. A similar procedure could be used to investigate whether the ability to attend selectively is influenced greatly by the similarity of the two messages. For example, are some kinds of music more disruptive of reading than others? Does music interfere with ability to work mathematical problems? Is it more difficult to attend selectively to one message when both messages are in the same modality (verbal) than when they are in different modalities (one verbal and one visual)? Are there other variables that influence a subject's ability to attend selectively?

One such variable is prior attention habits. The effect of trying to ignore well-learned habits can be demonstrated by constructing a task similar to one developed by Stroop (1935). Pens or pencils with different color inks or leads — say, red, black, green, yellow, and brown — are used to print the words *red, black, green, yellow,* and *brown* in rows. Each word should appear once in each row and the order of the words in each row should be random. Each word is printed in a color other than the color for which it is the label. For example, the word *red* could be printed in black, green, yellow, or brown, but not in red. The color for each word is changed each time the word is presented. The task for the subject is to name the color of each word (i.e., the color of the ink) as quickly as possible. The amount of time needed to complete the task can be the performance measure. The student who performs this task is likely to notice the interference. The interference results from the fact that there is a very strong tendency to respond (attend) to the word instead of to the color of the word. A test of this nature may be used to study individual differences in selective attention. Would you expect to find individual differences in the ability to attend selectively? Do you believe the ability to attend selectively is related to other cognitive abilities?

References

Cherry, C. *On Human Communication.* New York: Science Editions, 1957.
Howarth, C. I., & Bloomfield, J. R. Search and selective attention. *British Medical Bulletin,* 1971, 27, 253–257.
Lindsay, P. H., & Norman, D. A. *Human Information Processing: An Introduction to Psychology.* New York: Academic Press, 1972.
Moray, N. Attention in dichotic listening: Affective cues and the influence of instructions. *Quarterly Journal of Experimental Psychology,* 1959, 11, 56–60.
Neisser, U., & Becklen, R. Selective looking: Attending to visually specified events. *Cognitive Psychology,* 1975, 7, 480–494.
Stroop, J. R. Studies of interference in serial verbal reactions. *Journal of Experimental Psychology,* 1935, 18, 643–662.
Treisman, A. M. Monitoring and storage of irrelevant messages in selective attention. *Journal of Verbal Learning and Verbal Behavior,* 1964, 3, 449–459.

TOPIC 7. PUPIL DILATION

Pupil dilation has been used extensively as a measure of attitude by Hess and as a measure of mental effort by Kahneman. We will consider some of the work by Hess. Students interested in pupil dilation as a measure of mental effort can refer to Kahneman (1973). Hess has performed several experiments using pupil dilation, so we can only consider a few of his findings. One of his basic questions is whether pupil size reveals a person's attitudes or emotions. In order to obtain the pupil-size measures, the eye is photographed with a motion picture camera while subjects view slides. A control slide is viewed for ten seconds and the test slide is viewed for ten seconds. The average pupil size while viewing the test slide is compared with the average pupil size while viewing the control slide. Hess and his associates have found that there is greater pupil dilation relative to the control slide when the stimuli on the test slides are interesting (e.g., an attractive member of the opposite sex, a baby) than when the stimuli are less interesting (e.g., an attractive member of the same sex, a landscape).

Although pupil dilation can be a useful measure of emotion and mental effort, it is likely that few, if any, students have the equipment available to record changes in pupil size accurately. The need for elaborate equipment can be avoided if pupil size is studied as an independent variable. Hess presented photographs of complete faces, which were identical except for pupil size. For example, in one of his experiments he showed a photograph of an attractive young woman with either small or large pupils to male subjects. The woman with the small pupils was described as "hard" or "cold" by the male subjects. The woman with the large pupils was described as "soft" or "pretty." In another series Hess and his associates presented pictures of faces without pupils. The subjects were to draw in the size of the pupils which best fit the face. That is, pupil size was the dependent measure, but the pupils were drawn, not photographed. They found that subjects drew larger pupils for happy faces than for sad faces. In yet another experiment subjects were asked to select the happier of two faces which were identical except for pupil size. Subjects over fifteen years old tended to select the face with the larger pupils; younger subjects did not show a preference for the faces with the larger pupils.

A student can perform several pupil-size experiments without elaborate equipment. For example, one could present pictures that are identical except for pupil size and observe the preference for large or small pupils in subjects of different ages. Will babies look longer at faces with large or small pupils? If babies and adults prefer large pupils to small pupils, why did subjects below fifteen years of age not select the face with the larger pupils as the "happier" of the two faces? One might also ask whether the effect of pupil size is restricted to human faces. That is, will subjects show a pupil-size effect if asked to indicate a preference for animal pictures that are identical except for pupil size? Will the effect, if any, be obtained for all animal pictures or just those animals with binocular vision (i.e., animals with both eyes in the front, not one on each side)?

References

Hess, E. H. The role of pupil size in communication. *Scientific American,* 1975, 233 (5), 110–119.

Janisse, M. P., & Peavler, W. S. Pupillary response today: Emotion in the eye. *Psychology Today,* February, 1974, 60–63.

Kahneman, D. *Attention and Effort.* Englewood Cliffs, N.J.: Prentice-Hall, 1973.

TOPIC 8. READING

Reading is obviously a very important and, unfortunately, a very complicated phenomenon to understand. One important question concerns the size of the units that one processes while reading. Do you attend to individual letters, to syllables, to words, or to phrases each time your eyes fixate on the material to be read? Miller (1962) argues that the unit must be larger than single syllables because there is not time to process individual syllables and still read as fast as we do.

Miller suggests that we make one decision about every second while reading and, therefore, we probably read phrases rather than smaller units.

A number of experiments can be performed to investigate reading. For example, one could vary the difficulty of the material and note the effect on reading rate. The difficulty of the material can be influenced by manipulating the style or content of the passage. One could also investigate performance on the difficult and easy passages by requiring subjects to read the passage upside down. Is the effect of the difficulty manipulation greater when the passage is presented right side up or upside down? What is the effect of allowing the subjects to read the passage once before attempting to read it upside down? What does this effect tell you about reading?

References

Gibson, E. J., & Levin, H. *The Psychology of Reading.* Cambridge, Mass.: The MIT Press, 1975.
Kohler, P. A. Experiments in reading. *Scientific American,* 1972, 227, 84–91.
Kolers, P. Specificity of operations in sentence recognition. *Cognitive Psychology,* 1975, 7, 289–306.
Miller, G. A. Decision units in the perception of speech. *I. R. E. Trans.* Information Theory, 1962, IT–8, 81–83.
Slobin, D. I. *Psycholinguistics.* Glenview, Ill.: Scott, Foresman, 1971.
Vernon, M. D. *Reading and Its Difficulties: A Psychological Study.* Cambridge, England: Cambridge University Press, 1971.

TOPIC 9. MACHIAVELLIANISM

It is possible to administer a test to assess whether an individual has a Machiavellian view of others (Christie, 1970). A Machiavellian is someone who believes that people are no good so it is permissible to use guile and deceit to influence and control them. The items in the test are designed to assess how the individual views others (e.g., as good, honest, and kind, or as selfish, vicious, and dishonest). The results of the research reported by Christie revealed that people who score high on the Machiavellian scale are more likely to be young, male, from urban environments, and members of professions that manipulate people (lawyers, psychiatrists, and behavioral scientists, as opposed to accountants, surgeons, and natural scientists). The scores were not related to intelligence, personality variables, authoritarianism, occupational status, education, marital status, or birth order.

Christie reported a study conducted by Dorothea Braginsky in which children were given a Machiavellianism test designed for elementary school children. The children who had high scores on the test were compared with children who had low scores. The task was to persuade children who had middle scores to eat crackers soaked in quinine. As you probably know, crackers soaked in quinine have a very bitter taste. The subjects who were to be the persuaders were told they would receive one nickel for every quinine-soaked cracker their subject (victim?)

ate. The high Machiavellian persuaders out-performed the low Machiavellian persuaders.

There are a number of possible experiments that a student could perform to study Machiavellianism. For example, it is possible to assess the effect of flattery on behavior to determine whether it "pays" to be a Machiavellian. Or, Machiavellianism could be studied by using factorial experiments in which Machiavellianism (a subject variable) and a nonsubject variable are manipulated. For example, one could manipulate the reasons subjects are given for complying with a request. In one case the reasons are subject based (i.e., gains for the subject) and in the other case the reasons are altruistic (i.e., gains for others). The effect of the reasons manipulation can be expected to be different for high and low Machiavellians. For example, the experimenter could manipulate the reasons given for donating blood (money versus an altruistic appeal). The effectiveness of the two appeals should depend on whether high or low Machiavellians are asked to donate blood. You may be able to think of other nonsubject variables that will interact with Machiavellianism.

References

Christie, R. The Machiavellis among us. *Psychology Today,* November, 1970. 82–86.

Geis, F., & Christie, R. (Eds.). *Studies in Machiavellianism.* New York: Academic Press, 1970.

TOPIC 10. THE PRISONER'S DILEMMA

The prisoner's dilemma game has been used to study conflict and conflict resolution. The name of the game is believed to be based on the conflict situation that two individuals could face when picked up on suspicion of committing a crime (see Lindsay & Norman, 1972). The district attorney can interrogate each suspect separately and offer each a special deal for confessing. He may promise that the person who confesses will be set free and the person who does not will be prosecuted on the maximum charge. If both confess, then they will be prosecuted on a lesser charge. If neither confesses, then the district attorney will not have a good case so the probability of either of the suspects being convicted is quite small. In this case the most reasonable procedure is for neither suspect to confess. This poses a dilemma, however, in that it is necessary for the two suspects to trust each other for this strategy to work.

The game is played by two players. Each player has to select one of two alternatives on each trial. They have to choose simultaneously, usually by writing their choices on pieces of paper, so that neither player knows what the other will do. The amount that one player gains or loses is determined both by his own choice and the choice of the other player. This can be seen by examining a typical payoff matrix presented in Table B-1. If both players choose B, they both receive only one cent. If they both choose A, they both receive ten cents. If Player 2 chooses B and Player 1 chooses A, then Player 2 receives fifty cents and Player 1 loses five cents. The reverse is true if Player 1 chooses B and Player 2 chooses A. The game is usually played for a number of trials.

TABLE B-1

A Payoff Matrix for the Prisoner's Dilemma Game

		Player 1	
		Selects A	Selects B
Player 2	Selects A	+10¢ / +10¢	+50¢ / −5¢
	Selects B	−5¢ / +50¢	+1¢ / +1¢

Several variables can be studied with the prisoner's dilemma game. For example, one could compare choices when subjects are playing for keeps or when they have to return the money. One could look at performance over different stages of practice. That is, do the players arrive at a cooperative strategy or not? A confederate of the experimenter could be one of the players so that the choices of one player (the confederate) could be manipulated. The effect of the confederate's strategy on the selections of the subject could then be systematically investigated. A questionnaire could be given at the end of the experiment to determine how the subjects view each other; the actual subject would not know, of course, that the other "subject" is actually a confederate of the experimenter.

References

Lindsay, P. H., & Norman, D. A. *Human Information Processing: An Introduction to Psychology.* New York: Academic Press, 1972.

Wrightsman, L. S., O'Connor, J., & Baker, N. J. (Eds.). *Cooperation and Competition: Readings on Mixed-Motive Games.* Belmont, Calif.: Brook/Cole, 1972.

TOPIC 11. CLOTHES AND BEHAVIOR

There have been a number of experiments which demonstrate that clothes influence the way people are treated. In general, well-dressed people are treated better than poorly dressed people because most people associate clothes with social status. Bickman (1974) reported a series of experiments demonstrating that clothing influences honesty, willingness to sign petitions, and obedience. Uniforms are particularly effective in eliciting obedience even when the uniformed person is seeking obedience in an area outside his normal role. In one experiment, for example, a passerby was stopped and instructed to give a dime to a confederate standing by a parking meter. Participants were much more likely to comply if the person making the demand was in a guard uniform than if he was not in uniform, but well dressed.

A student can perform a number of experiments to assess further the relationship between clothes and behavior. Are there situations in which poorly dressed persons are treated better than well-dressed persons? Does clothing influence all aspects of interpersonal relations or just those requiring obedience and honesty? That is, do we assess a person's clothing when making judgments about intelligence, political views, morals, and personality? Does a person's clothing become an unimportant consideration once we get to know the person? Is the probability of "interacting effectively with members of the opposite sex" influenced by the nature of one's dress? Is it possible to investigate these problems without violating the ethical principles discussed in Chapter 1?

References

Bickman, L. Social roles and uniforms: Clothes make the person. *Psychology Today,* April, 1974, 48–51.

TOPIC 12. THE EYEWITNESS

There is considerable evidence to support the view that eyewitness testimony frequently leaves much to be desired. This point can be demonstrated by staging an incident in front of several observers (e.g., confederates could attack a professor while she is lecturing) and then question the witnesses. The usual result is that the witnesses do not agree about what happened. Let us consider why eyewitness testimony tends to be inaccurate.

One problem with eyewitness testimony is that the phrasing of the question can influence the response that is given. In one study (Loftus & Palmer, 1974) subjects were shown a short movie in which two cars collided. Later, subjects were asked how fast the two cars were going when they smashed, collided, bumped, hit, or contacted. That is, the verb was manipulated to determine if the phrasing of the question influenced the speed estimates that subjects gave. It did. The average speed estimate was 40.8 miles per hour when smashed was used and 31.8 miles per hour when contacted was used. And, although no broken glass was shown in the movie, twice as many subjects reported seeing broken glass in the "smashed" condition than in the "hit" condition. In another experiment (Loftus, 1975) subjects were shown a movie and then asked questions about the movie. Some subjects were asked questions containing false presuppositions. For example, one of the questions was, "Did you see the children getting on the school bus?" Since there was no school bus in the film, the presupposition of the question was false. A week later all subjects were asked direct questions about the presuppositions. For example, all subjects were asked whether they had seen a school bus in the film. The interesting result is that the subjects in the false presupposition condition were much more likely to respond yes (incorrectly) than subjects in the control conditions. Thus, asking a question with a false presupposition immediately following an event appears to be a particularly effective way to alter a person's memory for an event.

There are a number of ways for a student to study how memory for an event can be altered. One might, for example, assess the effect of time delay between the occurrence of the event and testifying about the event. Is the effect of questions with false presuppositions greater if the questions are asked immediately after an event or several days later? What other approaches could be used to alter a person's memory for an event? Is the use of false presuppositions more effective for altering a child's memory or an adult's memory? Are there ways to improve eyewitness testimony?

References

Loftus, E. F. The incredible eyewitness. *Psychology Today,* December, 1974, 116–119.
Loftus, E. F. Leading questions and eyewitness report. *Cognitive Psychology,* 1975, 7, 560–572.
Loftus, E. F., & Palmer, J. C. Reconstruction of automobile destruction: An example of the interaction between language and memory. *Journal of Verbal Learning and Verbal Behavior,* 1974, 13, 585–589.

appendix: tables

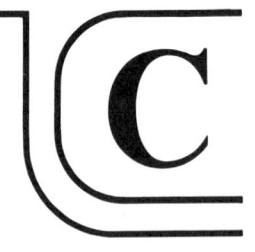

1. NUMBER TABLES FOR RANDOM ASSIGNMENT

	1	2	3	4	5	6	7	8	9	10	11	12	13	14	15	16	17	18	19	20
1	3	2	8	2	4	6	4	5	5	1	7	6	4	6	1	5	2	8	1	8
2	1	5	7	4	5	4	1	1	7	3	4	2	8	7	3	2	3	6	7	6
3	4	8	2	8	8	8	8	2	1	4	6	8	7	5	3	6	4	3	4	4
4	2	6	1	5	7	1	5	3	3	7	8	5	2	2	5	4	5	1	6	7
5	8	4	6	7	1	3	6	1	2	6	5	8	1	3	7	1	7	2	3	3
6	6	3	4	1	3	5	7	8	8	5	1	4	5	4	8	3	8	7	2	5
7	7	1	3	3	6	7	3	4	6	8	2	7	3	4	4	7	4	4	8	1
8	5	7	5	6	2	2	2	6	4	2	3	3	6	8	4	8	6	5	5	2

	21	22	23	24	25	26	27	28	29	30	31	32	33	34	35	36	37	38	39	40
21	1	6	3	2	5	1	3	5	5	7	8	2	1	6	1	7	7	1	6	4
22	3	8	1	1	6	3	6	3	7	1	7	8	3	8	4	6	1	5	3	2
23	7	4	4	6	8	6	5	8	2	8	3	7	4	7	5	2	5	8	1	6
24	6	2	7	3	3	5	4	2	6	3	2	6	5	5	7	5	6	4	4	8
25	2	3	6	2	4	4	8	6	3	2	5	1	8	3	6	3	3	2	5	3
26	4	7	8	7	2	7	1	7	1	4	7	8	7	2	3	8	4	6	7	7
27	5	1	5	5	1	8	1	1	8	5	6	4	2	1	2	1	2	7	8	5
28	8	5	2	8	7	6	2	4	4	6	4	5	6	4	8	4	8	3	2	1

	41	42	43	44	45	46	47	48	49	50	51	52	53	54	55	56	57	58	59	60
41	2	3	3	2	5	1	8	3	2	6	4	7	5	5	2	2	7	8	7	7
42	7	6	4	1	3	4	6	7	3	1	6	3	6	7	5	3	1	7	6	5
43	1	8	8	4	4	6	3	4	8	3	3	8	2	4	4	4	5	6	3	6
44	5	2	1	8	7	8	4	6	1	2	2	7	8	2	1	7	8	4	1	3
45	6	5	2	7	2	3	5	2	5	8	7	5	4	8	6	8	2	2	8	1
46	3	4	6	6	6	7	7	1	6	4	1	2	1	6	3	1	4	1	4	2
47	8	7	7	5	1	2	2	8	7	5	5	4	7	1	7	6	6	3	5	8
48	4	1	5	3	8	5	1	5	4	7	8	6	3	3	8	5	3	5	2	4

	61	62	63	64	65	66	67	68	69	70	71	72	73	74	75	76	77	78	79	80
61	4	4	2	8	5	7	5	7	2	1	8	4	7	1	8	3	3	5	5	2
62	5	8	1	5	2	2	6	6	5	7	2	7	5	7	5	8	5	6	2	4
63	8	7	4	1	1	6	8	3	6	3	5	5	2	4	6	7	8	3	3	8
64	6	3	3	2	7	5	7	2	7	5	7	1	3	8	7	2	2	4	6	7

328

1. Number Tables for Random Assignment

Row								
81	5	8	2	6	7	1	4	3
82	8	5	3	2	4	1	6	7
83	1	3	2	8	7	4	5	6
84	2	1	5	6	4	7	8	3
85	2	5	6	3	1	8	7	4
86	6	2	8	1	3	7	4	5
87	3	8	5	2	4	7	6	1
88	8	5	6	7	2	1	4	3
89	7	6	2	5	3	8	4	1
90	1	4	3	8	5	6	2	7
91	2	4	6	5	1	3	8	7
92	7	8	6	2	1	4	3	5
93	2	7	6	8	3	1	5	4
94	2	3	6	1	7	4	5	8
95	3	2	7	6	4	1	8	5
96	2	6	1	5	8	4	7	3
97	1	8	2	6	4	7	5	3
98	2	5	8	3	6	4	1	7
99	5	7	8	2	1	4	3	6
100	4	2	1	3	5	6	7	8

Row								
101	7	3	8	1	6	2	4	5
102	5	1	3	2	7	8	6	4
103	1	2	6	5	7	4	8	3
104	6	4	5	1	2	3	7	8
105	8	3	4	7	2	5	1	6
106	3	1	7	4	6	8	2	5
107	1	2	3	7	8	6	4	5
108	3	6	4	5	8	1	7	2
109	4	8	6	5	1	3	2	7
110	2	1	8	4	7	3	5	6
111	3	8	4	1	7	6	2	5
112	6	5	8	1	4	7	3	2
113	8	6	2	7	5	3	1	4
114	3	8	2	4	7	6	1	5
115	6	4	8	2	7	5	3	1
116	7	8	4	6	2	3	1	5
117	3	6	4	1	8	7	2	5
118	2	8	6	7	1	3	5	4
119	1	3	2	5	4	6	8	7
120	2	4	3	8	7	1	6	5

Row								
121	6	8	3	2	7	5	4	1
122	2	3	1	7	6	4	8	5
123	5	1	2	6	8	4	7	3
124	2	8	3	4	1	5	7	6
125	7	6	4	3	5	8	2	1
126	8	1	6	4	2	3	7	5
127	7	5	6	2	4	8	1	3
128	5	2	8	4	7	6	1	3
129	2	7	5	4	3	8	6	1
130	4	8	7	6	2	5	1	3
131	1	7	8	6	4	5	3	2
132	4	7	3	8	2	5	6	1
133	6	7	5	8	3	4	1	2
134	3	2	7	4	6	5	8	1
135	2	6	3	8	5	7	4	1
136	7	4	8	3	1	2	5	6
137	7	1	3	8	6	5	2	4
138	7	2	3	4	1	6	8	5
139	5	3	2	7	6	4	1	8
140	5	6	7	8	4	1	3	2

1. Number Tables for Random Assignment

141	142	143	144	145	146	147	148	149	150	151	152	153	154	155	156	157	158	159	160
2	6	7	2	4	5	2	7	2	6	3	8	1	3	6	1	4	6	7	2
4	4	6	4	8	7	7	1	7	8	4	3	2	5	2	7	7	5	4	6
7	5	1	7	5	6	5	8	3	3	5	7	6	1	1	2	1	7	1	7
5	3	4	5	2	1	6	4	5	2	1	2	8	8	7	5	3	8	3	3
3	7	2	6	3	2	3	2	8	5	7	5	4	7	4	8	6	3	8	1
8	8	5	1	6	3	8	3	4	4	6	6	5	2	3	3	8	2	6	5
1	2	3	8	7	8	4	6	6	1	8	1	7	6	8	4	5	1	2	4
6	1	8	3	1	4	1	5	1	7	2	4	7	4	5	6	2	4	5	8

161	162	163	164	165	166	167	168	169	170	171	172	173	174	175	176	177	178	179	180
7	8	8	4	3	4	6	4	1	5	3	7	6	8	6	2	6	3	7	3
3	7	2	7	1	5	2	3	2	4	1	2	4	5	5	1	4	1	6	7
4	4	6	8	8	6	1	1	4	7	5	1	2	7	3	6	2	2	8	4
6	2	3	3	5	8	4	6	7	6	8	6	3	4	2	7	5	4	5	2
1	3	1	1	6	3	8	7	5	8	4	4	7	2	7	5	1	5	4	6
8	6	4	6	2	2	5	5	8	3	7	8	1	1	4	4	7	7	1	8
5	5	5	2	7	1	7	8	6	2	6	5	5	3	8	8	3	6	2	1
2	1	7	5	4	7	—	2	3	1	2	3	8	6	1	3	8	8	3	5

181	182	183	184	185	186	187	188	189	190	191	192	193	194	195	196	197	198	199	200
1	8	2	5	7	4	5	2	4	7	6	8	8	5	7	1	4	6	5	7
5	3	6	6	6	5	8	8	1	8	5	5	5	3	6	2	5	1	1	5
6	7	7	3	3	6	4	4	7	2	7	1	6	7	1	4	7	4	8	8
2	6	4	4	5	1	6	6	3	6	8	7	3	4	5	3	3	3	6	4
4	2	1	7	1	8	3	3	2	5	1	4	4	8	2	8	2	5	4	3
7	4	3	2	2	2	7	7	5	3	4	3	2	2	8	6	8	8	7	2
3	5	8	1	4	7	2	1	6	4	2	6	7	1	4	5	6	2	6	1
8	1	5	8	8	3	1	5	8	1	3	2	1	6	3	7	1	7	3	6

201	202	203	204	205	206	207	208	209	210	211	212	213	214	215	216	217	218	219	220
5	4	8	2	6	7	1	8	4	2	3	2	5	2	7	6	6	5	4	8
1	1	2	3	3	4	8	2	8	3	1	3	4	1	6	5	1	4	2	2
2	7	5	4	1	5	7	3	7	1	5	1	7	7	1	1	7	8	8	6
4	3	7	8	8	3	2	1	6	5	7	6	2	6	8	4	4	7	5	4

7	5	4	7	5	2	6	7	3	4	8	5	3	8	2	2	5	1	1	7
3	8	1	5	4	6	4	4	2	8	2	7	6	5	4	8	3	2	7	3
6	6	6	6	2	1	5	5	1	7	4	8	1	4	3	7	2	6	3	5
8	2	3	1	7	8	3	6	5	6	6	4	8	3	5	3	8	3	6	1
221	*222*	*223*	*224*	*225*	*226*	*227*	*228*	*229*	*230*	*231*	*232*	*233*	*234*	*235*	*236*	*237*	*238*	*239*	*240*
7	4	4	3	5	3	6	4	7	6	8	6	5	1	2	6	3	4	6	5
5	2	8	8	1	4	4	3	1	7	4	5	8	4	8	3	2	2	3	4
2	7	7	1	4	2	1	5	6	8	7	2	6	5	6	2	5	7	1	7
6	8	2	6	6	8	7	2	2	2	5	7	1	7	3	1	8	6	7	8
3	1	5	4	7	6	3	7	8	1	3	4	3	8	4	7	1	5	4	3
4	3	1	7	3	7	8	1	4	4	2	1	7	6	5	5	7	1	5	2
8	5	3	2	8	1	5	8	3	5	1	8	2	3	7	4	6	8	2	1
1	6	6	8	2	5	2	6	5	3	6	3	4	2	1	8	4	3	8	6
241	*242*	*243*	*244*	*245*	*246*	*247*	*248*	*249*	*250*	*251*	*252*	*253*	*254*	*255*	*256*	*257*	*258*	*259*	*260*
8	3	7	4	1	1	8	5	1	1	4	5	6	7	5	3	2	7	4	7
4	6	8	1	8	6	1	4	4	4	1	3	3	8	7	7	4	8	1	5
3	8	3	3	2	3	5	2	5	7	5	6	5	6	6	1	5	5	8	2
6	1	4	2	7	2	3	6	6	2	7	7	8	3	1	5	3	2	2	6
5	5	2	8	6	5	4	7	3	6	6	4	2	2	8	8	7	6	7	3
1	4	5	5	5	7	7	8	8	8	3	1	1	1	3	2	8	3	3	1
2	2	6	6	4	8	2	1	7	5	8	2	4	4	2	4	6	4	5	4
7	7	1	7	3	4	6	3	2	3	2	8	7	5	4	6	1	1	6	8
261	*262*	*263*	*264*	*265*	*266*	*267*	*268*	*269*	*270*	*271*	*272*	*273*	*274*	*275*	*276*	*277*	*278*	*279*	*280*
7	1	5	4	2	2	3	4	5	2	2	6	2	7	2	8	1	4	3	3
8	6	7	1	6	7	7	8	1	5	3	2	8	3	7	7	8	2	6	2
4	8	3	6	5	6	5	2	4	7	6	8	3	4	8	3	7	1	7	7
3	2	8	5	4	8	1	3	7	6	7	3	4	6	5	6	6	7	4	8
6	3	1	8	6	4	6	1	8	8	8	5	1	1	1	4	4	5	8	1
2	4	6	7	7	3	2	6	3	3	1	7	6	2	4	2	2	3	2	4
1	5	4	2	1	5	8	5	6	4	4	4	7	8	3	1	5	8	1	6
5	7	2	3	3	1	4	7	2	1	5	1	5	5	6	5	3	6	5	5

2. TABLE OF CHI SQUARES

Degrees of Freedom df	Two-tail levels			
	p = .10	.05	.02	.01
1	2.706	3.841	5.412	6.635
2	4.605	5.991	7.824	9.210
3	6.251	7.815	9.837	11.341
4	7.779	9.488	11.668	13.277
5	9.236	11.070	13.388	15.086
6	10.645	12.592	15.033	16.812
7	12.017	14.067	16.622	18.475
8	13.362	15.507	18.168	20.090
9	14.684	16.919	19.679	21.666
10	15.987	18.307	21.161	23.209
11	17.275	19.675	22.618	24.725
12	18.549	21.026	24.054	26.217
13	19.812	22.362	25.472	27.688
14	21.064	23.685	26.873	29.141
15	22.307	24.996	28.259	30.578
16	23.542	26.296	29.633	32.000
17	24.769	27.587	30.995	33.409
18	25.989	28.869	32.346	34.805
19	27.204	30.144	33.687	36.191
20	28.412	31.410	35.020	37.566
21	29.615	32.671	36.343	38.932
22	30.813	33.924	37.659	40.289
23	32.007	35.172	38.968	41.638
24	33.196	36.415	40.270	42.980
25	34.382	37.652	41.566	44.314
26	35.563	38.885	42.856	45.642
27	36.741	40.113	44.140	46.963
28	37.916	41.337	45.419	48.278
29	39.087	42.557	46.693	49.588
30	40.256	43.773	47.962	50.892

This table is taken from Tables III and VI of Fischer: *Statistical Methods for Research Workers*, and Fischer and Yates: *Statistical Tables for Biological, Agricultural and Medical Research*, published by Oliver and Boyd, Edinburgh. Reprinted by permission of the authors and publishers.

3. CRITICAL VALUES OF T IN THE WILCOXON-MANN-WHITNEY SUM OF RANKS TEST

a. Two-tailed test, $p = .10$; one-tailed test, $p = .05$

N_1 (Smaller sample)

N_2	1	2	3	4	5	6	7	8	9	10	11	12	13	14	15	16	17	18	19	20
3			6																	
4			6	11																
5		3	7	12	19															
6		3	8	13	20	28														
7		3	8	14	21	29	39													
8		4	9	15	23	31	41	51												
9		4	9	16	24	33	43	54	66											
10		4	10	17	26	35	45	56	69	82										
11		4	11	18	27	37	47	59	72	86	100									
12		5	11	19	28	38	49	62	75	89	104	120								
13		5	12	20	30	40	52	64	78	92	108	125	142							
14		5	13	21	31	42	54	67	81	96	112	129	147	166						
15		6	13	22	33	44	56	69	84	99	116	133	152	171	192					
16		6	14	24	34	46	58	72	87	103	120	138	156	176	197	219				
17		6	15	25	35	47	61	75	90	106	123	142	161	182	203	225	249			
18		7	15	26	37	49	63	77	93	110	127	146	166	187	208	231	255	280		
19	1	7	16	27	38	51	65	80	96	113	131	150	171	192	214	237	262	287	313	
20	1	7	17	28	40	53	67	83	99	117	135	155	175	197	220	243	268	294	320	348

This table is taken from Table L in Tate, M. W., and Clelland, R. C.: *Nonparametric and Shortcut Statistics* (1957). Reprinted by permission of The Interstate Printers & Publishers, Inc., Danville, Illinois.

b. Two-tailed test, $p = .05$; one-tailed test, $p = .025$

N_1 *(Smaller sample)*

N_2	1	2	3	4	5	6	7	8	9	10	11	12	13	14	15	16	17	18	19	20
3																				
4				10																
5			6	11	17															
6			7	12	18	26														
7			7	13	20	27	36													
8		3	8	14	21	29	38	49												
9		3	8	14	22	31	40	51	62											
10		3	9	15	23	32	42	53	65											
11		3	9	16	24	34	44	55	68	81	96									
12		4	10	17	26	35	46	58	71	84	99	115								
13		4	10	18	27	37	48	60	73	88	103	119	136							
14		4	11	19	28	38	50	62	76	91	106	123	141	160						
15		4	11	20	29	40	52	65	79	94	110	127	145	164	184					
16		4	12	21	30	42	54	67	82	97	113	131	150	169	190	211				
17		5	12	21	32	43	56	70	84	100	117	135	154	174	195	217	240			
18		5	13	22	33	45	58	72	87	103	121	139	158	179	200	222	246	270		
19		5	13	23	34	46	60	74	90	107	124	143	163	182	205	228	252	277	303	
20		5	14	24	35	48	62	77	93	110	128	147	167	188	210	234	258	283	309	337

3. Critical Values of T

c. Two-tailed test, $p = .01$; one-tailed test, $p = .005$

N_1 (Smaller sample)

N_2	1	2	3	4	5	6	7	8	9	10	11	12	13	14	15	16	17	18	19	20
3																				
4																				
5					15															
6				10	16	23														
7				10	16	24	32													
8			6	11	17	25	34	43												
9			6	11	18	26	35	45	56											
10			6	12	19	27	37	47	58	71										
11			6	12	20	28	38	49	61	73	87									
12			7	13	21	30	40	51	63	76	90	105								
13			7	14	22	31	41	53	65	79	93	109	125							
14			7	14	22	32	43	54	67	81	96	112	129	147						
15			8	15	23	33	44	56	69	84	99	115	133	151	171					
16			8	15	24	34	46	58	72	86	102	119	136	155	175	196				
17			8	16	25	36	47	60	74	89	105	122	140	159	180	201	223			
18			8	16	26	37	49	62	76	92	108	125	144	163	184	206	228	252		
19		3	9	17	27	38	50	64	78	94	111	129	147	168	189	210	234	258	283	
20		3	9	18	28	39	52	66	81	97	114	132	151	172	193	215	239	263	289	315

4. F DISTRIBUTION

df for denom.	p	1	2	3	4	5	6	7	8	9	10
1	.05	161	200	216	225	230	234	237	239	241	242
2	.05	18.5	19.0	19.2	19.2	19.3	19.3	19.4	19.4	19.4	19.4
	.01	98.5	99.0	99.2	99.2	99.3	99.3	99.4	99.4	99.4	99.4
3	.05	10.1	9.55	9.28	9.12	9.10	8.94	8.89	8.85	8.81	8.79
	.01	34.1	30.8	29.5	28.7	28.2	27.9	27.7	27.5	27.3	27.2
4	.05	7.71	6.94	6.59	6.39	6.26	6.16	6.09	6.04	6.00	5.96
	.01	21.2	18.0	16.7	16.0	15.5	15.2	15.0	14.8	14.7	14.5
5	.05	6.61	5.79	5.41	5.19	5.05	4.95	4.88	4.82	4.77	4.74
	.01	16.3	13.3	12.1	11.4	11.0	10.7	10.5	10.3	10.2	10.1
6	.05	5.99	5.14	4.76	4.53	4.39	4.28	4.21	4.15	4.10	4.06
	.01	13.7	10.9	9.78	9.15	8.75	8.47	8.26	8.10	7.98	7.87
7	.05	5.59	4.74	4.35	4.12	3.97	3.87	3.79	3.73	3.68	3.64
	.01	12.2	9.55	8.45	7.85	7.46	7.19	6.99	6.84	6.72	6.62
8	.05	5.32	4.46	4.07	3.84	3.69	3.58	3.50	3.44	3.39	3.35
	.01	11.3	8.65	7.59	7.01	6.63	6.37	6.18	6.03	5.91	5.81
9	.05	5.12	4.26	3.86	3.63	3.48	3.37	3.29	3.23	3.18	3.14
	.01	10.6	8.02	6.99	6.42	6.06	5.80	5.61	5.47	5.35	5.26
10	.05	4.96	4.10	3.71	3.48	3.33	3.22	3.14	3.07	3.02	2.98
	.01	10.0	7.56	6.55	5.99	5.64	5.39	5.20	5.06	4.94	4.85
11	.05	4.84	3.98	3.59	3.36	3.20	3.09	3.01	2.95	2.90	2.85
	.01	9.65	7.21	6.22	5.67	5.32	5.07	4.89	4.74	4.63	4.54

df for numerator

4. F Distribution

12	.05 .01	4.75 9.33	3.89 6.93	3.49 5.95	3.26 5.41	3.11 5.06	3.00 4.82	2.91 4.64	2.85 4.50	2.80 4.39	2.75 4.30
13	.05 .01	4.67 9.07	3.81 6.70	3.41 5.74	3.18 5.21	3.03 4.86	2.92 4.62	2.83 4.44	2.77 4.30	2.71 4.19	2.67 4.10
14	.05 .01	4.60 8.86	3.74 6.51	3.34 5.56	3.11 5.04	2.96 4.69	2.85 4.46	2.76 4.28	2.70 4.14	2.65 4.03	2.60 3.94
15	.05 .01	4.54 8.68	3.68 6.36	3.29 5.42	3.06 4.89	2.90 4.56	2.79 4.32	2.71 4.14	2.64 4.00	2.59 3.89	2.54 3.80
16	.05 .01	4.49 8.53	3.63 6.23	3.24 5.29	3.01 4.77	2.85 4.44	2.74 4.20	2.66 4.03	2.59 3.89	2.54 3.78	2.49 3.69
17	.05 .01	4.45 8.40	3.59 6.11	3.20 5.18	2.96 4.67	2.81 4.34	2.70 4.10	2.61 3.93	2.55 3.79	2.49 3.68	2.45 3.59
18	.05 .01	4.41 8.29	3.55 6.01	3.16 5.09	2.93 4.58	2.77 4.25	2.66 4.01	2.58 3.84	2.51 3.71	2.46 3.60	2.41 3.51
19	.05 .01	4.38 8.18	3.52 5.93	3.13 5.01	2.90 4.50	2.74 4.17	2.63 3.94	2.54 3.77	2.48 3.63	2.42 3.52	2.38 3.43
20	.05 .01	4.35 8.10	3.49 5.85	3.10 4.94	2.87 4.43	2.71 4.10	2.60 3.87	2.51 3.70	2.45 3.56	2.39 3.46	2.35 3.37
22	.05 .01	4.30 7.95	3.44 5.72	3.05 4.82	2.82 4.31	2.66 3.99	2.55 3.76	2.46 3.59	2.40 3.45	2.34 3.35	2.30 3.26
24	.05 .01	4.26 7.82	3.40 5.61	3.01 4.72	2.78 4.22	2.62 3.90	2.51 3.67	2.42 3.50	2.36 3.36	2.30 3.26	2.25 3.17

4. F Distribution

| df for denom. | p | \multicolumn{10}{c}{df for numerator} |
		1	2	3	4	5	6	7	8	9	10
26	.05	4.23	3.37	2.98	2.74	2.59	2.47	2.39	2.32	2.27	2.22
	.01	7.72	5.53	4.64	4.14	3.82	3.59	3.42	3.29	3.18	3.09
28	.05	4.20	3.34	2.95	2.71	2.56	2.45	2.36	2.29	2.24	2.19
	.01	7.64	5.45	4.57	4.07	3.75	3.53	3.36	3.23	3.12	3.03
30	.05	4.17	3.32	2.92	2.69	2.53	2.42	2.33	2.27	2.21	2.16
	.01	7.56	5.39	4.51	4.02	3.70	3.47	3.30	3.17	3.07	2.98
40	.05	4.08	3.23	2.84	2.61	2.45	2.34	2.25	2.18	2.12	2.08
	.01	7.31	5.18	4.31	3.83	3.51	3.29	3.12	2.99	2.89	2.80
60	.05	4.00	3.15	2.76	2.53	2.37	2.25	2.17	2.10	2.04	1.99
	.01	7.08	4.98	4.13	3.65	3.34	3.12	2.95	2.82	2.72	2.63
120	.05	3.92	3.07	2.68	2.45	2.29	2.17	2.09	2.02	1.96	1.91
	.01	6.85	4.79	3.95	3.48	3.17	2.96	2.79	2.66	2.56	2.47
200	.05	3.89	3.04	2.65	2.42	2.26	2.14	2.06	1.98	1.93	1.88
	.01	6.76	4.71	3.88	3.41	3.11	2.89	2.73	2.60	2.50	2.41
∞	.05	3.84	3.00	2.60	2.37	2.21	2.10	2.01	1.94	1.88	1.83
	.01	6.63	4.61	3.78	3.32	3.02	2.80	2.64	2.51	2.41	2.32

This table is taken from Table 18 in Pearson, E. S. and Hartley, H. O.: *Biometrika Tables for Statisticians*, vol. 1, 2nd. Ed. (New York: Cambridge University Press, 1958). Reprinted by permission of Dr. E. S. Pearson.

5. VALUES OF *t* FOR GIVEN PROBABILITY LEVELS

df	\multicolumn{4}{c}{*Level of significance for a directional (one-tailed) test*}
	.05	.025	.01	.005
	\multicolumn{4}{c}{*Level of significance for a nondirectional (two-tailed) test*}
	.10	.05	.02	.01
1	6.314	12.706	31.821	63.657
2	2.920	4.303	6.965	9.925
3	2.353	3.182	4.541	5.841
4	2.132	2.776	3.747	4.604
5	2.015	2.571	3.365	4.032
6	1.943	2.447	3.143	3.707
7	1.895	2.365	2.998	3.499
8	1.860	2.306	2.896	3.355
9	1.833	2.262	2.821	3.250
10	1.812	2.228	2.764	3.169
11	1.796	2.201	2.718	3.106
12	1.782	2.179	2.681	3.055
13	1.771	2.160	2.650	3.012
14	1.761	2.145	2.624	2.977
15	1.753	2.131	2.602	2.947
16	1.746	2.120	2.583	2.921
17	1.740	2.110	2.567	2.898
18	1.734	2.101	2.552	2.878
19	1.729	2.093	2.539	2.861
20	1.725	2.086	2.528	2.845
21	1.721	2.080	2.518	2.831
22	1.717	2.074	2.508	2.819
23	1.714	2.069	2.500	2.807
24	1.711	2.064	2.492	2.797
25	1.708	2.060	2.485	2.787
26	1.706	2.056	2.479	2.779
27	1.703	2.052	2.473	2.771
28	1.701	2.048	2.467	2.763
29	1.699	2.045	2.462	2.756
30	1.697	2.042	2.457	2.750
40	1.684	2.021	2.423	2.704
60	1.671	2.000	2.390	2.660
120	1.658	1.980	2.358	2.617
∞	1.645	1.960	2.326	2.576

This table is abridged from Table III of Fisher and Yates, *Statistical Tables for Biological, Agricultural and Medical Research*, published by Longman Group Ltd., London by permission of the authors and publishers.

6. CRITICAL VALUES OF W FOR THE WILCOXON TEST[a]

N	\.05	.025	.01	.005	N	.05	.025	.01	.005
	.10	.05	.02	.01		.10	.05	.02	.01
5	0	—	—	—	28	130	116	101	91
6	2	0	—	—	29	140	126	110	100
7	3	2	0	—	30	151	137	120	109
8	5	3	1	0	31	163	147	130	118
9	8	5	3	1	32	175	159	140	128
10	10	8	5	3	33	187	170	151	138
11	13	10	7	5	34	200	182	162	148
12	17	13	9	7	35	213	195	173	159
13	21	17	12	9	36	227	208	185	171
14	25	21	15	12	37	241	221	198	182
15	30	25	19	15	38	256	235	211	194
16	35	29	23	19	39	271	249	224	207
17	41	34	27	23	40	286	264	238	220
18	47	40	32	27	41	302	279	252	233
19	53	46	37	32	42	319	294	266	247
20	60	52	43	37	43	336	310	281	261
21	67	58	49	42	44	353	327	296	276
22	75	65	55	48	45	371	343	312	291
23	83	73	62	54	46	389	361	328	307
24	91	81	69	61	47	407	378	345	322
25	100	89	76	68	48	426	396	362	339
26	110	98	84	75	49	446	415	379	355
27	119	107	92	83	50	466	434	397	373

Columns under "Level of significance for a directional (one-tailed) test": .05, .025, .01, .005
Columns under "Level of significance for a nondirectional (two-tailed) test": .10, .05, .02, .01

This table is taken from F. Wilcoxon, S. Katte, and R. A. Wilcox, *Critical Values and Probability Levels for the Wilcoxon Rank Sum Test and the Wilcoxon Signed Rank Test,* New York, American Cyanamid Co., 1963, and F. Wilcoxon and R. A. Wilcox, *Some Rapid Approximate Statistical Procedures,* New York, Lederle Laboratories, 1964 as used in Runyon and Haber, *Fundamentals of Behavioral Statistics,* 3rd edition, 1976, Addison-Wesley, Reading, Mass.

[a] For a given N (the number of pairs of scores), if the observed value is *equal to* or *less than* the value in the table for the appropriate level of significance, then reject H_0. The symbol W denotes the smaller sum of ranks associated with differences that are all of the same sign.

7. DISTRIBUTION OF F_{max} STATISTICS[a]

n−1	k = Number of variances								
	2	3	4	5	6	7	8	9	10
4	9.60	15.5	20.6	25.2	29.5	33.6	37.5	41.4	44.6
5	7.15	10.8	13.7	16.3	18.7	20.8	22.9	24.7	26.5
6	5.82	8.38	10.4	12.1	13.7	15.0	16.3	17.5	18.6
7	4.99	6.94	8.44	9.70	10.8	11.8	12.7	13.5	14.3
8	4.43	6.00	7.18	8.12	9.03	9.78	10.5	11.1	11.7
9	4.03	5.34	6.31	7.11	7.80	8.41	8.95	9.45	9.91
10	3.72	4.85	5.67	6.34	6.92	7.42	7.87	8.28	8.66
12	3.28	4.16	4.79	5.30	5.72	6.09	6.42	6.72	7.00
15	2.86	3.54	4.01	4.37	4.68	4.95	5.19	5.40	5.59
20	2.46	2.95	3.29	3.54	3.76	3.94	4.10	4.24	4.37
30	2.07	2.40	2.61	2.78	2.91	3.02	3.12	3.21	3.29
60	1.67	1.85	1.96	2.04	2.11	2.17	2.22	2.26	2.30
∞	1.00	1.00	1.00	1.00	1.00	1.00	1.00	1.00	1.00

This table is taken from Table 31 in Pearson, E. S. and Hartley, H. O.: *Biometrika Tables for Statistics*, vol. 1, 2nd. Ed. (New York: Cambridge University Press, 1958). Reprinted by permission of Dr. E. S. Pearson.

[a] $p = .05$.

8. CRITICAL VALUES OF r_s (RANK-ORDER CORRELATION COEFFICIENT)

Number of pairs	Level of significance		
	.10	.05	.01
5	.900	1.000	—
6	.829	.886	1.000
7	.714	.786	.929
8	.643	.738	.881
9	.600	.683	.833
10	.564	.648	.794
12	.506	.591	.777
14	.456	.544	.715
16	.425	.506	.665
18	.399	.475	.625
20	.377	.450	.591
22	.359	.428	.562
24	.343	.409	.537
26	.329	.392	.515
28	.317	.377	.496
30	.306	.364	.478

This table is taken from Olds, E. G.: "The 5 percent significance levels of sums of squares of rank differences and a correction," *Annals of Mathematical Statistics*, 20 (1949): 117-118, and from Olds, E. G.: "Distribution of sums of squares of rank differences for small numbers of individuals," *Annals of Mathematical Statistics*, 9 (1938): 113-148. Reprinted by permission of the Institute of Mathematical Statistics.

9. CRITICAL VALUES OF r (PEARSON PRODUCT-MOMENT CORRELATION)

Number of pairs minus two	Level of significance		
	.10	.05	.01
1	.98769	.99692	.999877
2	.90000	.95000	.990000
3	.8054	.8783	.95873
4	.7293	.8114	.91720
5	.6694	.7545	.8745
6	.6215	.7067	.8343
7	.5822	.6664	.7977
8	.5494	.6319	.7646
9	.5214	.6021	.7348
10	.4973	.5760	.7079
11	.4762	.5529	.6835
12	.4575	.5324	.6614
13	.4409	.5139	.6411
14	.4259	.4973	.6226
15	.4124	.4821	.6055
16	.4000	.4683	.5897
17	.3887	.4555	.5751
18	.3783	.4438	.5614
19	.3687	.4329	.5487
20	.3598	.4227	.5368
25	.3233	.3809	.4869
30	.2960	.3494	.4487
35	.2746	.3246	.4182
40	.2573	.3044	.3932
45	.2428	.2875	.3721
50	.2306	.2732	.3541
60	.2108	.2500	.3248
70	.1954	.2319	.3017
80	.1829	.2172	.2830
90	.1726	.2050	.2673
100	.1638	.1946	.2540

This table is taken from Tables III and VI of Fischer; *Statistical Methods for Research Workers*, and from Fischer and Yates: *Statistical Tables for Biological, Agricultural and Medical Research*, published by Oliver and Boyd. Reprinted by permission of the authors and publishers.

10. TABLE OF SQUARES AND SQUARE ROOTS

n	n^2	$\sqrt{n}$	$\sqrt{10n}$	n	n^2	$\sqrt{n}$	$\sqrt{10n}$
1.00	1.0000	1.00000	3.16228	1.50	2.2500	1.22474	3.87298
1.01	1.0201	1.00499	3.17805	1.51	2.2801	1.22882	3.88587
1.02	1.0404	1.00995	3.19374	1.52	2.3104	1.23288	3.89872
1.03	1.0609	1.01489	3.20936	1.53	2.3409	1.23693	3.91152
1.04	1.0816	1.01980	3.22490	1.54	2.3716	1.24097	3.92428
1.05	1.1025	1.02470	3.24037	1.55	2.4025	1.24499	3.93700
1.06	1.1236	1.02956	3.25576	1.56	2.4336	1.24900	3.94968
1.07	1.1449	1.03441	3.27109	1.57	2.4649	1.25300	3.96232
1.08	1.1664	1.03923	3.28634	1.58	2.4964	1.25698	3.97492
1.09	1.1881	1.04403	3.30151	1.59	2.5281	1.26095	3.98748
1.10	1.2100	1.04881	3.31662	1.60	2.5600	1.26491	4.00000
1.11	1.2321	1.05357	3.33167	1.61	2.5921	1.26886	4.01248
1.12	1.2544	1.05830	3.34664	1.62	2.6244	1.27279	4.02492
1.13	1.2769	1.06301	3.36155	1.63	2.6569	1.27671	4.03733
1.14	1.2996	1.06771	3.37639	1.64	2.6896	1.28062	4.04969
1.15	1.3225	1.07238	3.39116	1.65	2.7225	1.28452	4.06202
1.16	1.3456	1.07703	3.40588	1.66	2.7556	1.28841	4.07431
1.17	1.3689	1.08167	3.42053	1.67	2.7889	1.29228	4.08656
1.18	1.3924	1.08628	3.43511	1.68	2.8224	1.29615	4.09878
1.19	1.4161	1.09087	3.44964	1.69	2.8561	1.30000	4.11096
1.20	1.4400	1.09545	3.46410	1.70	2.8900	1.30384	4.12311
1.21	1.4641	1.10000	3.47851	1.71	2.9241	1.30767	4.13521
1.22	1.4884	1.10454	3.49285	1.72	2.9584	1.31149	4.14729
1.23	1.5129	1.10905	3.50714	1.73	2.9929	1.31529	4.15933
1.24	1.5376	1.11355	3.52136	1.74	3.0276	1.31909	4.17133
1.25	1.5625	1.11803	3.53553	1.75	3.0625	1.32288	4.18330
1.26	1.5876	1.12250	3.54965	1.76	3.0976	1.32665	4.19524
1.27	1.6129	1.12694	3.56371	1.77	3.1329	1.33041	4.20714
1.28	1.6384	1.13137	3.57771	1.78	3.1684	1.33417	4.21900
1.29	1.6641	1.13578	3.59166	1.79	3.2041	1.33791	4.23084
1.30	1.6900	1.14018	3.60555	1.80	3.2400	1.34164	4.24264
1.31	1.7161	1.14455	3.61939	1.81	3.2761	1.34536	4.25441
1.32	1.7424	1.14891	3.63318	1.82	3.3124	1.34907	4.26615
1.33	1.7689	1.15326	3.64692	1.83	3.3489	1.35277	4.27785
1.34	1.7956	1.15758	3.66060	1.84	3.3856	1.35647	4.28952
1.35	1.8225	1.16190	3.67423	1.85	3.4225	1.36015	4.30116
1.36	1.8496	1.16619	3.68782	1.86	3.4596	1.36382	4.31277
1.37	1.8769	1.17047	3.70135	1.87	3.4969	1.36748	4.32435
1.38	1.9044	1.17473	3.71484	1.88	3.5344	1.37113	4.33590
1.39	1.9321	1.17898	3.72827	1.89	3.5721	1.37477	4.34741
1.40	1.9600	1.18322	3.74166	1.90	3.6100	1.37840	4.35890
1.41	1.9881	1.18743	3.75500	1.91	3.6481	1.38203	4.37035
1.42	2.0164	1.19164	3.76829	1.92	3.6864	1.38564	4.38178
1.43	2.0449	1.19583	3.78153	1.93	3.7249	1.38924	4.39318
1.44	2.0736	1.20000	3.79473	1.94	3.7636	1.39284	4.40454
1.45	2.1025	1.20416	3.80789	1.95	3.8025	1.39642	4.41588
1.46	2.1316	1.20830	3.82099	1.96	3.8416	1.40000	4.42719
1.47	2.1609	1.21244	3.83406	1.97	3.8809	1.40357	4.43847
1.48	2.1904	1.21655	3.84708	1.98	3.9204	1.40712	4.44972
1.49	2.2201	1.22066	3.86005	1.99	3.9601	1.41067	4.46094

Reprinted by permission of the publisher from *Computational Handbook of Statistics* by James L. Bruning and L. B. Kintz. Copyright © 1968 by Scott, Foresman and Company.

10. Table of Squares and Square Roots

n	n^2	$\sqrt{n}$	$\sqrt{10n}$	n	n^2	$\sqrt{n}$	$\sqrt{10n}$
2.00	4.0000	1.41421	4.47214	2.50	6.2500	1.58114	5.00000
2.01	4.0401	1.41774	4.48330	2.51	6.3001	1.58430	5.00999
2.02	4.0804	1.42127	4.49444	2.52	6.3504	1.58745	5.01996
2.03	4.1209	1.42478	4.50555	2.53	6.4009	1.59060	5.02991
2.04	4.1616	1.42829	4.51664	2.54	6.4516	1.59374	5.03984
2.05	4.2025	1.43178	4.52769	2.55	6.5025	1.59687	5.04975
2.06	4.2436	1.43527	4.53872	2.56	6.5536	1.60000	5.05964
2.07	4.2849	1.43875	4.54973	2.57	6.6049	1.60312	5.06952
2.08	4.3264	1.44222	4.56070	2.58	6.6564	1.60624	5.07937
2.09	4.3681	1.44568	4.57165	2.59	6.7081	1.60935	5.08920
2.10	4.4100	1.44914	4.58258	2.60	6.7600	1.61245	5.09902
2.11	4.4521	1.45258	4.59347	2.61	6.8121	1.61555	5.10882
2.12	4.4944	1.45602	4.60435	2.62	6.8644	1.61864	5.11859
2.13	4.5369	1.45945	4.61519	2.63	6.9169	1.62173	5.12835
2.14	4.5796	1.46287	4.62601	2.64	6.9696	1.62481	5.13809
2.15	4.6225	1.46629	4.63681	2.65	7.0225	1.62788	5.14782
2.16	4.6656	1.46969	4.64758	2.66	7.0756	1.63095	5.15752
2.17	4.7089	1.47309	4.65833	2.67	7.1289	1.63401	5.16720
2.18	4.7524	1.47648	4.66905	2.68	7.1824	1.63707	5.17687
2.19	4.7961	1.47986	4.67974	2.69	7.2361	1.64012	5.18652
2.20	4.8400	1.48324	4.69042	2.70	7.2900	1.64317	5.19615
2.21	4.8841	1.48661	4.70106	2.71	7.3441	1.64621	5.20577
2.22	4.9284	1.48997	4.71169	2.72	7.3984	1.64924	5.21536
2.23	4.9729	1.49332	4.72229	2.73	7.4529	1.65227	5.22494
2.24	5.0176	1.49666	4.73286	2.74	7.5076	1.65529	5.23450
2.25	5.0625	1.50000	4.74342	2.75	7.5625	1.65831	5.24404
2.26	5.1076	1.50333	4.75395	2.76	7.6176	1.66132	5.25357
2.27	5.1529	1.50665	4.76445	2.77	7.6729	1.66433	5.26308
2.28	5.1984	1.50997	4.77493	2.78	7.7284	1.66733	5.27257
2.29	5.2441	1.51327	4.78539	2.79	7.7841	1.67033	5.28205
2.30	5.2900	1.51658	4.79583	2.80	7.8400	1.67332	5.29150
2.31	5.3361	1.51987	4.80625	2.81	7.8961	1.67631	5.30094
2.32	5.3824	1.52315	4.81664	2.82	7.9524	1.67929	5.31037
2.33	5.4289	1.52643	4.82701	2.83	8.0089	1.68226	5.31977
2.34	5.4756	1.52971	4.83735	2.84	8.0656	1.68523	5.32917
2.35	5.5225	1.53297	4.84768	2.85	8.1225	1.68819	5.33854
2.36	5.5696	1.53623	4.85798	2.86	8.1796	1.69115	5.34790
2.37	5.6169	1.53948	4.86826	2.87	8.2369	1.69411	5.35724
2.38	5.6644	1.54272	4.87852	2.88	8.2944	1.69706	5.36656
2.39	5.7121	1.54596	4.88876	2.89	8.3521	1.70000	5.37587
2.40	5.7600	1.54919	4.89898	2.90	8.4100	1.70294	5.38516
2.41	5.8081	1.55242	4.90918	2.91	8.4681	1.70587	5.39444
2.42	5.8564	1.55563	4.91935	2.92	8.5264	1.70880	5.40370
2.43	5.9049	1.55885	4.92950	2.93	8.5849	1.71172	5.41295
2.44	5.9536	1.56205	4.93964	2.94	8.6436	1.71464	5.42218
2.45	6.0025	1.56525	4.94975	2.95	8.7025	1.71756	5.43139
2.46	6.0516	1.56844	4.95984	2.96	8.7616	1.72047	5.44059
2.47	6.1009	1.57162	4.96991	2.97	8.8209	1.72337	5.44977
2.48	6.1504	1.57480	4.97996	2.98	8.8804	1.72627	5.45894
2.49	6.2001	1.57797	4.98999	2.99	8.9401	1.72916	5.46809

10. Table of Squares and Square Roots

n	n^2	$\sqrt{n}$	$\sqrt{10n}$	n	n^2	$\sqrt{n}$	$\sqrt{10n}$
3.00	9.0000	1.73205	5.47723	3.50	12.2500	1.87083	5.91608
3.01	9.0601	1.73494	5.48635	3.51	12.3201	1.87350	5.92453
3.02	9.1204	1.73781	5.49545	3.52	12.3904	1.87617	5.93296
3.03	9.1809	1.74069	5.50454	3.53	12.4609	1.87883	5.94138
3.04	9.2416	1.74356	5.51362	3.54	12.5316	1.88149	5.94979
3.05	9.3025	1.74642	5.52268	3.55	12.6025	1.88414	5.95819
3.06	9.3636	1.74929	5.53173	3.56	12.6736	1.88680	5.96657
3.07	9.4249	1.75214	5.54076	3.57	12.7449	1.88944	5.97495
3.08	9.4864	1.75499	5.54977	3.58	12.8164	1.89209	5.98331
3.09	9.5481	1.75784	5.55878	3.59	12.8881	1.89473	5.99166
3.10	9.6100	1.76068	5.56776	3.60	12.9600	1.89737	6.00000
3.11	9.6721	1.76352	5.57674	3.61	13.0321	1.90000	6.00833
3.12	9.7344	1.76635	5.58570	3.62	13.1044	1.90263	6.01664
3.13	9.7969	1.76918	5.59464	3.63	13.1769	1.90526	6.02495
3.14	9.8596	1.77200	5.60357	3.64	13.2496	1.90788	6.03324
3.15	9.9225	1.77482	5.61249	3.65	13.3225	1.91050	6.04152
3.16	9.9856	1.77764	5.62139	3.66	13.3956	1.91311	6.04979
3.17	10.0489	1.78045	5.63028	3.67	13.4689	1.91572	6.05805
3.18	10.1124	1.78326	5.63915	3.68	13.5424	1.91833	6.06630
3.19	10.1761	1.78606	5.64801	3.69	13.6161	1.92094	6.07454
3.20	10.2400	1.78885	5.65685	3.70	13.6900	1.92354	6.08276
3.21	10.3041	1.79165	5.66569	3.71	13.7641	1.92614	6.09098
3.22	10.3684	1.79444	5.67450	3.72	13.8384	1.92873	6.09918
3.23	10.4329	1.79722	5.68331	3.73	13.9129	1.93132	6.10737
3.24	10.4976	1.80000	5.69210	3.74	13.9876	1.93391	6.11555
3.25	10.5625	1.80278	5.70088	3.75	14.0625	1.93649	6.12372
3.26	10.6276	1.80555	5.70964	3.76	14.1376	1.93907	6.13188
3.27	10.6929	1.80831	5.71839	3.77	14.2129	1.94165	6.14003
3.28	10.7584	1.81108	5.72713	3.78	14.2884	1.94422	6.14817
3.29	10.8241	1.81384	5.73585	3.79	14.3641	1.94679	6.15630
3.30	10.8900	1.81659	5.74456	3.80	14.4400	1.94936	6.16441
3.31	10.9561	1.81934	5.75326	3.81	14.5161	1.95192	6.17252
3.32	11.0224	1.82209	5.76194	3.82	14.5924	1.95448	6.18061
3.33	11.0889	1.82483	5.77062	3.83	14.6689	1.95704	6.18870
3.34	11.1556	1.82757	5.77927	3.84	14.7456	1.95959	6.19677
3.35	11.2225	1.83030	5.78792	3.85	14.8225	1.96214	6.20484
3.36	11.2896	1.83303	5.79655	3.86	14.8996	1.96469	6.21289
3.37	11.3569	1.83576	5.80517	3.87	14.9769	1.96723	6.22093
3.38	11.4244	1.83848	5.81378	3.88	15.0544	1.96977	6.22896
3.39	11.4921	1.84120	5.82237	3.89	15.1321	1.97231	6.23699
3.40	11.5600	1.84391	5.83095	3.90	15.2100	1.97484	6.24500
3.41	11.6281	1.84662	5.83952	3.91	15.2881	1.97737	6.25300
3.42	11.6964	1.84932	5.84808	3.92	15.3664	1.97990	6.26099
3.43	11.7649	1.85203	5.85662	3.93	15.4449	1.98242	6.26897
3.44	11.8336	1.85472	5.86515	3.94	15.5236	1.98494	6.27694
3.45	11.9025	1.85742	5.87367	3.95	15.6025	1.98746	6.28490
3.46	11.9716	1.86011	5.88218	3.96	15.6816	1.98997	6.29285
3.47	12.0409	1.86279	5.89067	3.97	15.7609	1.99249	6.30079
3.48	12.1104	1.86548	5.89915	3.98	15.8408	1.99499	6.30872
3.49	12.1801	1.86815	5.90762	3.99	15.9201	1.99750	6.31664

n	n^2	$\sqrt{n}$	$\sqrt{10n}$	n	n^2	$\sqrt{n}$	$\sqrt{10n}$
4.00	16.0000	2.00000	6.32456	4.50	20.2500	2.12132	6.70820
4.01	16.0801	2.00250	6.33246	4.51	20.3401	2.12368	6.71565
4.02	16.1604	2.00499	6.34035	4.52	20.4304	2.12603	6.72309
4.03	16.2409	2.00749	6.34823	4.53	20.5209	2.12838	6.73053
4.04	16.3216	2.00998	6.35610	4.54	20.6116	2.13073	6.73795
4.05	16.4025	2.01246	6.36396	4.55	20.7025	2.13307	6.74537
4.06	16.4836	2.01494	6.37181	4.56	20.7936	2.13542	6.75278
4.07	16.5649	2.01742	6.37966	4.57	20.8849	2.13776	6.76018
4.08	16.6464	2.01990	6.38749	4.58	20.9764	2.14009	6.76757
4.09	16.7281	2.02237	6.39531	4.59	21.0681	2.14243	6.77495
4.10	16.8100	2.02485	6.40312	4.60	21.1600	2.14476	6.78233
4.11	16.8921	2.02731	6.41093	4.61	21.2521	2.14709	6.78970
4.12	16.9744	2.02978	6.41872	4.62	21.3444	2.14942	6.79706
4.13	17.0569	2.03224	6.42651	4.63	21.4369	2.15174	6.80441
4.14	17.1396	2.03470	6.43428	4.64	21.5296	2.15407	6.81175
4.15	17.2225	2.03715	6.44205	4.65	21.6225	2.15639	6.81909
4.16	17.3056	2.03961	6.44981	4.66	21.7156	2.15870	6.82642
4.17	17.3889	2.04206	6.45755	4.67	21.8089	2.16102	6.83374
4.18	17.4724	2.04450	6.46529	4.68	21.9024	2.16333	6.84105
4.19	17.5561	2.04695	6.47302	4.69	21.9961	2.16564	6.84836
4.20	17.6400	2.04939	6.48074	4.70	22.0900	2.16795	6.85565
4.21	17.7241	2.05183	6.48845	4.71	22.1841	2.17025	6.86294
4.22	17.8084	2.05426	6.49615	4.72	22.2784	2.17256	6.87023
4.23	17.8929	2.05670	6.50384	4.73	22.3729	2.17486	6.87750
4.24	17.9776	2.05913	6.51153	4.74	22.4676	2.17715	6.88477
4.25	18.0625	2.06155	6.51920	4.75	22.5625	2.17945	6.89202
4.26	18.1476	2.06398	6.52687	4.76	22.6576	2.18174	6.89928
4.27	18.2329	2.06640	6.53452	4.77	22.7529	2.18403	6.90652
4.28	18.3184	2.06882	6.54217	4.78	22.8484	2.18632	6.91375
4.29	18.4041	2.07123	6.54981	4.79	22.9441	2.18861	6.92098
4.30	18.4900	2.07364	6.55744	4.80	23.0400	2.19089	6.92820
4.31	18.5761	2.07605	6.56506	4.81	23.1361	2.19317	6.93542
4.32	18.6624	2.07846	6.57267	4.82	23.2324	2.19545	6.94262
4.33	18.7489	2.08087	6.58027	4.83	23.3289	2.19773	6.94982
4.34	18.8356	2.08327	6.58787	4.84	23.4256	2.20000	6.95701
4.35	18.9225	2.08567	6.59545	4.85	23.5225	2.20227	6.96419
4.36	19.0096	2.08806	6.60303	4.86	23.6196	2.20454	6.97137
4.37	19.0969	2.09045	6.61060	4.87	23.7169	2.20681	6.97854
4.38	19.1844	2.09284	6.61816	4.88	23.8144	2.20907	6.98570
4.39	19.2721	2.09523	6.62571	4.89	23.9121	2.21133	6.99285
4.40	19.3600	2.09762	6.63325	4.90	24.0100	2.21359	7.00000
4.41	19.4481	2.10000	6.64078	4.91	24.1081	2.21585	7.00714
4.42	19.5364	2.10238	6.64831	4.92	24.2064	2.21811	7.01427
4.43	19.6249	2.10476	6.65582	4.93	24.3049	2.22036	7.02140
4.44	19.7136	2.10713	6.66333	4.94	24.4036	2.22261	7.02851
4.45	19.8025	2.10950	6.67083	4.95	24.5025	2.22486	7.03562
4.46	19.8916	2.11187	6.67832	4.96	24.6016	2.22711	7.04273
4.47	19.9809	2.11424	6.68581	4.97	24.7009	2.22935	7.04982
4.48	20.0704	2.11660	6.69328	4.98	24.8004	2.23159	7.05691
4.49	20.1601	2.11896	6.70075	4.99	24.9001	2.23383	7.06399

10. Table of Squares and Square Roots

n	n^2	$\sqrt{n}$	$\sqrt{10n}$	n	n^2	$\sqrt{n}$	$\sqrt{10n}$
5.00	25.0000	2.23607	7.07107	5.50	30.2500	2.34521	7.41620
5.01	25.1001	2.23830	7.07814	5.51	30.3601	2.34734	7.42294
5.02	25.2004	2.24054	7.08520	5.52	30.4704	2.34947	7.42967
5.03	25.3009	2.24277	7.09225	5.53	30.5809	2.35160	7.43640
5.04	25.4016	2.24499	7.09930	5.54	30.6916	2.35372	7.44312
5.05	25.5025	2.24722	7.10634	5.55	30.8025	2.35584	7.44983
5.06	25.6036	2.24944	7.11337	5.56	30.9136	2.35797	7.45654
5.07	25.7049	2.25167	7.12039	5.57	31.0249	2.36008	7.46324
5.08	25.8064	2.25389	7.12741	5.58	31.1364	2.36220	7.46994
5.09	25.9081	2.25610	7.13442	5.59	31.2481	2.36432	7.47663
5.10	26.0100	2.25832	7.14143	5.60	31.3600	2.36643	7.48331
5.11	26.1121	2.26053	7.14843	5.61	31.4721	2.36854	7.48999
5.12	26.2144	2.26274	7.15542	5.62	31.5844	2.37065	7.49667
5.13	26.3169	2.26495	7.16240	5.63	31.6969	2.37276	7.50333
5.14	26.4196	2.26716	7.16938	5.64	31.8096	2.37487	7.50999
5.15	26.5225	2.26936	7.17635	5.65	31.9225	2.37697	7.51665
5.16	26.6256	2.27156	7.18331	5.66	32.0356	2.37908	7.52330
5.17	26.7289	2.27376	7.19027	5.67	32.1489	2.38118	7.52994
5.18	26.8324	2.27596	7.19722	5.68	32.2624	2.38328	7.53658
5.19	26.9361	2.27816	7.20417	5.69	32.3761	2.38537	7.54321
5.20	27.0400	2.28035	7.21110	5.70	32.4900	2.38747	7.54983
5.21	27.1441	2.28254	7.21803	5.71	32.6041	2.38956	7.55645
5.22	27.2484	2.28473	7.22496	5.72	32.7184	2.39165	7.56307
5.23	27.3529	2.28692	7.23187	5.73	32.8329	2.39374	7.56968
5.24	27.4576	2.28910	7.23878	5.74	32.9476	2.39583	7.57628
5.25	27.5625	2.29129	7.24569	5.75	33.0625	2.39792	7.58288
5.26	27.6676	2.29347	7.25259	5.76	33.1776	2.40000	7.58947
5.27	27.7729	2.29565	7.25948	5.77	33.2929	2.40208	7.59605
5.28	27.8784	2.29783	7.26636	5.78	33.4084	2.40416	7.60263
5.29	27.9841	2.30000	7.27324	5.79	33.5241	2.40624	7.60920
5.30	28.0900	2.30217	7.28011	5.80	33.6400	2.40832	7.61577
5.31	28.1961	2.30434	7.28697	5.81	33.7561	2.41039	7.62234
5.32	28.3024	2.30651	7.29383	5.82	33.8724	2.41247	7.62889
5.33	28.4089	2.30868	7.30068	5.83	33.9889	2.41454	7.63544
5.34	28.5156	2.31084	7.30753	5.84	34.1056	2.41661	7.64199
5.35	28.6225	2.31301	7.31437	5.85	34.2225	2.41868	7.64853
5.36	28.7296	2.31517	7.32120	5.86	34.3396	2.42074	7.65506
5.37	28.8369	2.31733	7.32803	5.87	34.4569	2.42281	7.66159
5.38	28.9444	2.31948	7.33485	5.88	34.5744	2.42487	7.66812
5.39	29.0521	2.32164	7.34166	5.89	34.6921	2.42693	7.67463
5.40	29.1600	2.32379	7.34847	5.90	34.8100	2.42899	7.68115
5.41	29.2681	2.32594	7.35527	5.91	34.9281	2.43105	7.68765
5.42	29.3764	2.32809	7.36206	5.92	35.0464	2.43311	7.69415
5.43	29.4849	2.33024	7.36885	5.93	35.1649	2.43516	7.70065
5.44	29.5936	2.33238	7.37564	5.94	35.2836	2.43721	7.70714
5.45	29.7025	2.33452	7.38241	5.95	35.4025	2.43926	7.71362
5.46	29.8116	2.33666	7.38918	5.96	35.5216	2.44131	7.72010
5.47	29.9209	2.33880	7.39594	5.97	35.6409	2.44336	7.72658
5.48	30.0304	2.34094	7.40270	5.98	35.7604	2.44540	7.73305
5.49	30.1401	2.34307	7.40945	5.99	35.8801	2.44745	7.73951

10. Table of Squares and Square Roots

n	n^2	$\sqrt{n}$	$\sqrt{10n}$	n	n^2	$\sqrt{n}$	$\sqrt{10n}$
6.00	36.0000	2.44949	7.74597	6.50	42.2500	2.54951	8.06226
6.01	36.1201	2.45153	7.75242	6.51	42.3801	2.55147	8.06846
6.02	36.2404	2.45357	7.75887	6.52	42.5104	2.55343	8.07465
6.03	36.3609	2.45561	7.76531	6.53	42.6409	2.55539	8.08084
6.04	36.4816	2.45764	7.77174	6.54	42.7716	2.55734	8.08703
6.05	36.6025	2.45967	7.77817	6.55	42.9025	2.55930	8.09321
6.06	36.7236	2.46171	7.78460	6.56	43.0336	2.56125	8.09938
6.07	36.8449	2.46374	7.79102	6.57	43.1649	2.56320	8.10555
6.08	36.9664	2.46577	7.79744	6.58	43.2964	2.56515	8.11172
6.09	37.0881	2.46779	7.80385	6.59	43.4281	2.56710	8.11788
6.10	37.2100	2.46982	7.81025	6.60	43.5600	2.56905	8.12404
6.11	37.3321	2.47184	7.81665	6.61	43.6921	2.57099	8.13019
6.12	37.4544	2.47386	7.82304	6.62	43.8244	2.57294	8.13634
6.13	37.5769	2.47588	7.82943	6.63	43.9569	2.57488	8.14248
6.14	37.6996	2.47790	7.83582	6.64	44.0896	2.57682	8.14862
6.15	37.8225	2.47992	7.84219	6.65	44.2225	2.57876	8.15475
6.16	37.9456	2.48193	7.84857	6.66	44.3556	2.58070	8.16088
6.17	38.0689	2.48395	7.85493	6.67	44.4889	2.58263	8.16701
6.18	38.1924	2.48596	7.86130	6.68	44.6224	2.58457	8.17313
6.19	38.3161	2.48797	7.86766	6.69	44.7561	2.58650	8.17924
6.20	38.4400	2.48998	7.87401	6.70	44.8900	2.58844	8.18535
6.21	38.5641	2.49199	7.88036	6.71	45.0241	2.59037	8.19146
6.22	38.6884	2.49399	7.88670	6.72	45.1584	2.59230	8.19756
6.23	38.8129	2.49600	7.89303	6.73	45.2929	2.59422	8.20366
6.24	38.9376	2.49800	7.89937	6.74	45.4276	2.59615	8.20975
6.25	39.0625	2.50000	7.90569	6.75	45.5625	2.59808	8.21584
6.26	39.1876	2.50200	7.91202	6.76	45.6976	2.60000	8.22192
6.27	39.3129	2.50400	7.91833	6.77	45.8329	2.60192	8.22800
6.28	39.4384	2.50599	7.92465	6.78	45.9684	2.60384	8.23408
6.29	39.5641	2.50799	7.93095	6.79	46.1041	2.60576	8.24015
6.30	39.6900	2.50998	7.93725	6.80	46.2400	2.60768	8.24621
6.31	39.8161	2.51197	7.94355	6.81	46.3761	2.60960	8.25227
6.32	39.9424	2.51396	7.94984	6.82	46.5124	2.61151	8.25833
6.33	40.0689	2.51595	7.95613	6.83	46.6489	2.61343	8.26438
6.34	40.1956	2.51794	7.96241	6.84	46.7856	2.61534	8.27043
6.35	40.3225	2.51992	7.96869	6.85	46.9225	2.61725	8.27647
6.36	40.4496	2.52190	7.97496	6.86	47.0596	2.61916	8.28251
6.37	40.5769	2.52389	7.98123	6.87	47.1969	2.62107	8.28855
6.38	40.7044	2.52587	7.98749	6.88	47.3344	2.62298	8.29458
6.39	40.8321	2.52784	7.99375	6.89	47.4721	2.62488	8.30060
6.40	40.9600	2.52982	8.00000	6.90	47.6100	2.62679	8.30662
6.41	41.0881	2.53180	8.00625	6.91	47.7481	2.62869	8.31264
6.42	41.2164	2.53377	8.01249	6.92	47.8864	2.63059	8.31865
6.43	41.3449	2.53574	8.01873	6.93	48.0249	2.63249	8.32466
6.44	41.4736	2.53772	8.02496	6.94	48.1636	2.63439	8.33067
6.45	41.6025	2.53969	8.03119	6.95	48.3025	2.63629	8.33667
6.46	41.7316	2.54165	8.03741	6.96	48.4416	2.63818	8.34266
6.47	41.8609	2.54362	8.04363	6.97	48.5809	2.64008	8.34865
6.48	41.9904	2.54558	8.04984	6.98	48.7204	2.64197	8.35464
6.49	42.1201	2.54755	8.05605	6.99	48.8601	2.64386	8.36062

10. Table of Squares and Square Roots

n	n^2	$\sqrt{n}$	$\sqrt{10n}$	n	n^2	$\sqrt{n}$	$\sqrt{10n}$
7.00	49.0000	2.64575	8.36660	7.50	56.2500	2.73861	8.66025
7.01	49.1401	2.64764	8.37257	7.51	56.4001	2.74044	8.66603
7.02	49.2804	2.64953	8.37854	7.52	56.5504	2.74226	8.67179
7.03	49.4209	2.65141	8.38451	7.53	56.7009	2.74408	8.67756
7.04	49.5616	2.65330	8.39047	7.54	56.8516	2.74591	8.68332
7.05	49.7025	2.65518	8.39643	7.55	57.0025	2.74773	8.68907
7.06	49.8436	2.65707	8.40238	7.56	57.1536	2.74955	8.69483
7.07	49.9849	2.65895	8.40833	7.57	57.3049	2.75136	8.70057
7.08	50.1264	2.66083	8.41427	7.58	57.4564	2.75318	8.70632
7.09	50.2681	2.66271	8.42021	7.59	57.6081	2.75500	8.71206
7.10	50.4100	2.66458	8.42615	7.60	57.7600	2.75681	8.71780
7.11	50.5521	2.66646	8.43208	7.61	57.9121	2.75862	8.72353
7.12	50.6944	2.66833	8.43801	7.62	58.0644	2.76043	8.72926
7.13	50.8369	2.67021	8.44393	7.63	58.2169	2.76225	8.73499
7.14	50.9796	2.67208	8.44985	7.64	58.3696	2.76405	8.74071
7.15	51.1225	2.67395	8.45577	7.65	58.5225	2.76586	8.74643
7.16	51.2656	2.67582	8.46168	7.66	58.6756	2.76767	8.75214
7.17	51.4089	2.67769	8.46759	7.67	58.8289	2.76948	8.75785
7.18	51.5524	2.67955	8.47349	7.68	58.9824	2.77128	8.76356
7.19	51.6961	2.68142	8.47939	7.69	59.1361	2.77308	8.76926
7.20	51.8400	2.68328	8.48528	7.70	59.2900	2.77489	8.77496
7.21	51.9841	2.68514	8.49117	7.71	59.4441	2.77669	8.78066
7.22	52.1284	2.68701	8.49706	7.72	59.5984	2.77849	8.78635
7.23	52.2729	2.68887	8.50294	7.73	59.7529	2.78029	8.79204
7.24	52.4176	2.69072	8.50882	7.74	59.9076	2.78209	8.79773
7.25	52.5625	2.69258	8.51469	7.75	60.0625	2.78388	8.80341
7.26	52.7076	2.69444	8.52056	7.76	60.2176	2.78568	8.80909
7.27	52.8529	2.69629	8.52643	7.77	60.3729	2.78747	8.81476
7.28	52.9984	2.69815	8.53229	7.78	60.5284	2.78927	8.82043
7.29	53.1441	2.70000	8.53815	7.79	60.6841	2.79106	8.82610
7.30	53.2900	2.70185	8.54400	7.80	60.8400	2.79285	8.83176
7.31	53.4361	2.70370	8.54985	7.81	60.9961	2.79464	8.83742
7.32	53.5824	2.70555	8.55570	7.82	61.1524	2.79643	8.84308
7.33	53.7289	2.70740	8.56154	7.83	61.3089	2.79821	8.84873
7.34	53.8756	2.70924	8.56738	7.84	61.4656	2.80000	8.85438
7.35	54.0225	2.71109	8.57321	7.85	61.6225	2.80179	8.86002
7.36	54.1696	2.71293	8.57904	7.86	61.7796	2.80357	8.86566
7.37	54.3169	2.71477	8.58487	7.87	61.9369	2.80535	8.87130
7.38	54.4644	2.71662	8.59069	7.88	62.0944	2.80713	8.87694
7.39	54.6121	2.71846	8.59651	7.89	62.2521	2.80891	8.88257
7.40	54.7600	2.72029	8.60233	7.90	62.4100	2.81069	8.88819
7.41	54.9081	2.72213	8.60814	7.91	62.5681	2.81247	8.89382
7.42	55.0564	2.72397	8.61394	7.92	62.7264	2.81425	8.89944
7.43	55.2049	2.72580	8.61974	7.93	62.8849	2.81603	8.90505
7.44	55.3536	2.72764	8.62554	7.94	63.0436	2.81780	8.91067
7.45	55.5025	2.72947	8.63134	7.95	63.2025	2.81957	8.91628
7.46	55.6516	2.73130	8.63713	7.96	63.3616	2.82135	8.92188
7.47	55.8009	2.73313	8.64292	7.97	63.5209	2.82312	8.92749
7.48	55.9504	2.73496	8.64870	7.98	63.6804	2.82489	8.93308
7.49	56.1001	2.73679	8.65448	7.99	63.8401	2.82666	8.93868

10. Table of Squares and Square Roots

n	n^2	$\sqrt{n}$	$\sqrt{10n}$	n	n^2	$\sqrt{n}$	$\sqrt{10n}$
8.00	64.0000	2.82843	8.94427	8.50	72.2500	2.91548	9.21954
8.01	64.1601	2.83019	8.94986	8.51	72.4201	2.91719	9.22497
8.02	64.3204	2.83196	8.95545	8.52	72.5904	2.91890	9.23038
8.03	64.4809	2.83373	8.96103	8.53	72.7609	2.92062	9.23580
8.04	64.6416	2.83549	8.96660	8.54	72.9316	2.92233	9.24121
8.05	64.8025	2.83725	8.97218	8.55	73.1025	2.92404	9.24662
8.06	64.9636	2.83901	8.97775	8.56	73.2736	2.92575	9.25203
8.07	65.1249	2.84077	8.98332	8.57	73.4449	2.92746	9.25743
8.08	65.2864	2.84253	8.98888	8.58	73.6164	2.92916	9.26283
8.09	65.4481	2.84429	8.99444	8.59	73.7881	2.93087	9.26823
8.10	65.6100	2.84605	9.00000	8.60	73.9600	2.93258	9.27362
8.11	65.7721	2.84781	9.00555	8.61	74.1321	2.93428	9.27901
8.12	65.9344	2.84956	9.01110	8.62	74.3044	2.93598	9.28440
8.13	66.0969	2.85132	9.01665	8.63	74.4769	2.93769	9.28978
8.14	66.2596	2.85307	9.02219	8.64	74.6496	2.93939	9.29516
8.15	66.4225	2.85482	9.02774	8.65	74.8225	2.94109	9.30054
8.16	66.5856	2.85657	9.03327	8.66	74.9956	2.94279	9.30591
8.17	66.7489	2.85832	9.03881	8.67	75.1689	2.94449	9.31128
8.18	66.9124	2.86007	9.04434	8.68	75.3424	2.94618	9.31665
8.19	67.0761	2.86182	9.04986	8.69	75.5161	2.94788	9.32202
8.20	67.2400	2.86356	9.05539	8.70	75.6900	2.94958	9.32738
8.21	67.4041	2.86531	9.06091	8.71	75.8641	2.95127	9.33274
8.22	67.5684	2.86705	9.06642	8.72	76.0384	2.95296	9.33809
8.23	67.7329	2.86880	9.07193	8.73	76.2129	2.95466	9.34345
8.24	67.8976	2.87054	9.07744	8.74	76.3876	2.95635	9.34880
8.25	68.0625	2.87228	9.08295	8.75	76.5625	2.95804	9.35414
8.26	68.2276	2.87402	9.08845	8.76	76.7376	2.95973	9.35949
8.27	68.3929	2.87576	9.09395	8.77	76.9129	2.96142	9.36483
8.28	68.5584	2.87750	9.09945	8.78	77.0884	2.96311	9.37017
8.29	68.7241	2.87924	9.10494	8.79	77.2641	2.96479	9.37550
8.30	68.8900	2.88097	9.11043	8.80	77.4400	2.96648	9.38083
8.31	69.0561	2.88271	9.11592	8.81	77.6161	2.96816	9.38616
8.32	69.2224	2.88444	9.12140	8.82	77.7924	2.96985	9.39149
8.33	69.3889	2.88617	9.12688	8.83	77.9689	2.97153	9.39681
8.34	69.5556	2.88791	9.13236	8.84	78.1456	2.97321	9.40213
8.35	69.7225	2.88964	9.13783	8.85	78.3225	2.97489	9.40744
8.36	69.8896	2.89137	9.14330	8.86	78.4996	2.97658	9.41276
8.37	70.0569	2.89310	9.14877	8.87	78.6769	2.97825	9.41807
8.38	70.2244	2.89482	9.15423	8.88	78.8544	2.97993	9.42338
8.39	70.3921	2.89655	9.15969	8.89	79.0321	2.98161	9.42868
8.40	70.5600	2.89828	9.16515	8.90	79.2100	2.98329	9.43398
8.41	70.7281	2.90000	9.17061	8.91	79.3881	2.98496	9.43928
8.42	70.8964	2.90172	9.17606	8.92	79.5664	2.98664	9.44458
8.43	71.0649	2.90345	9.18150	8.93	79.7449	2.98831	9.44987
8.44	71.2336	2.90517	9.18695	8.94	79.9236	2.98998	9.45516
8.45	71.4025	2.90689	9.19239	8.95	80.1025	2.99166	9.46044
8.46	71.5716	2.90861	9.19783	8.96	80.2816	2.99333	9.46573
8.47	71.7409	2.91033	9.20326	8.97	80.4609	2.99500	9.47101
8.48	71.9104	2.91204	9.20869	8.98	80.6404	2.99666	9.47629
8.49	72.0801	2.91376	9.21412	8.99	80.8201	2.99833	9.48156

n	n^2	$\sqrt{n}$	$\sqrt{10n}$	n	n^2	$\sqrt{n}$	$\sqrt{10n}$
9.00	81.0000	3.00000	9.48683	9.50	90.2500	3.08221	9.74679
9.01	81.1801	3.00167	9.49210	9.51	90.4401	3.08383	9.75192
9.02	81.3604	3.00333	9.49737	9.52	90.6304	3.08545	9.75705
9.03	81.5409	3.00500	9.50263	9.53	90.8209	3.08707	9.76217
9.04	81.7216	3.00666	9.50789	9.54	91.0116	3.08869	9.76729
9.05	81.9025	3.00832	9.51315	9.55	91.2025	3.09031	9.77241
9.06	82.0836	3.00998	9.51840	9.56	91.3936	3.09192	9.77753
9.07	82.2649	3.01164	9.52365	9.57	91.5849	3.09354	9.78264
9.08	82.4464	3.01330	9.52890	9.58	91.7764	3.09516	9.78775
9.09	82.6281	3.01496	9.53415	9.59	91.9681	3.09677	9.79285
9.10	82.8100	3.01662	9.53939	9.60	92.1600	3.09839	9.79796
9.11	82.9921	3.01828	9.54463	9.61	92.3521	3.10000	9.80306
9.12	83.1744	3.01993	9.54987	9.62	92.5444	3.10161	9.80816
9.13	83.3569	3.02159	9.55510	9.63	92.7369	3.10322	9.81326
9.14	83.5396	3.02324	9.56033	9.64	92.9296	3.10483	9.81835
9.15	83.7225	3.02490	9.56556	9.65	93.1225	3.10644	9.82344
9.16	83.9056	3.02655	9.57079	9.66	93.3156	3.10805	9.82853
9.17	84.0889	3.02820	9.57601	9.67	93.5089	3.10966	9.83362
9.18	84.2724	3.02985	9.58123	9.68	93.7024	3.11127	9.83870
9.19	84.4561	3.03150	9.58645	9.69	93.8961	3.11288	9.84378
9.20	84.6400	3.03315	9.59166	9.70	94.0900	3.11448	9.84886
9.21	84.8241	3.03480	9.59687	9.71	94.2841	3.11609	9.85393
9.22	85.0084	3.03645	9.60208	9.72	94.4784	3.11769	9.85901
9.23	85.1929	3.03809	9.60729	9.73	94.6729	3.11929	9.86408
9.24	85.3776	3.03974	9.61249	9.74	94.8676	3.12090	9.86914
9.25	85.5625	3.04138	9.61769	9.75	95.0625	3.12250	9.87421
9.26	85.7476	3.04302	9.62289	9.76	95.2576	3.12410	9.87927
9.27	85.9329	3.04467	9.62808	9.77	95.4529	3.12570	9.88433
9.28	86.1184	3.04631	9.63328	9.78	95.6484	3.12730	9.88939
9.29	86.3041	3.04795	9.63846	9.79	95.8441	3.12890	9.89444
9.30	86.4900	3.04959	9.64365	9.80	96.0400	3.13050	9.89949
9.31	86.6761	3.05123	9.64883	9.81	96.2361	3.13209	9.90454
9.32	86.8624	3.05287	9.65401	9.82	96.4324	3.13369	9.90959
9.33	87.0489	3.05450	9.65919	9.83	96.6289	3.13528	9.91464
9.34	87.2356	3.05614	9.66437	9.84	96.8256	3.13688	9.91968
9.35	87.4225	3.05778	9.66954	9.85	97.0225	3.13847	9.92472
9.36	87.6096	3.05941	9.67471	9.86	97.2196	3.14006	9.92975
9.37	87.7969	3.06105	9.67988	9.87	97.4169	3.14166	9.93479
9.38	87.9844	3.06268	9.68504	9.88	97.6144	3.14325	9.93982
9.39	88.1721	3.06431	9.69020	9.89	97.8121	3.14484	9.94485
9.40	88.3600	3.06594	9.69536	9.90	98.0100	3.14643	9.94987
9.41	88.5481	3.06757	9.70052	9.91	98.2081	3.14802	9.95490
9.42	88.7364	3.06920	9.70567	9.92	98.4064	3.14960	9.95992
9.43	88.9249	3.07083	9.71082	9.93	98.6049	3.15119	9.96494
9.44	89.1136	3.07246	9.71597	9.94	98.8036	3.15278	9.96995
9.45	89.3025	3.07409	9.72111	9.95	99.0025	3.15436	9.97497
9.46	89.4916	3.07571	9.72625	9.96	99.2016	3.15595	9.97998
9.47	89.6809	3.07734	9.73139	9.97	99.4009	3.15753	9.98499
9.48	89.8704	3.07896	9.73653	9.98	99.6004	3.15911	9.98999
9.49	90.0601	3.08058	9.74166	9.99	99.8001	3.16070	9.99500
				10.00	100.000	3.16228	10.0000

11. RANDOM NUMBERS

22 17 68 65 84	68 95 23 92 35	87 02 22 57 51	61 09 43 95 06	58 24 82 03 47
19 36 27 59 46	13 79 93 37 55	39 77 32 77 09	85 52 05 30 62	47 83 51 62 74
16 77 23 02 77	09 61 87 25 21	28 06 24 25 93	16 71 13 59 78	23 05 47 47 25
78 43 76 71 61	20 44 90 32 64	97 67 63 99 61	46 38 03 93 22	69 81 21 99 21
03 28 28 26 08	73 37 32 04 05	69 30 16 09 05	88 69 58 28 99	35 07 44 75 47
93 22 53 64 39	07 10 63 76 35	87 03 04 79 88	08 13 13 85 51	55 34 57 72 69
78 76 58 54 74	92 38 70 96 92	52 06 79 79 45	82 63 18 27 44	69 66 92 19 09
23 68 35 26 00	99 53 93 61 28	52 70 05 48 34	56 65 05 61 86	90 92 10 70 80
15 39 25 70 99	93 86 52 77 65	15 33 59 05 28	22 87 26 07 47	86 96 98 29 06
58 71 96 30 24	18 46 23 34 27	85 13 99 24 44	49 18 09 79 49	74 16 32 23 02
57 35 27 33 72	24 53 63 94 09	41 10 76 47 91	44 04 95 49 66	39 60 04 59 81
48 50 86 54 48	22 06 34 72 52	82 21 15 65 20	33 29 94 71 11	15 91 29 12 03
61 96 48 95 03	07 16 39 33 66	98 56 10 56 79	77 21 30 27 12	90 49 22 23 62
36 93 89 41 26	29 70 83 63 51	99 74 20 52 36	87 09 41 15 09	98 60 16 03 03
18 87 00 42 31	57 90 12 02 07	23 47 37 17 31	54 08 01 88 63	39 41 88 92 10
88 56 53 27 59	33 35 72 67 47	77 34 55 45 70	08 18 27 38 90	16 95 86 70 75
09 72 95 84 29	49 41 31 06 70	42 38 06 45 18	64 84 73 31 65	52 53 37 97 15
12 96 88 17 31	65 19 69 02 83	60 75 86 90 68	24 64 19 35 51	56 61 87 39 12
85 94 57 24 16	92 09 84 38 76	22 00 27 69 85	29 81 94 78 70	21 94 47 90 12
38 64 43 59 98	98 77 87 68 07	91 51 67 62 44	40 98 05 93 78	23 32 65 41 18
53 44 09 42 72	00 41 86 79 79	68 47 22 00 20	35 55 31 51 51	00 83 63 22 55
40 76 66 26 84	57 99 99 90 37	36 63 32 08 58	37 40 13 68 97	87 64 81 07 83
02 17 79 18 05	12 59 52 57 02	22 07 90 47 03	28 14 11 30 79	20 69 22 40 98
95 17 82 06 53	31 51 10 96 46	92 06 88 07 77	56 11 50 81 69	40 23 72 51 39
35 76 22 42 92	96 11 83 44 80	34 68 35 48 77	33 42 40 90 60	73 96 53 97 86
26 29 13 56 41	85 47 04 66 08	34 72 57 59 13	82 43 80 46 15	38 26 61 70 64
77 80 20 75 82	72 82 32 99 90	63 95 73 76 63	89 73 44 99 05	48 67 26 43 18
46 40 66 44 52	91 36 74 43 53	30 82 13 54 00	78 45 63 98 35	55 03 36 67 68
37 56 08 18 09	77 53 84 46 47	31 91 18 95 58	24 16 74 11 53	44 10 13 85 57
61 65 61 68 66	37 27 47 39 19	84 83 70 07 48	53 21 40 06 71	95 06 79 88 54
93 43 69 64 07	34 18 04 52 35	56 27 09 24 86	61 85 53 83 45	19 90 70 99 68
21 96 60 12 99	11 20 99 45 18	48 13 93 55 34	18 37 79 49 90	65 97 38 20 46
95 20 47 97 97	27 37 83 28 71	00 06 41 41 74	45 89 09 39 84	51 67 11 52 49
97 86 21 78 73	10 65 81 92 59	58 76 17 14 97	04 76 62 16 17	17 95 70 45 80
69 92 06 34 13	59 71 74 17 32	27 55 10 24 19	23 71 82 13 74	63 52 52 01 41
04 31 17 21 56	33 73 99 19 87	26 72 39 27 67	53 77 57 68 93	60 61 97 22 61
61 06 98 03 91	87 14 77 43 96	43 00 65 98 50	45 60 33 01 07	98 99 46 50 47
85 93 85 86 88	72 87 08 62 40	16 06 10 89 20	23 21 34 74 97	76 38 03 29 63
21 74 32 47 45	73 96 07 94 52	09 65 90 77 47	25 76 16 19 33	53 05 70 53 30
15 69 53 82 80	79 96 23 53 10	65 39 07 16 29	45 33 02 43 70	02 87 40 41 45
02 89 08 04 49	20 21 14 68 86	87 63 93 95 17	11 29 01 95 80	35 14 97 35 33
87 18 15 89 79	85 43 01 72 73	08 61 74 51 69	89 74 39 82 15	94 51 33 41 67
98 83 71 94 22	59 97 50 99 52	08 52 85 08 40	87 80 61 65 31	91 51 80 32 44
10 08 58 21 66	72 68 49 29 31	89 85 84 46 06	59 73 19 85 23	65 09 29 75 63
47 90 56 10 08	88 02 84 27 83	42 29 72 23 19	66 56 45 65 79	20 71 53 20 25
22 85 61 68 90	49 64 92 85 44	16 40 12 89 88	50 14 49 81 06	01 82 77 45 12
67 80 43 79 33	12 83 11 41 16	25 58 19 68 70	77 02 54 00 52	53 43 37 15 26
27 62 50 96 72	79 44 61 40 15	14 53 40 65 39	27 31 58 50 28	11 39 03 34 25
33 78 80 87 15	38 30 06 38 21	14 47 47 07 26	54 96 87 53 32	40 36 40 96 76
13 13 92 66 99	47 24 49 57 74	32 25 43 62 17	10 97 11 69 84	99 63 22 32 98

This table is taken from Table XXXIII of Fisher and Yates, *Statistical Tables for Biological, Agricultural and Medical Research*, published by Longman Group Ltd., London (previously published by Oliver and Boyd, Ltd., Edinburgh), and by permission of the authors and publishers.

11. Random Numbers 353

10 27 53 96 23	71 50 54 36 23	54 31 04 82 98	04 14 12 15 09	26 78 25 47 47
28 41 50 61 88	64 85 27 20 18	83 36 36 05 56	39 71 65 09 62	94 76 62 11 89
34 21 42 57 02	59 19 18 97 48	80 30 03 30 98	05 24 67 70 07	84 97 50 87 46
61 81 77 23 23	82 82 11 54 08	53 28 70 58 96	44 07 39 55 43	42 34 43 39 28
61 15 18 13 54	16 86 20 26 88	90 74 80 55 09	14 53 90 51 17	52 01 63 01 59
91 76 21 64 64	44 91 13 32 97	75 31 62 66 54	84 80 32 75 77	56 08 25 70 29
00 97 79 08 06	37 30 28 59 85	53 56 68 53 40	01 74 39 59 73	30 19 99 85 48
36 46 18 34 94	75 20 80 27 77	78 91 69 16 00	08 43 18 73 68	67 69 61 34 25
88 98 99 60 50	65 95 79 42 94	93 62 40 89 96	43 56 47 71 66	46 76 29 67 02
04 37 59 87 21	05 02 03 24 17	47 97 81 56 51	92 34 86 01 82	55 51 33 12 91
63 62 06 34 41	94 21 78 55 09	72 76 45 16 94	29 95 81 83 83	79 88 01 97 30
78 47 23 53 90	34 41 92 45 71	09 23 70 70 07	12 38 92 79 43	14 85 11 47 23
87 68 62 15 43	53 14 36 59 25	54 47 33 70 15	59 24 48 40 35	50 03 42 99 36
47 60 92 10 77	88 59 53 11 52	66 25 69 07 04	48 68 64 71 06	61 65 70 22 12
56 88 87 59 41	65 28 04 67 53	95 79 88 37 31	50 41 06 94 76	81 83 17 16 33
02 57 45 86 67	73 43 07 34 48	44 26 87 93 29	77 09 61 67 84	06 69 44 77 75
31 54 14 13 17	48 62 11 90 60	68 12 93 64 28	46 24 79 16 76	14 60 25 51 01
28 50 16 43 36	28 97 85 58 99	67 22 52 76 23	24 70 36 54 54	59 28 61 71 96
63 29 62 66 50	02 63 45 52 38	67 63 47 54 75	83 24 78 43 20	92 63 13 47 48
45 65 58 26 51	76 96 59 38 72	86 57 45 71 46	44 67 76 14 55	44 88 01 62 12
39 65 36 63 70	77 45 85 50 51	74 13 39 35 22	30 53 36 02 95	49 34 88 73 61
73 71 98 16 04	29 18 94 51 23	76 51 94 84 86	79 93 96 38 63	08 58 25 58 94
72 20 56 20 11	72 65 71 08 86	79 57 95 13 91	97 48 72 66 48	09 71 17 24 89
75 17 26 99 76	89 37 20 70 01	77 31 61 95 46	26 97 05 73 51	33 95 78 72 87
37 48 60 82 29	81 30 15 39 14	48 38 75 93 29	06 87 37 78 48	45 56 00 84 47
68 08 02 80 72	83 71 46 30 49	89 17 95 88 29	02 39 56 03 46	97 74 06 56 17
14 23 98 61 67	70 52 85 01 50	01 84 02 78 43	10 62 98 19 41	18 83 99 47 99
49 08 96 21 44	25 27 99 41 28	07 41 08 34 66	19 42 74 39 91	41 96 53 78 72
78 37 06 08 43	63 61 62 42 29	39 68 95 10 96	09 24 23 00 62	56 12 80 73 16
37 21 34 17 68	68 96 83 23 56	32 84 60 15 31	44 73 67 34 77	91 15 79 74 58
14 29 09 34 04	87 83 07 55 07	76 58 30 83 64	87 29 25 58 84	86 50 60 00 25
58 43 28 06 36	49 52 83 51 14	47 56 91 29 34	05 87 31 06 95	12 45 57 09 09
10 43 67 29 70	80 62 80 03 42	10 80 21 38 84	90 56 35 03 09	43 12 74 49 14
44 38 88 39 54	86 97 37 44 22	00 95 01 31 76	17 16 29 56 63	38 78 94 49 81
90 69 59 19 51	85 39 52 85 13	07 28 37 07 61	11 16 36 27 03	78 86 72 04 95
41 47 10 25 62	97 05 31 03 61	20 26 36 31 62	68 69 86 95 44	84 95 48 46 45
91 94 14 63 19	75 89 11 47 11	31 56 34 19 09	79 57 92 36 59	14 93 87 81 40
80 06 54 18 66	09 18 94 06 19	98 40 07 17 81	22 45 44 84 11	24 62 20 42 31
67 72 77 63 48	84 08 31 55 58	24 33 45 77 58	80 45 67 93 82	75 70 16 08 24
59 40 24 13 27	79 26 88 86 30	01 31 60 10 39	53 58 47 70 93	85 81 56 39 38
05 90 35 89 95	01 61 16 96 94	50 78 13 69 36	37 68 53 37 31	71 26 35 03 71
44 43 80 69 98	46 68 05 14 82	90 78 50 05 62	77 79 13 57 44	59 60 10 39 66
61 81 31 96 82	00 57 25 60 59	46 72 60 18 77	55 66 12 62 11	08 99 55 64 57
42 88 07 10 05	24 98 65 63 21	47 21 61 88 32	27 80 30 21 60	10 92 35 36 12
77 94 30 05 39	28 10 99 00 27	12 73 73 99 12	49 99 57 94 82	96 88 57 17 91
78 83 19 76 16	94 11 68 84 26	23 54 20 86 85	23 86 66 99 07	36 37 34 92 09
87 76 59 61 81	43 63 64 61 61	65 76 36 95 90	18 48 27 45 68	27 23 65 30 72
91 43 05 96 47	55 78 99 95 24	37 55 85 78 78	01 48 41 19 10	35 19 54 07 73
84 97 77 72 73	09 62 06 65 72	87 12 49 03 60	41 15 20 76 27	50 47 02 29 16
87 41 60 76 83	44 88 96 07 80	83 05 83 38 96	73 70 66 81 90	30 56 10 48 59

appendix: answers for problems in chapters 8 through 12 D

CHAPTER 8

1. a. Nominal
   b. Ordinal
   c. Ordinal or interval
   d. Ratio
   e. Ratio
   f. Ordinal
2. Mode = 13, median = 12.5, mean = 12.0.
3. Mode = 14 and 16, median = 15, mean = 15.0.
4. Mode = 3, median = 4.5, mean = 8.0.
5. Mean is greater than median for 8-2A, mean is less than median for 8-2B, and mean is equal to median for 8-2C.
7. Range = 13, variance = 15.11, and standard deviation = 3.89 for problem 2. Range = 2, variance = 1.11, and standard deviation = 1.05 for problem 3. Range = 17, variance = 45.11, and standard deviation = 6.72 for problem 4.
9. The first test.
10. The means are 11.8, 13.0, and 14.6 for the mnemonic group and 6.8, 9.4, and 12.6 for the control group.

CHAPTER 9

1. Phi = .47 or −.47.
2. Rank-order correlation = .806, product-moment correlation = .821.
3. Product-moment correlation = 1.00, no.
4. Product-moment correlation = −.95, yes.

354

CHAPTER 10

1. The expected frequencies are 25, 75, 37.5, 112.5, 37.5, and 112.5.
2. The obtained chi square of 9.37 exceeds the table value so the null hypothesis can be rejected.
4. Chi square = 10.09; you can reject the null hypothesis.
5. Chi square for females = .88; you cannot reject the null hypothesis. Chi square for males = 28.51; you can reject the null hypothesis.
7. Chi square for median test = 2.68 so you cannot reject the null hypothesis.
8. Smaller sum = 108 so you can reject the null hypothesis.

CHAPTER 11

2. $F = .80$; you cannot reject the null hypothesis. The t value for the comparison of groups I and II is 1.07 (either plus or minus depending on which way you subtracted the means), so you cannot reject the null hypothesis.
3. $F = 11.24$; you can reject the null hypothesis. The t value is plus or minus 3.354; you can reject the null hypothesis.
4. $F = 3.94$; you cannot reject the null hypothesis. The t value is plus or minus 1.987; you cannot reject the null hypothesis.
5. $F = 56.63$, you can reject the null hypothesis.
6. $F = 2.84$, you cannot reject the null hypothesis for the Group I versus Group III comparison. $F = 68.49$; you can reject the null hypothesis for the Group I versus Group II comparison. $F = 98.85$; you can reject the null hypothesis for the Group II versus Group III comparison. The mean square for within groups was taken from the overall analysis.
7. $F = 1.13$ for the humanitarian versus lawyer comparison, you cannot reject the null hypothesis. $F = 0.41$ for the type of appeal effect, you cannot reject the null hypothesis. $F = 191.35$ for the interaction, you can reject the null hypothesis.
8. $F = 0.32$ for anxiety level; you cannot reject the null hypothesis. $F = 146.29$ for the type of task effect; you can reject the null hypothesis. $F = 31.65$ for the interaction, you can reject the null hypothesis.

CHAPTER 12

1. $Q = 5.33$; you can reject the null hypothesis.
2. $Q = 3.57$; you cannot reject the null hypothesis.
3. The W (Wilcoxon) value = 7.5. Since you need a value of 5 or less for the .05 significance level with a nondirectional (two-tailed) test, you cannot reject the null hypothesis. For the analysis at the interval level, $F = 4.94$ for conditions; you cannot reject the null hypothesis.
4. $F = 41.50$ for treatments; you can reject the null hypothesis. The t value for the A versus B comparison is equal to 2.55, so you can reject the null hypothesis.
5. $F = 27.08$; you can reject the null hypothesis.

REFERENCES

Barber, T. X., & Silver, M. J. Fact, fiction, and the experimenter bias effect. *Psychological Bulletin Monograph,* 1968, 70 (6, Pt. 2), 1–29.

Beach, F. A. The snark was a boojum. *American Psychologist,* 1950, 5, 115–124.

Bennett, C. F. Marital agreement as a function of status-related agreement. *Social Forces,* 1971, 50, 249–255.

Cameron, P. Children's reactions to second-hand tobacco smoke. *Journal of Applied Psychology,* 1972, 56, 171–173.

Campbell, D. T. Factors relevant to the validity of experiments in social settings. *Psychological Bulletin,* 1957, 54, 297–312.

Campbell, D. T. Blind variation and selective retention in creative thought and in other knowledge processes. *Psychological Review,* 1960, 67, 380–400.

Campbell, D. T., & Stanley, J. C. *Experimental and Quasi-Experimental Designs for Research.* Chicago: Rand McNally, 1963.

Cavior, N., & Boblett, P. J. The physical attractiveness of dating vs. married couples. *Proceedings of the Annual Convention of The American Psychological Association,* 1972, 7 (Pt. 1), 175–176.

Chance, P. Ads without answers make the brain itch. *Psychology Today,* November, 1975, 9, 78.

Cochran, W. G. The comparison of percentages in matched samples. *Biometrika,* 1950, 37, 256–266.

Cohen, M., Liebson, I. A., & Faillace, L. A. A technique for establishing controlled drinking in chronic alcoholics. *Diseases of the Nervous System,* 1972, 33, 46–49.

Crano, W. D., & Brewer, M. B. *Principles of Research in Social Psychology.* New York: McGraw-Hill, 1973.

Crano, W. D., Kenny, D. A., & Campbell, D. T. Does intelligence cause achievement? A cross-lagged panel analysis. *Journal of Educational Psychology,* 1972, 63, 258–275.

Cronbach, L. J. *Essentials of Psychological Testing* (3rd ed.). New York: Harper & Row, 1970.

Cronbach, L. J. Beyond the two disciplines of scientific psychology. *American Psychologist,* 1975, 30, 116–127.

Dabbs, J. M. Sex, setting, and reactions to crowding on sidewalks. *Proceedings of the Annual Convention of The American Psychological Association,* 1972, 7 (Pt. 1), 205–206.

Hanley, C., Personal Communication, 1969.

Hussar, D. A. Drug interactions 1. *American Journal of Pharmacy,* 1973, 145, 65–116.

Johnson, D. A., Porter, R. J., & Marteljan, P. Racial discrimination in apartment rentals. *Journal of Applied Social Psychology,* 1971, 1, 364–377.

Koch, M. D., & Arnold, W. J. Effects of early social deprivation on emotionality in rats. *Journal of Comparative and Physiological Psychology,* 1972, 78, 391–399.

Kruskal, W. H., & Wallis, W. A. Use of ranks in one criterion variance analysis. *Journal of American Statistical Association,* 1952, 47, 583–621.

Labovitz, S., & Hagedorn, R. *Introduction to Social Research.* New York: McGraw-Hill, 1971.

Lockard, R. B. The albino rat: A defensible choice or a bad habit? *American Psychologist,* 1968, 23, 734–742.

Marshall, A. J., & Disney, H. J. de S. Experimental induction of the breeding season in a xerophilous bird. *Nature,* 1957, 180, 647–649.

Mednick, S. A., & Mednick, M. T. *Examiner's Manual: Remote Associates Test.* Boston: Houghton Mifflin, 1967.

Neisser, U. *Cognitive Psychology.* New York: Appleton-Century-Crofts, 1967.

Norris, D. Crying and laughing in imbeciles. *Developmental Medicine and Child Neurology,* 1971, 13, 756–761.

Orne, M. T. The nature of hypnosis: Artifact and essence. *Journal of Abnormal and Social Psychology,* 1959, 58, 277–299.

Orne, M. T. On the social psychology of the psychological experiment: With particular reference to demand characteristics and their implications. *American Psychologist,* 1962, 17, 776–783.

Rosenthal, R. On the social psychology of the psychological experiment: The experimenter's hypothesis as unintended determinant of experimental results. *American Scientist,* 1963, 51, 268–283.

Rosenthal, R. *Experimenter Effects in Behavioral Research.* New York: Appleton-Century-Crofts, 1966.

Schusterman, R. J., & Gentry, R. L. Development of a fatted male phenomenon in California sea lions. *Developmental Psychobiology,* 1971, 4, 333–338.

Siegel, S. *Nonparametric Statistics for the Behavioral Sciences.* New York: McGraw-Hill, 1956.

Stevens, S. S. Mathematics, measurement, and psychophysics. In S. S. Stevens (Ed.), *Handbook of Experimental Psychology.* New York: Wiley, 1951.

Underwood, B. J. Individual differences as a crucible in theory construction. *American Psychologist,* 1975, 30, 128–134.

Webb, E. J., Campbell, D. T., Schwartz, R. D., & Sechrest, L. *Unobtrusive Measures: Nonreactive Research in the Social Sciences.* Chicago: Rand McNally, 1966.

Wolf, M. M., & Risley, T. M. Reinforcement: Applied research. In R. Glaser (Ed.), *The Nature of Reinforcement.* New York: Academic Press, 1971.

GLOSSARY

Abscissa: the X or horizontal axis in a graph.

Alpha: in hypothesis testing, the probability of rejecting the null hypothesis when the null hypothesis is true; the probability of a Type 1 error. The alpha level is equal to the significance level.

Analysis of variance: a statistical test appropriate for analyzing interval data obtained with between-subject and within-subject experimental designs.

Assumption: a basic tenet of a theory that is taken for granted from which other tenets are derived; condition that must be met before certain conclusions are warranted (e.g., the assumptions of a statistical test).

Bar graph: a frequency distribution in which the height of bars is used to indicate the frequency of each score or each class of scores.

Beta: in hypothesis testing, the probability of failing to reject the null hypothesis when it is false; the probability of making a Type 2 error.

Between-group variance: a measure of the fluctuations between groups based on group means.

Between-subject design: an experimental design in which each subject is tested under only one level of each independent variable.

Chance: in probability, the lack of any systematic effect influencing the outcome of an event. All events are equally likely.

Chi square test: a statistical test appropriate for analyzing nominal data obtained with between-subject designs.

Cochran Q test: a statistical test appropriate for analyzing nominal data obtained with within-subject designs.

Combination: a group of r objects or events in which the order of the objects or events within the group is not important.

Confounding variable: a variable not manipulated as an independent variable that systematically varies with an independent variable so that the effect of the confounding variable and the effect of the independent variable cannot be separated.

Constant: a term in a mathematical formula that does not vary.

Control group: the group that does not receive the treatment. The performance of the no treatment group (control) is compared to the treatment group (experimental) to assess the effect of the treatment.

Correlation: a measure of the extent to which two variables are related, not necessarily in a causal relationship. The magnitude of a correlation can vary from −1.00 to +1.00.

Counterbalancing: a technique used to distribute order and time-related effects over all conditions equally by systematically varying the order of the conditions within or across subjects.

Criterion: a standard used to assess the predictive validity of a test.

Data: the scores obtained on a dependent variable or performance measure.

Degrees of freedom: the number of values that are free to vary if the sum of the values and the number of values are fixed.

Demand characteristics: those cues available to a subject in an experiment that may enable him to determine the "purpose" of the experiment; the cues that allow the subject to infer what the experimenter "expects" of him; one type of confounding variable.

Dependent variable: the variable the investigator measures to assess the effect of the independent variable; in an experiment, the variable whose level is not determined by the experimenter.

Descriptive statistics: methods for summarizing, organizing, and communicating data.

Determinism: an assumption of science asserting that events have a finite number of causes that can be discovered.

Dichotomous variable: a variable with two and only two mutually exclusive categories (e.g., male-female, yes-no).

Differential transfer: in a within-subject design, differential transfer occurs when the effect of one treatment is dependent on the treatment that preceded it; an interaction of treatment by order of treatment.

Distribution: a set of values for an attribute or variable.

Double-blind: a design in which neither the subject nor the experimenter knows which subjects are in which treatment condition.

Eidetic imagery: a visual image of a visual stimulus that is retained for a short time after the stimulus is removed. The image is almost photographic in clarity.

Equivalent groups: groups are said to be equivalent if the probability of the obtained group differences if only chance is operating is greater than the significance level.

Ethologist: a zoologist or naturalist whose main interest is in behaviors specific to a species.

Experimental design: a plan for obtaining and treating data in which the experimental method is used.

Experimental method: a method used to study phenomena in which one or more independent variables are manipulated, and performance on one or more dependent variables is measured.

Explanation: a specification of the antecedent condition necessary to demonstrate a phenomenon.

Factorial (!): $N!$ indicates the operation of multiplying together all of the counting numbers from 1 to N. For instance, $5! = 5 \times 4 \times 3 \times 2 \times 1 = 120$.

Factorial design: an experimental design in which each level of each independent variable occurs with each level of every other independent variable.

Fixed effects model: a statistical model that necessitates that the conclusions drawn from the experiment be limited to the actual levels of the independent variable that were manipulated because the levels manipulated have not been randomly selected from the population of possible levels.

Frequency distribution: a set of scores arranged in ascending or descending order. The number of times each score occurs is indicated.

F_{max} *statistic:* a statistical test appropriate for determining whether the probability of the obtained differences between sample variances is less than the significance level.

Generalization: in experimentation, being able to extend the results of an experiment beyond the sample tested to the population from which the sample was drawn. In order to generalize the results to the population the sample must have been randomly selected from the population.

Heterogeneous: dissimilar.

Histogram: a bar graph.

Homogeneous: similar, alike.

Hypothesis: a proposed explanation for a phenomenon.

Independent variable: a variable in an experiment whose level is determined by the experimenter; a variable systematically manipulated by the experimenter in order to determine the effect of one variable on another.

Interaction: the effect of one independent variable on performance is dependent on the level of another independent variable.

Interval scale: a scale in which the scale values are related by a single, underlying, quantitative dimension and there are equal intervals between successive scale values.

Kurtosis: the degree of peakedness of a distribution.

Leptokurtic: a distribution or curve that is steep.

Linear relationship: a relationship between two variables in which an increase in one variable is always accompanied by a constant increase or is always accompanied by a constant decrease in the other.

Longitudinal study: a method in which individuals are studied over time and measurements are obtained on the individuals at various intervals.

Matched-groups design: a between-subject design in which groups are equated on the variable(s) selected for matching in an attempt to obtain equal groups or to reduce the within-group chance fluctuations.

Mean ($\bar{X}$): a descriptive measure of central tendency appropriate for interval data; the sum of all the scores divided by the number of scores.

Mean square (MS): in analysis of variance, an estimate of population variance if the null hypothesis is true.

Median: a descriptive measure of central tendency; the value that divides the distribution in half.

Median Test: a statistical test appropriate for analyzing ordinal data obtained with between-subject designs.

Mesokurtic: a curve or distribution that is neither peaked nor flat. The normal distribution is mesokurtic.

Mnemonic system: a memory improving system.

Mode: a descriptive measure of central tendency; the most frequently occurring value.

Monotonic relationship: a relationship between two variables on which an increase in one variable is always accompanied by an increase or is always accompanied by a decrease in the other variable.

Nominal measurement: placement of subjects into qualitatively different categories.

Nonreactive measure: a measure of behavior in which the subject is not aware of being observed and the subject's behavior is not changed by the observation process.

Normal distribution: a symmetric, mesokurtic, bell-shaped curve. If scores on a measure are distributed normally, the greater the difference between a score and the mean, the less the probability of obtaining the score.

Null hypothesis: the assertion that the independent variable will not have an effect on the dependent variable.

Null hypothesis sampling distribution: a distribution of sample values that can be expected if only chance is operating.

Observational techniques: a method of research based on observing behavior of organisms without the systematic manipulation of an independent variable.

One-tailed test: a procedure for testing the null hypothesis in which the entire rejection area is placed at one end of the appropriate sampling distribution.

Operational definition: a definition of a concept in terms of the operations that must be performed in order to demonstrate the concept.

Order: an assumption of science asserting that events follow each other in regular sequences.

Ordinal scale: a scale in which scale values are related by a single, underlying quantitative dimension but it is not possible to assume that the differences between successive scale values are of equal magnitude.

Ordinate: the Y or vertical axis in a graph.

Permutation: an ordered sequence of objects or events.

Phenomenon: a fact or event that is observable.

Placebo: a substance or treatment having no effect that is given to a control group in place of a drug or experimental treatment to minimize demand characteristics.

Platykurtic: a curve or distribution that is flat.

Population: the potential units for observation from which the sample to be observed is drawn.

Probability: an estimate of the likelihood that a particular event will occur; the ratio of the number of favorable events to the total number of possible events if only chance is operating.

Random assignment: a procedure used to place subjects in groups or to order events such that only chance determines the placement or ordering.

Random-groups design: a between-subject design in which random assignment is used to assign subjects to conditions.

Random sampling: a procedure used to obtain representative samples from a population. In complete random sampling, each subject in the population must have an equal chance of being selected and the selection or nonselection of one subject cannot influence the selection or nonselection of any other subject.

Range: a descriptive measure of variability; the difference score obtained by subtracting the smallest score in the distribution from the largest score in the distribution.

Ratio scale: a scale in which scale values are related by a single, underlying, quantitative dimension; there are equal intervals between scale values, and there is an absolute zero.

Reactive measure: a measure of behavior obtained when the observee is aware that his behavior is being observed or there is reason to believe that the observation or measurement procedures *may* influence the observee's behavior.

Reliability: the consistency of a test or a measurement instrument, usually determined by computing a correlation between scores obtained by the same subjects on two forms of the test, scores on the same test at two points in time, or scores obtained on each half of the test.

Research hypothesis: the assertion that the independent variable will have an effect on the dependent variable.

Rho (ρ): the rank-order correlation for a population; r_s is an estimate of rho.

Sample: the group of subjects selected from the population.

Scale: a set of numbers assigned to objects or events indicating the relative amounts of some characteristic that the objects or events possess.

Scattergram: a plot of the scores made by the same individuals on two different variables, providing a pictorial representation of the degree of correlation between two variables.

Significance: statistical significance refers to whether the obtained results are a rare or common event if only chance is operating. Psychological significance refers to the quality of the idea, the adequacy of the test of the idea, and the clarity of the results.

Significance level: the probability used to define an experimental outcome as a rare event if chance only is operating and to define what is meant by equivalent groups.

Skewed distribution: a nonsymmetrical distribution. In a negatively skewed distribution extreme scores are below the mean. In a positively skewed distribution extreme scores are above the mean.

Standard deviation: a descriptive measure of variability obtained by taking the square root of the variance; a unit of measurement, or a standard way of describing scores in terms of their relation to the mean.

Standard error: the standard deviation of the sampling distribution.

Stereotaxic procedure: a procedure for immobilizing and positioning the head of an organism in order to stimulate, record, or destroy brain tissue.

Subject: the object or organism on which a manipulation or observation is being made.

Subject variable: a characteristic of a subject that can be measured.

Theory: a tentative explanation for a phenomenon or set of phenomena.

Two-tailed test: a procedure for testing the null hypothesis in which the rejection area is placed at both ends of the appropriate sampling distribution.

Type 1 error: an error that occurs if the null hypothesis is rejected when it is true.

Type 2 error: an error that occurs if the null hypothesis is not rejected when it is false.

Validity: the extent to which an instrument measures what it is purported to measure.

Variable: a thing or event that can be measured or manipulated.

Variance (s^2): a descriptive measure of variability within a sample; the sum of the squared deviations of each score from the mean divided by the number of scores minus one.

Wilcoxon-Mann-Whitney Test: a statistical test appropriate for analyzing ordinal data obtained with within-subject designs.

Within-group variance: a measure of the fluctuations between subjects in the same group.

Within-subject design: an experimental design in which each subject is tested under more than one level of the independent variable.

index

American Humane Association, 16
American Psychological Association
   Committee on Ethical Standards in Psychological Research, 16
   Committee on Precautions and Standards in Animal Experimentation, 16
   style manual, 284
American Psychologist, 16, 17
analysis, relation of, to design, 72. *See also* statistical analysis
animals, use of, in research, 16, 27
Army General Classification Test, 176
Arnold, W. J., 47
assignment, random, 62–63, 81
association, 37
audience, selection of, 283–284
Azrin, N. H., 318

Bandura, A., 318
Barber, T. X., 150
bar graph, 180–181, 187
Beach, F. A., 145
behavioral measure, 161
Bennett, C. F., 46
between-groups estimate of population variance, 308–309
between-group variables, 99–101
between-subject designs, 71, 72, 83–101
   analysis of, 212–229
      by interval data, 233–262
   confounding with, 152–154, 156
   median test in, 222–225, 229
   and Wilcoxon-Mann-Whitney test, 226–229
Bickman, L., 325
Boblett, P. J., 49
Braginsky, Dorothea, 323
Bugelski, B. R., 316

Cameron, P., 45

Campbell, D. T., 6, 7, 9, 10, 26, 33, 38, 44, 122, 123, 129, 137
categorical measurement, 162, 187
causality
   and multiple correlations, 38, 57
   and subject variables, 42–43, 57
Cavior, N., 49
central tendency
   means as, 166–167, 187
   median as, 165, 167, 187
   mode as, 165, 185
Chance, P., 49
chance, 64, 81
chance fluctuations, 67, 108, 117
Cherry, C., 320
chi square
   computation of, 214, 217, 220–221, 222, 224, 229
   evaluation of, 214–215, 217–218, 220–221, 222, 224, 229
   median test application of, 222–225, 229
   and nonsubject variables, 221–225
   obtained and expected frequencies in, 213–214, 216–217, 219–220
   and phi coefficient, 218–219
   restrictions on use of, 225–226, 229
   and subject variables, 215–221
   table, 214–215, 229
   test, 213–226, 229
Christie, R., 323
Cochran Q test, 268–269, 277
combinations, 307
computers, role of, in research, 142, 155
conditions, representation of, 147–148
confounding, 92, 143–144
   with between-subject design, 152–154, 156
   and demand characteristics, 149–152, 156
   and number of experimenters, 149
   with within-subject design, 154, 156

construct validity, 25–26, 27
content validity, 24
control group design, nonequivalent, 134–136
control groups, 40
Cook, Stuart W., 18
correlation. *See also* correlation research
 of abilities, 314–316
 and discovery, 39
 and estimation, 202
 and range restriction, 207–209
 and relationship between variables, 199–200
 variance and, 203–207, 209
correlation coefficients, computing, 190–196
correlation research. *See also* correlation
 and causality, 37–39, 57
 and discovery, 39, 57
 interpreting, 37–38
 nature of, 34–35, 57
 and prediction, 35–36, 57
 rank-order, 193–194, 209
counterbalancing
 complete, 110–111
 nature and purpose of, 109–110
 partial, 111–112
Crano, W. D., 38
Cronbach, L. J., 7, 26

Dabbs, J. M., 48
degrees of freedom, 214
demand characteristics, 109, 117
 controlling, 151–152
 experimenter attitude and, 150–151
 influence on nonexperimental designs, 125, 139
 nature of, 149–152, 156
 pervasiveness of, 150, 156
dependent measure, 98, 161
dependent variable. *See* variables, dependent
derived scores, 175–176
designs
 between-subject. *See* between-subject designs
 classification of, 136–137
 comparison of, 136–138
 experimental, 71–72
  compared with quasi-experimental designs, 136–138
  and generality, 114–115

 matched-groups. *See* matched-groups designs
 nonequivalent, control-group, 134–136
 nonexperimental, 120–129, 136–139
  compared with quasi-experimental designs, 136–138
  evaluation of, 129
  examples of, 120–122
  factors influencing adequacy of, 122–129, 139
  single group, 120–121
  static groups, 121–122
 quasi-experimental, 129–139
  compared with experimental and nonexperimental designs, 136–138
  examples of, 130–136
  logic of, 129–130, 139
  nonequivalent, control-group, 134–136
  time-series, 130–134
 random-groups. *See* random-groups design
 relation to analysis, 72
 time-series, 130–134
 validity of, 137–138
 within-subject. *See* within-subject designs
determination, coefficient of (r^2), 207, 209
determinism, as assumption of scientific approach, 7, 26
deviation. *See* variance
deviation formulas, 239
deviation method, 168–170. *See also* standard deviation
differential regression, 135
differential transfer, 112–113
discovery, and correlation, 39, 57
Disney, H. J. de S., 33
distributions
 frequency, 64–67
 nonnormal, 173–175
 normal, 172–173
 sampling, 67–70, 81
double-blind experiments, 91

ego, 14
empiricism, as assumption of scientific approach, 8, 26
equivalent groups, 71, 74, 152–153
 subject variables and, 43, 57
Eron, L. D., 319
error, experimental, 75–76
estimation, 60, 70, 81
 and correlation, 202

Ethical Principles in the Conduct of Research with Human Participants (American Psychological Association), 17–18
ethics, 16–21
  and use of animals, 15–16
  and use of human subjects, 16–18
experimental designs. *See* designs, experimental
experimental error, 75–76
experimental groups, 40
experimental method. *See also* experiments
  and analysis of experiments, 72
  basic proproties of, 39–41, 57
  compared with quasi-experimental method, 44–45
  and experiments with one independent variable, 50–51, 57
  and experiments with two independent variables, 51–56, 57
  and hypothesis testing, 70–72
  independent and dependent variables in, 39–40, 57
  logic of, 40–41, 57
  and performing the experiment, 72
  and research with one subject, 115–116, 118
  and subject variables, 41–43, 57
experiments. *See also* experimental method; research
  demand characteristics of, 149–152, 156
  describing results of, 176–186
    using interval data, 179–186, 187
    using nominal data, 176–177, 187
    using ordinal data, 177–179, 187
  validity of, 26
external validity, 27

factorial design, 180
figures, use of, in describing results of experiments, 180–181
Fisher, Sir Ronald, 243
Fisher-Yates Exact Probability Test, 226
fixed effects models, 92–93
flatness (of distributions), 173
follow-up tests in analysis of variance, 244–245
format, 284
freedom, degrees of, 242
frequencies, calculation of, 213–214, 216–217, 219–220

frequency distributions
  and probability, 66–67
  types of, 65–66
Freud, Sigmund, 14
F-test
  relation to t-test, 245–247, 277
F value, 243, 262

generalities, establishment of, 113–115
Graduate Record Examination, 176
graphic phobia, 282–283
Guide for Laboratory Animal Facilities and Care (American Psychological Association), 16

Hagedorn, R., 37
Hake, D. F., 318
Hanley, C., 150
Hess, E. H., 321, 322
history, influence of, on nonexperimental designs, 122–123, 139
homogeneity of variance, 260–261, 262
Huesmann, L. R., 319
human subjects, use of, in research, 16–18, 27
Hussar, D. A., 95
Hutchinson, R. R., 318
hypothesis testing. *See also* theory
  and experimental method, 60, 70–72, 81

id, 14
ideas. *See also* theory
  criteria for evaluating, 13–22
    testability and comparability of, 14–15, 26–27
    testability and ethical considerations of, 15–20, 27
    testability and operational definitions of, 13, 26–27
    testability and practical considerations of, 15, 26–27
    testability and refutability of, 14, 26–27
  generation of, 12
  importance of, 21–22
  quality of, 281
independent variable. *See* variables, independent
interactions, 254–260
  definition of, 255
  importance of, 255–256

Index 367

of independent variables, 51–54, 57
   relationship between, and main effects, 256–260
internal validity, 27
interval data, 163
   analysis of, 271–277
   in analysis of between-subject designs, 233–262
   and product-moment correlation, 195–196
   use of, 179–186, 187
interval measurement, 163, 187
intervention
   nonreactive measures with, 33–34, 56–57
   nonreactive measures without, 32–33, 56–57
investigators, 10–11

Johnson, D. A., 46

Kahneman, D., 321
Kenny, D. A., 38
Kidd, E., 316
Koch, M. D., 47
Kosslyn, S. M., 316
Kruskal, W. H., 228
kurtosis, 173

laboratories
   and confounding, 143, 155
   and within-group variance, 144, 155
Labovitz, S., 37
large treatment effect, 86–88
least squares, method of, 202
Lefkowitz, M. M., 319
leptokurtic curve, 173, 174
Lindsay, P. H., 324
line graph, 180, 187
linear relationships, 198
Lockard, R. B., 145
Loftus, E. F., 326

main effects, 55
   and interactions, 256–260
manuscript, preparation of, for publication, 290
Marler, P., 319
Marshall, A. J., 33

Marteljan, P., 46
matched-groups designs, 71, 96–101, 102
   analysis of, 266–277
   and nonsubject variables, 98–99, 102
      matching procedures, 99–101, 102
   and subject variables, 97–98, 102
matching
   prerequisite for, 98
   reasons for, 98
   subject by subject, 101
matching procedures
   and nonsubject variables
      reducing between-group variance, 101, 102
      reducing within-group variance, 99–100, 102
maturation, influence of, on nonexperimental designs, 123–124, 139
mean, 83
mean, overall, 86
meaning units, 317–318
mean score, 166–167, 187
mean square, 242–243
measurement. *See also* measures
   importance of, 22
   influence of, on nonexperimental designs, 124–125, 139
   interval, 163, 187
   levels of, 162–164
      determining, 164
      and performance variables, 161–164, 187
   nominal, 162, 187
   ordinal, 162–163, 187
   ratio, 164, 187
   and reliability, 22–24
   validity of, 24–26, 27
measures. *See also* measurement
   descriptive, 161, 164–165, 187
      of central tendency, 165–167, 187
      of variability, 167–171, 187
median score, 165, 167, 187
median test, 222–225, 229
Mednick test, 315
memory test, 315
mesokurtic curve, 173, 174
Milgram technique, 313–314
Miller, G. A., 322, 323
mode score, 165, 187
Monitor, The, 18
monotonic relationships, 198
Moray, N., 320
multiplication rule, 305–306

Neisser, U., 150
nominal data, 162
    analysis of, 266–267, 277
        in between-subject designs, 212–229
    and phi coefficient, 190–192, 209
    use of, 176–177, 187
nominal measurement, 162, 187
nonequivalent, control group design, 134–136
nonexperimental designs. *See* designs, nonexperimental
nonmanipulated variables, controlling, 109
nonreactive measures, 56
    with intervention, 33–34, 57
    without intervention, 32–33
nonspurious relation, 37
nonsubject variables, 95–96
    and chi square test, 221–225
    manipulation of, 55–56, 58, 248
    and matched-groups designs, 98–99, 102
    matching procedures and, 99–101, 102
    within-subject manipulations of, 105–106, 117
normality assumption, 261–262
Norman, D. A., 324
no treatment effect, 88
null hypothesis, 70–71, 73, 74, 81, 307–309
    rejection of, 75–79
        in sampling distribution, 76–79
            and experimental error and rejecting, 76–79

observational techniques
    observer in, 30–31, 56–57
    for nonreactive measures, 32–33, 57
    for reactive measures, 31, 56
observer, the, 30–31, 56–57
odds, 63–64
one-tailed tests, 79–80
    advantages of, 80
    misuse of, 80
order, as assumption of scientific approach, 7, 26
ordinal data, 162–163
    analysis of, 269–271, 277
        in between-subject designs, 212–229
    effect of independent variable on, 178
    use of, 177–179, 187
ordinal measurement, 162–163, 187
Orne, M. T., 149
overall mean, 86

parsimony, as assumption of scientific approach, 7–8, 26
Palmer, J. C., 326
parameters, 70
peakedness (of distributions), 173
Pearson product-moment correlation, 199
performance measure, 161
permutations, 306–307
personality structure, Freudian view of, 14
phi (ϕ) coefficient
    and chi square, 218–219
    and nominal data, 190–192, 209
platykurtic curve, 173, 174
population, definition of, 61
population variance, estimates of, 85–89, 168, 237–238, 262
    between-group, 86, 102
    independent, 307–309
    within-group, 86, 102
Porter, R. J., 46
prediction and correlation, 35–36, 57
predictive validity, 24–25, 27
pretest-posttest design, 121, 124, 128–129
probability, 63–70, 81, 305–307
    common sense view of, 63
    definition of, 64
problem
    limiting scope of, 12
    selecting, 11
product-moment correlation, 207, 209
    computation of, 194–196
    magnitude of, 196
psychological significance, 280–282, 290
public opinion, assessment of, 313–314

qualitative manipulations, representation of, 180, 187
quantitative manipulations, representation of, 180, 187
quasi-experimental approach, 44–45, 57–58
    compared with experimental, 44–45
quasi-experimental designs. *See* designs, quasi-experimental
Q value, computation of, 268–269

r^2 (coefficient of determination), 207, 209
random assignment, 62–63, 81, 143
random-groups design, 71, 90–96, 102
    analysis of variance with, 84, 85, 101
    experiments with, 91–95
    logic of, 90–91
    properties of, 90

Index

randomization, 61–63, 81
randomized block design, 143
random sampling, 61–62, 81
range, as measure of variability, 167–171, 187
range restriction, and correlation, 207–209
rank-order correlation, 209
    computation of, 193–194
    magnitude of, 194
rare event, 74, 81
ratio data, use of, 179–186
ratio measurement, 164, 187
rationale, 37
raw scores, 175
reactive measures, 56
    nature of, 31
    usefulness of, 31–32
regression
    differential, 135
    influence of, on nonexperimental designs, 126–129, 139
regression line, 200–202, 209
relation, nonspurious, 37
relative standing, 176
reliability, 126–129
    and measurement, 22–24, 27
Remote Associates Test, 315
research. *See also* research methodology
    confounding of, 149–154, 156
    criteria for evaluating ideas in, 13–22, 26–27
    with established baselines, 116–117
    ethical considerations of, 16–21, 27
    evaluating and reporting results of, 186–187, 280–291
    examples of, involving ethical issues, 18–21
    facilities, special skills and equipment for, 141–145, 155–156
    importance of ideas in, 21–22
    the investigator in, 10–11
    methods and procedures for describing results of, 161–188
    with one subject, 115–116
    purpose of, 10
    reevaluating psychological significance of, 280
        adequacy of test, 281
        definitiveness of results, 281–282
        quality of ideas, 281
    reporting findings of
        decision to report, 282–283
        the discussion section, 288–289, 291
        factors to consider before writing, 283–284
        general comment about writing, 289–290
        the introduction section, 284–285, 290
        the method section, 285–286, 291
        preparing manuscript for publication, 290
        the results section, 286–288, 291
    selecting a laboratory for, 142–144
    selecting the problem area for, 11
    standard procedures for, 144–145, 155
    subjects, 145–148
        human, 16–18, 27, 145
        individual or group testing of, 147–148, 155
        number of, per condition in, 146–147, 155
        selection of, 145–146, 155
    testing the subjects in, 154–155
    theories and, 10–12
research findings, generality of, 113–115
research hypothesis, 70–71, 75
research methodology. *See also* research
    and the citizen, 3–5
    classifying according to, 45–50
    correlational techniques of, 34–39, 57
    experimental, 39–45, 57
    and majors in psychology, 5–6
    observational approach to, 29–34, 56
    quasi-experimental approach to, 44–45, 57–58
    rationale for studying, 3–6
    scientific approach to, 6–10, 26
research topics, 313–327
    abilities, correlation of, 314–316
    aggression, 318–319
    clothes and behavior, 325–326
    cocktail party phenomenon, 320–321
    eyewitness testimony, 326–327
    information processing, 317–318
    lost letter technique, 313–314
    Machiavellianism, 323–324
    mnemonic systems, 316–317
    prisoner's dilemma, 324–325
    pupil dilation, 321–322
    reading, 322–323
results, definitiveness of, 281–282
Risley, T. M., 116
Rosenthal, R., 149
Ross D., 318
Ross, S. A., 318

samples, 67–68, 70
sampling, random, 61–62, 81
sampling distributions, 67–70, 76–79, 81
  empirical, 67–69
  mathematical, 69–70
scattergrams, and correlation, 196–202, 209
scatter-plot. See scattergrams
Schwartz, R. D., 33
science, goal of, 8–9
scientific approach
  assumptions of, 6–8, 26
    determinism, 7
    empiricism, 8
    order, 7
    parsimony, 7–8
scores. See also distributions
  derived, 175–176
  equivalent, 175
  raw, 175
  z, 171–176
Sechrest, L., 33
Segman, J., 316
selection, influence of, on nonexperimental designs, 124, 139
sensitization, influence of, on nonexperimental designs, 124, 125, 139
Siegel, S., 261
significance level, 73–74
significance tests. See tests, statistical
significant differences, 73
Silver, M. J., 150
skew, 173–175
squared deviations from the mean, sum of, 234, 308–309, 309–310
standard deviation, 175–176, 180
  relation to variance, 171, 187
  as unit of measurement, 171–176, 187
standard error, 308–309
standardized tests, 176
standard normal distribution, 173
Stanley, J. C., 6, 7, 9, 10, 44, 122, 123, 129
statistical analysis
  logic of, 73–80
  and one-tailed versus two-tailed tests, 79–80
  and sampling distributions, experimental error and rejecting null hypothesis, 76–79
statistical significance, 280, 290
statistics, 70
Stevens, S. S., 22
Stroop, J. R., 321

subject by subject matching, 101
subjects, research, 145–148
subject variable experiments, 95–96
subject variable manipulations, classification of, 43
subject variables
  and causality, 42–43, 57
  and chi square test, 215–221
  definition of, 41–42, 57
  and equivalent groups, 43, 57
  experimental manipulation of, 42–43, 57
  manipulation of, 55–56, 248
  and matched-groups designs, 97–98, 102
sum of squared deviations from the mean, 234, 308–309, 309–310
sum of squares, computation of, 239–241
Sundel, Martin, 49
superego, 14

tables, use of, in describing results of experiments, 180, 187
Terman, L. M., 314
testing
  individual or group, 147–148, 155
  subjects in research, 154–155
tests
  chi square, 213–226, 229
  Cochran Q, 268–269, 277
  F, 243, 245–247, 262, 277
  median, 222–225, 229
  Mednick, 315
  memory, 315
  one-tailed versus two-tailed, 79–80
  Remote Associates, 315
  statistical, 73–75, 222–229
    selecting, 212–213, 229
    significance level of, 73–74
  t, 233–236, 245–247, 261, 262, 272–274, 277
  Wilcoxon, 270–271, 277
  Wilcoxon-Mann-Whitney, 226–229
theories, and research, 10–12
theory
  definition of, 9–10, 26
  functions of, 10
  importance of, 9–10
time priority, 37
time-series design, 130–134
topics, research. See research topics
treatment effects, 86–89
treatment manipulation, 115–116, 118
Treisman, A. M., 320

t-test, 233–236, 261
   and analysis of interval data, 272–274, 277
   compared with *F*-test, 277
   computation of, 234–235, 262
   relation to *F*-test, 245–247
t-value, evaluation of, 236–262
two-tailed tests, 79–80, 215

Ulrich, R. E., 318
Underwood, B. J., 26

validity
   construct, 25–26, 27
   content, 24
   of experiments, 26, 27
   external, 26, 27
   internal, 26, 27
   predictive, 24–25, 27
variability, measures of, 167–171, 187
   deviation method, 168–170
   range, 167–168, 187
   standard deviation, 171, 175–176, 180, 187
   variance, 168–170
variable, definition of, 34, 57
variable manipulations, 248
variables. *See also* variance
   confounding, 143
   dependent, 39–40, 57
   independent, 39–40, 50–56, 57–58, 71, 78–79
      in describing results of experiments, 180, 187
      effect on ordinal data, 178
      experiments with one, 91–93
      experiments with two, 93–95
      interacting, 51–54, 57
      main effects of, 55
      noninteracting, 54–55
   nonmanipulated, control of, 109, 153–154
   nonsubject, 41, 57, 58
   subject, 41, 57
variance, 168–170, 187. *See also* population variance; variables; variance, analysis of
   concept of, 83–85
   and correlation, 203–207, 209
   definition of, 83–85
   relation of standard deviation to, 171, 187

variance, analysis of. *See also* population variance; variables; variance
   assumptions of, 260–261
   between-group, 85, 102
   computation of, 310–311, 311–312
   and experimental design, 90
   homogeneity of, 260–261, 262
   logic of, 83–90, 237
   and matched-groups or within-subject designs, 274–277
   with one independent variable, 238–247, 262
      follow-up tests, 244–245
      sum of squares, 239–241
      table, 241–243
   with two independent variables, 247–254, 262
      computation of, 249–253
      and interactions, 254–260, 262
      manipulations, 248–249
      table, 253–254
   within-group, 85, 101–102
variance, source of, 242

Walder, L. O., 319
Wallis, W. A., 228
Webb, E. J., 33
Wechsler Adult Intelligence Scale, 176
Wilcoxon-Mann-Whitney test
   characteristics of, 228–229
   computation of, 226–227
   evaluation of, 227–228
Wilcoxon test, 270–271, 277
within-group estimate of population variance, 308
within-group variables, 99–101
within-group variance, 144, 155
within-subject designs, 71, 72, 104–118
   advantages of, 106–108
   analysis of, 266–277
   confounding with, 154, 156
   efficiency of, 107–108
   limitations of, 105, 108–109, 117
   methodological problems in, 109–115
      counterbalancing, 109–112
      differential transfer, 112–113
      generality of research findings, 113–115
   and nonsubject variable manipulations, 105–106, 117
   properties of, 104–106, 117
   selection of, 115

uses of, 115, 118
and within-subject manipulations, 104–105
within-subject manipulations, 104–105, 117
Wolf, M. M., 116
writing, 289–290
W value, 271

z-scores, 171–176
  formula for computing, 171
  and nonnormal distributions, 173–175
  and normal distributions, 172–173
  use of, 171–172